Marching West

NO ON 14
NO ON 14
ON TO --
WASHINGTON!
PRAYER-
PILGRIMAGE
Police
Brutality
MUST STOP NOW
WE ALL
CAN'T GO
UNDERGROUND
THE ROAD TO LASTING PEACE
EQUAL RIGHTS
FOR ALL AMERICANS
IN DIXIE TOO
THIS IS 1962
W... CAN'T GO
UNDERGROUND
THE ROAD TO LASTING PEACE
MUST BE FOUND
ASHES to ASHES DUST to DUST
A DYNAMIC STRONG UNITED NATIONS
IS A MUST or WE ALL GO BUST!
JIM
CROW
MUST
GO!
ALL GO BUST!

Marching West

The Los Angeles Civil Rights Movement in Photographs

Karin L. Stanford with Mark Speltz

GETTY PUBLICATIONS
LOS ANGELES

Published by Getty Publications, Los Angeles
1200 Getty Center Drive, Suite 500
Los Angeles, California 90049-1682
getty.edu/publications

Elizabeth S. G. Nicholson and Darryl Oliver, *Project Editors*
Sharon Shahid, *Manuscript Editor*
Jon Grizzle, *Designer*
Molly McGeehan, *Production*
Nancy Rivera, *Image and Rights Acquisition*

Distributed in the United States and Canada by the University of Chicago Press

Distributed outside the United States and Canada by Yale University Press, London

Printed in Singapore

Library of Congress Cataloging-in-Publication Data
Names: Stanford, Karin L., 1961- author | Speltz, Mark contributor
Title: Marching west : the Los Angeles civil rights movement in photographs / by Karin L. Stanford with Mark Speltz.
Description: Los Angeles : Getty Publications, [2026] | Includes index. | Summary: "A visual history of the people and organizations who led the fight for change during the civil rights era in Los Angeles"– Provided by publisher.
Identifiers: LCCN 2025041890 | ISBN 9781606069899 hardback | ISBN 9781606069905 pdf | ISBN 9781606069912 epub
Subjects: LCSH: Civil rights movements–California–Los Angeles–History–20th century | African Americans–Civil rights–California–Los Angeles–History–20th century | Photography in social change–California–Los Angeles–History–20th century | Documentary photography–Social aspects–California–Los Angeles–History–20th century | Photojournalism–Social aspects–California–Los Angeles–History–20th century
Classification: LCC F869.L89 A275 2026
LC record available at https://lccn.loc.gov/2025041890

Front cover: Charles Williams, 1960. Martin Luther King Jr. leads a protest at an F. W. Woolworth store on Crenshaw Boulevard, p. 59.

The complete manuscript of this work was peer reviewed through a single-masked process in which the reviewers were anonymous.

The images in this volume are drawn from a range of historical sources. Variations in appearance may reflect material aging; period retouching practices, including those used in newsrooms; and other characteristics inherent to vintage prints of the era.

Authorized Product Safety Representative in the European Union:
Easy Access System Europe, Mustamäe tee 50, 10621 Tallinn, Estonia, gpsr.requests@easproject.com

MIX
Paper | Supporting responsible forestry
FSC® C167869

Contents

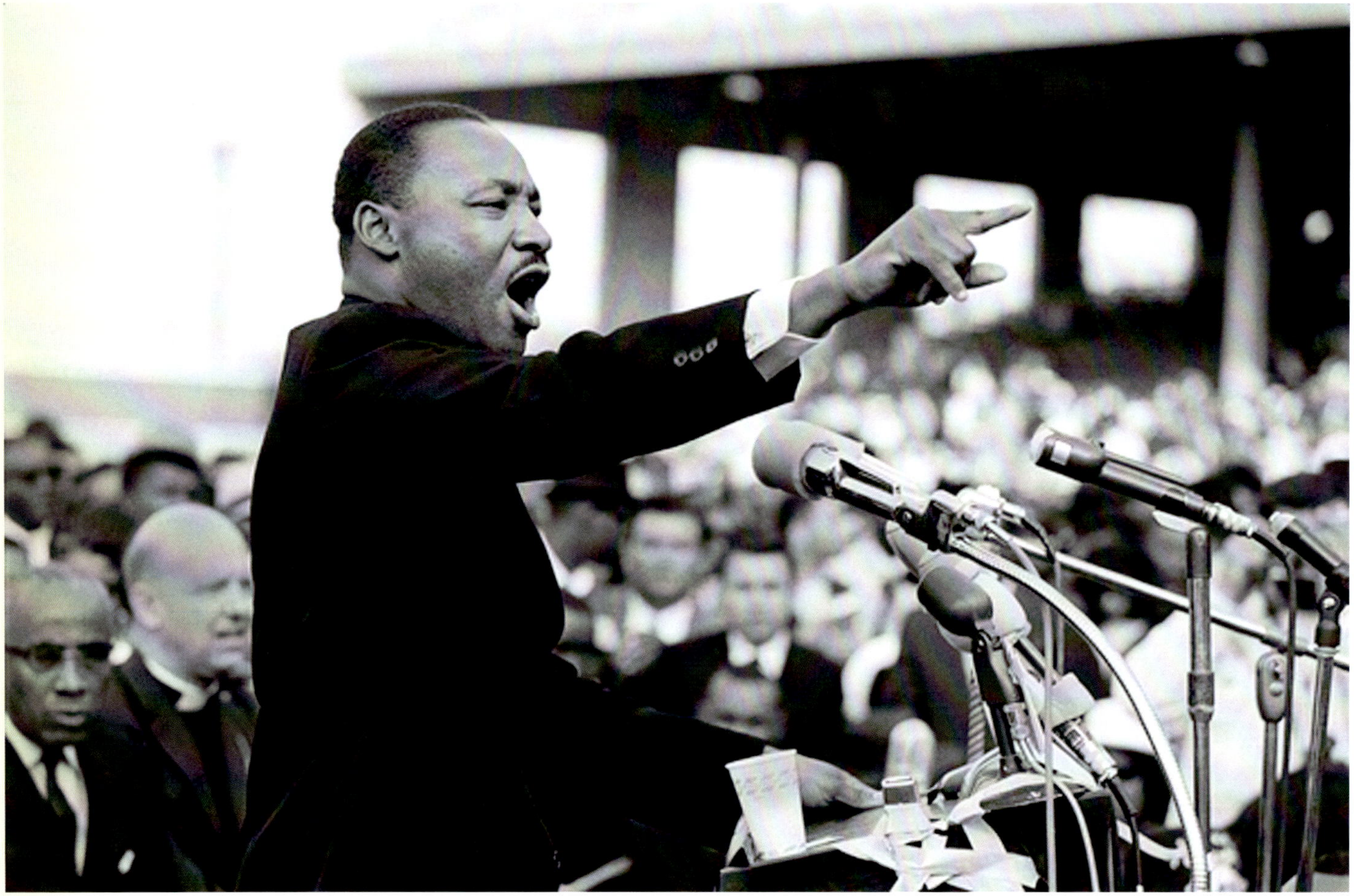

Introduction

One of the most iconic photographs of civil rights leader Martin Luther King Jr. was taken in Los Angeles, California, on May 26, 1963 (fig. 1). Speaking at the Freedom Rally to an estimated audience of forty thousand, the young orator is shown gripping the lectern with his left hand as he projects his voice and his right hand toward the crowd, appearing at once firmly grounded and dynamic. This powerful photo was taken by Julian Wasser for *Time* magazine, and it expresses the dignity and passion of those who fought for equality during the civil rights era, not just in the American South but across the country. Years later, a print was acquired by President Barack Obama and displayed in the White House.

King was in Los Angeles that spring day to generate support for the campaign to end discrimination in Birmingham, Alabama. In the preceding weeks, Angelenos had been riveted by photographs and news clips showing Birmingham police and firemen attacking nonviolent protesters with German shepherds and high-pressure hoses. At Wrigley Field, a minor-league baseball stadium in South Los Angeles, King spoke before an overflow crowd. He thanked the Western Christian Leadership Conference (WCLC) for supporting desegregation efforts in the South and invited everyone to join the upcoming March on Washington for Jobs and Freedom (more than a thousand Southern Californians would attend; fig. 2). He then answered a question that had been posed to him by Angelenos: "You asked me what Los Angeles can do to help us in Birmingham. The most important thing that you can do is to set Los Angeles free because you have segregation and discrimination here and police brutality."[1] King often stated, "The racial issue we confront in America is not a sectional but a national problem," and he shared that message on his many visits to Los Angeles between 1956 and 1968 (fig. 3).[2] During that period, he joined a vibrant community of religious and political leaders, academics, and activists including Rev. J. Raymond Henderson, Marnesba Tackett, Maurice Dawkins, Gwendolyn Green, Rev. Arthur Atlas Peters, Rev. L. Sylvester Odom, Rev. Hamel Hartford Brookins, and Rev. Thomas Kilgore, and worked not only to bring attention to civil rights campaigns in the South but also to combat injustice in Los Angeles.

Photographs taken in L.A. were rarely included in early studies of the civil rights movement, which typically focused on Southern states and left the imagery

Fig. 1 JULIAN WASSER, 1963. Martin Luther King Jr. speaks to an estimated crowd of forty thousand at the 1963 Freedom Rally.

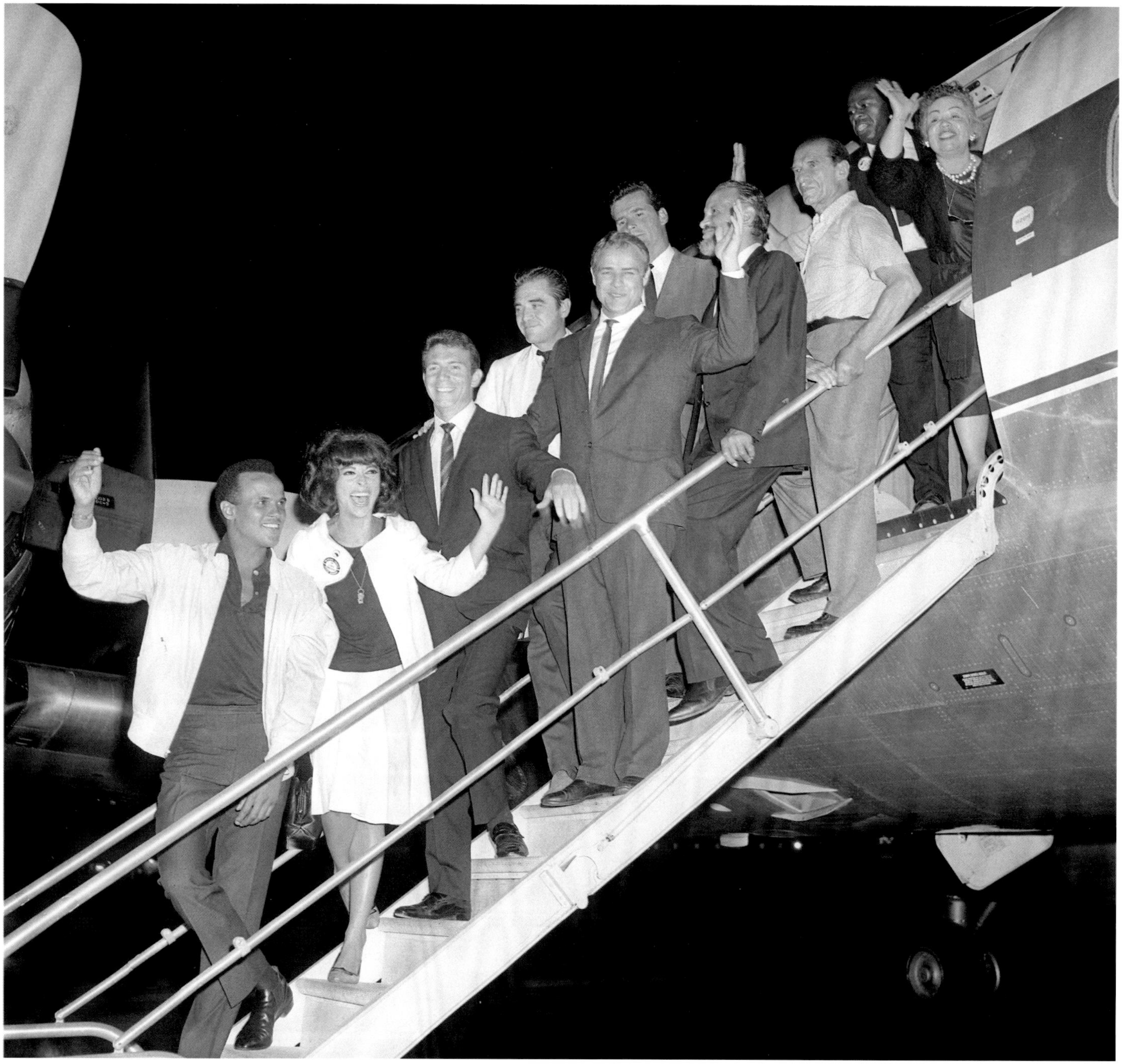

Fig. 2 Hollywood stars and L.A. civil rights leaders board a plane to Washington, DC, to participate in the March on Washington, 1963. *From left*: Harry Belafonte, Rita Moreno, Tony Franciosa, Steve Cochran, Marlon Brando, James Garner, Frank Silvera, two unidentified travelers, and Marnesba Tackett.

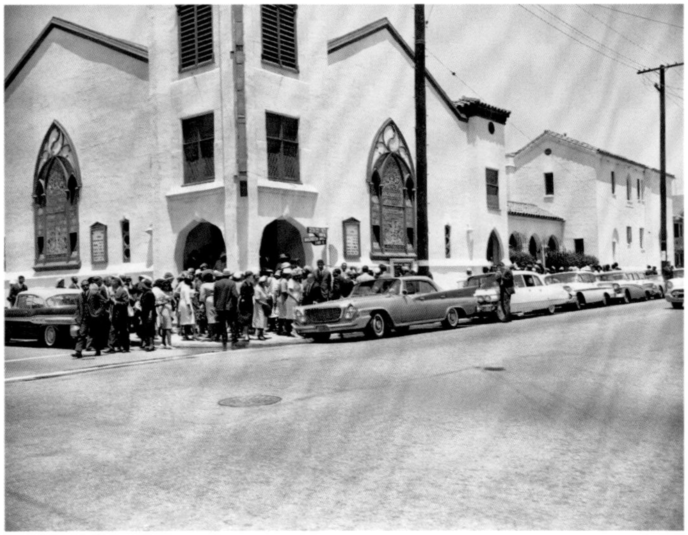

Fig. 3 CHARLES WILLIAMS, 1962. Parishioners gather outside Los Angeles's Ward AME Church preparing to listen to Martin Luther King Jr. speak on Freedom Sunday.

and impact of people and institutions in other parts of the country out of the narrative. In recent decades, an updated approach has encompassed the social and political activism of the 1950s and 1960s in Northern and Western cities. Reflecting on issues and mobilizations all over the United States provides a broader understanding of Jim Crow as a nationwide system of oppression. Equally important is recognizing the interconnectedness of regional movements that helped to make Southern victories possible by intensifying political pressure and contributing essential resources and helping hands over decades. Photojournalism was an important means of communication among the far-flung movements; pictures in newspapers, magazines, and on television showed what was happening on the ground and compelled people to act.

The African American civil rights movement in Los Angeles and the photography that both witnessed and played a role in its progress merit significant attention. Though many Black Angelenos experienced degrees of prosperity and political rights far beyond what was possible elsewhere in the country, historian Douglas Flamming described Black Los Angeles—from its beginnings into the twentieth century—as a "half-free environment."[3] Discrimination was widespread and included restrictive housing covenants, segregated schools, and brutal treatment by law enforcement (fig. 4). African Americans, from factory workers to famous Hollywood entertainers, were legally barred from a variety of hotels, business establishments, swimming pools, and public beaches. Camouflaged among palm trees and birds of paradise, the harsh reality of Black life in an ostensibly liberal city was the kind of open secret that made change difficult to achieve and obscured the local movement from national view.

In fact, Black residents of Los Angeles had built an activist community that challenged discrimination long before the advent of the modern civil rights movement in 1955. Since the founding of the First African Methodist Episcopal (AME) Church of Los Angeles in 1872, the establishment of several Black-owned newspapers between 1879 and 1933, and the increase in local groups and branches of national organizations throughout the twentieth century, including the Afro-American Council and the Los Angeles NAACP, Black voices have been raised in support of equality and against injustice.

Nevertheless, accounts of the civil rights era in Los Angeles often foreground the Watts Uprising of 1965 and feature pictures of billowing smoke and police rifles pointed at Black residents. Though important to the historical record, these images shift the focus away from the long-standing issues that sparked the uprising and overshadow the preceding decades of nonviolent protest and civic engagement.

Marching West uses close examination of the era's powerful imagery—as well as archival research, oral histories, and interviews—to illuminate the inspiring story of African American organizing and activism in Los Angeles, from its earliest days through the civil rights era to Black Power and beyond. It also reveals

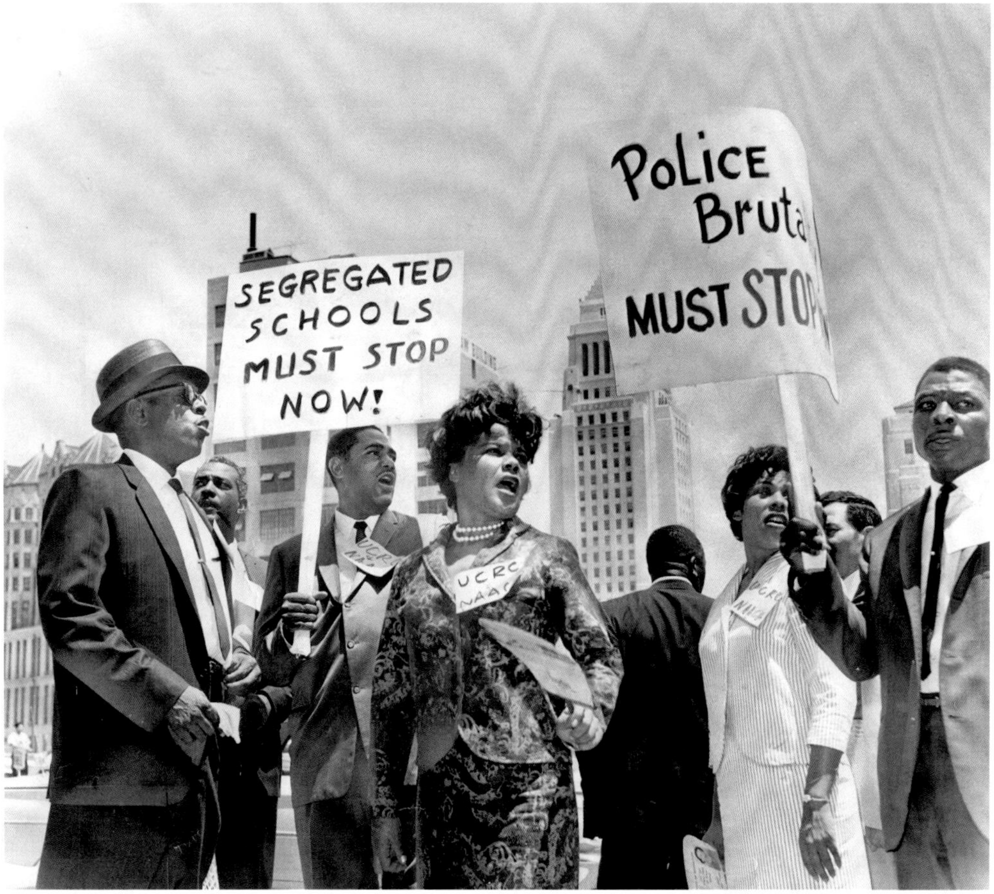

Fig. 4 Integrationists protest near Los Angeles City Hall, 1963.

the mundane and shocking racism that necessitated this chronicle of resistance. Central to the narrative are the talented photojournalists and activist photographers who wielded their cameras as powerful tools for social change, including those who contributed impactful images to L.A.'s Black newspapers, such as the *California Eagle* and the *Los Angeles Sentinel*.

This volume grew from the collections of the Tom & Ethel Bradley Center at California State University, Northridge (CSUN), which holds thousands of photographs documenting African American social, cultural, and political life in Southern California and includes works by notable Black photographers Harry Adams (fig. 5), Guy Crowder, Jack Davis, Joe Flowers, Vera Jackson, Charles Williams, and others. Additional photos selected from the J. Paul Getty Museum, Getty Research Institute, Los Angeles Public Library, and numerous archives, museums, and private collections seek to present a more representative view of civil rights struggles and achievements in the city.

Marching West is both a retrospective and a starting point, inviting a new generation of readers and scholars into the fascinatingly vast archives of the era and contributing to a greater understanding of the historical and ongoing fight for equality in Los Angeles and beyond.

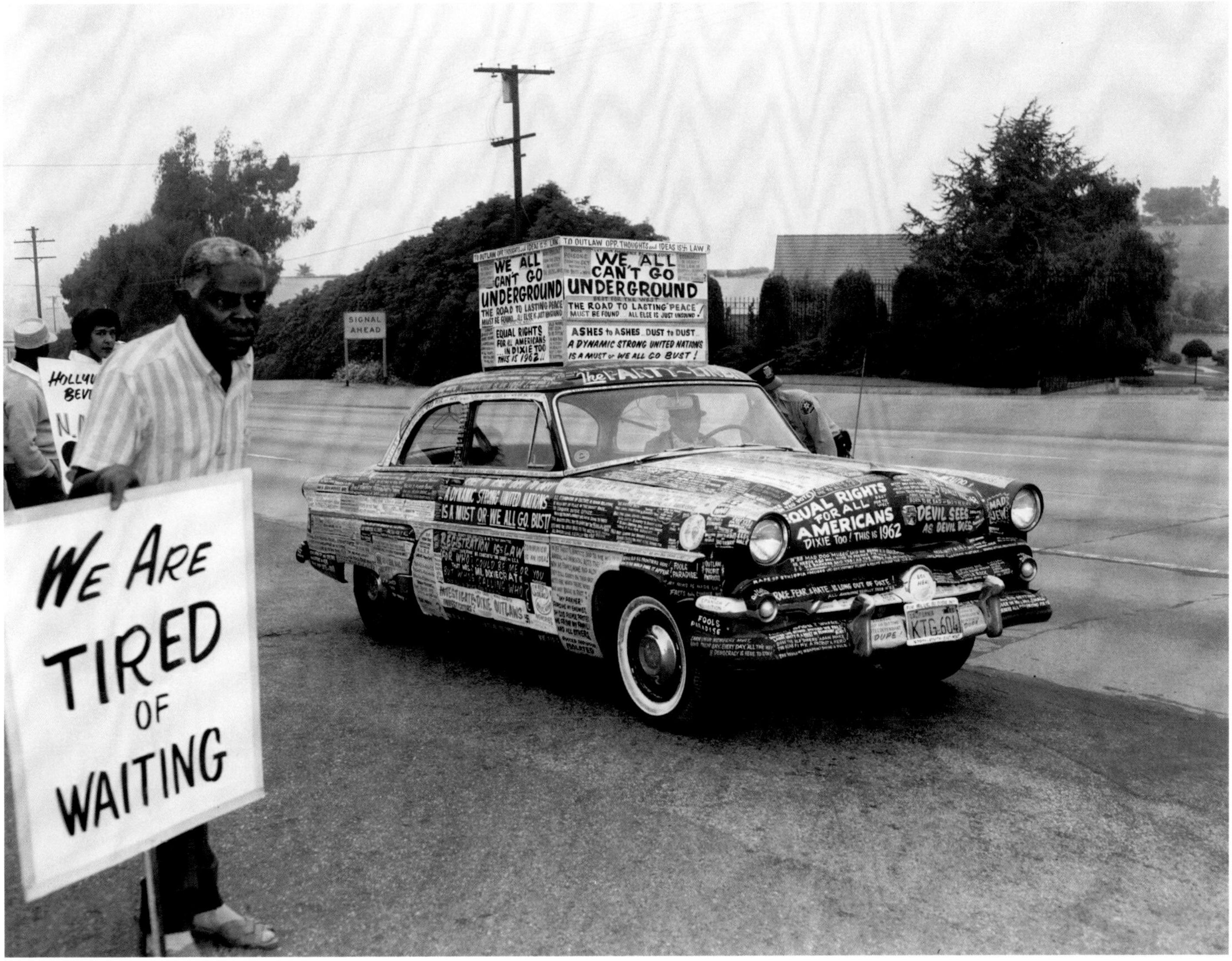

Fig. 5 HARRY ADAMS, 1962. A California car covered in protest signage.

NOTE TO THE READER

Marching West **contains photographs and textual examinations of the history of the civil rights movement in Los Angeles, largely during the nineteenth and twentieth centuries. To encourage a deeper understanding of the movement and the period, some themes and imagery include racial discrimination, violence, and protest. Outdated terms, including those used to identify Black Americans, frequently appear in records of the past. They are mentioned in this book only when used within historical context or in quotations.**

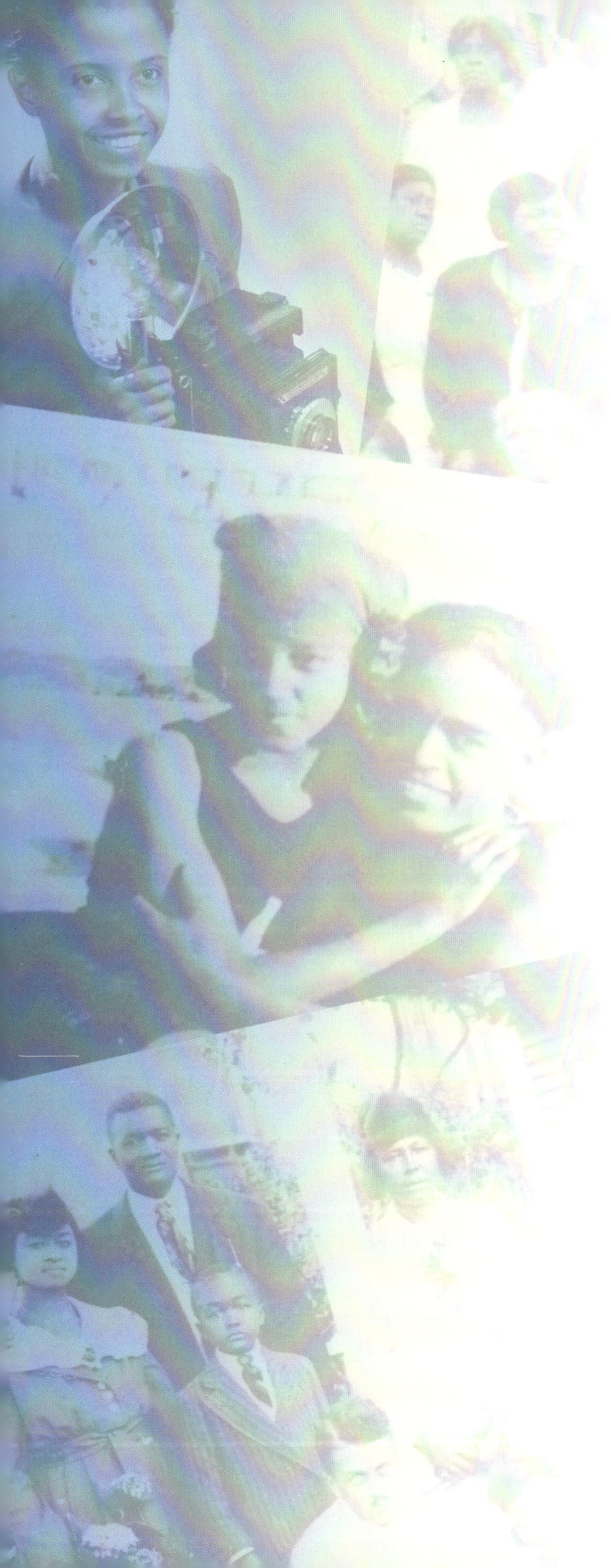

1

Picturing a Community Movement in the West

THE POWER OF SELF-IDENTITY

Photography, in the form of the daguerreotype method, arrived in North America from Europe in December 1839 and spread west during the 1840s. At the time, pervasive racial bigotry and the institution of slavery were ongoing in the United States,[1] and the new technology exposed not only enslavement's cruelties but also the humanity of the Black people who were forced to endure it. African American leaders such as abolitionist and social justice trailblazer Frederick Douglass quickly recognized photography's potential to influence public perception and empower Black individuals to project their own identities. "Men of all conditions may see themselves as others see them," said Douglass, who himself was formerly enslaved. "What was once the exclusive luxury of the rich and great is now within reach of all."[2]

In Los Angeles, Black residents gained access to the new art form as the century progressed. Notable figures, including Bridget "Biddy" Mason (plate 1) and John Ballard (fig. 6), stepped outside their homes or into photography studios to have their pictures taken and their accomplished lives engraved into the city's history. Mason arrived in Los Angeles enslaved but successfully sued for her freedom in 1856. Over time, she established a thriving business based on her reputation as a skilled herbalist, midwife, and nurse. She made wise investments in real estate, acquiring multiple properties including land on what is now Spring Street in downtown Los Angeles. Ballard, a formerly enslaved laborer from Kentucky, became a trader and blacksmith and settled in Los Angeles in 1859 before moving to Agoura Hills, northwest of the city. Both Mason and Ballard were among the civic leaders who helped to establish the earliest African American congregation in Los Angeles, the First African Methodist Episcopal (AME) Church, in 1872. Their rise from enslaved people to entrepreneurs and philanthropists inspired others to go west to escape the oppression of the post–Civil War American South,[3] a path made easier by the extension of the Santa Fe Railway to Los Angeles in 1887. Black-owned newspapers, surreptitiously distributed in the South by Pullman porters, actively promoted the benefits of moving to Los Angeles, emphasizing improved health, less racial violence, and the chance to own property. New arrivals sent encouraging reports back home, and the idea of a fresh start on the West Coast spread throughout the country.

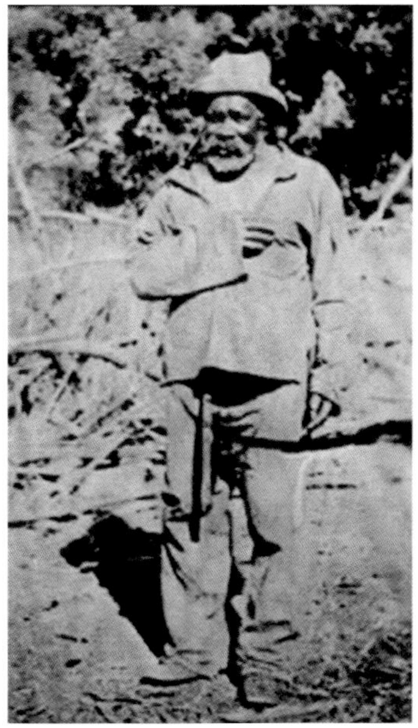

Fig. 6 John Ballard, a formerly enslaved person from Kentucky and one of the cofounders of Los Angeles's First AME Church, on his homestead in Agoura Hills, ca. 1900.

BLACK AMERICA IN PRINT

America's Black-owned newspapers grew in importance during the late nineteenth and early twentieth centuries. Influential Black papers such as Baltimore's *Afro-American* (est. 1892) and the *Pittsburgh Courier* (est. 1907) chronicled local affairs, reported on national news, and campaigned against discrimination. Early issues included engravings, and later ones photos, of Black community leaders, politicians, and newsmakers ranging from athletes and entertainers to soldiers and society's best. The *Chicago*

Defender (est. 1905) and others ran stories about the opportunities available beyond the South, fueling the Great Migration, which saw millions of Black people relocate to Northern and Western states between 1910 and 1970.

While Black Angelenos could obtain Western editions of some major Black papers, they were also served by an expanding Black-owned local press. The *California Eagle* remains perhaps the best-known Black newspaper in Los Angeles history, founded in 1879 by John Neimore. Charlotta Spears joined the staff in 1910 and became owner and managing editor after Neimore's death in 1912 (plate 2). She hired journalist Joseph Bass as editor, and the two eventually married. Over four decades, Charlotta Bass guided the *Eagle*'s weekly coverage of pressing social justice issues, society life, and the everyday concerns of Black citizens. As a civil rights activist, Bass infused the *Eagle* with her political mission, strategically wielding it as a powerful weapon against oppression. Her activism included initiating letter-writing campaigns, leading pickets, confronting the Ku Klux Klan (KKK), establishing new organizations, and running for political office.[4] Angelenos also had access to the early Black-owned paper *New Age Dispatch* (est. 1912) and newsmagazine *The Liberator* (est. 1900), both of which covered local politics and promoted educational, social, and economic uplift in the community.

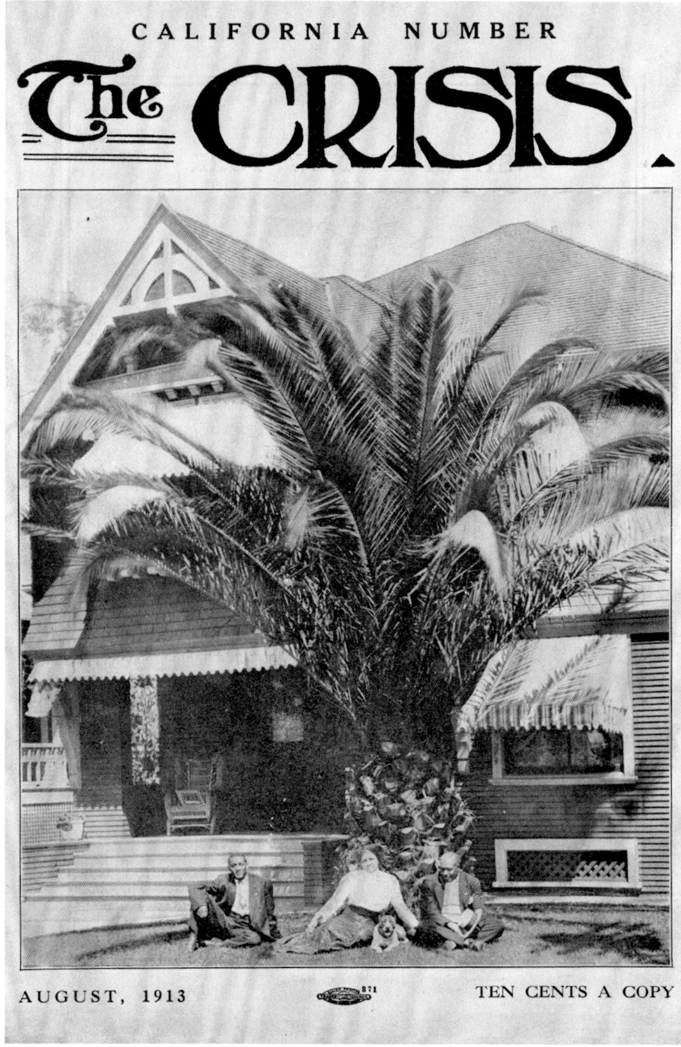

Fig. 7 Home of Mr. and Mrs. William Foster, featured on the cover of *The Crisis* magazine, 1913.

MAKING L.A. HOME

By the turn of the twentieth century, Los Angeles was home to 2,131 African Americans, constituting 2 percent of the city's population and representing the largest Black community in California.[5] At that time, thanks to comparatively inexpensive real estate and new construction, rates of homeownership for Black people in Los Angeles were greater than in other parts of the country. Affluent families embraced photography as a means of recording their social progress and family legacy. In 1910, for example, the Rozier family posed for a group portrait outside their L.A. bungalow (plate 3).

Early in the century, Black Angelenos established numerous community support organizations. The Los Angeles Sunday Forum was created in 1903 and led by individuals including John Wesley Coleman, founder of an employment agency; Jefferson Lewis Edmonds, founder of *The Liberator*; Rev. Jarrett E. Edwards, pastor of First AME Church; and Frederick Madison Roberts, future state assemblyman and owner of the *New Age Dispatch*. The forum supported westward migration among Southern African Americans through charitable initiatives, relief programs, scholarships, and job placement assistance.[6] The city also boasted several branches of national and statewide organizations, including the Afro-American Council and the National Association of Colored Women's Clubs (plate 4).

L.A.'s growing Black community enjoyed visits from prominent national leaders. Author and educator Booker T. Washington arrived by train on New Year's Day, 1903, on a fundraising tour for the Tuskegee Institute (now Tuskegee University), the Black college he established in Alabama in 1881. In Los Angeles, he spoke to an integrated audience of three thousand to four thousand people. Commenting on his trip, he observed, "The colored people of the Pacific coast, as a general thing, so prosperous, so intelligent and so well informed not only as to matters pertaining to the race in the country as a whole but particularly as regarding the history and work of Tuskegee."[7]

In 1913, W. E. B. Du Bois, distinguished African American sociologist, author, and cofounder of the National Association for the Advancement of Colored People (NAACP), visited Los Angeles to rally support for the organization. After his trip, he published an article titled "Colored California" in the NAACP magazine, *The Crisis*. He commented on the beauty, fresh air, sunlight, and hospitality he experienced, and he wrote: "These colored people are pushing and energetic. They are without doubt the most beautifully housed group of colored people in the United States."[8] *The Crisis* employed photography to increase its popularity with readers and further its mission, alternating its visual focus between the dark realities of racism and celebrations of Black accomplishment. The August 1913 cover featured the picturesque home of Mr. and Mrs. William Foster (fig. 7). Nearly filling the frame is a lush palm tree, a symbol of the California dream.

The following spring, a chapter of the NAACP was officially established in Los Angeles. John Somerville, a dentist and the first African American graduate of the University of Southern California (USC), was one of the new chapter's founders. His wife, Vada Watson Somerville, was also active in the NAACP and in 1918 was the first Black woman to receive a degree from USC's School of Dentistry.

Photography grew more accessible and personal in the early twentieth century. Smaller cameras that were affordable and easy to use made taking snapshots a popular hobby for amateurs. In a picture taken about 1920, Los Angeles teen Ernestine Jones points a hand-held camera toward the photographer snapping her photo (fig. 8).

SEPARATE TOGETHER

The NAACP's goal of a fully integrated society gained broad support in Los Angeles. At the same time, some African Americans favored building independent communities, proving their ability to pioneer and run their own municipalities.[9] Col. Allen Allensworth (fig. 9), with William A. Payne, organized the California Colony and Home Promoting Association and established California's first all-Black town in 1908. The town was envisioned as a self-governed, Black-led community where residents could live with dignity, free from the discrimination that defined much of the era. Historian Susan D. Anderson described it as "a civic model so that Americans couldn't have any justification for Jim Crow."[10]

Colonel Allensworth was born enslaved in 1842 and rose to become a buffalo soldier, chaplain, and the highest-ranking Black officer in the US Army before retiring in 1906. He wrote: "We encourage our people to develop the best there is in them under the most

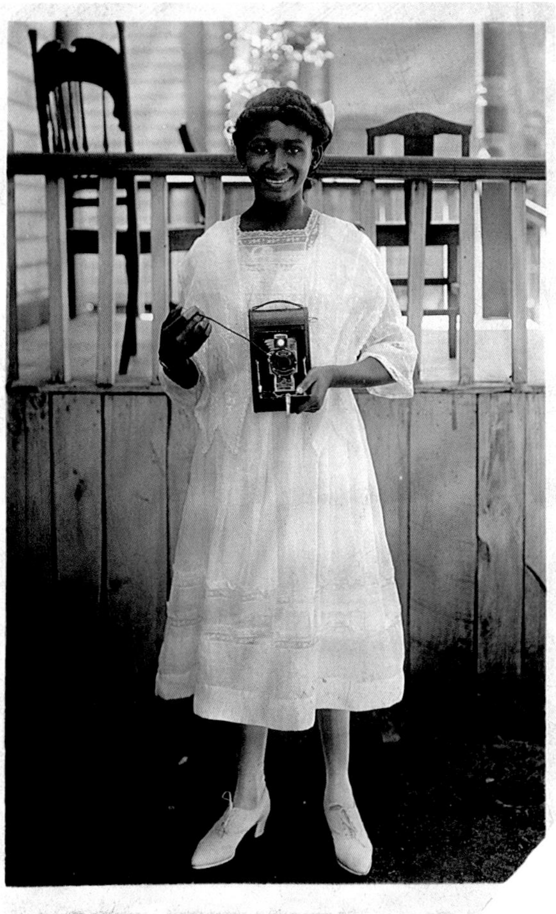

Fig. 8 Thirteen-year-old Ernestine Jones holds a camera outside a Los Angeles home, ca. 1920.

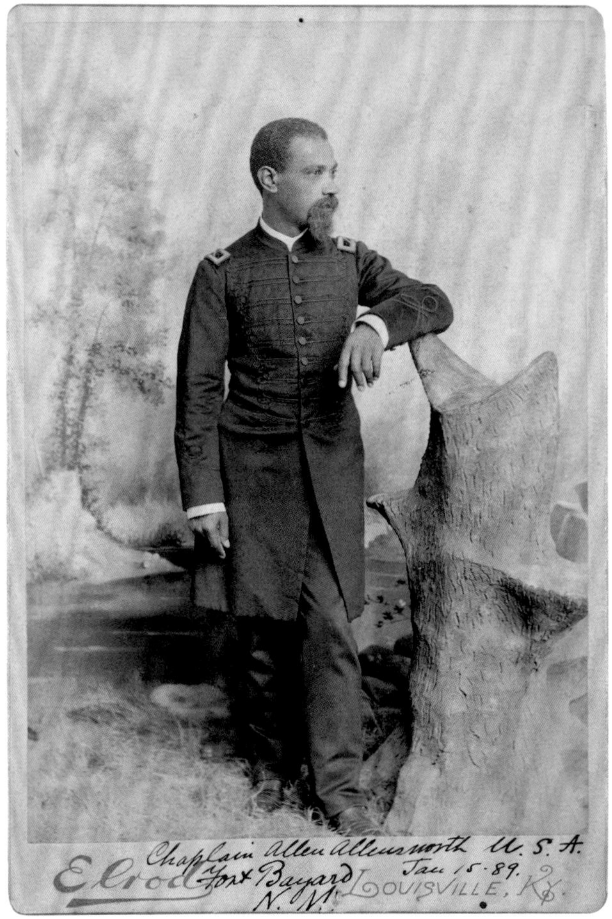

Fig. 9 Carte de visite of Col. Allen Allensworth in military uniform, 1889.

favorable conditions of mind and body. This we have in California, as you are aware."[11]

The town of Allensworth, about thirty miles north of Bakersfield, initially thrived, boasting a school, courthouse, church, businesses, and a bustling economy. Payne, an educator from West Virginia and a graduate of Denison University, spearheaded the establishment of the Allensworth Public School, which became its own county school district in 1912, enabling the Black community to govern its educational system and access public funding. However, the town faced a series of setbacks. The Santa Fe Railway altered its route to bypass Allensworth, and drought and a failing water supply presented significant challenges. Colonel Allensworth was struck by a motorcycle and killed in 1914. These factors led to the town's decline, prompting most residents to leave by the end of World War I.[12]

The pursuit of Black independence continued when several Black residents of Los Angeles established a local chapter of Marcus Garvey's Universal

Negro Improvement Association (UNIA) in 1920. The national organization had been founded six years earlier, in 1914, driven by the ideals of racial pride, economic self-sufficiency, and the establishment of a sovereign Black nation outside the borders of the United States.[13]

HOLLYWOOD AND RACISM

The NAACP grew into one of the most influential civil rights organizations in the city. Backed by its national office with funding and a team of experienced civil rights lawyers, the L.A. chapter fought legally and societally encoded rules that blocked marginalized groups from progressing socially, economically, and politically. It attracted national attention with its active opposition to the film *The Birth of a Nation*. Released in 1915, the Civil War epic was the most technically and artistically advanced movie of its time, and it remains a landmark in the emergence of the Hollywood film industry. But its blatantly racist portrayal of Southern African Americans and heroic depiction of the KKK raised moral objections and safety concerns in the Black community. Wrote Du Bois: "A new art was used deliberately to slander and vilify a race.... We decided to try to make the authorities stop the picture on the grounds that it was a public menace, that it was not art but vicious propaganda."[14] Bass referred to the film as "The Big Lie" in her *Eagle* column. She filed unsuccessfully for an injunction against it while it was still in production.[15] The Los Angeles NAACP called on the local censorship board to stop the film's premiere; met with the mayor, chief of police, and city council; and took its case to court. Though the city council favored a ban, a California Supreme Court judge ruled that there were no legal means to enforce it. The L.A. chapter persisted in its opposition, which raised awareness and led to a national effort to ban the film, though it was met with limited success.

In 1916, the brothers Noble and George Johnson founded the Lincoln Motion Picture Company, partly in response to the racism of *The Birth of a Nation* (plate 5). Lincoln, possibly the first all-Black movie production company in the United States, made films that showcased Black talent and appealed to African American audiences (plate 6). The nuanced Black characters in Lincoln movies inhabited dignified roles and costumes, in contrast to many mainstream Hollywood movies in which Black roles were played by white actors in blackface, usually for comedic or derogatory effect. Lincoln films were shown in churches, schools, and "colored-only" theaters, and though they received positive reviews in the Black press and were popular with Black audiences, segregation prevented them from achieving wider recognition. The company remained in operation until 1923.

The KKK had been defunct for almost fifty years when the pending release of *The Birth of a Nation* contributed to a resurgence of the white supremacist organization and its practices of intimidation and extralegal violence. The revived Klan's popularity peaked in the 1920s and continued into subsequent decades, and L.A.'s Black community was subjected to cross burnings, kidnappings, and lynchings (plate 7). In 1922, the anti-Klan district attorney Thomas Lee Woolwine issued a warrant to search the organization's Los Angeles headquarters. A list of members was discovered that included the names of city and county law enforcement and government officials, some of whom had condemned the Klan in public.[16]

ORGANIZING UNITY

The 1920s would prove a productive decade for Black organizing in Los Angeles. The year 1921 saw the founding of the Los Angeles Urban League, a local chapter of a national organization chartered to help African Americans who had migrated to urban centers find employment, housing, and social services. The Urban League also launched educational initiatives and advocated for better schools in Black neighborhoods. In 1925, the Brotherhood of Sleeping Car Porters (BSCP) was established as a national union representing Pullman porters and other attendants serving passengers on the railways. The Los Angeles branch was founded in 1926 as a result of BSCP founder

A. Philip Randolph's efforts to establish local divisions throughout the United States. However, the local group struggled to build a strong presence, primarily because city leaders were unfriendly to organized labor. This anti-union environment was compounded by the open racism of the American Federation of Labor (AFL), which prompted fear that Black workers would be targeted. In addition, direct competition from the Dining Car Employees Union divided potential membership among railway workers.[17]

Working alongside the Urban League and the BSCP was the UNIA Division 156 in Los Angeles, which by 1921 had become the largest UNIA chapter in the Western region with a membership of over a thousand.[18] Its members were associated with key financial institutions like Liberty Savings and Loan Association, Unity Finance Company, and Golden State Mutual Life Insurance Company to empower the Black community with financial resources and capital.[19] The organization was established by John Wesley Coleman, J. D. Gordon, W. H. "Pop" Saunders, and Charlotta and Joseph Bass. Noah Thompson, the only Black journalist at the *Los Angeles Evening Express*, and Charlotta Bass were elected president and "lady president," respectively. The local UNIA's collaborative approach extended to diverse racial groups. For example, UNIA members in Los Angeles actively protested the 1913 Alien Land Act, which prohibited "aliens ineligible for citizenship" from owning land and effectively discriminated against the city's Japanese immigrant community.[20]

Following accusations of financial impropriety at the national office in 1921, local members declared independence from the UNIA and formed the Pacific Coast Universal Negro Improvement Association (PCUNIA). However, Marcus Garvey remained a popular figure; when he visited the city in 1922, he received a warm welcome and appeared in an automobile parade down Central Avenue with Frederick Madison Roberts,[21] who had been elected to the California State Assembly in 1918 (fig. 10).

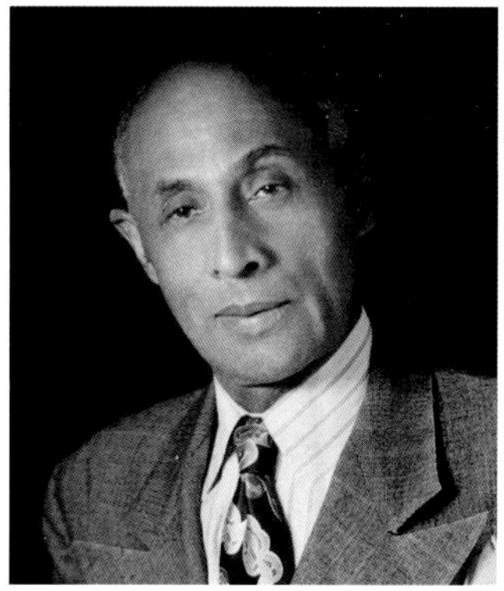

Fig. 10 Frederick Madison Roberts, founder of the *New Age Dispatch* and California's first Black state legislator, ca. 1930–40. Roberts was the great-grandson of Thomas Jefferson and Sally Hemings.

While the PCUNIA contemplated its work without a parent organization, the NAACP made significant strides in court against segregation. In 1925, the NAACP filed suit against the Los Angeles Playground and Recreation Commission to end a new policy that restricted access to city swimming pools for people of color to one designated day per week. At that time, most of Southern California's beaches were also effectively off limits to African Americans, with the exception of segregated Bay Street Beach, derisively nicknamed the "Inkwell," located near Pico Boulevard in Santa Monica (plate 8). Bruce's Beach, a Black-owned resort, opened in 1912 but was shut down in 1924 by the City of Manhattan Beach, which used eminent domain to seize the property from its owners and then left it sitting undeveloped for decades.

The city pool lawsuit was initiated by George Cushnie with the support of NAACP attorney E. Burton Ceruti. Cushnie and his three children lived near the Exposition Park pool and used it often before the new segregation policy was enforced. Though Cushnie's case was dismissed, it inspired activists to raise funds to continue the fight. Led by Betty Hill, a founding member of the Los Angeles NAACP and an organizer of the Westside Property Owners Association, they aided Ethel Prioleau in her lawsuit *Ethel Prioleau v. Board of Playground and Recreation Commissioners*, filed after her family was denied access to the public

Fig. 11 Postcard featuring the Hotel Somerville, built by John Somerville to host the 1928 NAACP national convention in Los Angeles, 1928. The stock market crash of 1929 would force Somerville to sell the hotel, which was renamed the Dunbar and became the epicenter of the West Coast jazz scene from the 1930s through the 1950s.

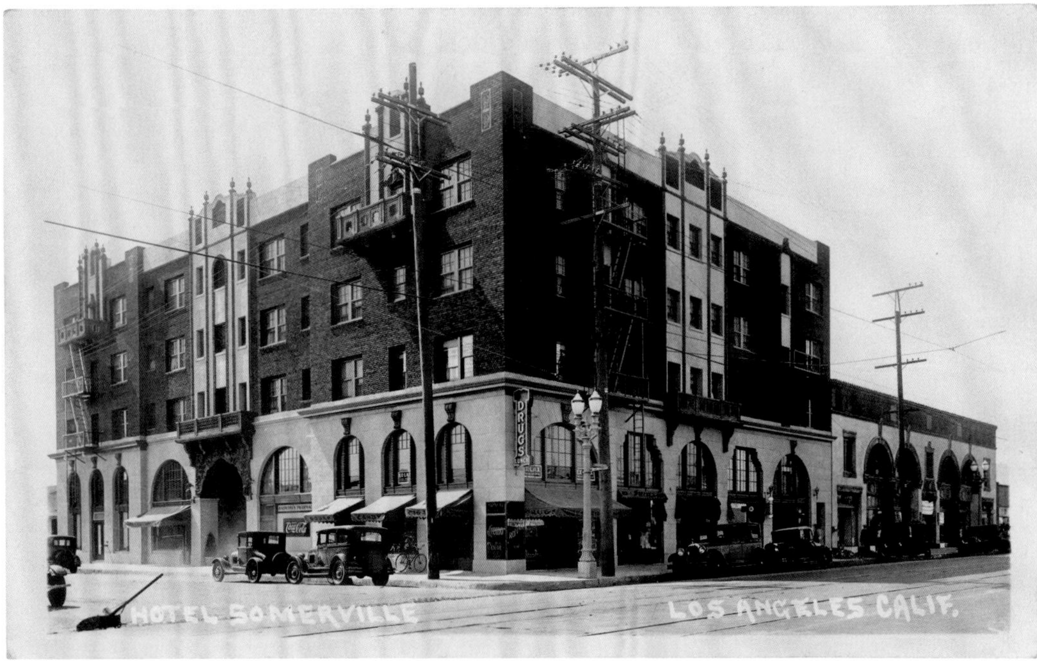

bathhouse at Lake Cabrillo in Los Angeles in 1929.[22] In 1931, Los Angeles County Superior Court Judge Walter S. Gates ruled that the commission had violated California civil rights laws, and all of the city's swimming pools were desegregated. Claude Hudson, president of the Los Angeles branch of the NAACP, wrote about the national importance of the decision, stating that "the humiliation of children daily does such harm that it is impossible to calculate."[23] In 1927, an NAACP legal effort led to a court decision upholding equal access to all public beaches in California.

NATIONAL STAGE

The size and accomplishments of the Los Angeles NAACP chapter were critical factors in the city's selection to host the organization's national convention in 1928, the first time that this major civil rights gathering was held west of the Mississippi. John Somerville's pledge to construct a hotel specifically to accommodate visiting NAACP delegates was instrumental in securing the convention. Located in the heart of L.A.'s African American community, the Hotel Somerville offered a luxurious reprieve from the discrimination Black travelers typically faced. The brick building was beautiful, with a main entrance leading to an open-air courtyard highlighted by Spanish tile, a lovely fountain, and leafy palms arching from each corner (fig. 11).[24] The delegates arrived from forty-four states. Hudson and Los Angeles Mayor George Cryer welcomed the guests, and Du Bois gave the keynote address. Second Baptist Church hosted panels and workshops during the day, and evening entertainment unfolded on lively Central Avenue. Du Bois called the 1928 NAACP conference "a jewel done with loving hands."[25] The Los Angeles NAACP convention played an important role in connecting East Coast and West Coast participants in the civil rights movement.

One national victory affected many Los Angeles residents in the 1930s: the BSCP secured its first major contract with the Pullman Company.

A. Philip Randolph engaged community organizations and media outlets such as the *New Age Dispatch* and the *Eagle* to denounce what they saw as Pullman's "master and slave relationship" with its employees.[26] The 1937 contract marked the first time a predominantly African American union won collective bargaining rights with a major US corporation.[27] It secured better wages and reduced working hours for Black porters in Los Angeles, bolstering the city's growing African American middle class.

EXPANDING COVERAGE OF THE COMMUNITY

In 1930, Leon Washington was persuaded by his cousin, journalist, groundbreaking civil rights attorney (and later *Eagle* owner) Loren Miller, to move to Los Angeles from Kansas (fig. 12). After two years as an advertising salesman at the *Eagle*, Washington started his own publication, the *Eastside Shopper*, which would become the *Los Angeles Sentinel*. Washington's background in sales supported the business side of the venture, and he also became well known for his reporting and editorials. During the Great Depression, Washington confronted employment discrimination with a "Don't Spend Where You Can't Work" campaign. His research, photography, and reportage mobilized readers to boycott businesses that catered to Black customers but refused to hire Black workers.

During the 1930s, the NAACP and other civil rights groups increased their use of photography to drive change or represent the goals and ideals of their organizations. They often issued prints along with press releases to augment the impact of their messaging, and they included images in their own publications. *The Crisis* continued to lead by example, featuring outstanding work by California photographer Frank Cloud, among others.

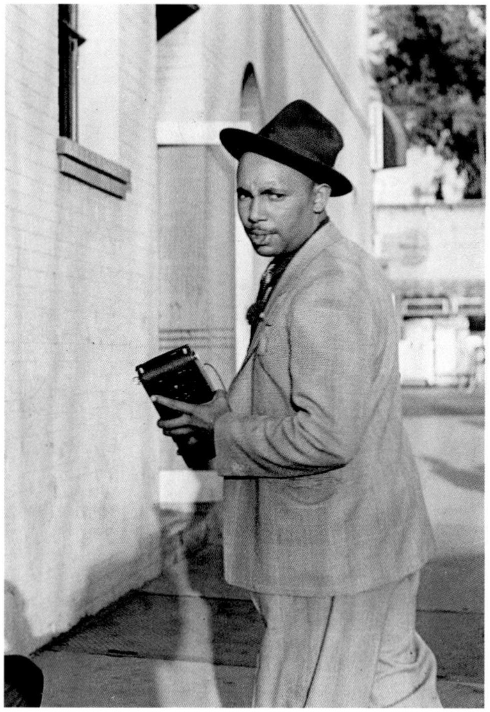

Fig. 12 Leon Washington, founder of the *Los Angeles Sentinel*, ca. 1930s.

WARTIME LOS ANGELES

Following the 1941 entry of the United States into World War II, California became a critical hub for war industry production. African Americans and others seeking employment arrived by the thousands. However, in Los Angeles and nationwide, Black men and women faced employment discrimination in both military and government-contracted roles. Randolph of the BSCP leveraged the threat of a massive march on Washington to challenge this injustice. His pressure compelled President Franklin D. Roosevelt to take action, resulting in Executive Order 8802, which prohibited racial discrimination in the defense industry and established the Fair Employment Practices Committee (FEPC).[28]

VERA JACKSON

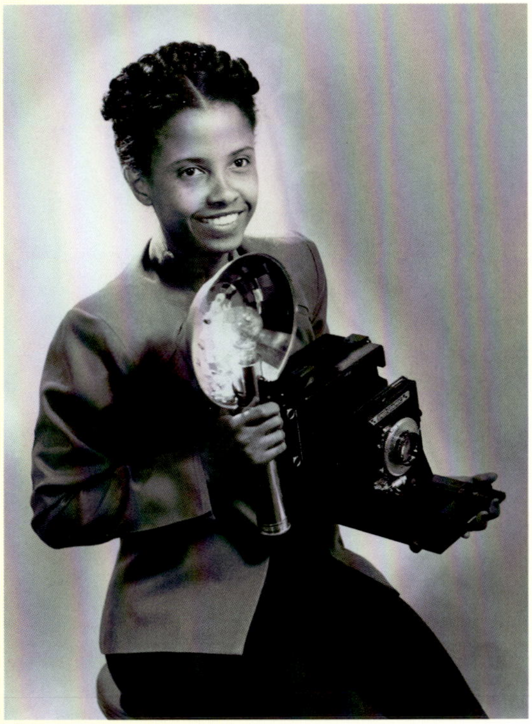

Vera Jackson (1911–1999) moved with her family to Corona, California, when she was a child (fig. 13). Jackson's father was an amateur photographer who inspired her interest in the medium. She learned the craft in a Depression-era photography workshop and in classes at Frank Wiggins Trade School in Los Angeles. Her printing skills earned her a job as an assistant to photographer Maceo Sheffield, whose images appeared in the *California Eagle.* Jackson was hired as a staff photographer at the *Eagle* after meeting editor and publisher Charlotta Bass, becoming one of a few professional Black female photographers in the United States at the time. Working with society page editor Jessica Mae Brown and Bass, Jackson aimed to counter stereotypical portrayals of Black people in Los Angeles and in popular culture. "We had a feeling that we were somebody important, so we really tried to make our subjects look extra good," she said. Jackson's coverage of L.A.'s early civil rights movement complemented Bass's crusade for racial justice. "Mrs. Bass was a real fighter, way ahead of her time.... She'd write ... the editorials and illustrate it with our pictures."[31]

Fig. 13 Vera Jackson, ca. 1940s.

In Los Angeles in 1942, civil rights activist Walter Williams, with Joseph James, president of the San Francisco NAACP, cofounded the Shipyard Workers Committee for Equal Participation, which advocated for equal opportunities for Black workers through rallies and petition drives. When the Boilermakers Union resisted cooperating with the FEPC, Williams and James filed lawsuits against the shipyards and the union.[29] In *James v. Marinship* (1944), the California Supreme Court ruled that Black people could not be arbitrarily excluded from joining the union, and in the case of *Williams v. Int. etc. of Boilermakers* (1946), a judge banned unequal policies and discrimination.[30] Ultimately, civil rights advocacy pressured the Roosevelt administration to desegregate shipyard jobs in Los Angeles and nationwide, opening tens of thousands of jobs to Black workers.

During World War II, Black Angelenos joined the "Double V" campaign, a movement begun by the *Pittsburgh Courier* to recognize that African Americans bravely fighting overseas or otherwise engaged in the war effort still endured racial discrimination at home. The goal of the movement was a "double victory" over fascism abroad and racism in the United States. The

HOWARD MOREHEAD

Howard Morehead (1926–2003) arrived in Los Angeles after training with the Army Air Corps at Tuskegee Airfield during World War II. The war ended before he could become a Tuskegee Airman. After studying photography at Los Angeles City College, Morehead began freelancing and then joined the *Los Angeles Sentinel* in 1950. In 1958, he became the first West Coast staff photographer at Johnson Publishing Company, owner of *Ebony* and *Jet* magazines. His longtime interest in jazz brought him into contact with many music icons, and he later shot album covers for singer Ray Charles. In 1970, Morehead became the first Black cameraman at an L.A. television station—KTLA-TV—and worked in the industry for nearly twenty years. He is well known for his glamour photography and for the Miss Bronze beauty pageant beginning in 1958, which provided Black women in Los Angeles with modeling opportunities during a time when they faced significant discrimination elsewhere.

campaign was actively promoted in the *Sentinel* and *Eagle*, and the energy of the protests was conveyed in the images of photographer Vera Jackson (plate 9).

Rev. Clayton Russell of the People's Independent Church in Los Angeles founded the Negro Victory Committee (NVC) in July 1941. Working with the Congress of Industrial Organizations (CIO) and the NAACP, the NVC confronted discrimination within the United States Employment Service (USES). Russell led a direct-action protest at local USES offices, accompanied by hundreds of Black women ready to apply for defense jobs. Eventually, USES representatives from Washington were sent to L.A. to ensure equal-opportunity hiring. The action paved the way for similar results in the Bay Area.[32]

Performer Hattie McDaniel, who won an Academy Award for Best Supporting Actress for her role in the film *Gone with the Wind*, served as chair of the Negro Division of the Hollywood Victory Committee. She and other entertainers performed for Black soldiers at hospitals, military bases, and bond rallies (plate 10).

HARMONIZING FOR JUSTICE

Los Angeles was the West Coast hub for jazz music, the original African American art form, from the 1920s through the 1950s. Music rang out from the Dunbar Hotel and clubs up and down Central Avenue, made by local musicians and such visiting luminaries as Louis Armstrong, Duke Ellington, and Billie Holiday. Photographers including Howard Morehead and Bob Douglas captured the excitement of the era and created sophisticated portraits for album covers, newspapers, and popular magazines (plates 11, 12).

Yet, just as the movie industry reinforced Hollywood's racial hierarchies, the wider Los Angeles music industry was also fraught with inequality. The American Federation of Musicians Local 47, established in 1897, was exclusively for white musicians, and Local 767 served Black musicians. Local 47 controlled access to Hollywood's best-paying jobs in recording studios, radio shows, and top venues, while talented Black musicians like Buddy Collette, Charles Mingus, and members of Local 767 were limited to lower-paying gigs despite their tremendous contributions to the city's music scene.[33] The push for change began in the early 1950s, when activists such as Marl Young joined forces with musicians including Collette, Bill Douglass, and Benny Carter to form a committee advocating for a merger of the two unions.[34] Their three-year campaign, supported by the interracial group Musicians for Amalgamation and NAACP representatives such as Lester Bailey, successfully pressured the two unions to merge in 1953.[35] While this historic agreement was supposed to guarantee equal treatment for all musicians, informal discrimination continued, making the merger just the first step toward real equality rather than an instant solution to decades of racial exclusion.[36]

THE FIGHT FOR FAIR HOUSING

By the end of World War II, about a half million African Americans had moved to Los Angeles from the South, from states such as Louisiana, Texas, and Mississippi. While some were able to earn a decent salary, it was still difficult for many Black families to find adequate housing. Segregation resulted in overcrowding and unsafe conditions in minority neighborhoods, an issue brought to wider attention through pictures.

Bass felt that an important "step then was to arouse the interest of all the people by taking photographs of some of the worst spots on the Eastside and printing them and their stories in the *Eagle*."[37] In January 1946, the *Sentinel* highlighted deplorable housing conditions in a Black neighborhood near 45th Street and Central Avenue. The article's subtitle read: "Overcrowding, Sanitation Lack, High Rents in 'Ghetto' Districts Create Scandalous Situation." Seven published images showed piles of garbage, families doubled up in apartments or living in storefronts, and substandard housing without working plumbing.[38]

Photojournalist Leonard Nadel began taking pictures of the city's public housing projects, including the Pueblo del Rio complex built in the early 1940s to house defense industry workers. His photos came to the attention of the Housing Authority of the City of Los Angeles (HACLA), which hired him in 1949 to document living conditions in deteriorating neighborhoods as well as in housing projects built during and after the war (plate 13).

In Los Angeles and other cities throughout the United States, housing discrimination was codified with restrictive housing covenants—clauses written into property deeds in specific neighborhoods to prevent the sale, lease, or rental of homes to African Americans and often to other ethnic and religious groups such as Asian Americans, Mexican Americans, and Jewish Americans. Even Black families with significant financial means still had difficulty purchasing homes. Those who managed to do so were often harassed by angry mobs or the KKK (plates 14, 15).

In 1945, O'Day H. Short, a civil rights activist from Mississippi, purchased land in Fontana, a town roughly forty-six miles east of Los Angeles. He was confronted by white vigilantes, who threatened violence if he refused to leave. Despite reporting the threats to the FBI and the local sheriff, Short received no protection. The Fontana Chamber of Commerce offered to buy Short's home and relocate his family to North Fontana, where other African Americans resided, but Short defiantly refused. On December 16, 1945, Short's home was set on fire with his family inside, resulting in the deaths of his wife, Helen Short, and the couple's two children. Short survived the fire but later died of his injuries.[39]

Also in 1945, eight white homeowners in the Los Angeles neighborhood of West Adams Heights sued to evict their Black neighbors, claiming violations of restrictive covenants. The first African American resident of the neighborhood was Norman O. Houston, cofounder of the Golden State Mutual Life Insurance Company. Established in 1925, it was the only company providing quality life insurance to Black residents in California, and at one point, it was considered the largest Black-owned insurance company in the West.[40]

After he purchased a mansion in 1938, Houston paved the way for other Black professionals and entertainers who wished to live in the area. Eventually, West Adams Heights was rechristened Sugar Hill, in reference to the affluent Black neighborhood in Harlem, New York, that had been home to notable figures including future Supreme Court Justice Thurgood Marshall and jazz legend Duke Ellington. In 1941, Hattie McDaniel purchased a mansion in Sugar Hill. Her arrival attracted white and Black celebrities to the area to participate in her famous soirées and salons.

The 1945 lawsuit brought by the white homeowners asserted that "if restrictive covenants were not enforced, their property would lose value and racial clashes would inevitably ensue."[41] In response, McDaniel, actress Louise Beavers, singer Ethel Waters, and thirty other Black residents contested the lawsuit. Under the leadership of attorney and former Los Angeles NAACP president Claude Hudson, NAACP lawyer Loren Miller argued against restrictive covenants in court. As a result, on December 5, 1945, Judge Thurmond Clarke of the Los Angeles Superior Court issued a landmark decision declaring restrictive covenants a violation of the Equal Protection Clause of the Fourteenth Amendment. Miller, along with Marshall, would go on to successfully argue the issue before the US Supreme Court. The *Shelley v. Kraemer* decision of 1948 outlawed restrictive covenants nationwide.[42]

CONFRONTING POLICE BRUTALITY

Los Angeles's Black newspapers fearlessly and consistently addressed the ongoing issue of police brutality. However, violent incidents were rarely caught on film, so editors used a wide variety of pictures and strategies to bear witness and raise awareness. Black veterans beaten by police posed for news photographers wearing their military uniforms. Mothers stood beside their bandaged children. The August 26, 1948, issue of the *Sentinel* covered a particularly brutal incident in which "one man was clubbed to death, one hospitalized, and another jailed after a dance. All were brothers and members of a family highly respected in the community.... Special police officers, sided by two members of the Los Angeles Police Department, it is alleged, turned in a gory night's work" (fig. 14).[43]

The Los Angeles NAACP chapter investigated cases of police brutality and included photographic evidence of victims' wounds in its documentation. Written reports detailing the attacks mentioned that photographs were available, though only the Black press would publish the shocking images. In 1991, former *Eagle* and *Sentinel* reporter Brad Pye Jr. discussed the difficulty of covering police brutality: "The police officers were never wrong. Unfortunately, there weren't any videos." Pye continued, "During the Rodney King testimony, there was a guy who came up to me with the front page of the *California Eagle* where he was beaten up just like Rodney King, and nobody covered it but the Black press."[44]

MULTICULTURAL SOLIDARITY

As Los Angeles rapidly expanded in the 1930s and 1940s, informal bigotry and codified restrictions resulted in widespread segregation, with Asian, Black, Latino, Jewish, and European-immigrant communities squeezed into separate neighborhoods. Overcrowding created competition for housing, employment, and political power and the potential for both conflict and collaboration.[45] In the Central Avenue district and downtown, proximity created natural contact points between different groups, though most developed parallel institutions, including churches, newspapers, and business associations.

Little Tokyo was home to a thriving population of thirty-five thousand by 1942. But the Japanese attack on Pearl Harbor on December 7, 1941, followed by President Roosevelt's signing of Executive Order 9066 on February 19, 1942, turned it into a ghost town. The order enabled the US government to cruelly and forcibly move Japanese Americans from their homes to remote internment camps. The newly vacated area provided room for growth to African Americans living in adjacent overcrowded neighborhoods and housing for those streaming into the city to fill wartime jobs.[46]

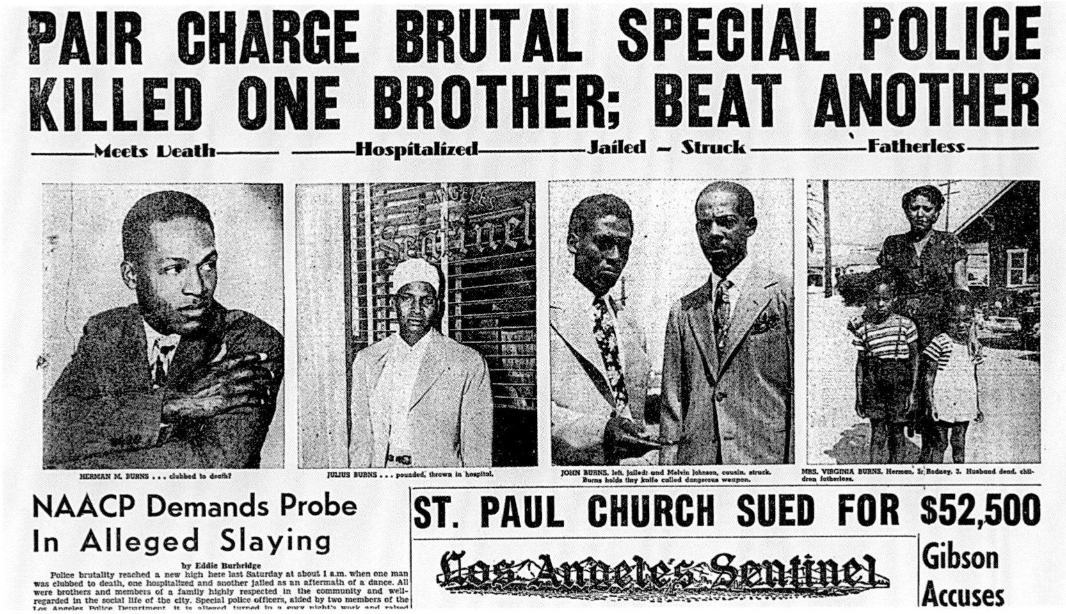

PAIR CHARGE BRUTAL SPECIAL POLICE KILLED ONE BROTHER; BEAT ANOTHER

—Meets Death— —Hospitalized— —Jailed – Struck— —Fatherless—

HERMAN M. BURNS . . . clubbed to death?

JULIUS BURNS . . . pounded, thrown in hospital,

JOHN BURNS, left, jailed: and Melvin Johnson, cousin, struck. Burns holds tiny knife called dangerous weapon.

MRS. VIRGINIA BURNS, Herman, 5; Rodney, 3. Husband dead, children fatherless.

NAACP Demands Probe In Alleged Slaying

by Eddie Burbridge

Police brutality reached a new high here last Saturday at about 1 a.m. when one man was clubbed to death, one hospitalized and another jailed as an aftermath of a dance. All were brothers and members of a family highly respected in the community and well-regarded in the social life of the city. Special police officers, aided by two members of the

ST. PAUL CHURCH SUED FOR $52,500

Los Angeles Sentinel

Gibson Accuses

Fig. 14 Front page of the August 26, 1948, issue of the *Los Angeles Sentinel.*

Temporarily dubbed Bronzeville, it became for three years a vibrant and evolving ecosystem.

As the war progressed, there was a shift in coverage in the Black news media, including the *Eagle*. In an editorial on November 11, 1943, it apologized for its initially meek response to internment and forcefully called the "persecution of the Japanese-American minority . . . one of the disgraceful aspects of the nation's conduct of the People's War." [47]

When Japanese Americans returned after the war, some white Angelenos predicted that racial violence would erupt between the area's Japanese American and Black residents. Though there were some disagreements, wrote historian Scott Kurashige, the "vast majority of Little Tokyo/Bronzeville denizens coexisted with nothing more than differences of opinion." Many Black and Japanese residents organized into groups and advocated for interracial interaction. For example, Hugh Macbeth Sr., a prominent Black attorney in Los Angeles, organized a "Negro-white committee" with the mission "to champion the cause of the disenfranchised Americans of Japanese ancestry," and he also provided legal assistance. In mid-1945, the Common Ground Committee of Caucasians, Japanese, and Negroes launched a project through the Pilgrim House youth agency to identify service needs in Little Tokyo/Bronzeville. Common Ground was one of a number of interracial groups that had been formed in the aftermath of the so-called Zoot Suit Riots.[48]

Relegated to Los Angeles's Eastside, Mexican Americans built a strong community during the early twentieth century despite persistent discrimination, including a program in 1929 that deported even US citizens to Mexico. During the 1930s, many Mexican immigrants came to L.A. seeking employment, along with many Black and white workers.[49]

By the 1940s in Los Angeles, the zoot suit had become popular among young Mexican American,

Filipino American, and African American men as a statement of identity and pride. This flamboyant style, characterized by a long jacket with wide lapels paired with loose pegged pants, evolved from the drape suits common in Harlem dance halls in the 1930s. The style unfortunately became associated with local street gangs and turned into a catalyst for racial violence. On August 1, 1942, a fight broke out at a party held near the Sleepy Lagoon reservoir. The following morning, a Mexican American man named José Díaz was found unconscious near the site, with blunt-force injuries, and he died shortly after. Despite scant evidence, the Los Angeles Police Department (LAPD) alleged that Díaz's death was related to gang activity. It cited the case as evidence of a Mexican American crime wave and used it as an excuse to round up hundreds of so-called zoot suiters for questioning. Eventually, twenty-two defendants were put on trial in a case that infamously became known as the Sleepy Lagoon murder case.

The trial, marred by bias, stoked anti-Mexican sentiment throughout the city. The growing tensions led to an attack by white servicemen on a group of Mexican American teenagers wearing zoot suits near Chinatown in early June 1943. Days later, dozens of sailors from the Naval Reserve Armory formed a vigilante group, attacking anyone in the streets wearing a zoot suit. The victims were often badly beaten. The Zoot Suit Riots ended on June 8, when military authorities confined US servicemen to their barracks. The Los Angeles City Council banned zoot suits, a decision that appeared to target the victims.[50]

The local news media played a significant role in fanning the flames as sailors and military personnel rioted and attacked the diverse youths. In addition to biased language and an editorial applauding zoot suits being ripped from young men, a front-page *Los Angeles Times* headline read: "Zoot Suiters Learn Lesson in Fights with Servicemen." The *Times* published images of injured service members, police, or citizens. Save for one picture of two youths who were beaten and stripped of their suits, all other Mexican zoot suiters were overwhelmingly pictured behind bars or in custody (plate 16). The *Eagle* highlighted the media bias by publishing a cartoon showing a male figure with the words "LA Newspapers" on it placing a noose over the head of a zoot suit–clad figure labeled "Minority Youth." The *Eagle* also reported on how the NAACP's Junior Council protested banning zoot suits in high schools, along with a bold headline, "City-Wide Youth Meet to Hit Bias Tomorrow."[51]

By January 13, 1943, seventeen of the twenty-two defendants in the Sleepy Lagoon case had been convicted of murder or assault.[52] In response to what was perceived as a grave injustice, a diverse coalition of Mexican American, Black, white, and Jewish attorneys and community leaders worked together on behalf of the Mexican American youths. Among many others were attorneys George Shibley, Ben Margolis, and Manuel Ruiz Jr., one of the few Mexican American attorneys practicing in Los Angeles at the time, along with A. L. Wirin of the American Civil Liberties Union (ACLU) and California Attorney General Robert W. Kenny. The Sleepy Lagoon Defense Committee was powered by Carey McWilliams, LaRue McCormick, and Alice McGrath. Charlotta Bass used her newspaper to raise awareness about the injustice. Activist Josefina Fierro de Bright mobilized Latino communities throughout Southern California. Dorothy Healey helped forge alliances with progressive labor unions. Actors Anthony Quinn and Rita Hayworth, both of Hispanic heritage, lent their celebrity status to raise funds and public awareness. Together, this multiethnic coalition collaborated to challenge the racially biased prosecution and eventually secured the reversal of the convictions by the California Court of Appeals in 1944.

The year 1949 saw the landmark election of Edward R. Roybal as the first Mexican American on the Los Angeles City Council since 1881. His victory resulted from a growing Mexican American population during World War II and years of grassroots organizing. A progressive coalition including labor, Jewish leaders, and African American groups lent their support to his campaign through coordinated, multiracial organizing.[53]

CHALLENGING DISPARITIES AND DISCRIMINATION IN EDUCATION

During the early 1930s, African American students attended Jefferson High School near Central Avenue and Jordan High School in Watts alongside white and Jewish students and a multitude of immigrants and racial groups. By the end of World War II, under pressure from white parents, local school boards had allowed transfer policies that enabled de facto segregation and created virtually all-white schools.[54] Nonwhite students were then more likely to attend overcrowded schools that operated double sessions to manage enrollment demands. White educators dominated the teaching staff, and schools serving predominantly minority populations received significantly fewer resources compared to those in white neighborhoods.[55] The curriculum structure channeled minority students into vocational tracks rather than college preparatory programs, and instructional materials included racist depictions of African Americans and "happy slave tales."

The NAACP and the ACLU tried to work with the Los Angeles Board of Education, but board members cited "color-blindness" as the official policy, stating that racial segregation in housing patterns was beyond their control and that they did not keep enrollment data by race.[56] However, segregation was deeply entrenched at Jordan and South Gate High Schools. Court challenges to the school district's policies revealed that during the 1950s, Jordan was 98 percent Black, while South Gate had only five Black students out of eighteen hundred.[57] Opposition to desegregation efforts was strong. In 1947, a group of students staged a strike at John C. Fremont High School, walking out to protest the attendance of a few Black children. A chilling photo shows the ringleaders hanging an effigy of a Black person from a lamppost at the corner of 77th and San Pedro Streets (plate 17). School board president J. Paul Elliott dismissed the incident as a "red herring" and "trumped up case of racial discrimination."[58]

That same year, the courts rendered a landmark decision in *Mendez v. Westminster* (1947), which ended the segregation of Mexican American students in California. When Gonzalo and Felicitas Mendez moved to the Orange County town of Westminster in 1944, they were prevented from registering their three children at the local school and were told the children would have to attend a "Mexican school" farther away. The Mendez family hired civil rights attorney David Marcus to help them sue the school district, and he recommended involving other families in a class-action lawsuit.[59] A multiracial legal team supported the case, including Harold Ward of the Mexican American movement; NAACP lawyers Marshall and Miller; William E. Guilford of the League of United Latin American Citizens (LULAC); and Wirin of the ACLU.[60] The US District Court found the separate schools to be unconstitutional. The ruling set an important precedent and laid the legal groundwork for *Brown v. Board of Education* (1954), the landmark Supreme Court case that declared state laws allowing separate public schools for Black and white students violated the Equal Protection Clause of the Fourteenth Amendment.

1

Plates

The arrival of photography in the United States in 1839 attracted the interest and participation of African Americans from the beginning. Countering racist caricatures, photography allowed Black Americans more control over their visual representation. They could shape images to their liking—selecting styles of dress, posture, and settings that best reflected their self-identities. Black thinkers such as Frederick Douglass and W. E. B. Du Bois understood the democratizing potential of the accessible, affordable tool and became proponents of the medium.

Black Angelenos approached photography with enthusiasm. Community leaders had their portraits made inside studios where they could pose amid finely crafted furniture, elegant tapestries, and specific props to project refinement and success. By the turn of the twentieth century, families assembled in front of their houses to record generational progress and prosperity. As the technology advanced, more affordable handheld cameras assumed a role in daily life. A snapshot from the 1920s shows a young couple sunbathing on the beach. Photography became convenient and personal, used for home display, or family albums, or as keepsakes.

Beyond the home, photographers documented the evolution of Black Los Angeles's social, educational, and religious institutions. Everything from building dedications and local parades to costume balls and concerts warranted a picture. Black Hollywood stars and entertainers were celebrated in print and photographs. Jazz musicians and the city's nightlife bopped and buzzed, and several aspiring picturemakers got their start in jazz clubs along Central Avenue. The community's interests and social engagements in all their vitality and significance came alive in influential weekly Black newspapers, including the *California Eagle* and the *Los Angeles Sentinel*. These uplifting views of a thriving community went all but unseen in mainstream newspapers such as the *Los Angeles Times*.

In contrast, the housing struggle faced by Black Angelenos played out visually on the pages of the city's non-Black newspapers. Black residents were relegated to overcrowded, segregated neighborhoods with inferior housing. Some of the worst buildings had no indoor plumbing. African Americans who could afford housing in upscale neighborhoods—including entrepreneurs like Norman O. Houston, cofounder of the Golden State

Mutual Life Insurance Company–faced roadblocks, racial covenants, or worse. Angry white crowds gathered outside homes that were sold, or even just rumored to be sold, to Black buyers. Outlawed by 1948, restrictive racial covenants were not themselves easy to illustrate. But violence by white supremacists against Black residents who challenged racial boundaries generated dramatic photos that made news. Images of broken windows and bombed houses showed the dangers that faced community members seeking to improve their living conditions. When South Dunsmuir Avenue residences were dynamited on March 16, 1952, the *Times*, the *Sentinel*, the *Los Angeles Herald Examiner*, and the *Eagle* all provided photographic coverage.

One of Los Angeles's leading champions of racial justice was Charlotta Bass, who became owner and managing editor of the *Eagle* in 1912. The *Eagle* published countless photographs highlighting the agency, brave protests, and determination of the Black community. Images showed lines of picketers in front of hiring offices and businesses that refused to hire Black workers. Photos of charred crosses and police brutality infuriated citizens who then filled churches and halls to rally against injustice. There were also independent photographers who recorded the activism of neighborhood, veteran, and other groups that organized to combat hate. Photographer Marion Palfi captured a protest outside an L.A. home where the Ku Klux Klan had struck. The community hoped unity, action, and photographic evidence would end KKK terror and force politicians to investigate.

Photographers wielded the camera both to document and to celebrate. They combated long-standing visual narratives with alternative perspectives of dignity, unity, and agency. And they embraced the power of photography to bear witness to injustice and inspire activism in Los Angeles and beyond.

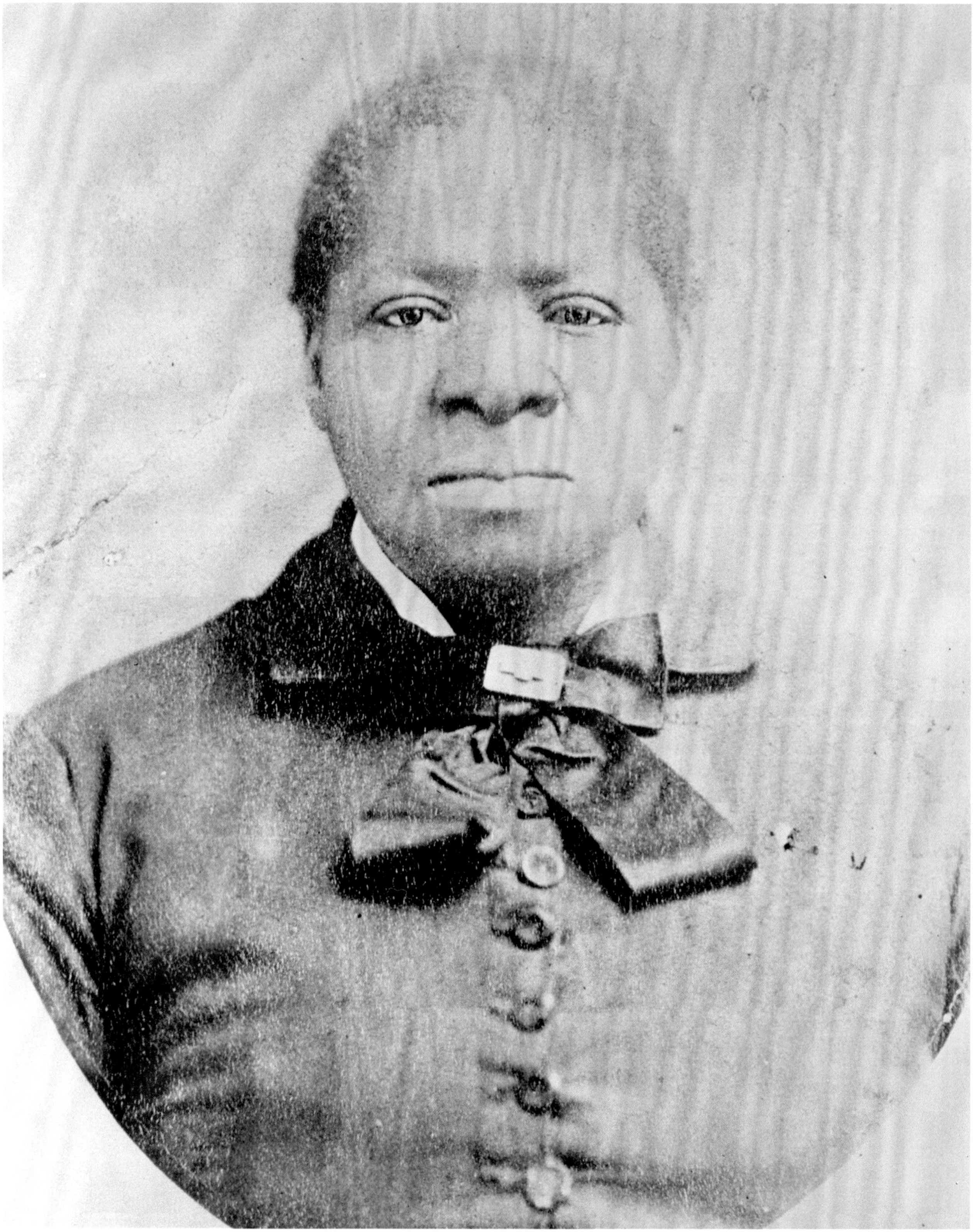

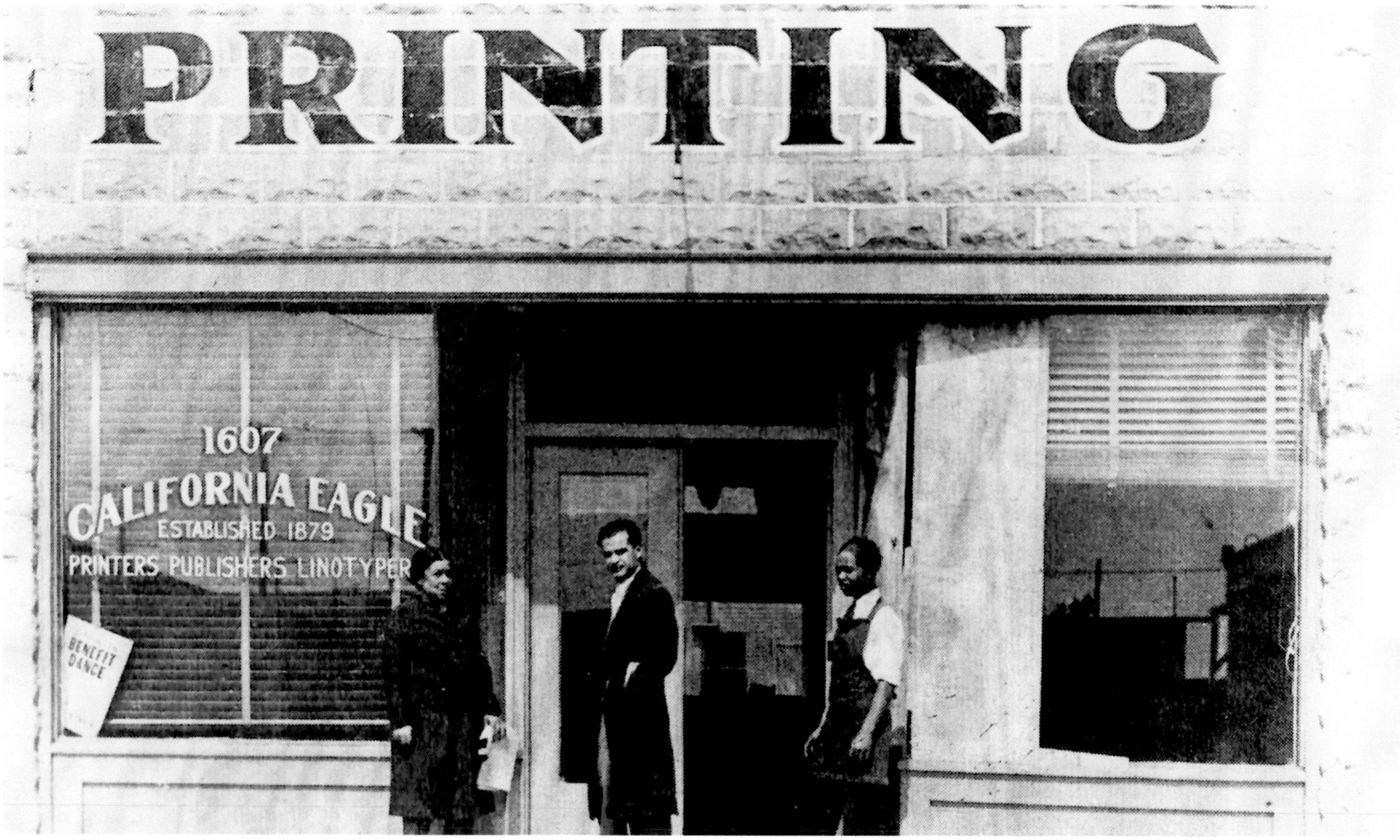

Plate 1 UNKNOWN PHOTOGRAPHER, ca. 1860–70

Bridget "Biddy" Mason arrived in California enslaved in 1851, twelve years after photography was introduced in the United States. She sued and won freedom for herself and thirteen family members, eventually becoming a landowner, philanthropist, and one of Los Angeles's earliest Black leaders. Mason's proud and determined pose reflects her esteemed standing in the community.

Plate 2 UNKNOWN PHOTOGRAPHER, ca. 1930s

Charlotta Bass (*far left*), managing editor of *The California Eagle*, stands with two employees in front of the newspaper's printing plant on East 103rd Street in Watts. As the *Eagle*'s outspoken owner, Bass covered issues affecting Black Angelenos and printed photographs that made housing discrimination, police abuse, and school desegregation visible for readers. Her tactical use of photography to inspire and persuade became more common during the 1930s, in part because lighter cameras and improved film made news photography easier.

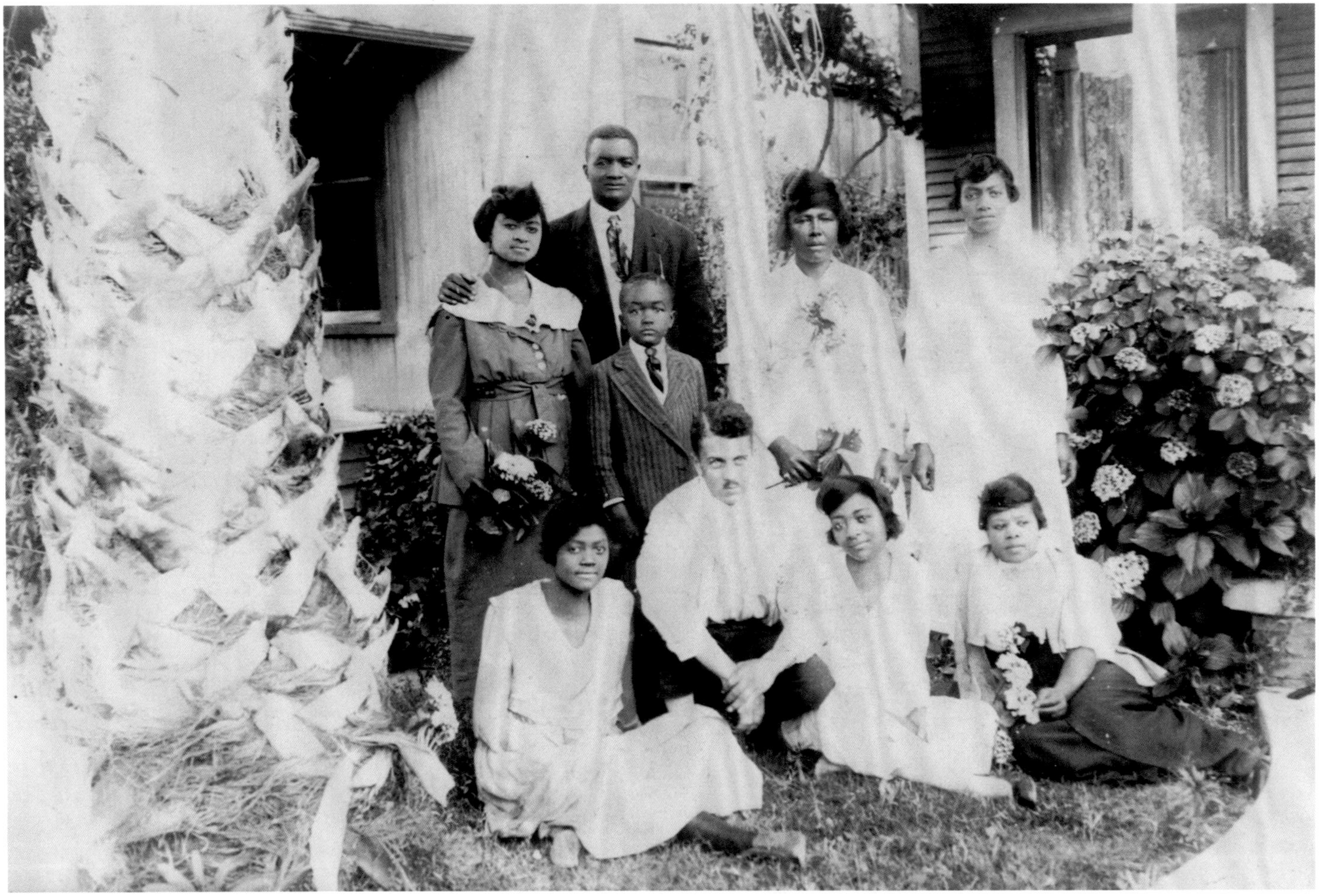

Plate 3 UNKNOWN PHOTOGRAPHER, 1910

Members of the Rozier family pose between a palm tree and a hydrangea bush on the front lawn of their Los Angeles bungalow. The family operated a grocery store at 51st Street and Holmes Avenue and were active in the community. Pictures like these were casually posed but projected Black success, affluence, and pride in homeownership.

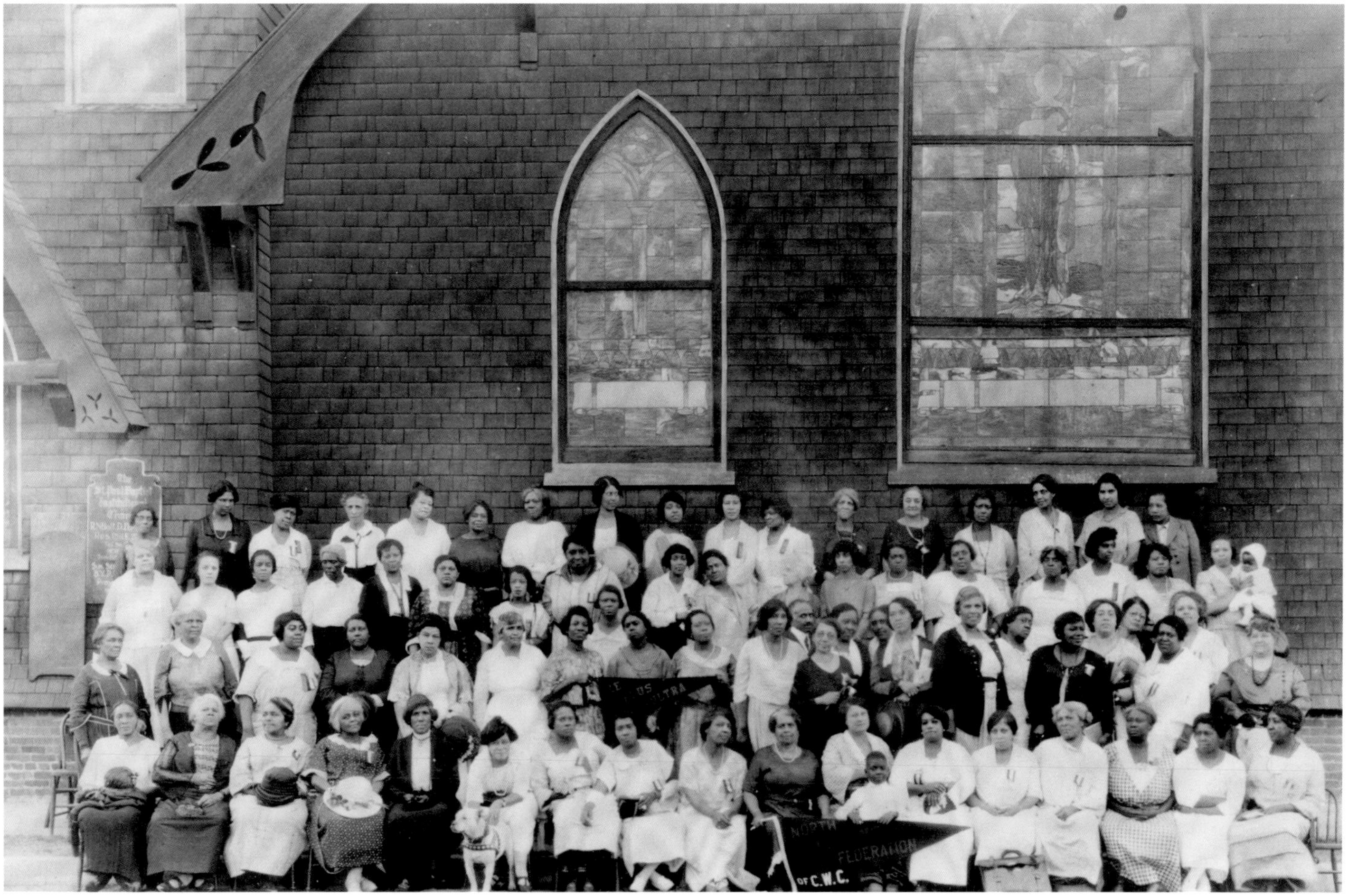

Plate 4 E. L. MERER, 1923

Over seventy-five attendees at the Third Biennial Convention of the Northwest Association of Colored Women's Clubs (NACWC) pose outside St. Paul Baptist Church in Los Angeles. NACWC members worked to empower women and support families, while also vigorously opposing segregated public transportation and facilities, lynching, and discrimination nationwide.

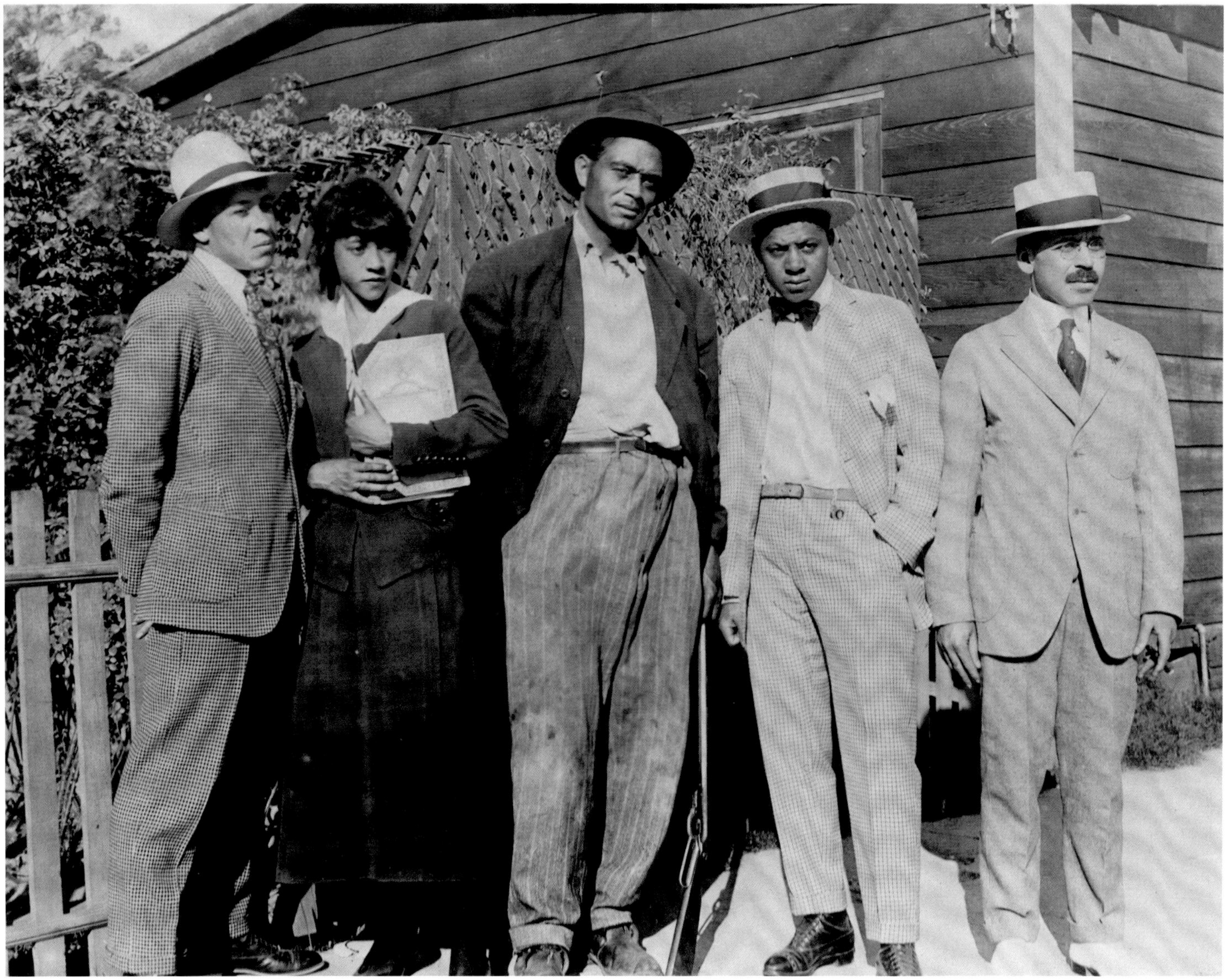

Plate 5 UNKNOWN PHOTOGRAPHER, ca. 1920

The Lincoln Motion Picture Company is often cited as the country's first all-Black movie production company. From 1916 to 1923, it showcased Black talent and presented uplifting stories exclusively to Black audiences. This staff picture, taken in Los Angeles, includes (*from left*) Clarence Brooks, actor and company secretary; Beulah Hall, actor; Noble Johnson, company cofounder and president; Dudley Brooks, assistant secretary; and James Smith, treasurer.

Plate 6 Still from the film *By Right of Birth*, produced by the Lincoln Motion Picture Company, 1921.

Plate 7 GEORGE WATSON, ca. 1930s

This staged photo of Ku Klux Klan members was taken in Inglewood by George Watson, who was the first photographer hired by the *Los Angeles Times*.

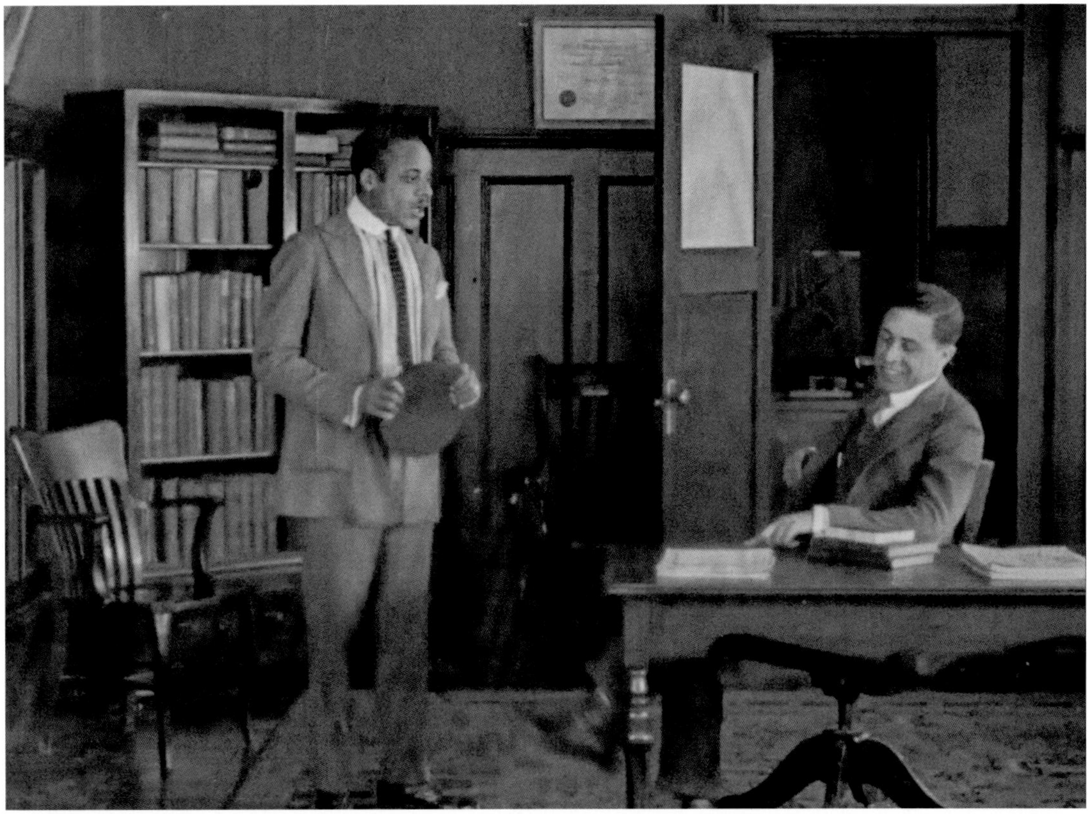

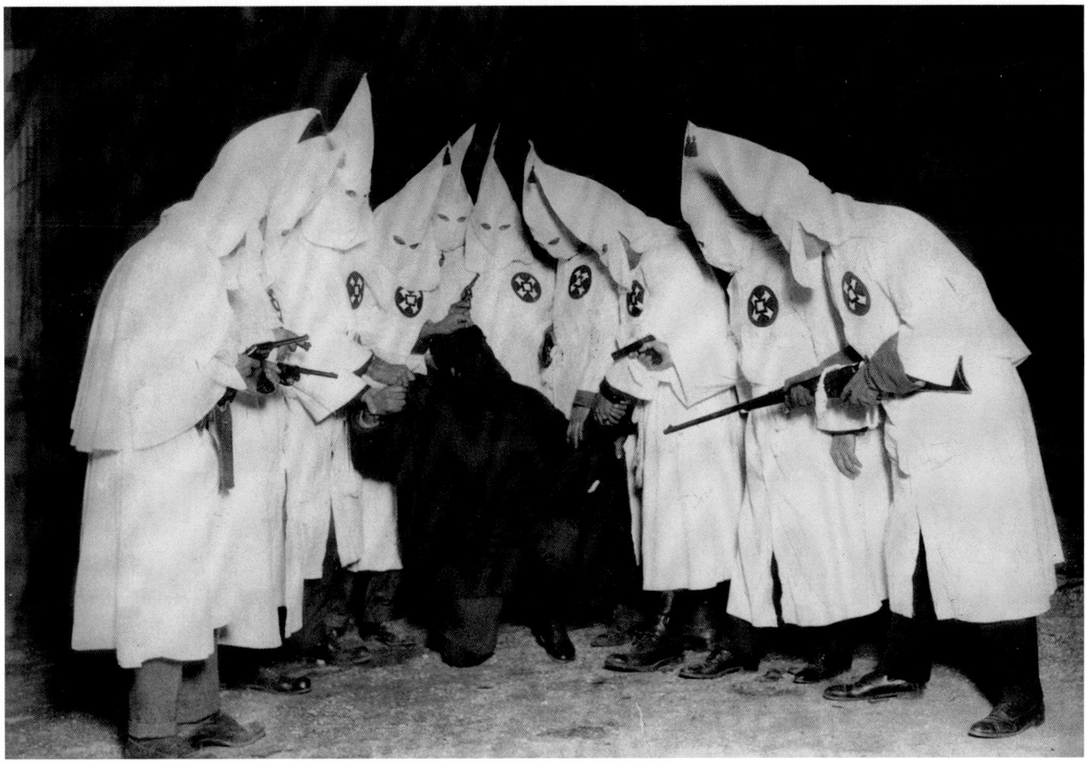

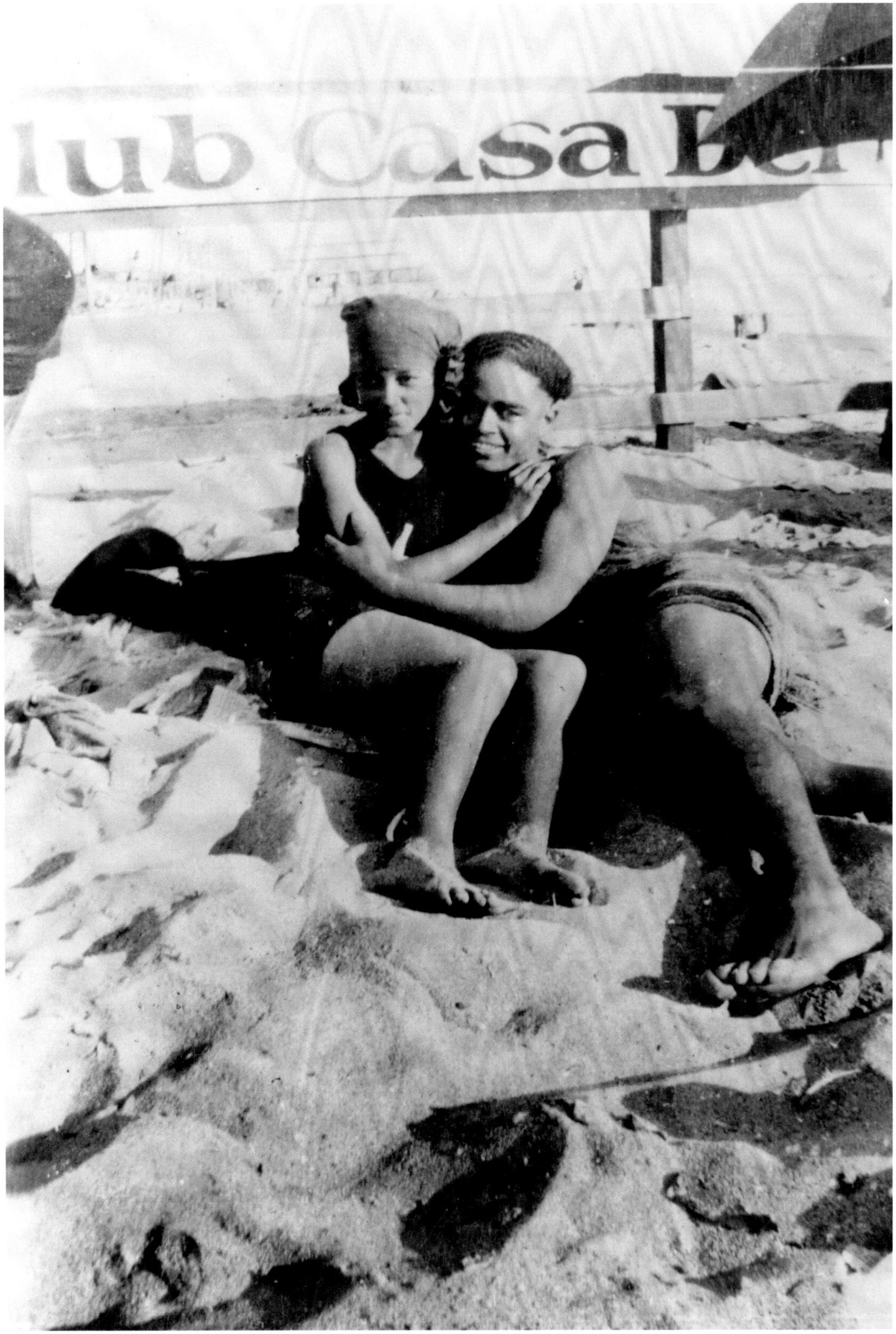
lub Casa

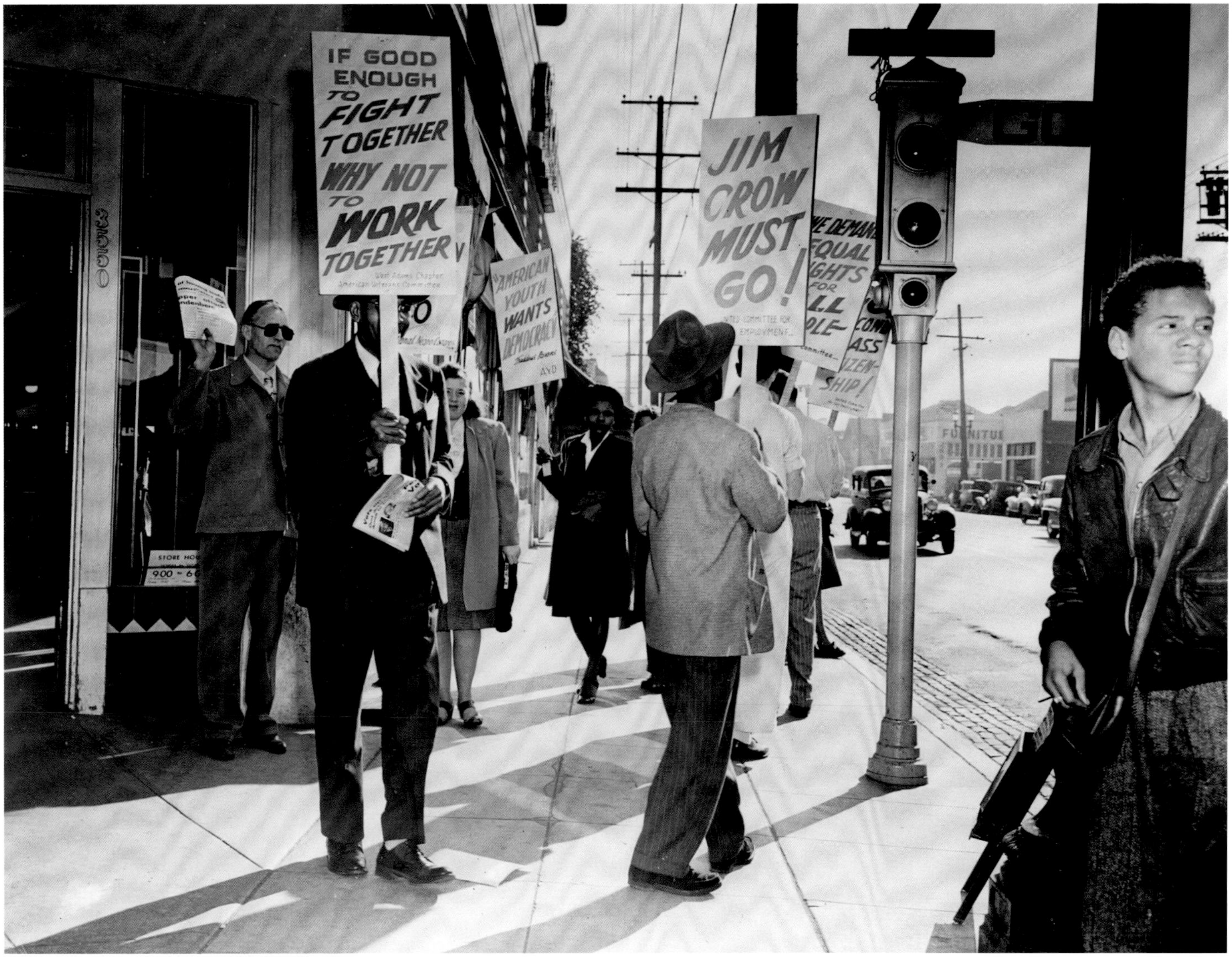

Plate 8 UNKNOWN PHOTOGRAPHER, 1924

Verna Deckard and Arthur Lewis enjoy a day at the beach in Santa Monica shortly before they married in 1924. Relegated to a segregated section called the "Inkwell," the couple pose in front of a sign for the Club Casa del Mar, an adjoining property that barred Black members. This simple snapshot captured both a joyous memory and a reminder of discrimination.

Plate 9 VERA JACKSON, 1939–45

A multiracial group protests employment discrimination outside a corner business during World War II. Each sign includes the name of a different activist organization, such as the American Youth for Democracy, the West Adams chapter of the American Veterans Committee, and the International Negro Congress. Vera Jackson's tight focus captures the movement and determination of the picketers.

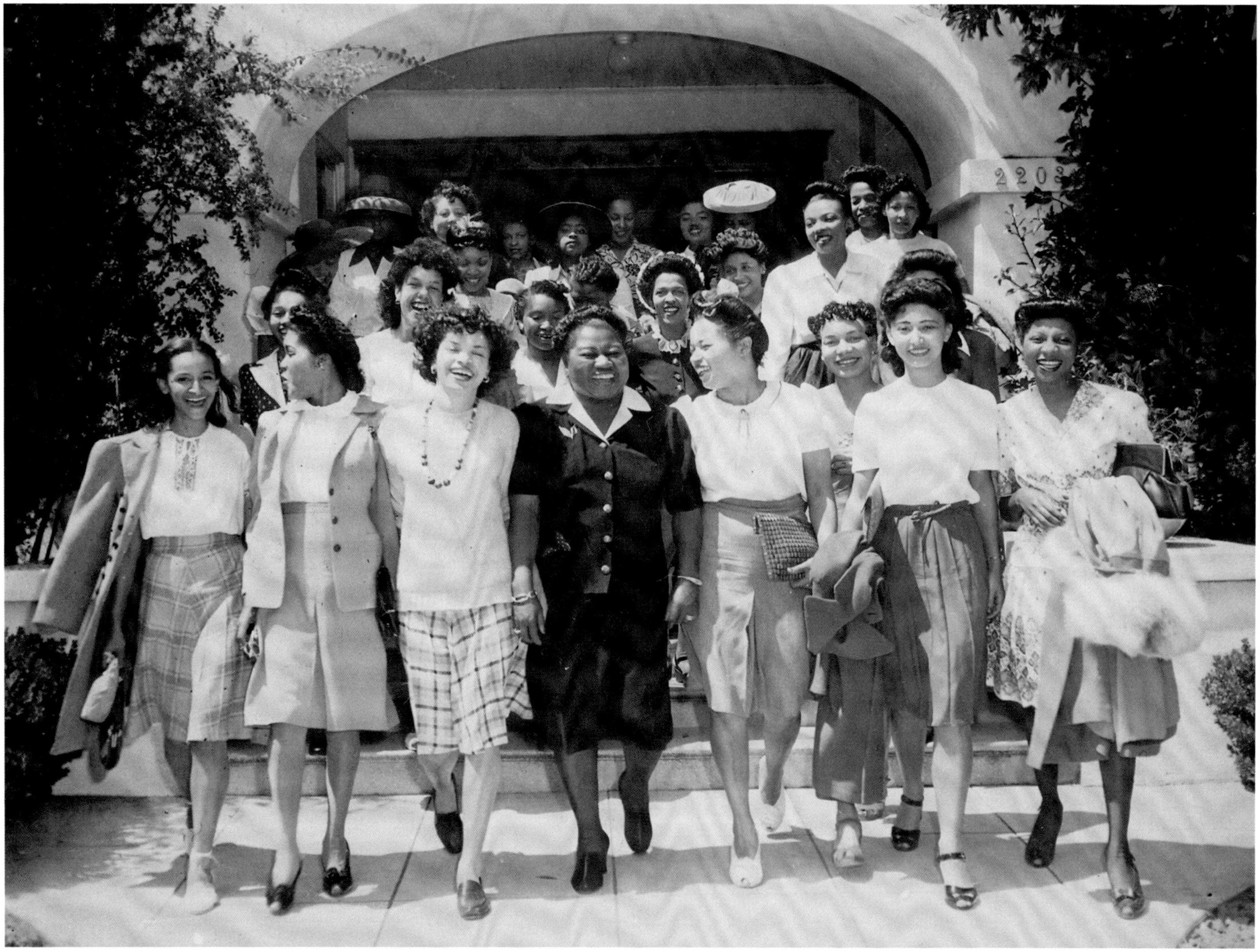

Plate 10 UNKNOWN PHOTOGRAPHER, 1941

Hattie McDaniel (*front, center*) leads a group of entertainers from her house at 2203 South Harvard Boulevard in the West Adams Heights (Sugar Hill) neighborhood to Minter Field, where they would perform a vaudeville and dance show for World War II soldiers. McDaniel, chair of the Negro Division of the Hollywood Victory Committee, and other Black celebrities challenged a lawsuit by white homeowners over racially restrictive covenants in the neighborhood.

Plate 11 BOB DOUGLAS, 1952

Jazz icon Billie Holiday sings during a record-breaking stint at the Tiffany Club in 1952. Bob Douglas's up-close work enhanced Holiday's beauty and the glitter of jewelry and beaded musical notes on her gown. Saxophonist Wardell Gray and Ronnell Bright at the piano accompany the singer.

Plate 12 HOWARD MOREHEAD, ca. 1955–58

Morehead snapped this smoke-filled scene featuring saxophonist Dexter Gordon at the California Club in the Crenshaw District. The image appeared on the cover of Gordon's album *Dexter Blows Hot & Cool.*

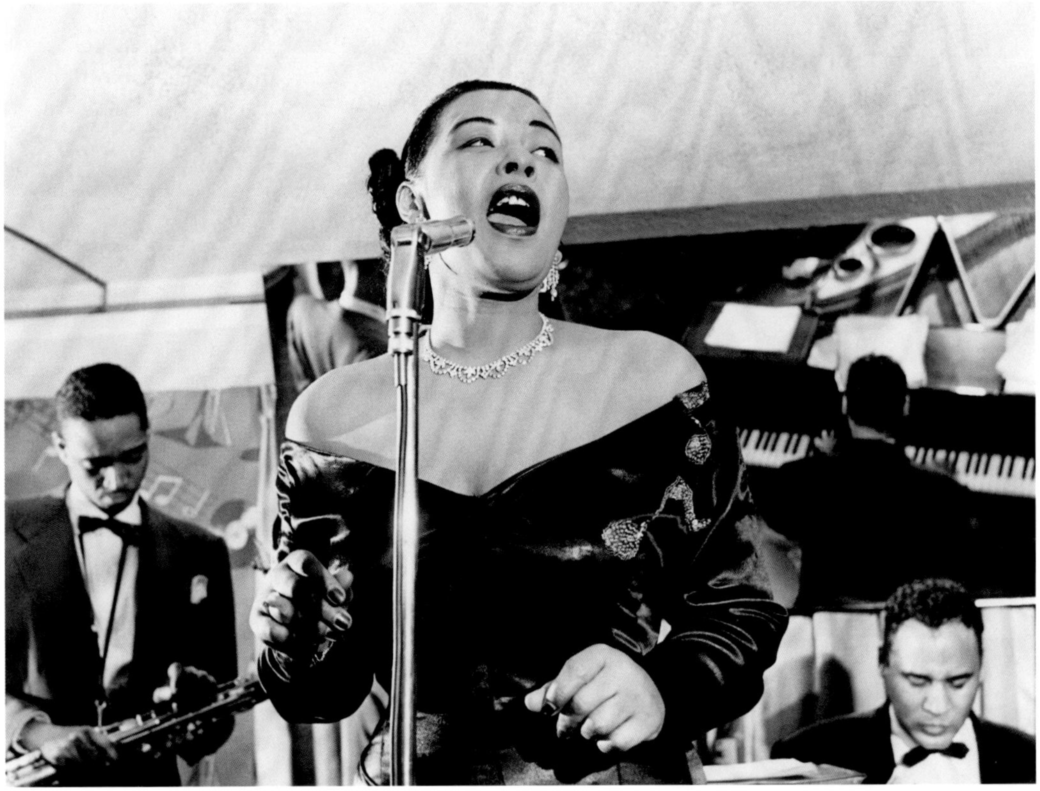

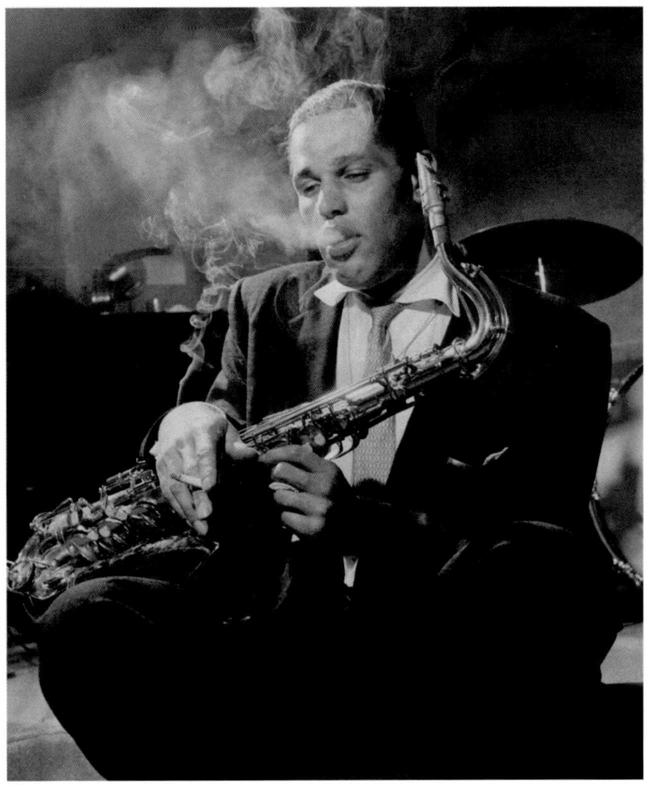

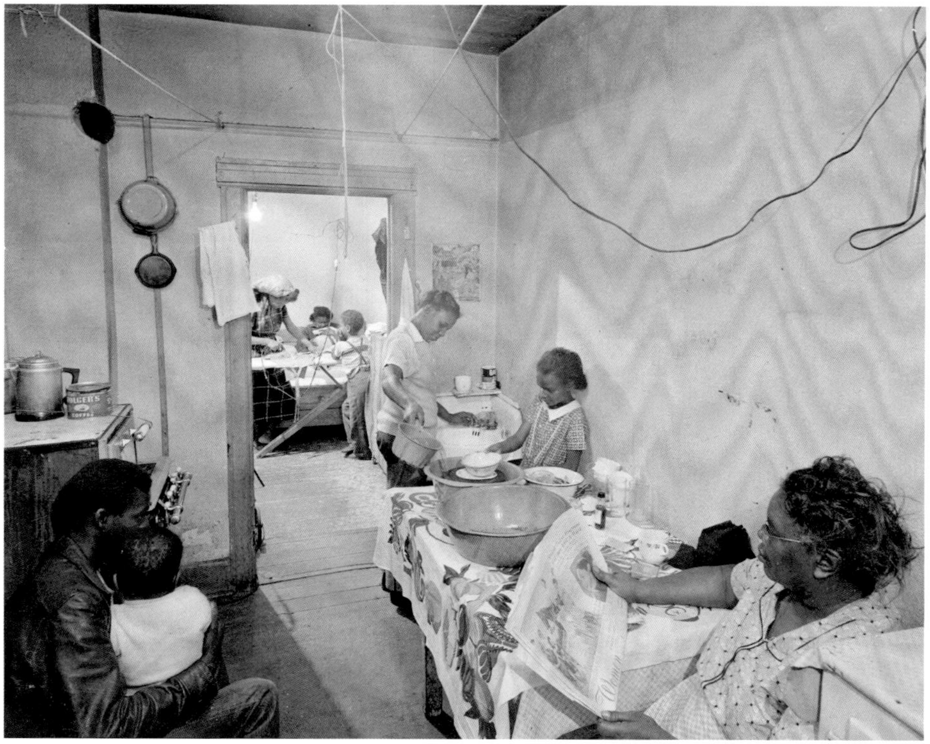

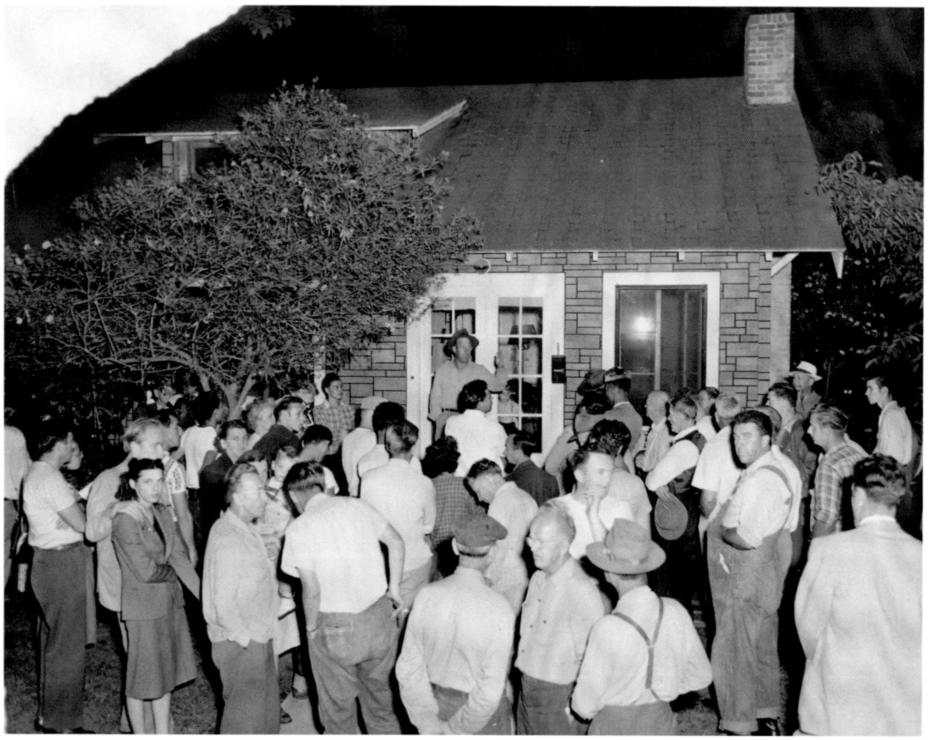

Plate 13 LEONARD NADEL, 1950

Several generations of the Chaney family occupy a single-story Hewitt Street dwelling in Los Angeles. Leonard Nadel, a photographer for the Housing Authority of the City of Los Angeles, documented conditions in deteriorating Black neighborhoods, where many poor Black families lived in overcrowded housing.

Plate 14 UNKNOWN PHOTOGRAPHER, 1949

An angry mob gathers on the front lawn of an East 70th Street home that the white owner planned to sell to a Black family. Several members of the crowd stare at the photographer as the nighttime flash makes the scene more visible. Mobs often damaged property and threatened violence against white and Black homeowners to maintain segregated neighborhoods.

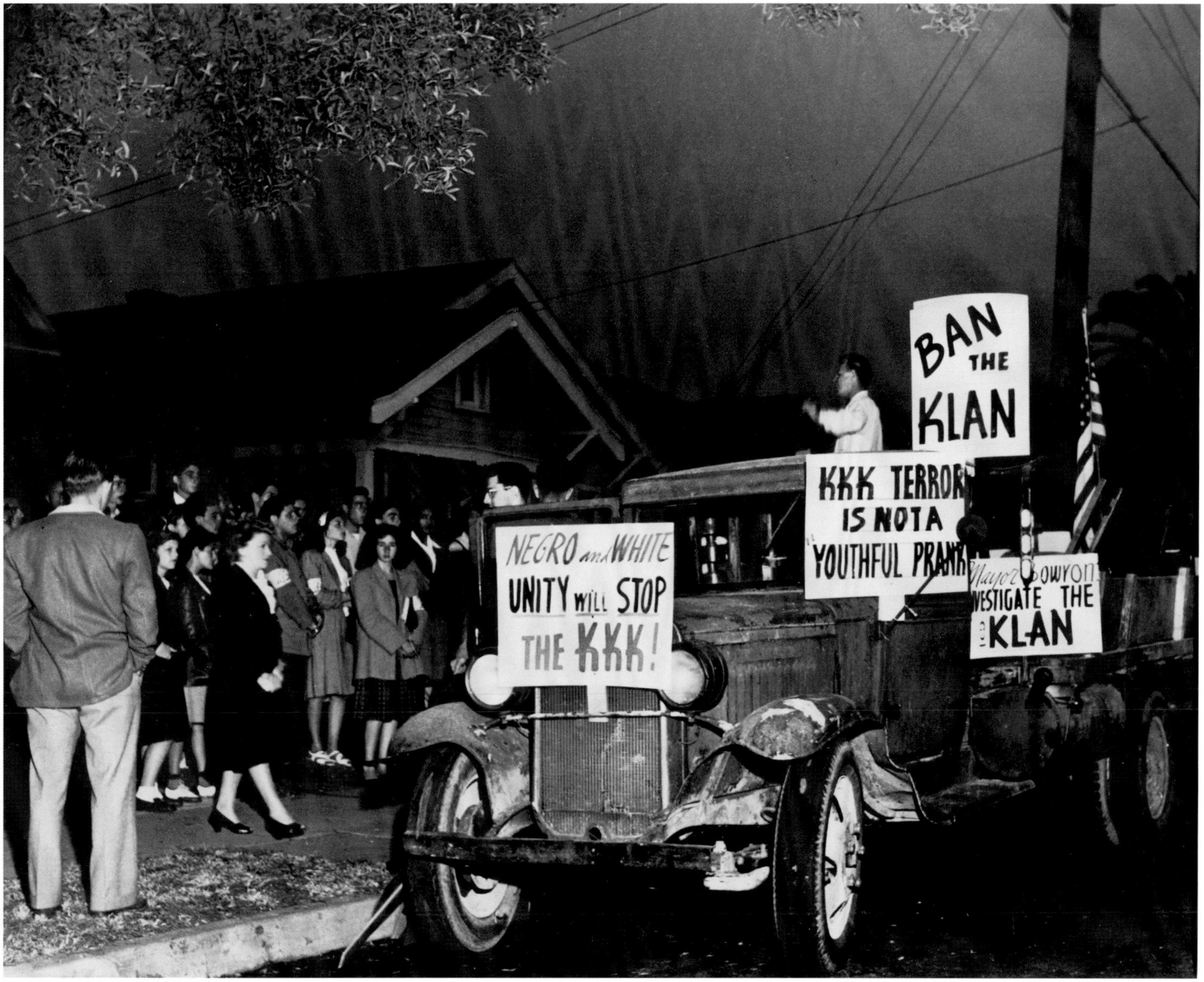

Plate 15 MARION PALFI, 1946–49

An anti-Klan rally unfolds outside a Los Angeles home where the KKK tried to intimidate residents. A speaker standing on top of the truck bed denounces the Klan's actions, surrounded by signs condemning the white supremacist group's tactics and calling for its demise. Marion Palfi's picture captures an interracial movement unified against the Klan and housing discrimination in postwar Los Angeles.

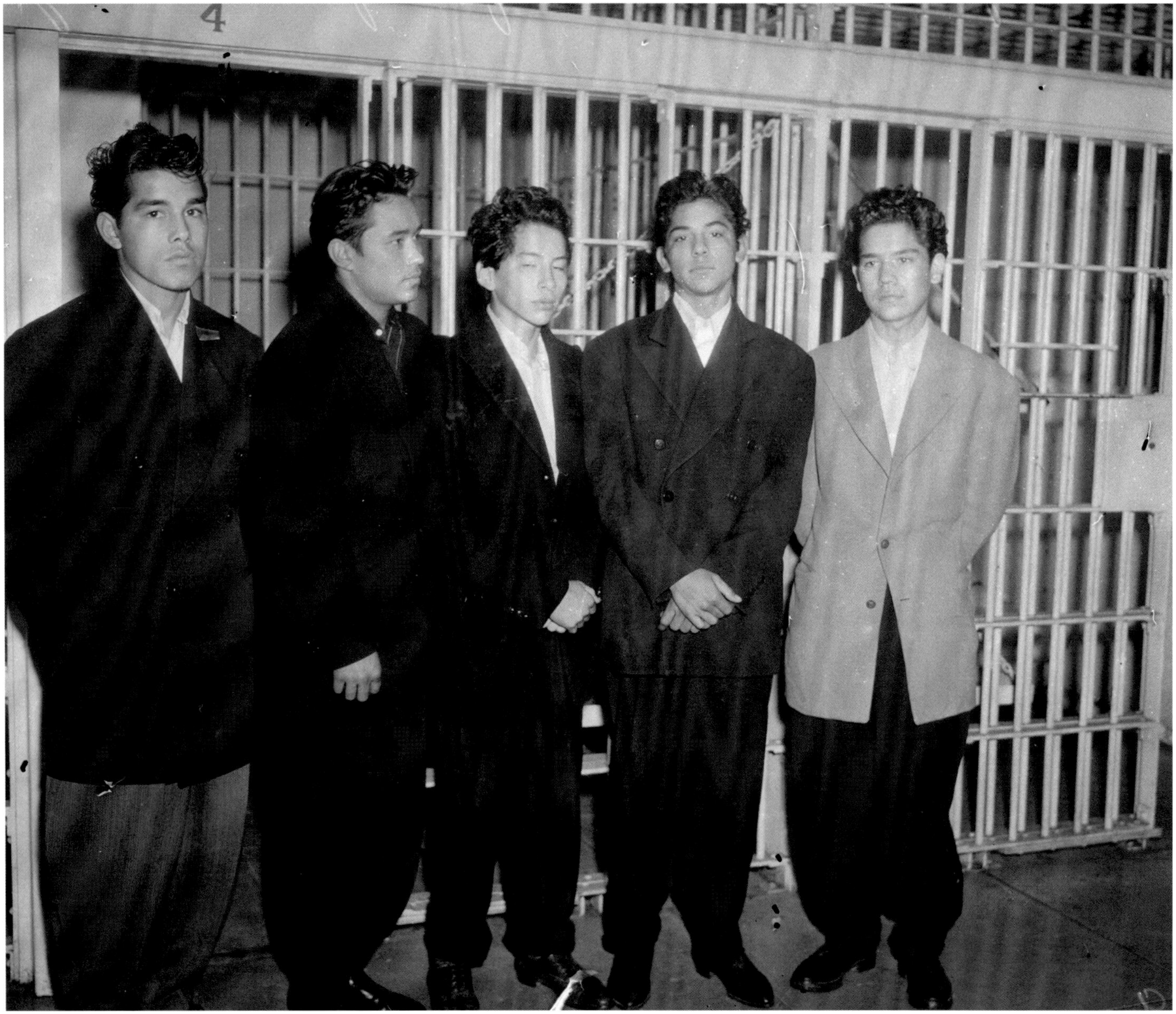

Plate 16 UNKNOWN PHOTOGRAPHER, ca. 1943

Mexican American youths in distinctive long jackets and baggy trousers, known as zoot suits, stand in front of a jail cell after being detained for questioning following a brawl. In 1943, racial tensions between Black and Mexican American "zoot suiters" and white servicemen exploded into the Zoot Suit Riots. This picture from the *Los Angeles Daily News* illustrates how the zoot suiters were typically depicted in L.A.'s mainstream newspapers—under suspicion and in jail.

Plate 17 UNKNOWN PHOTOGRAPHER, 1947

A student hangs an effigy on a lamppost across the street from John C. Fremont High School to protest the handful of Black students enrolled there. About three hundred students—10 percent of the student body—participated, and most received only a one-day suspension. Taken by a *Los Angeles Daily News* photographer, this image highlights the harassment Black students endured in neighborhood schools.

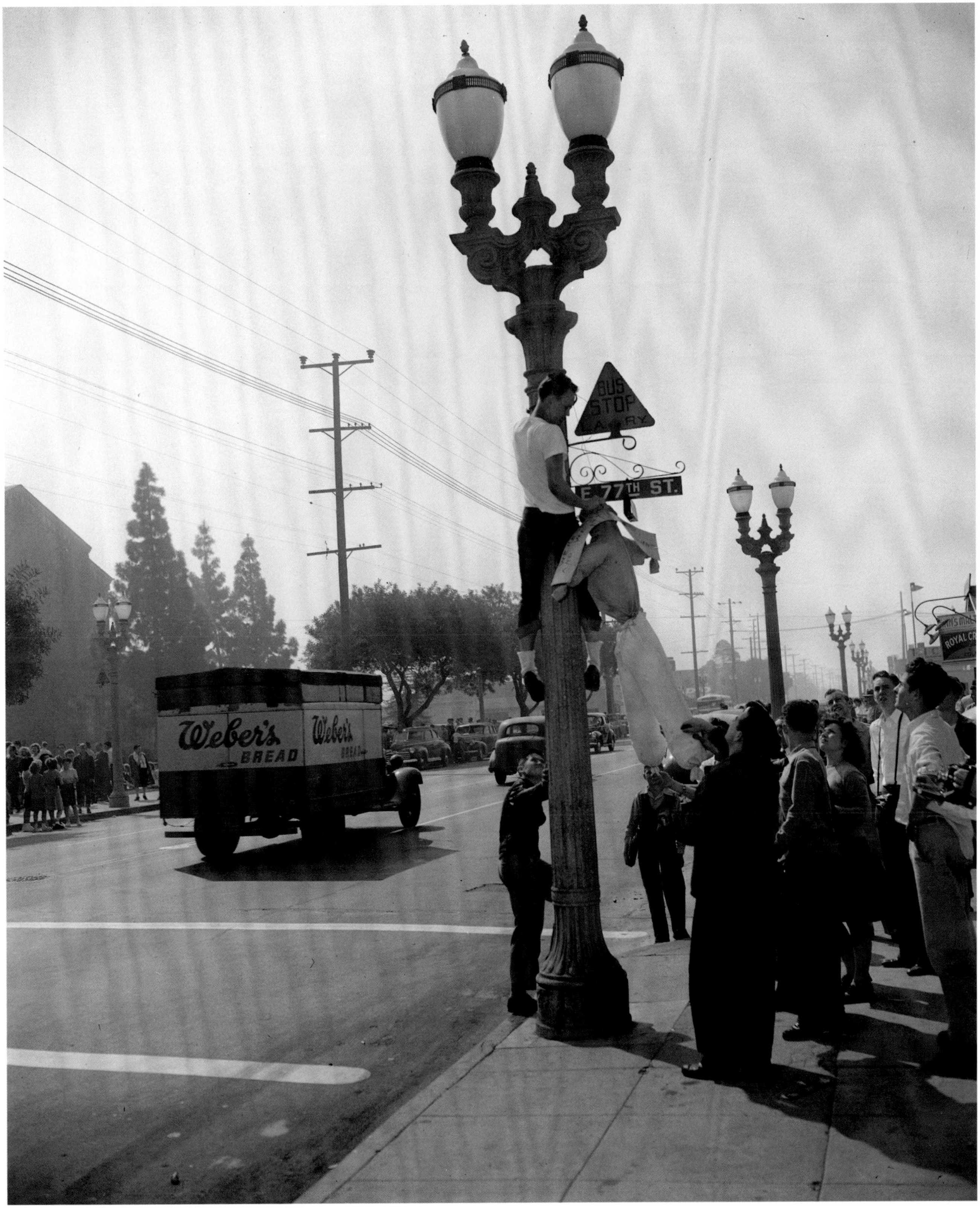
Weber's
BREAD
Weber's
BUS
STOP
E 77TH ST.

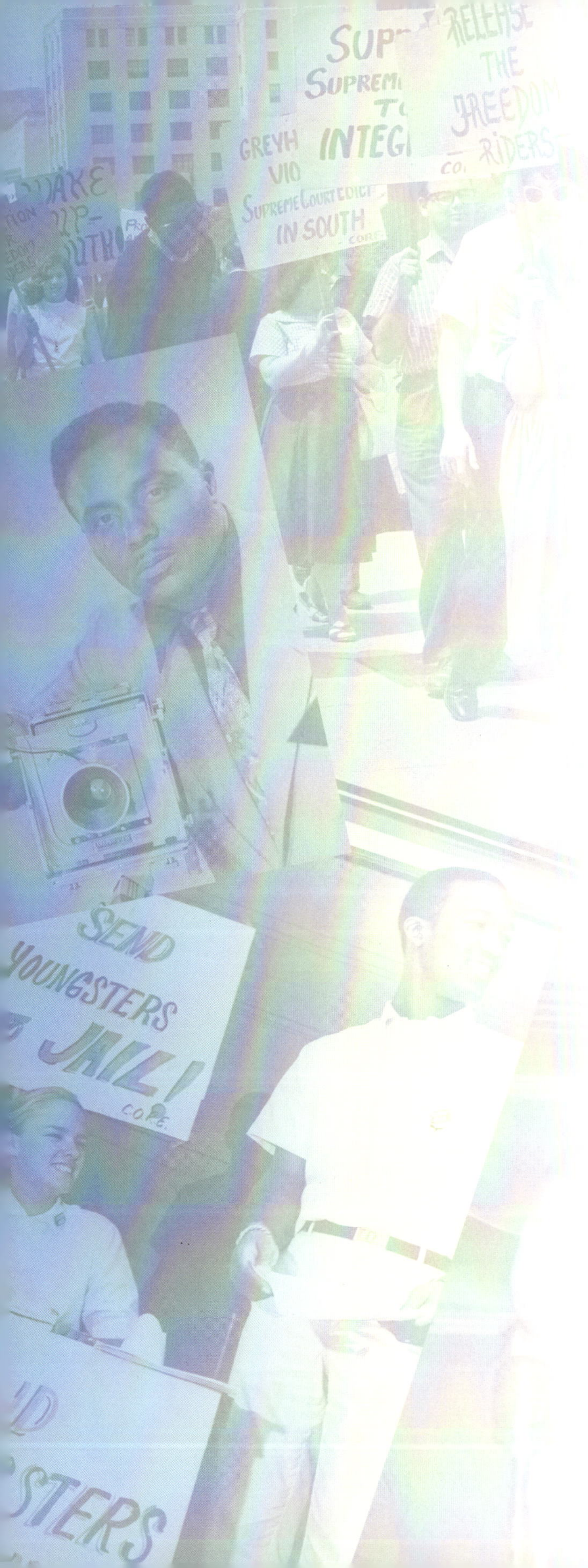

2

Witnessing the Fight for Freedom

Photographs from a child's funeral ignited the modern civil rights movement in 1955. That summer, a fourteen-year-old Black boy from Chicago named Emmett Till was visiting family in Money, Mississippi (fig. 15). On August 24, while Till was in Bryant's Grocery and Meat Market, he offended a white woman named Carolyn Bryant.[1] The precise nature of the interaction remains ambiguous, but Till was accused of whistling at her. In the early morning hours of August 28, Bryant's husband and brother-in-law kidnapped, tortured, and murdered the boy. Till's bereaved mother, Mamie Till-Mobley, brought his body back to Chicago for the funeral. She insisted on an open casket so the world could see "what they did to my boy."[2] When *Jet* magazine published photographs of Till's mutilated face, it shocked the nation and spurred people to action.

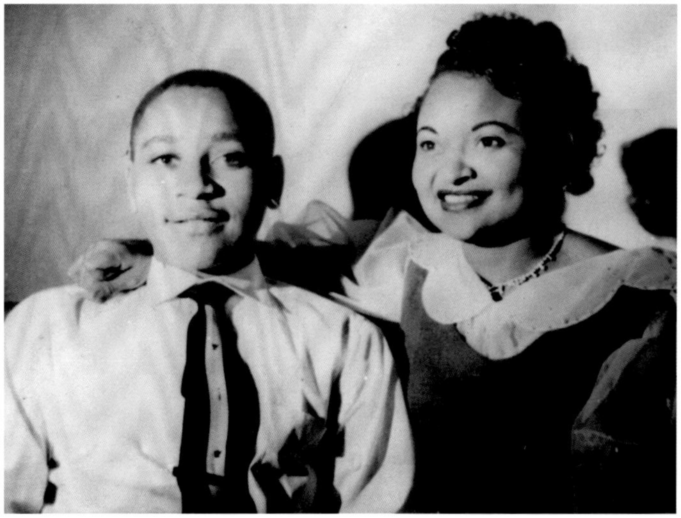

Fig. 15 Emmett Till with his mother, Mamie Till-Mobley, ca. 1953–55.

The *California Eagle*'s coverage of Till's murder played a critical role in mobilizing Los Angeles activists. A poignant image of Till-Mobley grieving for her son appeared in the *Eagle* (plate 18), but no similar photography ran in the *Los Angeles Times*. Its minimal reporting on the brutal killing amounted to short updates—for example, when a trial date was set or the verdict was announced. Despite its status as the multicultural city's leading newspaper, the *Times* in the 1950s largely ignored the issues facing L.A.'s African American community. Concerns such as school segregation and police brutality were overlooked or buried. The editorials that did run frequently questioned the decisions of local Black leaders. Decades later, Bob Douglas, a photojournalist for *Jet* and *Ebony* as well as the *Eagle* and the *Los Angeles Sentinel* during the civil rights era, said: "White newspapers would not print Black news. Nobody would've known there [were] lynchings if it'd been left up to the white newspapers."[3]

The acquittal of Till's killers by an all-white jury triggered a wave of outrage across the United States and Europe. Black Angelenos jammed into mass meetings, including one featuring Moses Wright, Till's great-uncle, who had bravely testified during the September trial and was no longer safe in his home state. "I'm through in Mississippi. Colored people in Mississippi have no protection," he said.[4] By December, African American churches in Los Angeles collected over $5,000 to help families in Mississippi caught in the violent aftermath of the trial. In support of the Southern Black cause, an *Eagle* editorial proclaimed: "Mississippi is caught in the throes of lawlessness, and as long as that mood lasts, no Negro's life is safe, no Negro's rights are secure."[5]

Black Angelenos were well prepared to support the burgeoning Southern movement by the time Rosa Parks—an NAACP member, women's rights activist, and assistant tailor at the Montgomery Fair Department Store—was arrested on December 1, 1955, in Montgomery, Alabama, for refusing to surrender her seat to a white passenger on a city bus. As a seasoned strategist, one of her goals was to transform the Montgomery NAACP into a more militant activist organization, in which she succeeded. After her arrest, Southern ministers and leaders used her act of defiance as the impetus to organize the Montgomery Bus Boycott. The Montgomery Improvement

Association (MIA) was formed to facilitate the boycott, and a young pastor from Atlanta—Martin Luther King Jr.—was elected president. Rev. Ralph Abernathy, a Baptist minister and a close friend of King's, served under his leadership. The boycott began on December 5, 1955, and Abernathy was dispatched to Los Angeles in March 1956 to meet with community leaders and raise funds to support the growing protest.

Upon Abernathy's arrival, seven thousand Angelenos attended a solidarity rally at the Olympic Auditorium. Abernathy reported on the status of the boycott and shared the sentiments of its participants. "Our cups are full, we are tired of being kicked around," he said. "There is only one way to stop this movement, and that is to give us justice."[6] The Los Angeles community raised $7,500 at the rally to help sustain the boycott. Later that month, Victory Baptist Church held a banquet in Abernathy's honor and presented him with a check for nearly $6,000.[7] Rev. Arthur Atlas Peters was the pastor of Victory Baptist Church. Born in Slidell, Louisiana, in 1908, Peters moved to Los Angeles in 1936 and founded the church in 1943. A talented gospel musician, he became known for Victory's music programs and the "Voice of Victory" radio broadcast that he started in 1949.

Shortly after Abernathy's visit, Parks herself traveled to Los Angeles. On April 8, 1956, more than three thousand people gathered at Second Baptist Church to hear her share her experiences and discuss the desegregation campaign (plate 19). To capitalize on her presence, the local NAACP initiated a membership drive and connected its activism with Montgomery's (plate 20). Parks led a walk alongside members of the executive board of the local chapter: attorney Thomas Neusom, the local NAACP president; entertainer Sammy Davis Jr., honorary chair of the membership drive; and Marnesba Tillmon Tackett, official chair of the drive. Tackett was born in St. Louis, Missouri, and moved to Los Angeles with her husband in 1952. She was an especially prominent member of the Los Angeles movement, leading the fight to desegregate the city's public schools. She was well connected and was serving as the local NAACP's education chair when Parks visited Los Angeles (fig. 16).[8] Tackett and Parks were among the few women to hold important leadership positions within the movement during a time when men typically held the reins of power. Tackett, acutely aware of her platform, highlighted the importance of listening to women's voices when she was quoted in the *Los Angeles Sentinel*: "In every situation, there is a woman. You have heard Rev. Ralph Abernathy; now come and hear a woman's side of the disgraceful story of injustice in the South and the

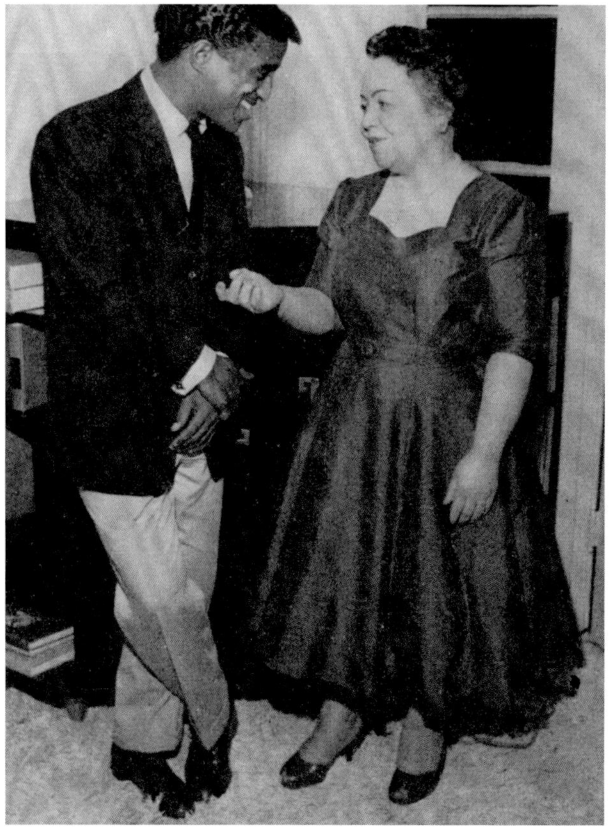

Fig. 16 Marnesba Tillmon Tackett (*right*) and Sammy Davis Jr., chair and honorary chair, respectively, of the Los Angeles NAACP 1956 membership drive, featured in *The Crisis* magazine, March 1956.

second-class citizenship accorded Negroes who call the South their home."[9] After tallying the numbers, Tackett reported 11,068 new memberships, bringing the total to 20,101 and making the Los Angeles NAACP one of the largest chapters in the country.[10] There are only a few photographs of Parks's trip to Los Angeles because the city's mainstream newspapers failed to cover her impactful visit, missing hints of deepening connections between Los Angeles and the Southern struggle for civil rights.

DR. KING ARRIVES IN LOS ANGELES

Abernathy and Parks primed Los Angeles for King's first known visit to the city in June 1956. King and his wife, Coretta Scott King, drove across the country with Abernathy and his wife, Juanita Jones Abernathy, "to enjoy the first of many summer vacations they would spend together during the tensions of the movement," daughter Donzaleigh Abernathy would write.[11] During the Jim Crow era, travel was especially dangerous for African Americans, and hotels and motels commonly refused service to Black travelers. After their safe arrival, the two couples enjoyed the county fair.

Thanks to a family connection with Rev. J. Raymond Henderson of Second Baptist Church, King gave several sermons there in June 1956. Before Henderson moved to Los Angeles in 1941, both he and King's father, Rev. Martin Luther King Sr., had been church pastors in Atlanta.[12] Henderson facilitated King's engagement with the Black community in L.A., and he quickly became a stalwart supporter of the bus boycott and King's vision of nonviolent direct action. As the movement grew, Second Baptist Church became a crucial hub for the fledgling civil rights movement.[13] Completed in 1926, the building was designed by African American architect Paul R. Williams with Norman Marsh and is now listed on the National Register of Historic Places.

THE PRAYER PILGRIMAGE

Following the *Browder v. Gayle* (1956) Supreme Court decision that declared bus segregation in Alabama unconstitutional, the MIA voted to end the 381-day bus boycott. This success inspired transportation desegregation initiatives throughout the South, leading to the formation of a regional organization to coordinate disparate groups and local movements. The Southern Christian Leadership Conference (SCLC), founded in January 1957, united grassroots activism across the South and became a beacon of centralized leadership for other locales.

Rev. Maurice Dawkins served as president of the Los Angeles branch of the NAACP during the early years of the SCLC. Born in Chicago to parents who were active in the NAACP, Dawkins later graduated from Columbia University and Union Theological Seminary.[14] In May 1954, he became pastor of the People's Independent Church of Christ in Los Angeles. By 1957, as local NAACP president, Dawkins established a long-standing and significant partnership with the newly formed SCLC. The strength of this association was visible during preparations for the nationally organized Prayer Pilgrimage for Freedom in Washington, DC. Calling attention to the third anniversary of *Brown v. Board of Education* (1954), the Supreme Court case that ruled public school segregation unconstitutional, the pilgrimage protested delays in implementing the law and President Dwight Eisenhower's refusal to make a public statement on the issue. Abernathy traveled to Los Angeles to generate support for the event. At a press conference at the Statler Hotel, he invited Angelenos to join the pilgrimage and add their voices to demands for voting rights, fair employment, and desegregation at the national level. "We will go to the Lincoln Memorial, and we will kneel there and raise our voices in prayers for freedom," Abernathy declared.[15]

The Los Angeles NAACP and local clergy eagerly accepted the invitation to participate. Henderson and Peters helped lead the organizing effort. Dawkins served as West Coast coordinator for the pilgrimage, working alongside organizers as far away as Oakland. The coalition of religious leaders successfully persuaded the Los Angeles City Council and California Govenor Goodwin Knight to endorse the march as well.[16]

The California contingent joined King, SCLC members, and two thousand clergy members on transportation chartered by Dawkins. Among the twenty-five thousand participants who marched in Washington on May 17, 1957, were members of the United Auto Workers and AFL-CIO labor unions, and celebrities such as Mahalia Jackson and Harry Belafonte. King delivered an address at the Lincoln Memorial titled "Give Us the Ballot" with his characteristic charisma and rhetorical flair.[17]

Los Angeles's leading Black newspapers amplified the event by covering the extensive advanced planning, while the *Times* ran a short Associated Press article afterward.[18] The *Eagle* dispatched executive editor Grace E. Simons and photographer Harry Adams to the nation's capital. A special report appeared in the May 23, 1957, issue, with Adams's photographs of the California contingent (plate 21) and the massive Washington crowd on the front page. The prominent coverage showed Los Angeles residents just how effective organizing could be. For many, the gathering at the Prayer Pilgrimage may have been the largest number of African Americans they had ever seen photographed in one place. Eight more photographs inside featured Parks, Jackson, Davis, Ruby Dee, and Belafonte. Additional pictures captured the close relationships the California travelers maintained with King, Abernathy, and others involved. One snapshot documented Dawkins sitting in a place of honor among platform guests. The visual display celebrated the important role Black Angelenos from clergy to Hollywood celebrities played in staging the rally.

"DON'T YOU GET WEARY!"

King visited Los Angeles several times in 1958 after the success of the Prayer Pilgrimage. His first visit of the year occurred in February, when he was once again invited by Henderson to speak at Second Baptist Church—cementing the prominence of both the church and the reverend in the local movement. While preaching to concerned parishioners in overflowing pews, King referenced the protracted nature of the battle for civil rights and justice, as he shouted: "Don't you get weary!" The *Eagle* reported that King's rousing final words brought the packed church to its feet for a "tumultuous round of applause."[19] Adams skillfully captured the moment; his image of King speaking that day caught the young preacher midsentence as he unintentionally duplicated Jesus's pose in the mural behind him. This striking photograph conveyed King's magnetism and gravitas to those not present at the event (plate 22).

King's address publicized the Los Angeles NAACP's new three-part strategy: a voter registration drive with a goal of fifty thousand new African American voters, a continued boycott of Anheuser-Busch beer in response to the company's racist hiring practices, and a renewed NAACP membership drive.[20] By the late 1950s, King had resolved to fight for the rights of Black Angelenos as he had for those of the Black citizens in Montgomery, believing that there was one cause—freedom and justice—uniting all African Americans in the United States.

STUDENT ACTIVISM

The power of the Los Angeles–based movement was strengthened by student activists who played a critical role in antidiscrimination battles across campuses and communities. In particular, those who were members of the Congress of Racial Equality (CORE) became the backbone of the nascent student movement. CORE had been established in Chicago in 1942 as an outgrowth of a large international pacifist organization, the Fellowship of Reconciliation. The multiracial group of students who founded CORE advocated for the use of nonviolent direct action as their primary tactic in affecting change. The first Los Angeles chapter was launched soon after the end of World War II by Black draft resister Manuel Talley and a few fellow pacifists.[21] The fledgling group won

HARRY ADAMS

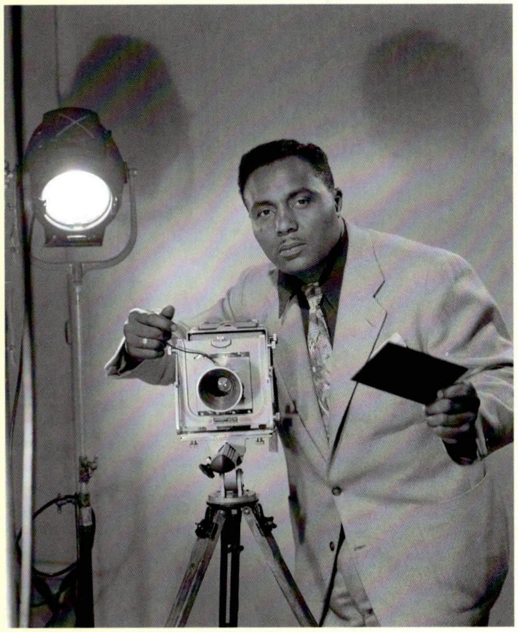

Harry Adams (1918–1985) began making photographs after receiving a Kodak Brownie camera at the age of twelve (fig. 17). Adams settled in Los Angeles in 1947 after serving in World War II. He enrolled in barber school, and in 1950 he began attending the Fred Archer School of Photography. He subsequently attended the California School of Photography and Graphic Design run by Charles Williams. Adams maintained a studio on Avalon Boulevard and later near Central Avenue and 43rd Street, and his freelance work appeared in the *Los Angeles Sentinel* and the *California Eagle*. Adams's ability to compose a picture, direct his subjects, and produce an image with often only one exposure earned him the nickname "One Shot Harry." His subjects ranged from Black political leaders and civil rights protests to local church and school events. His photographs, taken across three decades, are a vivid and invaluable record of postwar Black Los Angeles.

Fig. 17 Harry Adams, 1952.

some victories against local restaurants, and members engaged in direct picketing, organized boycotts, joined legal suits, and supplied aid to the Southern movement.[22] Talley later became CORE's Western field organizer and subsequently participated in two winning Supreme Court cases that strengthened free speech. Most famously, in *Talley v. California* (1960), the Supreme Court ruled that a Los Angeles ordinance requiring that protest materials identify the person or organization distributing handbills was unconstitutional and in violation of the First Amendment. This was not only a victory for Talley—who faced prosecution for distributing handbills—but also a victory for the civil rights movement at large.[23]

After a period of inactivity, the Los Angeles CORE branch saw a revival during the summer of 1955 led by Herbert Kelman, a white pacifist and CORE field representative from Baltimore, and Henry Hodge, a Black social worker and former chair of the St. Louis branch. One notable achievement was dismantling racist practices at Union Station train terminal, where a barbershop and coffee shop had previously denied service to nonwhite patrons. CORE also achieved modest successes by challenging employment discrimination and facilitating the hiring of Black sales employees at downtown Los Angeles stores. Still, their most visible—and arguably most successful—protest was the active campaign against Anheuser-Busch, brewer of Budweiser and other beers. Los Angeles CORE collaborated with the NAACP to boycott the company in an effort to create job opportunities for Black truck drivers. Although African Americans constituted about 8 percent of the population in Los Angeles, Anheuser-Busch only employed two Black drivers and refused to hire others. Dawkins saw the boycott as analogous to the bus boycott in Montgomery—a mass action against segregation and injustice. The *Eagle* proclaimed: "The fight for fair job opportunities is one of the most significant aspects of the struggle for equality on the West Coast made especially important by the current layoffs in industry and mounting unemployment."[24] The boycott quickly spread across the state to Northern cities, including San Francisco.[25] The effort resulted in the hiring of three new Black drivers by Anheuser-Busch in 1958.

In March 1960, CORE field secretary James McCain launched a West Coast tour to rally support for the civil rights movement's new and emerging tactics: sit-ins and Freedom Rides. Black students in cities like Baltimore and Wichita had already successfully used sit-ins and other direct-action methods against segregated lunch counters in the 1950s. On February 1, 1960, four freshmen from North Carolina Agricultural and Technical University in Greensboro entered an F. W. Woolworth store and quietly sat at the lunch counter reserved for whites only. Despite being refused service, they stayed in their seats until the store closed for the day. The following morning, they returned with more students, sparking a wave of sympathy protests against Woolworth by students from colleges and universities nationwide. Photographs of sit-ins showed well-dressed students calmly but resolutely occupying seats. Some read and studied. But it was the pictures that hinted at violence or showed harassment of the nonviolent protesters that generated the most exposure and, in turn, elicited sympathy. They also prompted more supporters to join. The early Los Angeles sympathy protests in March garnered photographic coverage in multiple issues of the *Sentinel* and *Eagle*, and at least twice in the *Times* (fig. 18). A March 26 *Times* editorial stated that demonstrating in a city where lunch-counter discrimination did not exist was "simply foolish."[26] Nevertheless, picketing in the city drew attention to the national movement while raising awareness of discriminatory practices occurring closer to home, such as ongoing housing and employment discrimination.

Around the same time as McCain's visit, Earl Walter, an African American social worker who was viewed by young activists as "the grandfather of the militant direct-action movement in Los Angeles,"[27] revitalized the local CORE branch. The latest iteration had a membership that was initially three-fourths white, and it was allied with a coalition of groups, including the NAACP, American Jewish Congress, United Auto Workers, and International Ladies' Garment Workers' Union (ILGWU), that were all engaged in picketing Woolworth stores. McCain's arrival in Los Angeles garnered the interest of various students and activists across the city, including Robert Singleton, an economics major at the University of California, Los Angeles (UCLA), who headed the campus NAACP chapter and would later chair a local CORE branch.

DIRECT-ACTION PROTESTS

Born in Philadelphia in 1936, Singleton was raised by his mother until she was hospitalized for four years after contracting tuberculosis in 1949. After high school and military service, Singleton moved to Los Angeles in 1958 to attend UCLA, where he was confronted with pervasive discrimination that stood in stark contrast to the city's national image as a "land of opportunity."[28] He discovered a place marked by racial division, including housing segregation, racist service practices, and low Black student enrollment. Singleton knew that his best chance to effect change rested in a leadership position, and he vied for and won the presidency of UCLA's NAACP chapter. One of his initiatives was a campaign challenging barbershops that refused service to Black men and boys. Despite explicit instructions from the national headquarters in New York City to avoid confrontation, Singleton's group

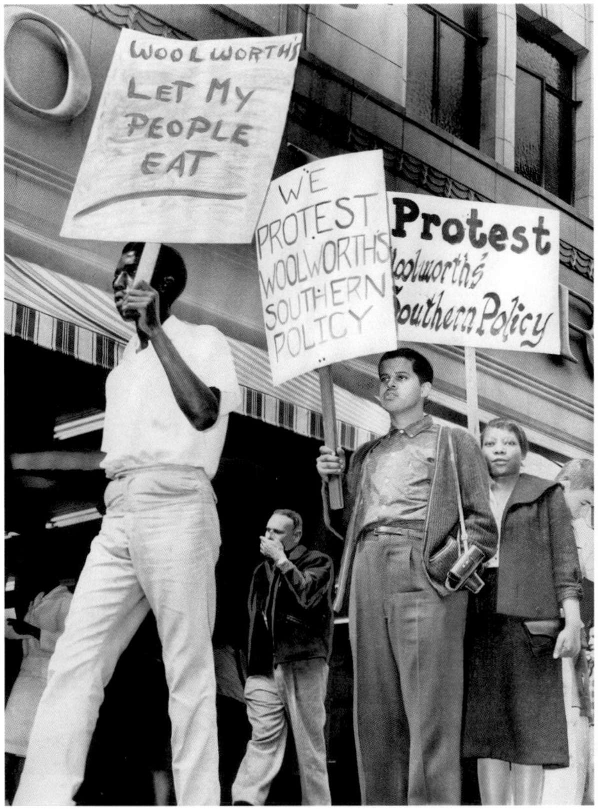

Fig. 18 Protesters march in front of a local F. W. Woolworth store to support the Southern boycott against segregation at the retail chain. *Los Angeles Times*, 1960.

picketed the barbershops. Their tenacious efforts drew the attention of California Governor Edmund G. "Pat" Brown's office, which provided them with crucial legal support. Eventually, the barbershops relented, opening their doors to patrons of all races.

The barbershop win resulted in a surge in membership for the "Bruin" NAACP chapter, which next turned its attention to housing discrimination near UCLA. "I saw that there were some problems in the community surrounding the campus," said Singleton. "I did some research and ... was able to make recommendations on how to stop some of the housing discrimination and job discrimination. And as a result, I became known all over campus as a troublemaker."[29] During the civil rights era, most African Americans were forced to live in Los Angeles's segregated Eastside neighborhoods, creating long commutes to UCLA's Westwood campus for Black students. The Bruin NAACP chapter employed a strategy in which Black and white students submitted inquiries about nearby apartments available for lease. When discrimination was identified, the NAACP exposed the biased landlords and compelled them to revise their rental policies. Eventually, UCLA Chancellor Charles E. Young began to acquire apartment complexes around the campus and opened access to all students regardless of racial background.[30]

Attracted to CORE's aggressive approach, Singleton joined forces with the Los Angeles CORE chapter as it engaged in boycotting local Woolworth stores. One example of the boycott's ability to encourage dialogue occurred when the owner of a Woolworth in Santa Monica made an agreement with CORE to urge the national office to address charges of racism before substantial financial losses caused his and other stores to close. Although he wrote a letter to the company's national headquarters, he told the activists that he received no response.[31]

NATIONAL POWER IN LOCAL POLITICS

The 1960 Democratic National Convention was held from July 11 to July 15 at the Los Angeles Memorial Sports Arena. Black Angelenos affiliated with the Democratic Party, including its community-based organizations and clergy, became immersed in politics during this period to influence the 1960 national elections. Their goal was to force Democrats to distance themselves from segregationist Dixiecrats within the party and to persuade the party to adopt a strong civil rights agenda. The March on Conventions, a strategic initiative with high-visibility demonstrations, protests, and rallies, was the vehicle for their efforts.

The March on Conventions was led by King and A. Philip Randolph, who drafted a joint statement on the march, declaring that

> at present, no candidate for the presidency has measured up to the courage of the Southern students. All of them have looked the other way when their parties have tolerated racists or made deals with racists. We are going to present a list of questions to all the candidates. We are going to demand specific answers and a specific program to implement them. The time of compromise and empty generalities is over. The time for action is now. The heroic students of the South have shown the way, and the least we can do is to carry their demands, and those of all Negroes who are denied the right to vote, directly to the political conventions.[32]

Negotiations with party leaders took place inside the convention, while simultaneous protests and rallies outside demanded action. For example, King and New York Congressman Adam Clayton Powell joined the picket lines protesting hiring discrimination at a local Woolworth store (plate 23).

The role of Los Angeles activists was vital in on-the-ground mobilization. Dawkins said: "A call has gone out to the Board of Rabbis and to the Roman Catholic hierarchy, as well as the general public, to be present at the mass prayer rally. It is expected that the historic rally and mass march will serve as a reminder to those convening delegates and both parties that a peaceful Christian people deserve fair Christian decisions."[33] Later, Powell preached a sermon, "What's in Your Hand," to motivate participants at Dawkins's church. Their presence on the picket lines, rallies, and marches, with the subsequent photographic documentation, allowed citizens across the city to see that the protesting students had the backing and support of civil rights leaders. While these protests were taking place, Democratic party presidential candidates, including Sen. John F. Kennedy, attended an NAACP rally, where civil rights leaders spoke. Kennedy, an adept politician, keenly understood the power of the media and was not shy about being photographed ingratiating himself with the local community. His visit was documented by photographers including Jack Davis, who often covered civil rights events in the city (plates 24, 25). Outside the convention, six thousand protesters marched to the Shrine Auditorium, where Dawkins delivered remarks before the Democratic Platform Committee.

Like Kennedy and his advisers, King and other civil rights leaders recognized the emerging significance of television and the valuable opportunity the heavy media presence for the convention offered to call attention to local and national concerns. With television sets in roughly 90 percent of American homes by 1960, nightly newscasts enjoyed unprecedented reach and visibility. Even more, snippets of demonstrations often conveyed a sense of urgency and intimacy unmatched by most print coverage. However, it would take a few more years for a confluence of significant conflicts and demonstrations, longer-form news reporting, and Hollywood stars to align for a more dramatic impact.[34]

During his acceptance speech after receiving the Democratic nomination for president, Kennedy affirmed his commitment to civil rights: "The rights of man—the civil and economic rights essential to the human dignity of all men—are indeed our goal and our first principles."[35] The newly negotiated Democratic platform embraced several proposals from King and Randolph—endorsed by the official committee—promising to address discrimination and ensure equal opportunities. It also included an acknowledgment of the Southern civil rights movement; a pledge to give the attorney general power to obtain injunctions against public officials who engaged in discrimination; a commitment to end the use of poll taxes and literacy tests; and a promise to use the executive powers of the administration to ensure equal employment throughout the federal government. The Democratic Party's willingness to champion civil rights contributed to Kennedy's victory over Richard M. Nixon, with 70

JACK DAVIS

Jack Davis (1920–2004) hopped a freight train headed west in the late 1930s and landed in Los Angeles. After serving in the US Navy during World War II, he settled in L.A. permanently in 1946. Like many other local Black photographers, Davis got his start hustling pictures in Central Avenue's bustling music clubs. In addition to photographing the jazz greats, he sold pictures to club patrons. Davis took classes at the Art Center School of Design to hone his skills and became a freelance photographer in the late 1940s. He operated the Modern Arts Studio of Photography for more than four decades, specializing in portrait and commercial photography. He also captured community and national events throughout the civil rights era, selling his pictures to the *Los Angeles Times*, *Los Angeles Sentinel*, and *Los Angeles Herald Examiner* newspapers, and to *Ebony*, *Jet*, and *Sepia* magazines. "My camera was my passport," he often mused.[36]

percent of the African American vote going to Kennedy. Following their electoral support for Kennedy, Black activists continued to press his administration for federal laws to secure integration, voting rights, and economic equality during his term of office.

AN ORGANIZATIONAL HUB

In January 1961, after the 1960 presidential election, King presided over the founding of the Western Christian Leadership Conference (WCLC), the West Coast counterpart to the SCLC (fig. 19). Civil rights leaders in Los Angeles came to understand that to assertively and effectively advocate for civil rights at the local and national levels, they needed a more formal organizational hub. Some clergy were inclined to ground the local movement in the Black church; however, a combination of religious and secular organizations prevailed, leading to the formation of the WCLC. Encouraged by King, Dawkins formally announced plans to form this new entity in the SCLC newsletter, stating: "The general program of the Western Christian Leadership Conference is to provide financial and moral support to the SCLC in its general crusade to bring first-class citizenship to all Americans."[37]

Of the more than one hundred ministers who attended the WCLC founding conference, a few prominent California figures emerged to lead the organization in its early years. Rev. L. Sylvester Odom of Ward AME Church in Los Angeles was elected president. A prominent graduate of Northwestern, Howard, and Yale Universities, Odom edited and managed the AME Church's official newspaper, the *Christian Recorder*, and eventually led the Sacramento and Oakland NAACP branches before moving to Los Angeles. Rev. Edward Stovall of Progressive Baptist Church in Berkeley served as vice president, and Rev. Arthur Atlas Peters of Victory Baptist Church in Los Angeles was elected president of the board of directors. After his election, Peters said: "The Los Angeles branch's primary objective is to pursue a program of spiritual rearmament, training in nonviolence,

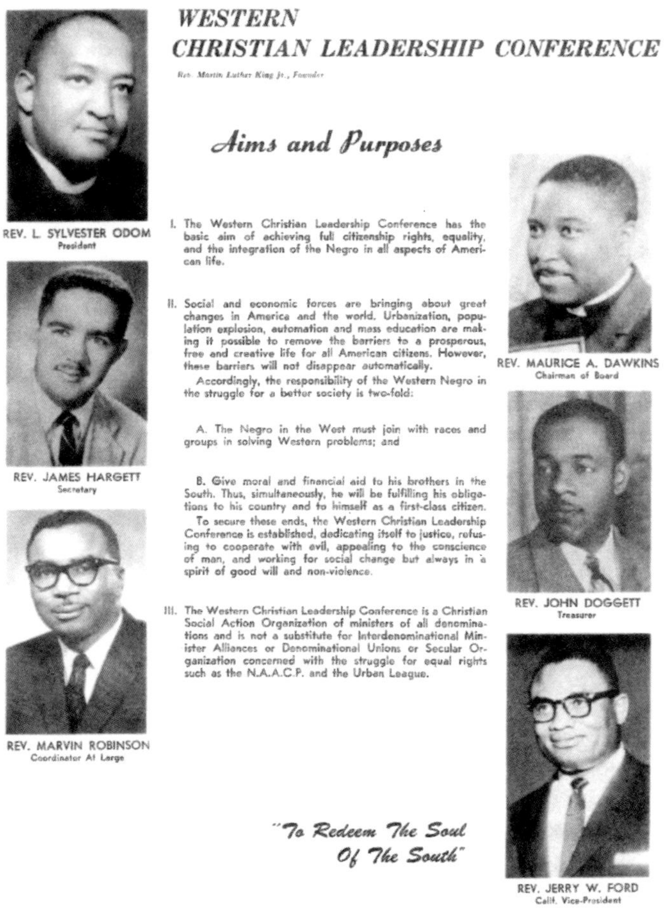

WESTERN
CHRISTIAN LEADERSHIP CONFERENCE

Rev. Martin Luther King Jr., Founder

Aims and Purposes

I. The Western Christian Leadership Conference has the basic aim of achieving full citizenship rights, equality, and the integration of the Negro in all aspects of American life.

II. Social and economic forces are bringing about great changes in America and the world. Urbanization, population explosion, automation and mass education are making it possible to remove the barriers to a prosperous, free and creative life for all American citizens. However, these barriers will not disappear automatically.

Accordingly, the responsibility of the Western Negro in the struggle for a better society is two-fold:

A. The Negro in the West must join with races and groups in solving Western problems; and

B. Give moral and financial aid to his brothers in the South. Thus, simultaneously, he will be fulfilling his obligations to his country and to himself as a first-class citizen.

To secure these ends, the Western Christian Leadership Conference is established, dedicating itself to justice, refusing to cooperate with evil, appealing to the conscience of man, and working for social change but always in a spirit of good will and non-violence.

III. The Western Christian Leadership Conference is a Christian Social Action Organization of ministers of all denominations and is not a substitute for Interdenominational Minister Alliances or Denominational Unions or Secular Organization concerned with the struggle for equal rights such as the N.A.A.C.P. and the Urban League.

"To Redeem The Soul Of The South"

REV. L. SYLVESTER ODOM
President

REV. JAMES HARGETT
Secretary

REV. MARVIN ROBINSON
Coordinator At Large

REV. MAURICE A. DAWKINS
Chairman of Board

REV. JOHN DOGGETT
Treasurer

REV. JERRY W. FORD
Calif. Vice-President

Fig. 19 Booklet commemorating the founding of the WCLC, 1961.

mass demonstrations, voter registration, selective buying, and aid the Southern Christian Leadership Conference."[38] Initially, as implied by both Dawkins and Peters, the WCLC acted as a local subsidiary of the SCLC, providing crucial human and monetary support to the Southern movement. However, as time went on, the organization would focus its efforts on building a national civil rights movement united by the common goals of integration and socioeconomic equity. Eventually, the WCLC instituted branches across California and in six surrounding states.

THE FREEDOM RIDES

The Freedom Rides were catalyzed by the *Boynton v. Virginia* Supreme Court ruling of 1960, which established that racial segregation in interstate travel facilities, including terminals and restaurants, was illegal under federal law. Despite this legal victory, many Southern states continued to ignore the ruling and maintained segregated facilities. In response, CORE organized the Freedom Rides in May 1961 to test compliance with the decision and bring national attention to ongoing segregation throughout the South.[39] Originating from various cities across the country, the Freedom Rides confronted segregation at bus terminals in the Jim Crow South and attempted to integrate "whites-only" restrooms, lunch counters, and waiting rooms at bus stations along their routes. After arriving in Southern cities, riders engaged in picketing, voter registration initiatives, and civil disobedience designed to fill jails to capacity (plate 26). Many of the Freedom Riders, including those originally based in the South and those arriving from elsewhere, were trained by Rev. James Lawson, a CORE leader who had traveled to India to study satyagraha—a form of nonviolent resistance developed by Mahatma Gandhi.

Beginning on June 25, 1961, Los Angeles CORE organized multiple Freedom Rides. Many who engaged in the first L.A. rides were students.[40] The second L.A. contingent arrived in Jackson on July 9 and were arrested like those before them. Second Baptist Church sponsored the third L.A. group of Freedom Riders, whose departure was heralded on the front page of the *Sentinel*.[41] They were jailed on July 15. One of the most noted Freedom Rides to originate in Los Angeles occurred on July 30 from New Orleans to Jackson, Mississippi, and involved eleven volunteers, including Robert Singleton and his wife, Helen Singleton, who were likewise arrested upon arrival (plates 27, 28). Helen Singleton recalls: "The policeman simply said, 'Are y'all gonna move?' He asked us one more time, and we didn't. We were taken to the city jail. The person booking us … said, 'What school do you go to?' I said, 'Santa Monica City College.' He said, 'How do you spell Santa Monica?' I was young at the time and thought he should know how to spell."[42] Because the local jails were overcrowded, the protesters were forced to spend several weeks at the notorious Mississippi State Penitentiary in Parchman.

Robert Farrell, a student at UCLA and a close friend of Robert Singleton's who would later become a Los Angeles City Council member, participated in the ride that left Los Angeles on August 9, 1961. The group also set out for Jackson, with a planned stop in Houston, Texas, to join ranks with students from Texas Southern University affiliated with the Progressive Youth Association (plate 29).[43] One objective of the journey was to desegregate a coffee shop at Houston's Union Station. Just forty-five minutes after the riders sat down at the whites-only counter, police arrived demanding that the protesters leave or face imminent arrest. Farrell recalled: "We were booked into the Harris County Jail, segregated by gender and race. We Black males were welcomed as heroes by the men in our tank once they learned we were Freedom Riders.... The white men ... were beaten bloody by other prisoners and carried physical and mental scars for the rest of their lives. Like many Freedom Riders, they paid a personal price to secure the right for all of us to travel without racial restrictions. We spent a few weeks in jail. As soon as our lawyers saw how the white riders were being abused, we were bailed out."[44] The group was eventually found guilty of misdemeanor "unlawful assembly" charges that were later overturned.

The Freedom Rides had generated significant news coverage nationwide and made a lasting impact in Los Angeles by reenergizing CORE among young people and on college campuses. On May 21, the *Times* reprinted two United Press International (UPI) pictures depicting the violence the bus riders encountered in Montgomery. One showed a Black student being attacked, while another pictured a bloodied white rider. The next day, the *Times* printed the headline "Martial Law Declared in Alabama's Capital," along with a picture of National Guard troops arriving and an article about a Whittier College student attending Fisk University who was present. A UPI photo inside the paper showed the white transfer student being interviewed by a reporter. The coverage no doubt created awareness and possibly generated interest and sympathy. The *Times* failed to print any pictures, nor much ink at all, related to the five organized L.A.-based contingents who risked their lives for freedom in the Deep South. The *Sentinel* and *Eagle*, by contrast, actively publicized the rides, encouraged fundraising support, and documented rallies. The certainty of jail, and the possibility of much worse, tested the courage of upward of fifty known Angelenos who participated as Freedom Riders. The many who stayed behind to participate in the collective action through fundraising, prayer, and protest charged Los Angeles's local freedom struggle with even more energy (plate 30).

THE 1961 FREEDOM RALLY

The WCLC held a Freedom Rally in Los Angeles on June 18, 1961, to raise money for the Freedom Rides. King headlined the rally, but he also engaged in a whirlwind of other appearances. He was the featured speaker at a press conference at the Los Angeles International Airport (LAX), toured Compton and Watts, and taped a segment for Channel 2 News, all on the first day of his visit.

An estimated forty thousand people, including California's governor, attended the rally held at the Los Angeles Memorial Sports Arena, which the LAPD labeled "the largest assembly of Negroes in Los Angeles within memory (plate 31)."[45] Organizers had planned for an audience of twelve thousand, and the venue could accommodate eighteen thousand. Many participants remained outside to listen via loudspeaker. King gave two separate speeches on the same topic to allow as many people as possible an opportunity to listen. Backed by opening music from gospel singer Mahalia Jackson, he stood before the massive audience and stressed the uniquely American qualities of the struggle for civil rights in a time of "world revolution." He called for national unity, commenting that the American dream "is being scarred not only in

Mississippi but in New York and other Northern cities as well."[46]

WCLC public relations coordinator Jim Goodrich thanked the press for its cooperation in publicizing the event in the *Times*, highlighting its importance.[47] *Sentinel* correspondent Wanda Joyner Dorsey recalled that she "had never seen an audience so anxious and so inquisitive." [48] King called the Los Angeles event "the greatest civil rights rally that has ever been held in the US."[49] Meanwhile, the *Eagle* filled its front page with pictures of the rally. Two images of the vast crowd sit atop the enormous headline "40,000 at Greatest Rally" (fig. 20). Another prominent picture shows celebrities Jackson, Davis, and Dick Gregory handling a mass of envelopes and donations, dubbed "Dollars for Freedom."[50]

The photographic and media coverage of the civil rights activism in Los Angeles in the late 1950s and early 1960s demonstrates just how large the movement had grown. Students and celebrities, Black residents and white allies, and religious leaders and government officials rallied throughout the state to support the national movement.

Los Angeles CORE continued to expand in 1961 and 1962. The branch engaged in a nearly yearlong campaign at the Greyhound bus terminal, which ended in August 1962 when the Greyhound company hired two Black bus drivers.[51] Also in 1962, CORE organized a Monterey Park sit-in in response to a real estate developer's refusal to sell land to a Black physician.

A success in equal education occurred in the fall of 1962, when the NAACP issued a call to picket outside of several Los Angeles schools. Negotiations between the NAACP and the L. A. Board of Education led to the admittance of two African American students to Baldwin Hills Elementary School. The children, Todd and Randall Garr, were the first of an anticipated fifty students who would transfer to the school (plate 32).

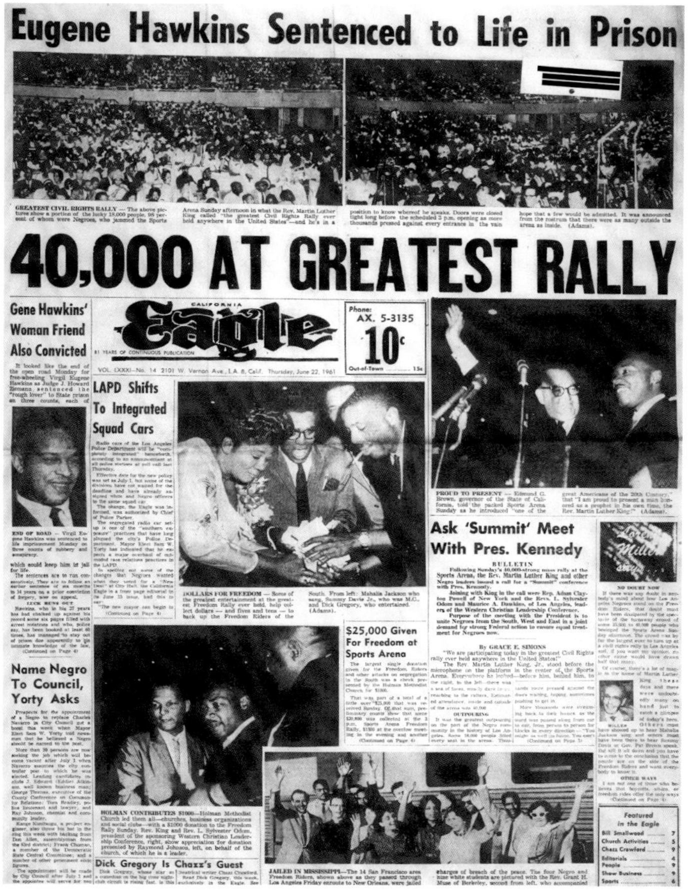

Eugene Hawkins Sentenced to Life in Prison

40,000 AT GREATEST RALLY

California Eagle

Phone: AX. 5-3135

10¢

Gene Hawkins' Woman Friend Also Convicted

LAPD Shifts To Integrated Squad Cars

Ask 'Summit' Meet With Pres. Kennedy

$25,000 Given For Freedom at Sports Arena

Name Negro To Council, Yorty Asks

Dick Gregory Is Chazz's Guest

Fig. 20 Front page of the June 22, 1961, issue of the *California Eagle* covering the pivotal 1961 Los Angeles Freedom Rally.

A BROAD COALITION

In particular, King's celebrity was instrumental in galvanizing local community members and drawing national support and media attention while he simultaneously led civil rights activism in the South. The early 1960s would prove an active time for King in Los Angeles as he broadened his outreach to religious leaders and communities across the city. In February 1960, King spoke to an audience at Temple

Isaiah in West Los Angeles after being introduced by Rabbi Albert M. Lewis, a well-known advocate for underserved groups. "In our nation, we have a long, long way to go," King said to the Jewish congregation. "And I am convinced that God is not interested merely in the freedom of Black men and Brown men … but God is interested in the freedom of the whole human race."[52] Lewis compared King's leadership to that of Moses leading the Israelites out of Egypt: "Since the Civil War, there has been no single action that has so galvanized the Negro people and stirred up the rest of the country as the direct positive action which Martin Luther King Jr. initiated in Montgomery, Alabama. And we trust that when he told his people to go, and they went, that it will have the same effect on the Negro people as Moses's command had upon the Jewish people."[53] With their own experiences of discrimination, the Jewish community was closely connected to the civil rights movement in Los Angeles. For example, the Emma Lazarus Jewish Women's Clubs of Los Angeles actively supported the Woolworth boycott and proudly signed a national petition in 1960 calling for Woolworth stores to end their discriminatory policies.[54] Additionally, Jewish students in particular were early antiracist activists as members of university chapters of CORE across the country.

Members of the Orange Grove Friends Meeting, a Quaker congregation established in Pasadena in 1907, openly advocated the Quaker ideals of equality and nonviolence and took part in Freedom Rides in the South and in the fight to desegregate local schools during the 1960s. Nationally known Quaker activist Rev. Ashton Jones participated in the Monterey Park sit-in, and he partnered with local Black ministers to organize support drives and protests. In August 1962, Jones and Dawkins knelt side by side in prayer on the steps of Los Angeles City Hall in support of King and his role in an ongoing desegregation campaign in Albany, Georgia.[55] Three years later, while attending Friendship Baptist Church in Pasadena, Jones was introduced to King, sparking an ongoing friendship.[56]

On January 15, 1961, at the invitation of Rev. Fred Owens Doty, King gave two sermons at Woodland Hills Community Church and later spoke at Canoga Park High School. The later engagement was given extensive, objective coverage in the *Valley Times* newspaper and accompanied by a photograph. All three speeches were aimed at largely white audiences. "It is always a great pleasure for me to come to the state of California," King said in the opening of his Canoga Park speech, "because I know that we have real friends here."[57]

2

Plates

Mamie Till-Mobley's decision to share her private grief over the 1955 murder of her fourteen-year-old son, Emmett Till, changed history. The African American boy was brutally beaten following accusations that he whistled at a white woman while visiting Mississippi. When Till-Mobley allowed *Jet* magazine to publish pictures of Emmett's disfigured face taken at his funeral, the images horrified the nation and ignited the modern civil rights movement.

Readers of the *California Eagle* saw Till-Mobley's despair on the paper's front page. Her pain became a call to action to fight discrimination everywhere. In the following months, Angelenos read of the rising tide of discontent spreading in the South and beyond. Los Angeles's Black churches hosted rallies to raise awareness and generate funds for desegregation efforts. Newspapers highlighted overflowing churches as civil rights leaders including Martin Luther King Jr. and Rev. Ralph Abernathy visited the city regularly. Photographers captured them boarding planes, speaking to the press, and preaching from pulpits.

Many Black Angelenos maintained deep connections to the South despite having fled its oppression and racial violence for safer and more prosperous lives in the West. Some found that, while still an improvement, California wasn't entirely the promised land they hoped it might be.

The rich archive of early civil rights imagery reveals the vital role women played in the movement. In April 1956, Rosa Parks came to Los Angeles to share her story of civil disobedience at a rally at Second Baptist Church and in smaller meetings at women's homes. She explained that her decision to keep her seat on a segregated public bus was not a spontaneous choice at the end of a long workday but a planned civil action. Her participation in a local fund drive drove excitement and new NAACP memberships.

Images of the student-led Southern sit-in movement of 1960 sparked waves of activism nationwide. In Los Angeles, college students picketed seventeen F. W. Woolworth and S. H. Kress stores in one day in late March. Black newsweeklies kept the story visible and contextualized the issue for readers. Some people wondered why protests happened in L.A. at all, including a curious woman who asked a picketer: "Why do you march in Pasadena, we don't have any discrimination here. Do you?" An attorney in a *Los Angeles Sentinel* article countered: "There are 36 existing establishments in Pasadena where a Negro cannot receive service."[58]

Freelancer Charles Williams snapped dozens of pictures of King and local ministers in July 1960 picketing outside a Woolworth on Crenshaw Boulevard. The ongoing visual documentation of Southern civil rights leaders supporting local campaigns reminded readers that their cities were part of a broader freedom struggle. King's trip to Los Angeles included marching at the Democratic National Convention and seeking to influence the civil rights platform and the nominee, Sen. John F. Kennedy. Photographer Jack Davis captured JFK attracting large crowds and the overwhelming support of Black voters.

The 1961 Freedom Rides pressured the new administration to act when activists were attacked while trying to desegregate Southern bus stations. Angelenos supported the protests, and dozens became Freedom Riders themselves, traveling by bus and train to the Deep South, risking arrest and potentially their lives. Photojournalists documented a CORE recruitment table with signs reading: "Help Send LA Youngsters to Jail!!" A cohort of young Freedom Riders boarding a train at L.A.'s Union Station smiled and waved to supporters. Pictures like these made their dedication and commitment visible to all. Within days of their departure, nearly fifty different Freedom Riders from Los Angeles were arrested, photographed for mug shots, and imprisoned.[59] Two of those activists were Robert and Helen Singleton, who were photographed on July 30, 1961, at the Jackson, Mississippi, police station. After being booked, Helen wryly noticed an LAPD recruiting poster on a nearby wall with a picture of Chief William Parker beckoning: "I Want You!" The Singletons, like many of the Freedom Riders, returned home even more determined to make Los Angeles a beacon of liberty and justice for all.

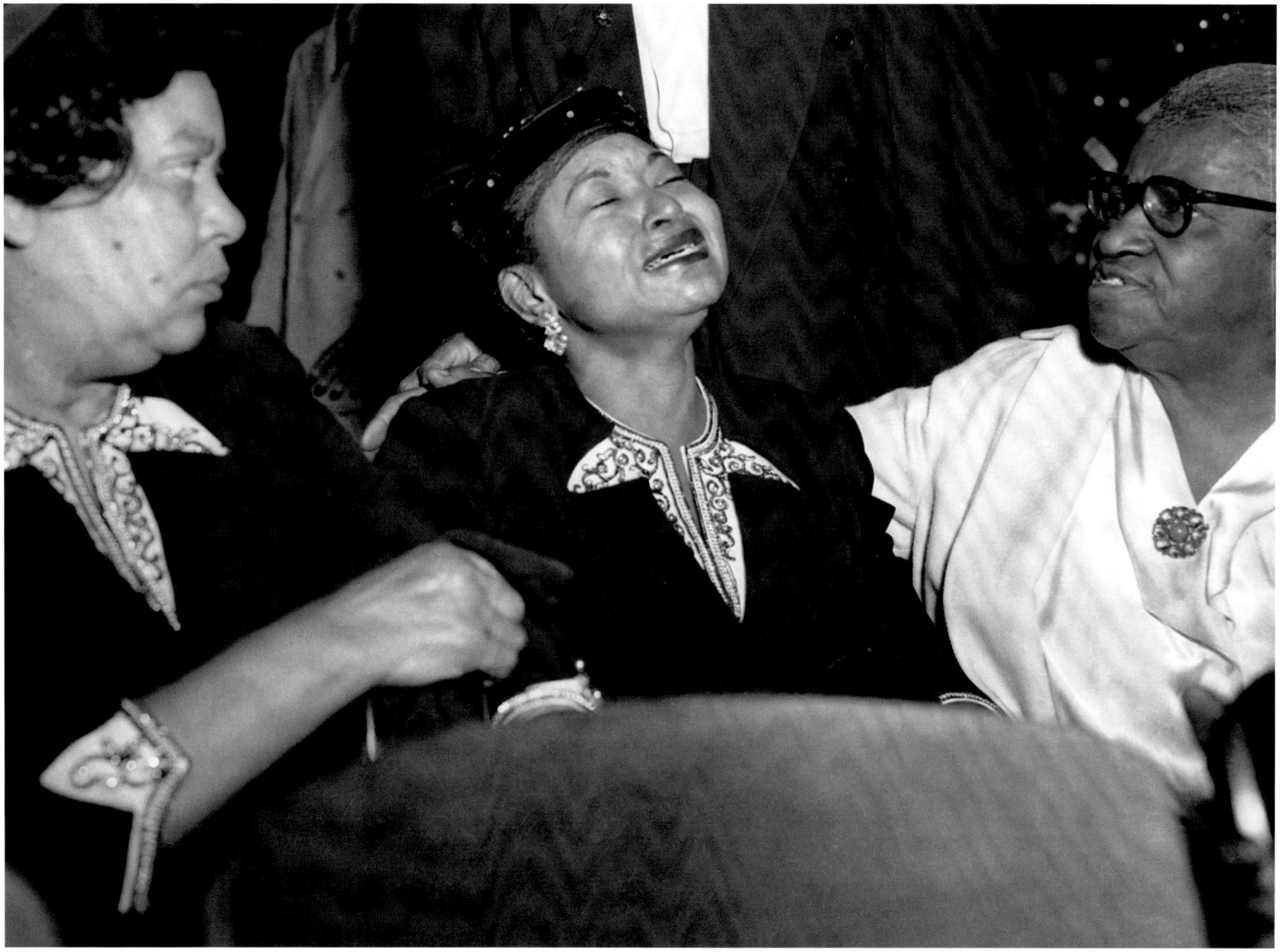

Plate 18 UNKNOWN PHOTOGRAPHER, 1955
A grief-stricken Mamie Till-Mobley at the funeral of her murdered son, Emmett Till, in Chicago. The *California Eagle* published this UPI photograph on its front page. Till-Mobley's decision to allow pictures of the open-casket funeral helped galvanize the rising civil rights movement. "The whole nation had to bear witness to this," she said.[60]

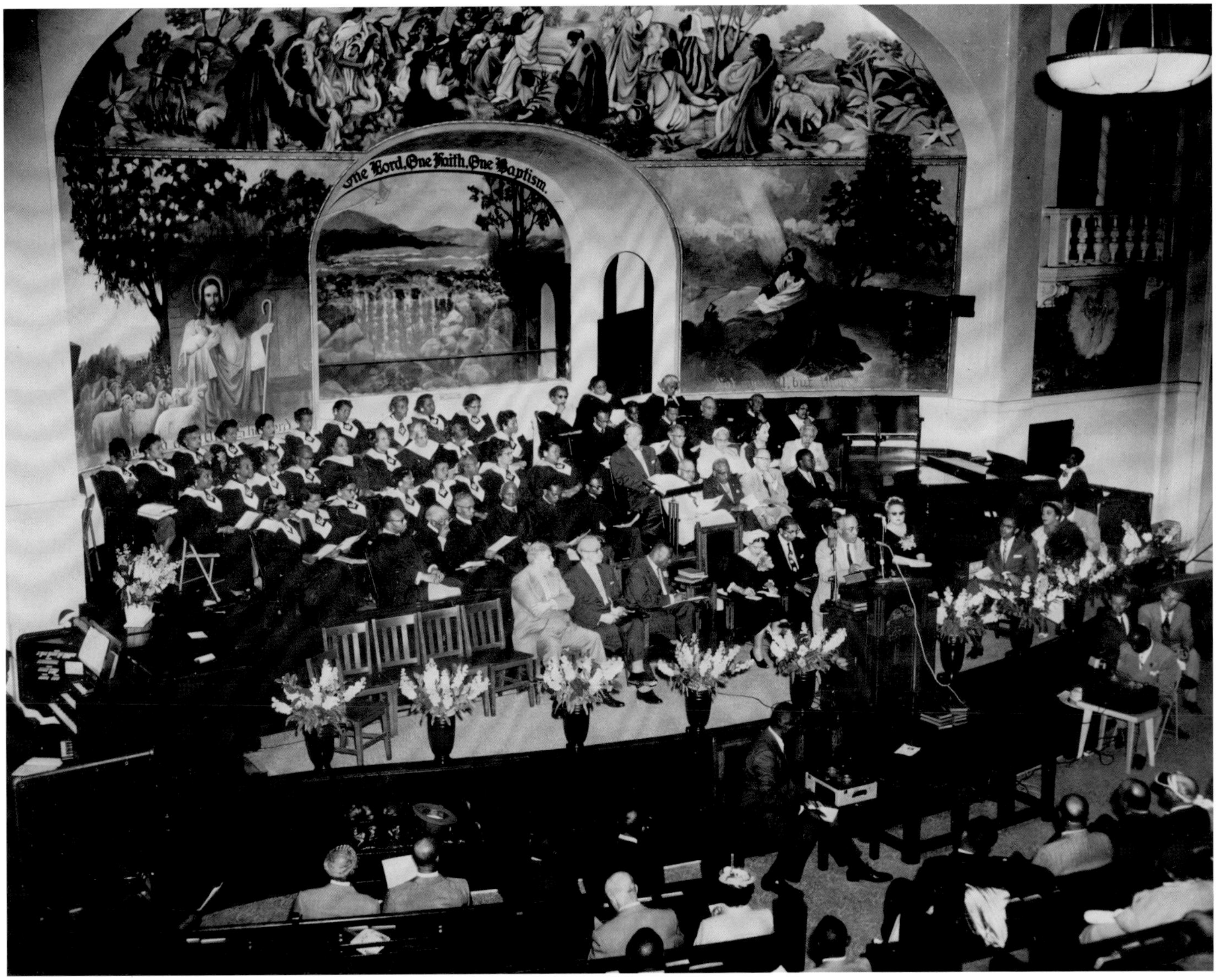

Plate 19 MCLAIN'S PHOTO SERVICE, 1956

Civil rights activist Rosa Parks, seated behind the speaker, is introduced at Second Baptist Church during a Sunday afternoon membership rally for the Los Angeles NAACP. Parks attracted an overflow crowd of more than three thousand eager to hear how her refusal to give up her bus seat instigated the Montgomery Bus Boycott in December 1955.

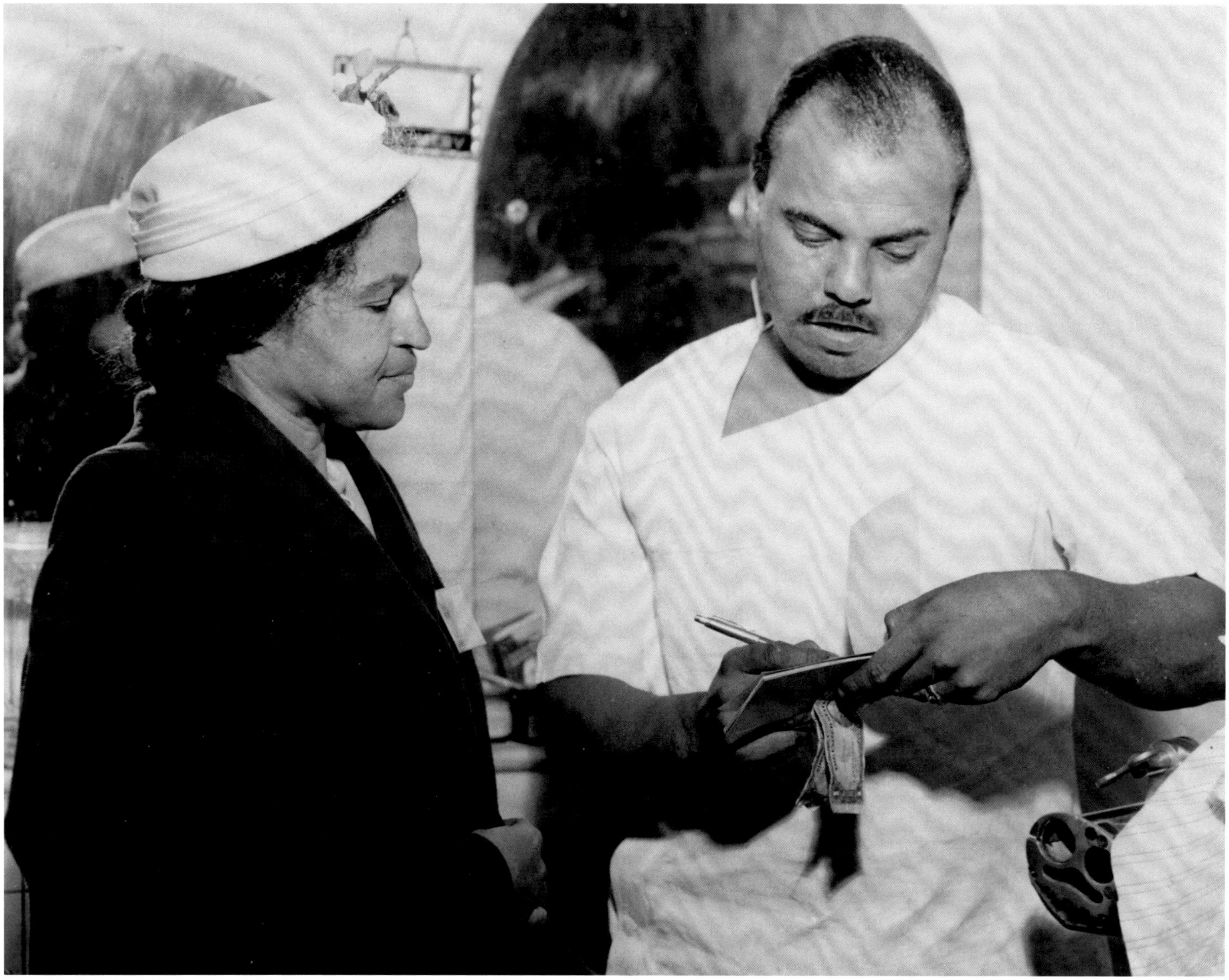

Plate 20 MCLAIN'S PHOTO SERVICE, 1956
Rosa Parks helps collect $2 membership dues for the NAACP at a local barbershop as part of a Los Angeles membership drive. The *Los Angeles Times* did not cover the civil rights leader's visit.

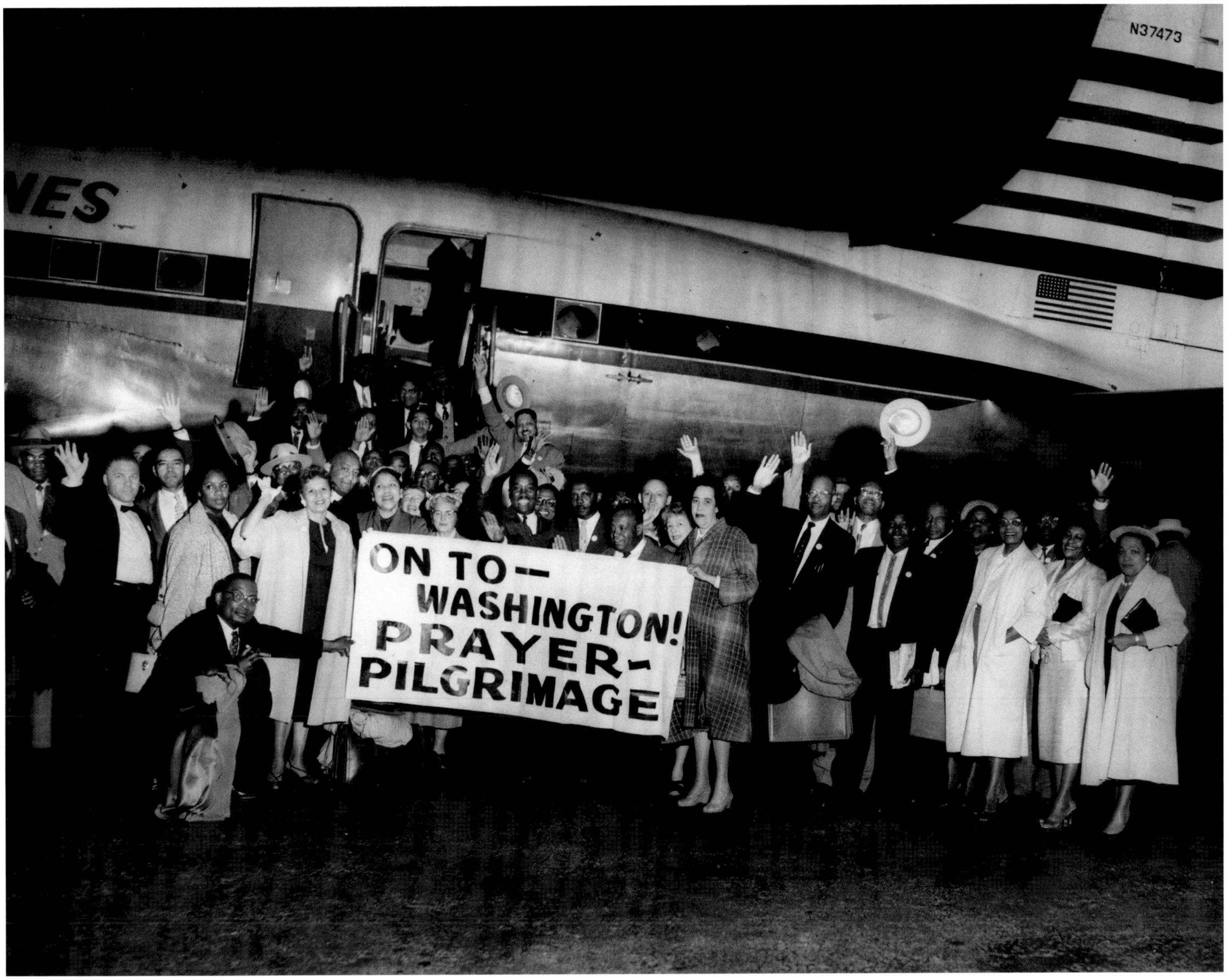

Plate 21 HARRY ADAMS, 1957

Harry Adams captured a jubilant contingent of Californians on their way to the Prayer Pilgrimage for Freedom in Washington, DC. West Coast coordinator Rev. Maurice Dawkins waves from directly behind the banner. The *California Eagle* provided extensive coverage of the demonstration at the Lincoln Memorial for readers back home. This picture ran on the front page of the *Eagle*'s May 23, issue.

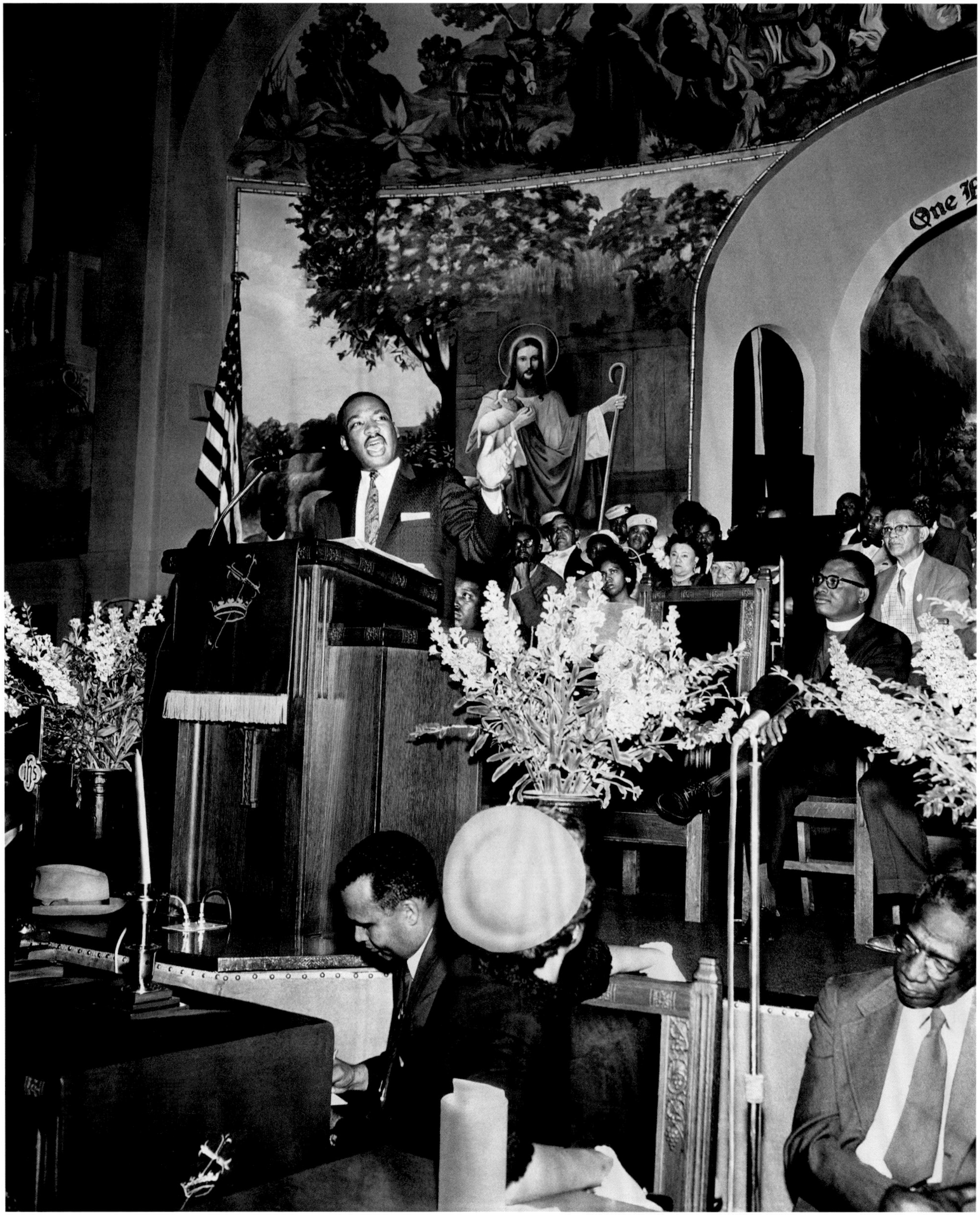
One

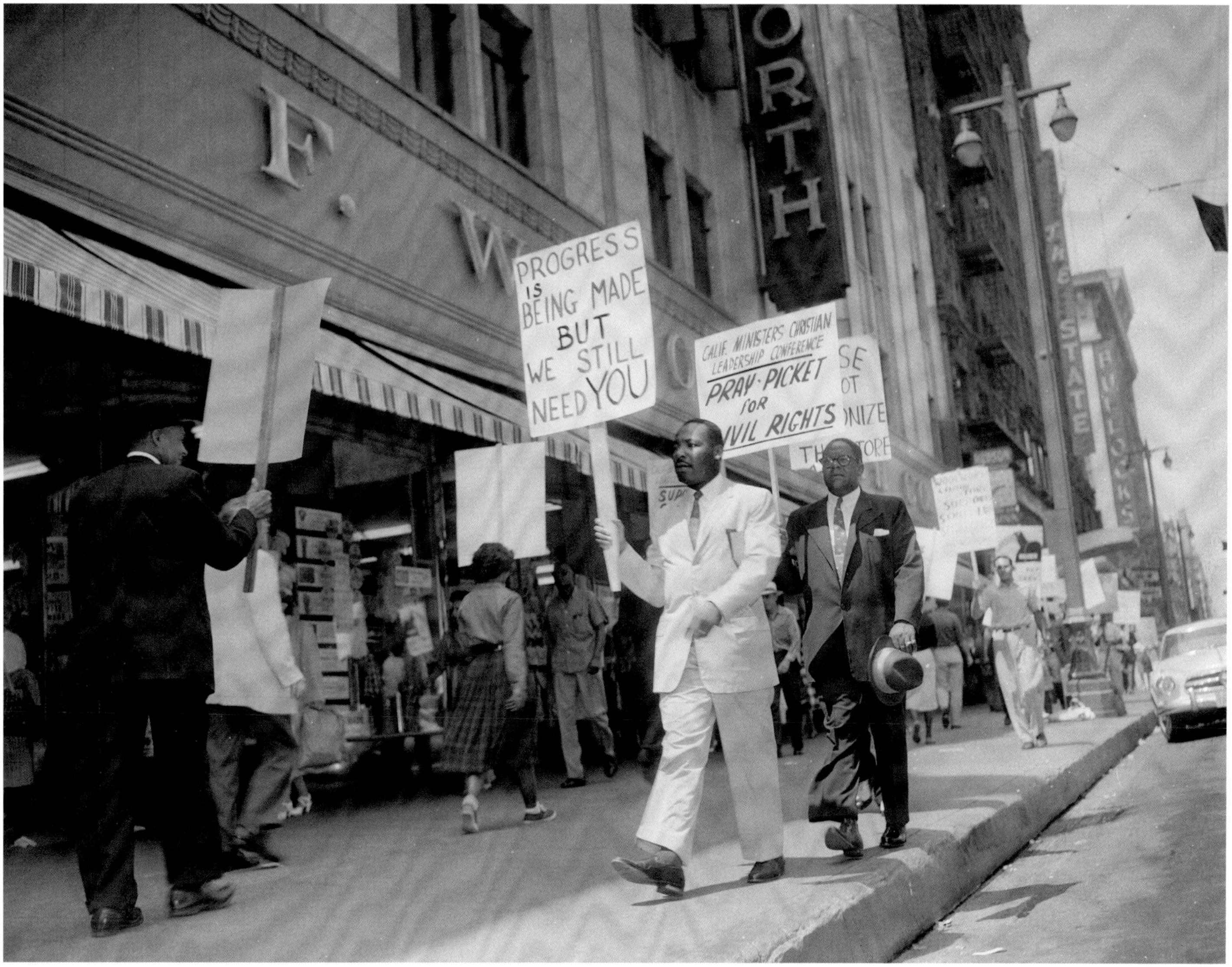

Plate 22 HARRY ADAMS, 1958

Martin Luther King Jr. speaks to a crowd of three thousand at Second Baptist Church. He urged the audience to "take the most decisive step—the short walk to the voting booth!"[63] Harry Adams's picture of King in a pose similar to that of Jesus depicted behind him appeared on the front page of the February 27 issue of the *California Eagle*.

Plate 23 CHARLES WILLIAMS, 1960

Martin Luther King Jr. leads local ministers and protesters in a demonstration outside an F. W. Woolworth store along Crenshaw Boulevard on July 9. King's picket sign notes that "Progress Is Being Made But We Still Need You." His participation drew photographers like Charles Williams, who had one of his pictures printed in the *California Eagle*. The next day, King led a march of five thousand demonstrators to the L.A. Memorial Sports Arena.

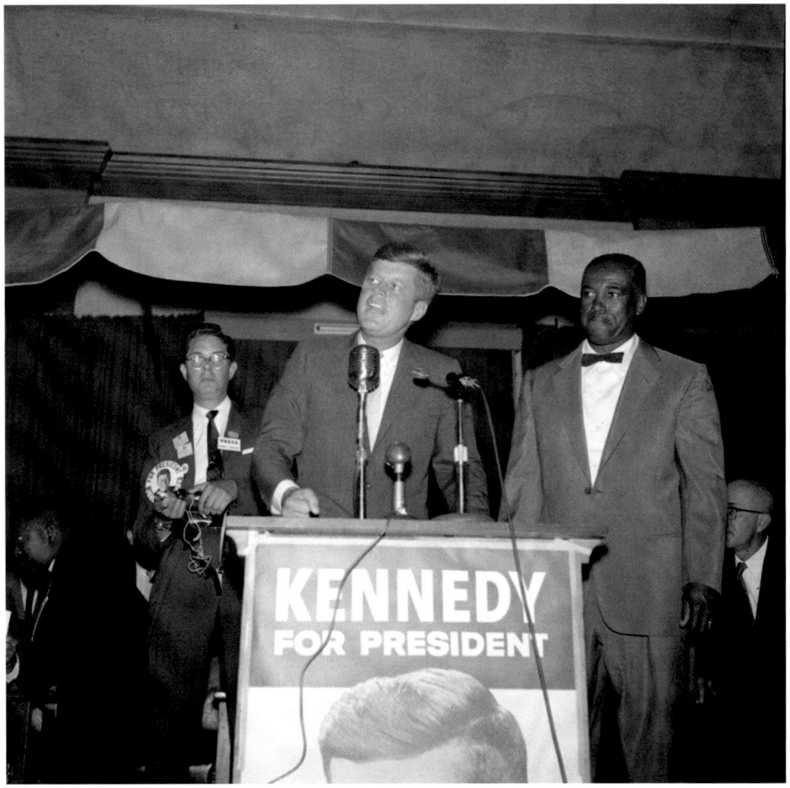

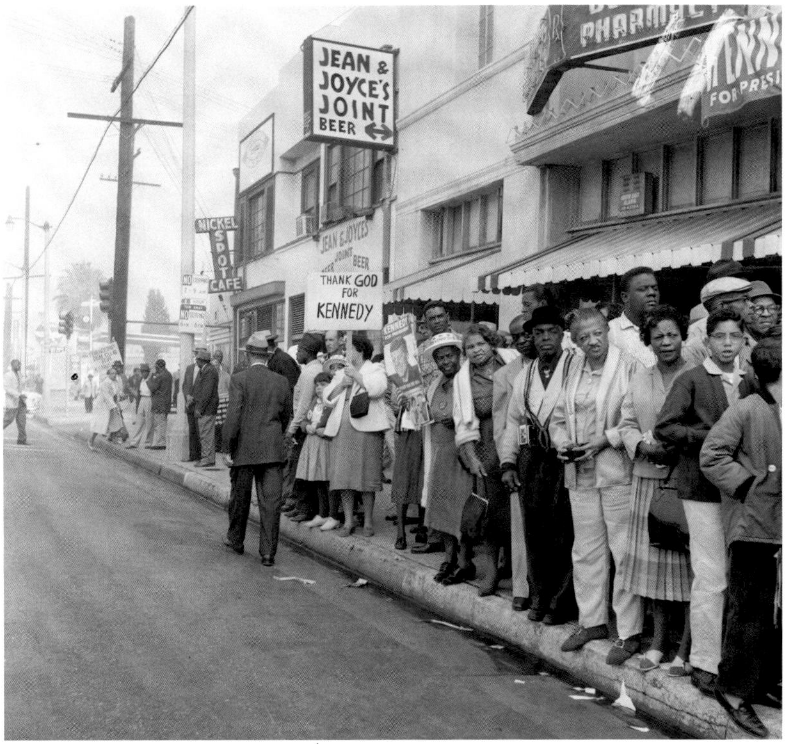

Plate 24 JACK DAVIS, 1960

Sen. John F. Kennedy speaks to supporters during a rally for the Democratic ticket before the November election. Two of Los Angeles's assembly districts with the largest concentration of Black voters overwhelmingly voted for Kennedy, as did heavily Hispanic and Jewish districts.

Plate 25 JACK DAVIS, 1960

Sen. John F. Kennedy drew significant crowds, as seen in Jack Davis's picture of a long line of people waiting to see the Democratic candidate's motorcade. One supporter holds a sign proclaiming "Thank God for Kennedy." The senator was more sympathetic to the civil rights movement than his Republican rival, Vice President Richard Nixon, a California native who went on to carry the state in the election.

Plate 26 UNKNOWN PHOTOGRAPHER, 1961

Members of Valley CORE recruit local participants to travel on Freedom Rides to challenge segregated public transportation facilities in the South. One of their goals was to overwhelm the judicial system by filling the jails with arrested Riders.

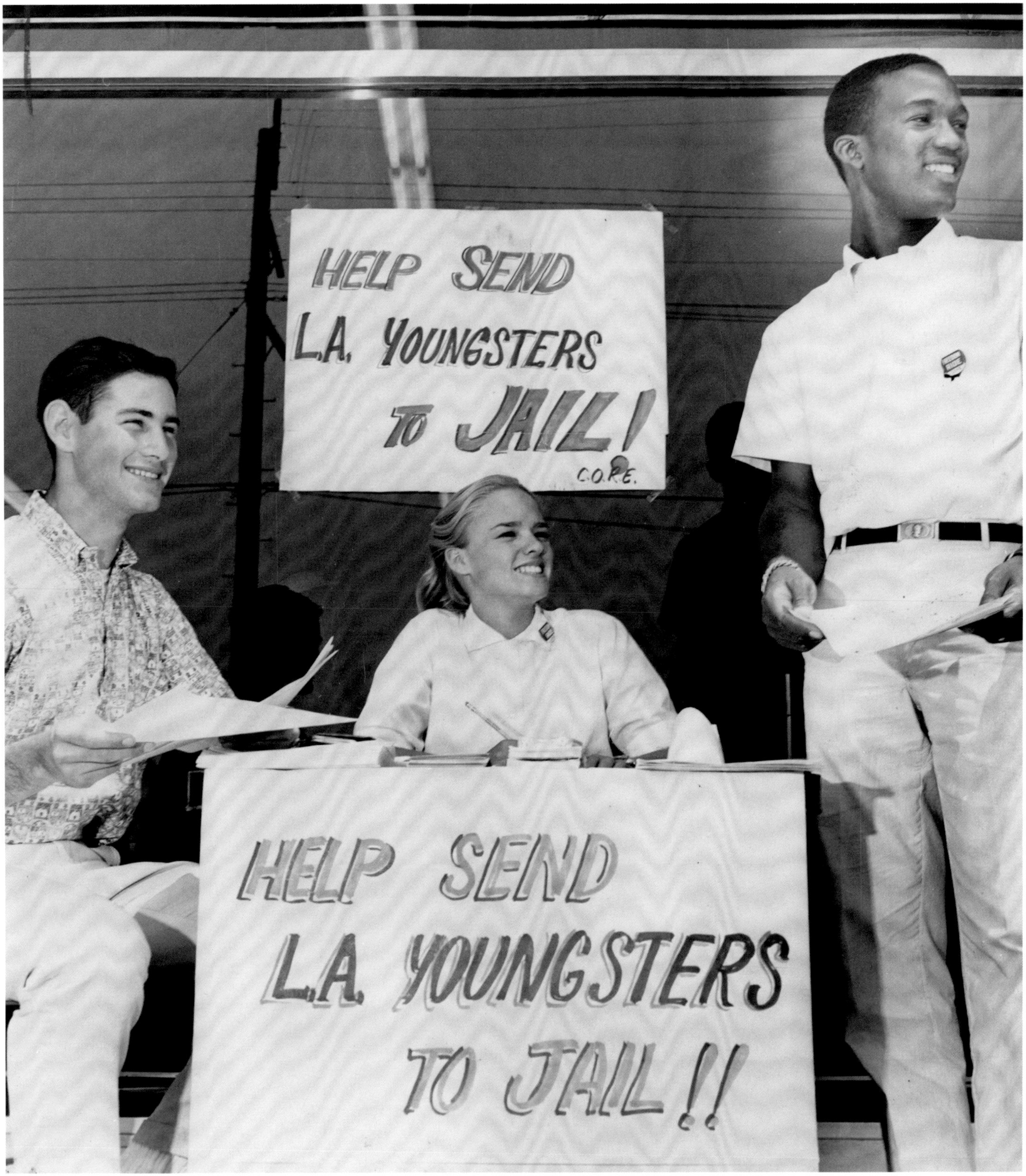
HELP SEND
L.A. YOUNGSTERS
TO JAIL!
C.O.R.E.
HELP SEND
L.A. YOUNGSTERS
TO JAIL!!

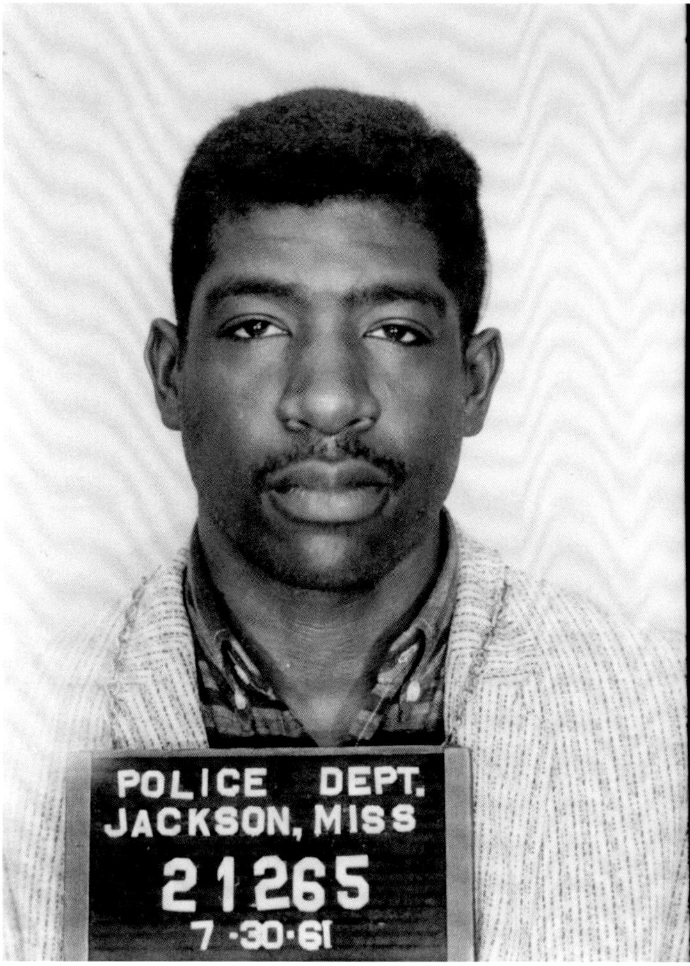

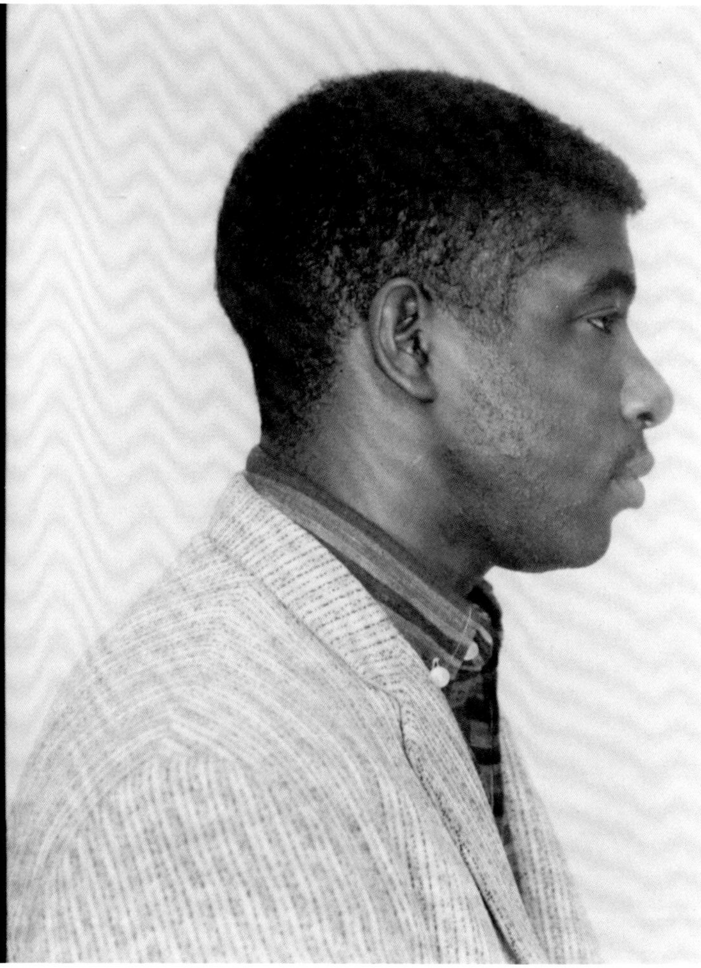

Plates 27, 28 UNKNOWN PHOTOGRAPHER, 1961
Robert and Helen Singleton in mug shots taken July 30 in Jackson, Mississippi. The couple helped recruit many L.A. activists for the Freedom Rides and understood the risks. "I knew that there was danger. I knew I would probably end up in prison," Helen recalled. "But … they can't stop you if you know you are on the right side of history."[62] The Singletons and more than three hundred other Freedom Riders were charged with "breach of peace."

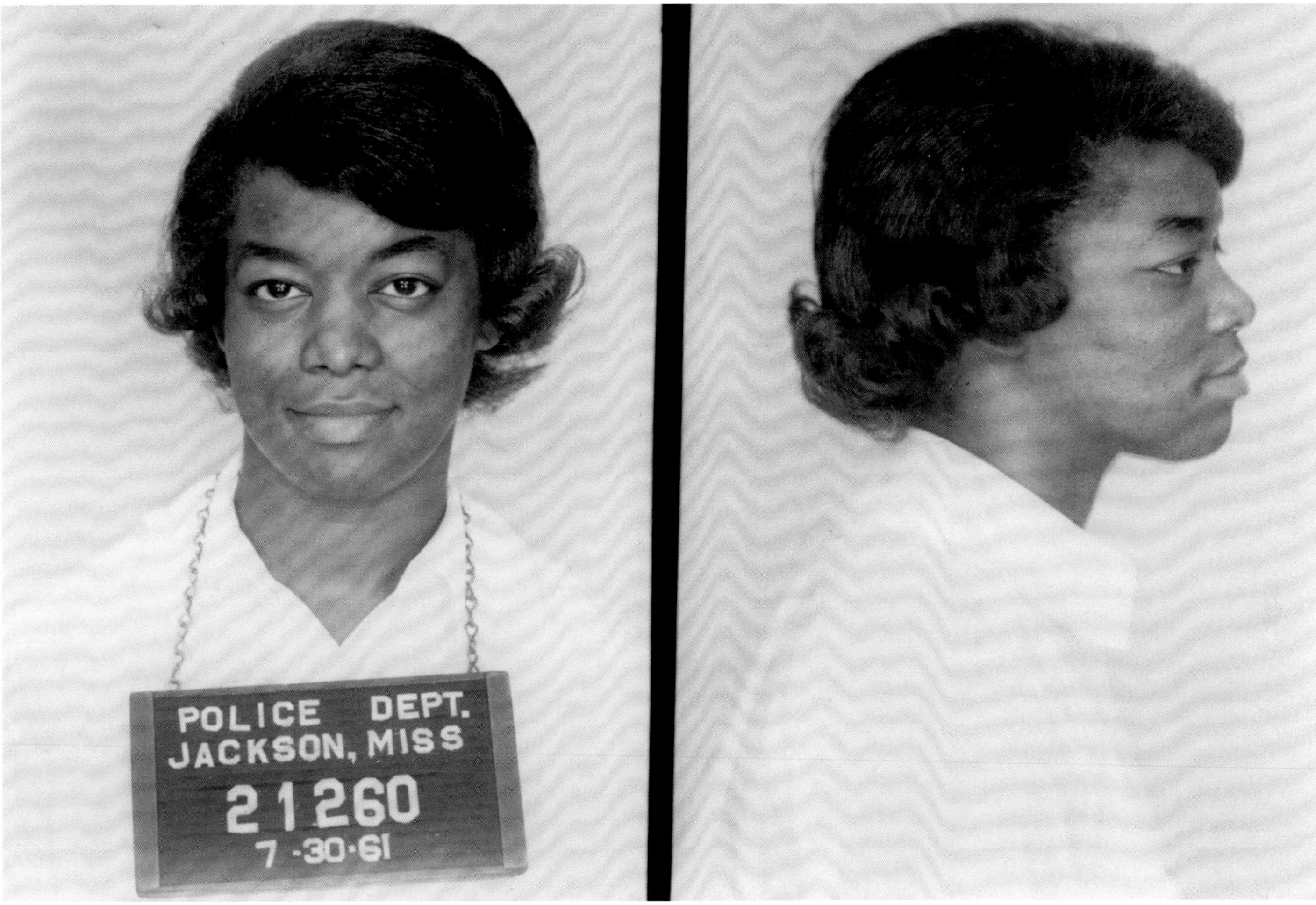
POLICE DEPT.
JACKSON, MISS
21260
7-30-61

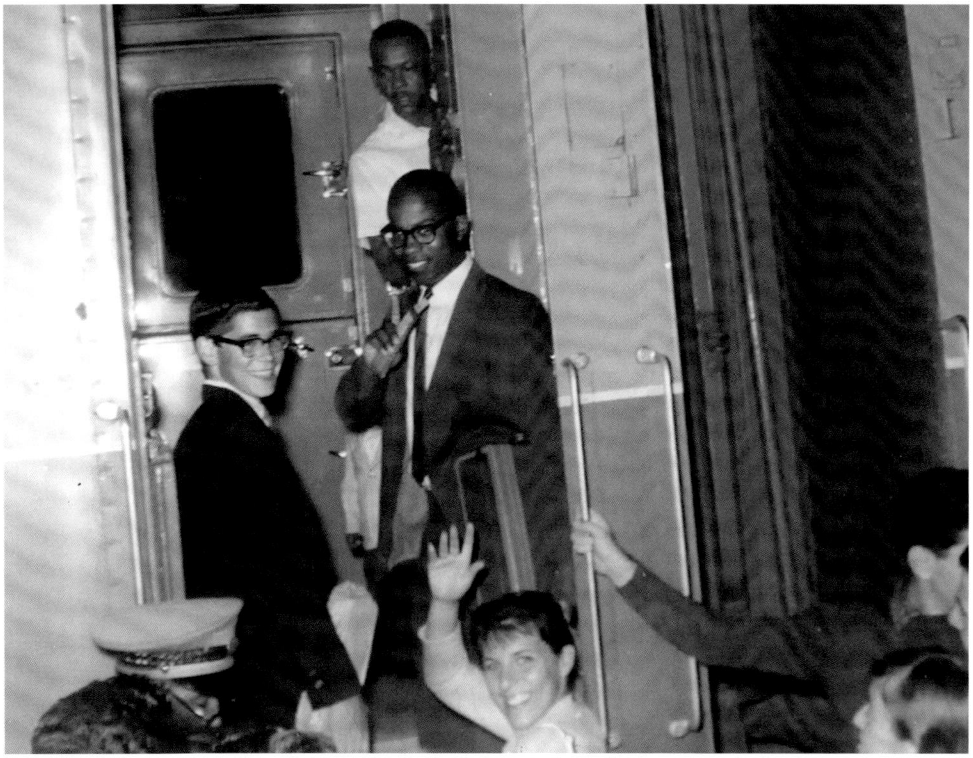

Plate 29 UNKNOWN PHOTOGRAPHER, 1961

Three Freedom Riders from Los Angeles board a train with eight others headed for Jackson, Mississippi, on August 9. The activists, Joe Stevenson (*left*), Charles Berrard (*center, with suitcase*), and Patricia Kovner (*waving*), were arrested during a sit-in at a coffee shop at Union Station in Houston, Texas.

Plate 30 UNKNOWN PHOTOGRAPHER, 1961

CORE members and supporters of the Freedom Riders protest the beatings and arrests of civil rights activists in the South. The protests erupted after two Greyhound and Trailways buses carrying Freedom Riders were attacked and firebombed in May near Anniston, Alabama, attracting international attention. By raising awareness and recruiting committed activists, CORE and other organizations in California sent more Freedom Riders to the South than almost any other state.

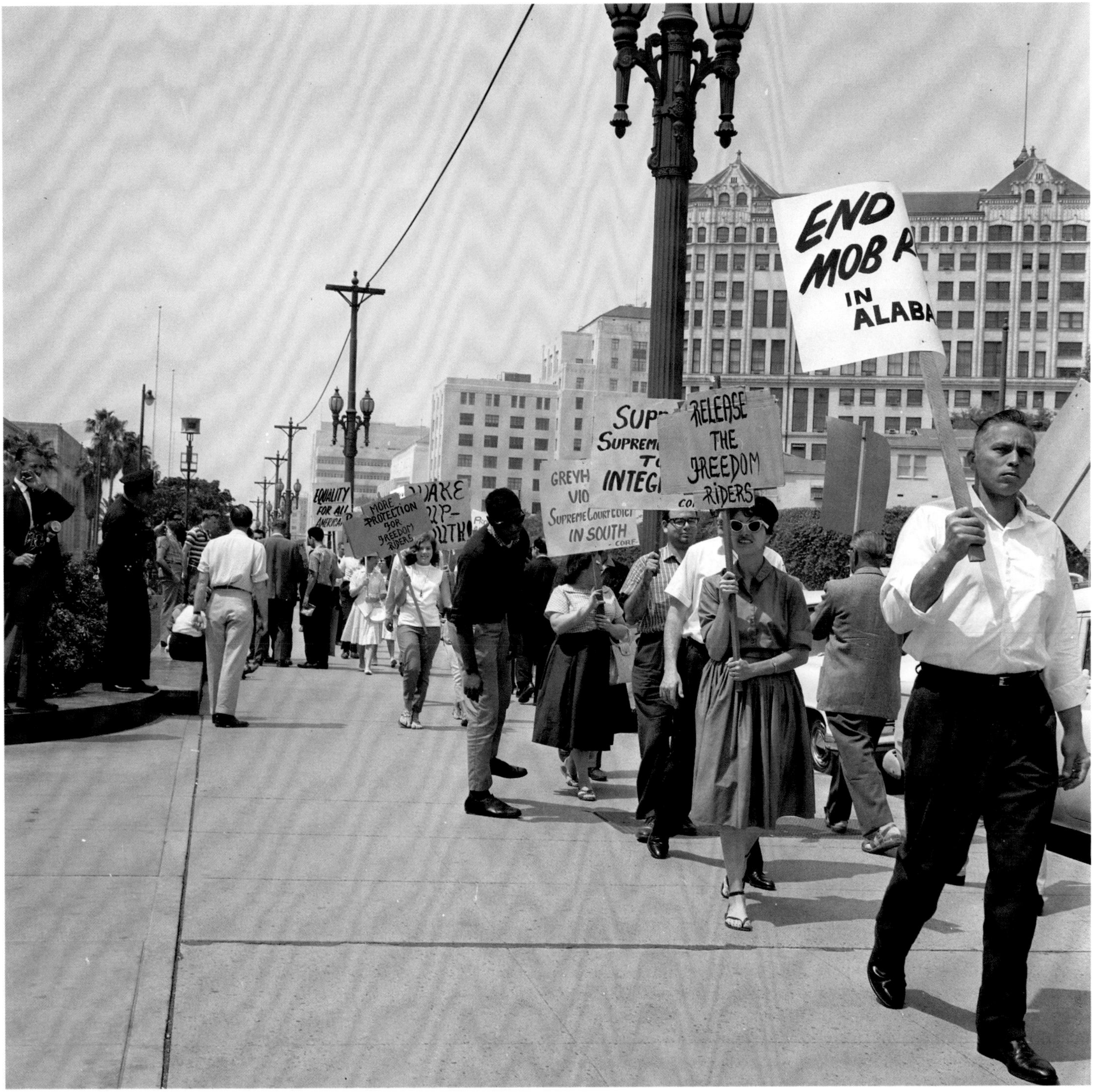
END
MOB R
IN
ALABA
RELEASE
THE
FREEDOM
RIDERS
MORE
PROTECTION
FOR
FREEDOM
RIDERS
IN SOUTH

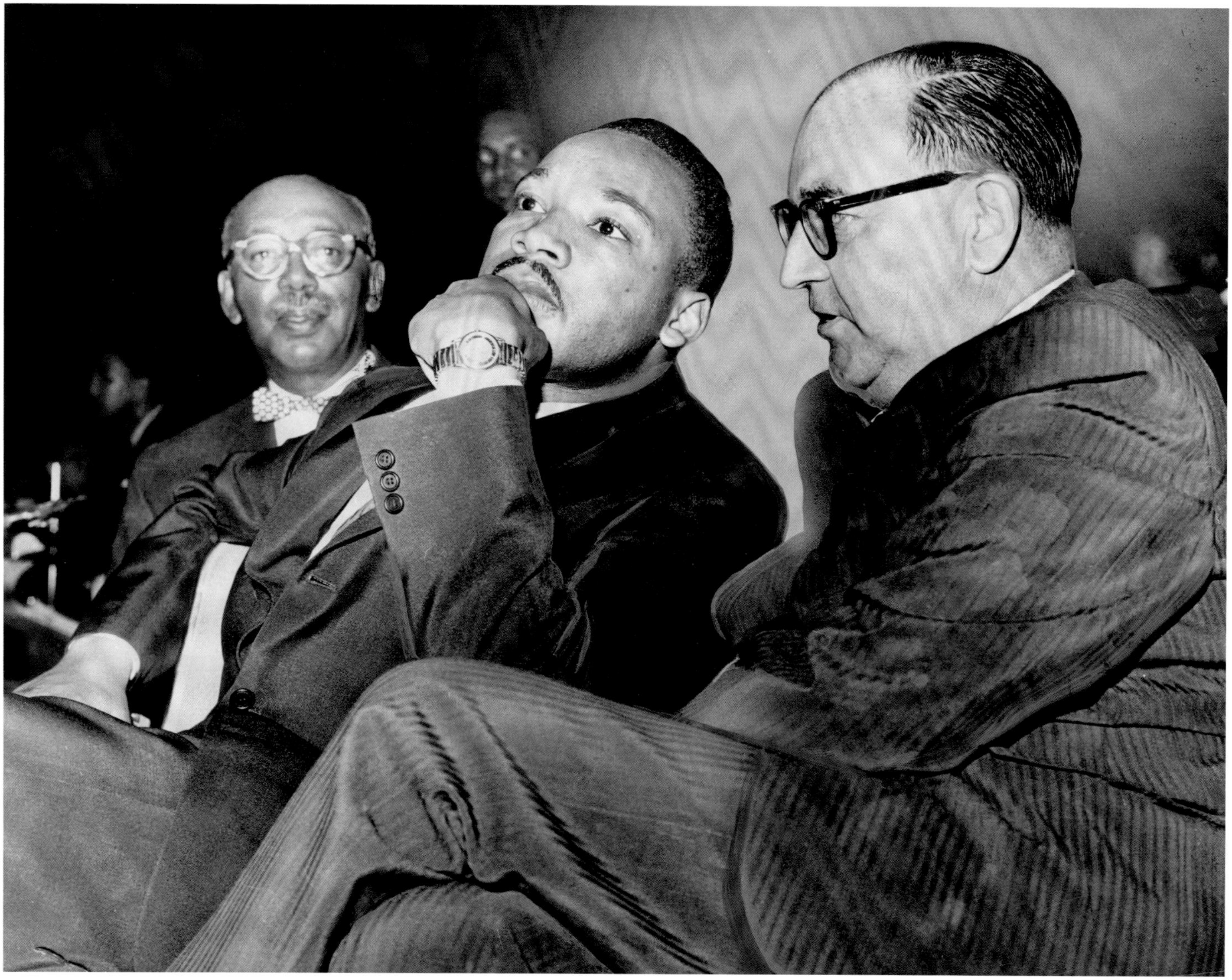

Plate 31 UNKNOWN PHOTOGRAPHER, 1961

Martin Luther King Jr. sits with Gov. Edmund G. "Pat" Brown (*right*) during the 1961 Freedom Rally at the Los Angeles Memorial Sports Arena on June 18. King spoke twice, and speakers were set up outside for the thousands who were unable to get inside the eighteen-thousand-person venue to hear King's talk. Brown, who introduced the civil rights leader as a man honored as a prophet in his own time, also remarked: "Americans must avoid the self-righteousness of considering the civil rights problem a 'sin of the South.'"[63]

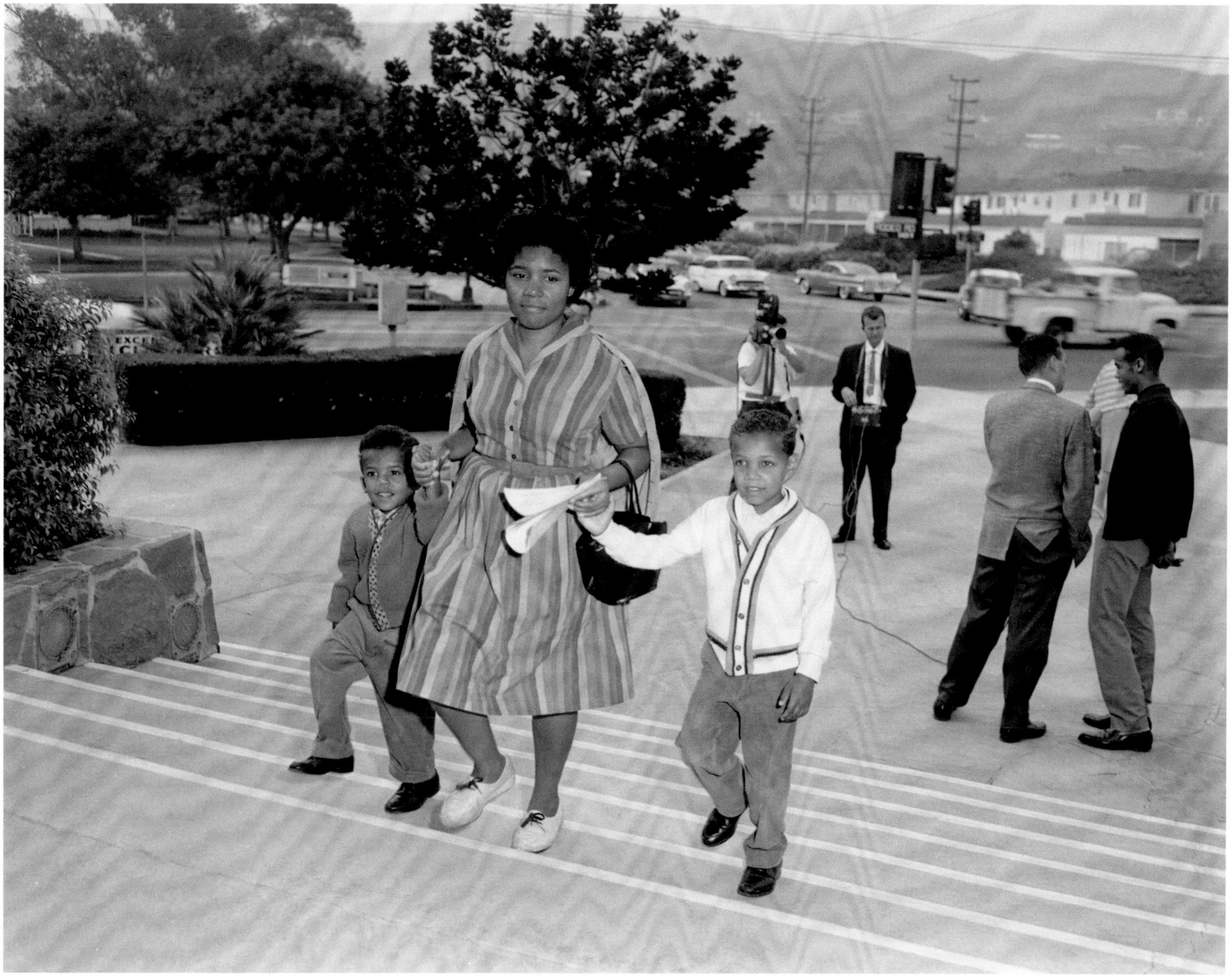

Plate 32 HARRY ADAMS, 1962

On the first day of the school year, Alyce Garr walks her sons, Todd and Randall, up the stairs of Baldwin Hills Elementary School. This photo appeared on the front page of the *California Eagle*, along with an article touting the success of a threatened NAACP picket in achieving the integration of the previously all-white school.

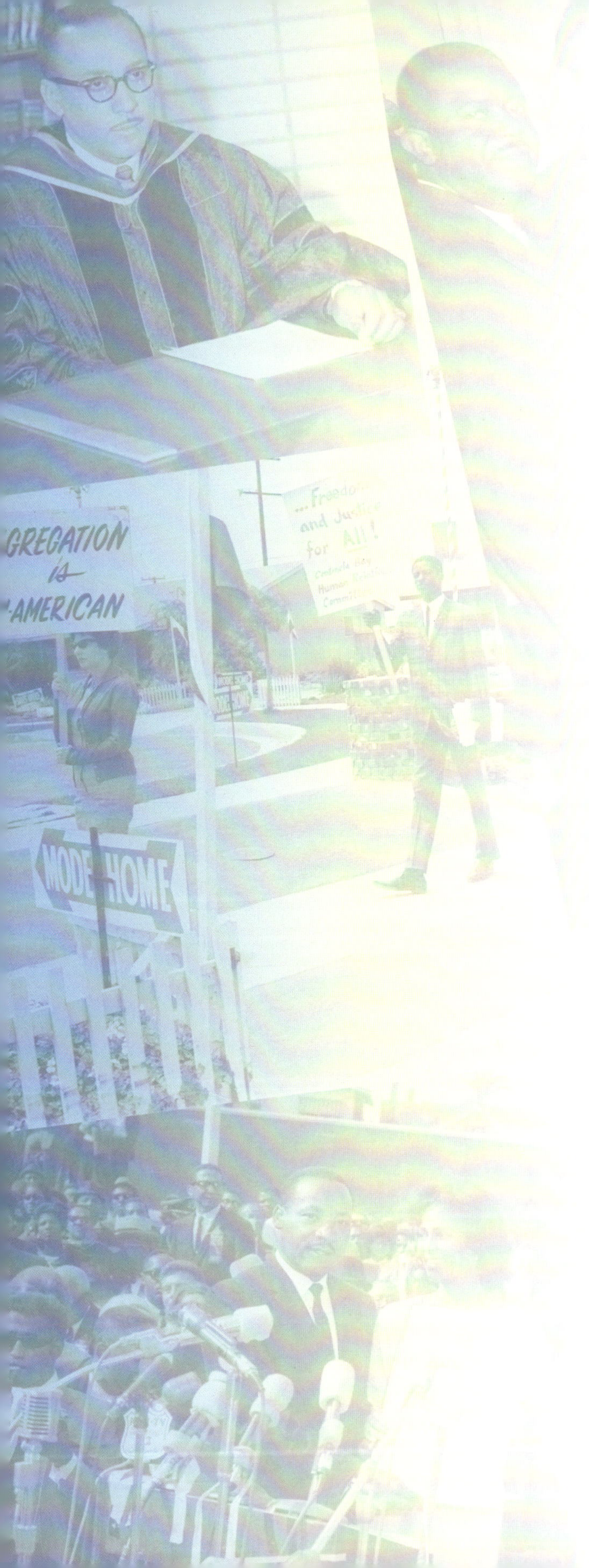

3

"Powers Greater than Violence"

TRAGEDY AT MOSQUE NO. 27

A deadly confrontation outside Muhammad's Mosque No. 27 on April 27, 1962, sent shock waves through the city. *Los Angeles Herald Examiner* photographer Howard Ballew arrived later that night, and as he clicked the shutter of his camera, three Muslim men lay splayed across the blood-splattered sidewalk as an armed officer looked impassively into the lens (plate 33). Ballew's photograph was later reprinted on the front page of the newspaper *Muhammad Speaks* below the headline "Seven Unarmed Negroes Shot in Cold Blood by Los Angeles Police."[1] The image was circulated nationally to reinforce the Nation of Islam's charge that police targeted them and, by implication, all Black Americans.

How and why the conflict began was disputed by both sides. Officers Frank Tomlinson and Stanley Kensic said they confronted two Nation of Islam (NOI) members who were removing clothes from a car around midnight about a block away from Mosque 27. According to police reports, the officers questioned the men because of recent burglaries in the area.[2] The two men asserted that they were bringing clothes into the mosque as part of a dry-cleaning delivery service.

The situation escalated, attracting bystanders and drawing out other NOI members from the mosque. Ronald Stokes heard the confrontation from inside the mosque (fig. 21). He told his wife, Delores Stokes, "I'm going out here to see what this commotion is about. Just wait here for me."[3] That was the last time she saw her husband alive. Officer Donald Weese fatally shot twenty-nine-year-old Stokes from six feet away as he walked toward the officer with his hands raised in the air as if in surrender. Another member, William Rogers, was shot in the back and paralyzed. One of the other men, Monroe Jones, was able to wrestle a gun away from one of the officers during the turmoil.[4] Police backup units arrived on the scene and dozens of officers forced their way into the mosque, shooting indiscriminately and beating members as the night wore on.

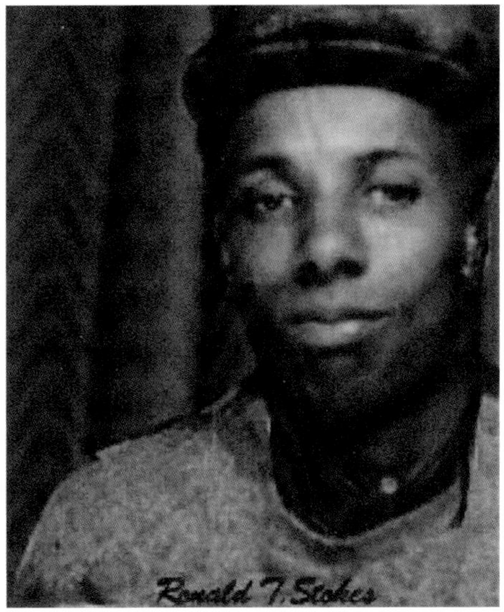

Fig. 21 Ronald Stokes, NOI member and secretary of Mosque No. 27.

By the time the violence ended, one person was dead, one was paralyzed, five sustained minor gunshot wounds, and many others were hospitalized for injuries due to physical battery. The police justified firing into the mosque as a response to shots they alleged were fired from inside; however, no weapons were found on the premises.[5] Fourteen NOI members were ultimately charged with felony assault and resisting arrest with force.

MALCOLM X ARRIVES

Malcolm X, the charismatic Muslim leader and national spokesman for the NOI who had helped establish Mosque 27 in 1957, flew to Los Angeles on May 4 and held a nearly thirty-minute press conference at the Statler Hotel in response to the violence. He defended the unarmed victims and vehemently condemned the police assault, likening the LAPD to "storm troopers" and the Gestapo of Nazi Germany.[6] An avid amateur photographer who knew the power of an image, Malcolm X arrived at the press conference armed with autopsy photos of Stokes's body showing a bullet hole in his chest and a hole in the back of his head, which Malcolm X said was caused by an officer's club. "This did not happen in Hitler's Nazi Germany," he told the assembled reporters. "This happened to innocent Black men in Los Angeles, California."[7]

The tragedy personally impacted Malcolm X because he and Stokes were childhood friends; Stokes had moved from Boston, where he and Malcolm X had met as teenagers, to Los Angeles to support the growth and stability of Mosque 27. Malcolm X believed his friend epitomized the devout and moral qualities of an upstanding citizen.[8] Ronald Stokes had been married to Delores for less than two years on the night of his death, leaving behind a three-month-old daughter, Saudia, for Delores to raise without him. At the funeral the day after the press conference, Malcolm X eulogized his friend before a crowd of two thousand. Photographer Harry Adams documented the funeral for the *California Eagle*, which printed three pictures below the headline "Muslims Bury Their First Martyr (plate 34)".[9]

THE NATION OF ISLAM

While Christian spiritual leaders organized large-scale events to gain support for civil rights activism and attract media attention, the Black Muslim community—led by the NOI—directly engaged with media and photography through the publication of their own newspaper, *Muhammad Speaks*. The NOI understood how the mainstream media shaped—and often distorted—the perception of the Black community in America. After the debut of *Muhammad Speaks* in 1960, the NOI was able to control its messaging and visual representation via regular nationally distributed issues. Malcolm X was often seen wearing a camera around his neck, which photographer Gordon Parks described as Malcolm's way of "collecting evidence."[10] He was pictured in a Los Angeles courtroom with one and later chatted with reporters while snapping "pictures of a murderer" during a recess (fig. 22).[11] Malcolm X's passion for photography, with which he engaged as both photographer and subject, allowed him to define himself and the causes for which he stood on his own terms while countering portrayals thrust upon him and the Black Muslim community by the traditionally white media.[12]

The NOI was founded thirty years prior to the first issue of *Muhammad Speaks*, in 1930 by Wallace D. Fard Muhammad in Detroit, to introduce African Americans to Islam and use the religion as a foundation for combating racial discrimination. Under the eventual leadership of Elijah Muhammad, Fard Muhammad's successor, the NOI began promoting Black nationalism and racial separatism as core doctrines within the organization's interpretation of Islam, which was specifically tailored to the experiences of Black people in the United States.[13] With the civil rights movement in full swing by the time the NOI founded its twenty-seventh mosque, the group became a significant player in the struggle for Black freedom in Los Angeles. Malcolm X had long desired to set up a mosque on the West Coast. The post–World War II demographic shift in Los Angeles resulted in a growing and economically stable Black population, further justifying his efforts to establish a mosque in the city.[14]

Before the tragedy in April 1962, Mosque 27 had drawn national attention for another high-profile confrontation with the LAPD. Certainly, the LAPD found the NOI's anti–white supremacy posture and the paramilitary Fruit of Islam (FOI) security force alarming. The FOI was known for its military-style drills and formations at public events, providing security at NOI gatherings, and protecting NOI leaders and members. The organization was created to enforce moral codes within its own community while serving as the protective arm of the movement.[15]

Tensions escalated into violence on September 2, 1961, when mosque members clashed with police while selling *Muhammad Speaks* newspapers outside a Safeway store. Even though the members were obeying all local ordinances, they were accosted by police officers. Five NOI members were

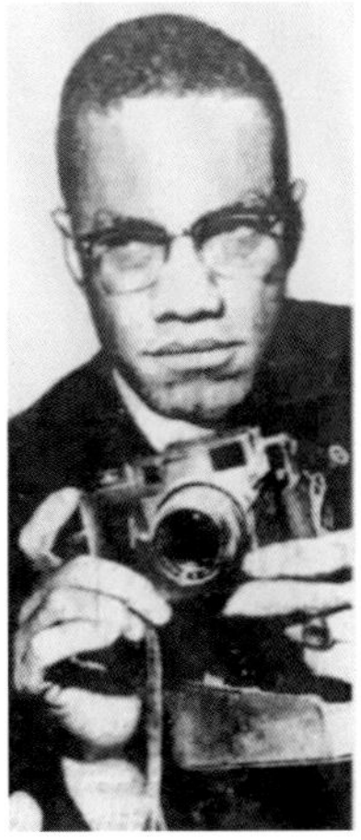

Fig. 22 Malcolm X holds a camera in the spectator section of a Los Angeles courtroom at the 1963 trial of NOI members. *Los Angeles Times*, 1963.

arrested, along with one bystander, and charged with assault and battery. But an all-white jury acquitted them based on affidavits from the store's owner and manager.[16]

FIGHTING BACK

After the tragedy at Mosque 27, Malcolm X pushed for the NOI to aggressively confront the LAPD over the murder of Stokes and their repeated instances of brutality. However, Muhammad insisted on a more tempered response. He issued directives to Malcolm X and Mosque 27 members urging them to refrain from engaging in open criticism and violence. Disappointed but following Muhammad's instructions, Malcolm X told the Los Angeles congregants: "The message from Elijah Muhammad is not to begin a war with the devil. Instead, we are going to sell newspapers."[17] The NOI printed news and images their followers needed to see, and by selling newspapers on busy sidewalks nationwide, they could also potentially engage thousands of others daily. The eye-catching headlines and dramatic imagery gained attention and conveyed a perspective not visible elsewhere (plate 35).

While some members acquiesced to Muhammad's directive and sold newspapers featuring Stokes on the cover, others refused. Hakim Jamal, a cousin of Malcolm X by marriage who also hailed from Boston, formed bands with other NOI members and attacked white people in various spaces across Los Angeles.[18] Meanwhile, Malcolm X worked with Black leaders outside the Muslim community to organize a unified response to the police attack on the mosque. Mainstream civil rights organizations, including the NAACP, SCLC, Urban League, and CORE, met with the NOI leader. National leaders such as James Farmer of CORE and Roy Wilkins of the NAACP openly condemned the LAPD's attack and indicated they would stand with human rights organizations against police brutality.[19] The cooperation of such a vast coalition was significant, as NOI tactics for fighting racism differed from those of the more traditional civil rights organizations. Malcolm X explained as much at his press conference after the tragedy. "The NAACP is against any type of brutality," he said. The organization "is for integration. We're for separation. We agree on the objective, but we disagree on the method. What both of us want is human dignity for the Black people in this country."[20]

Several local clergy, elected officials, and Black professionals began to organize support for the NOI and strategize on how to effectively address the issue of police abuse, going so far as to have a sit-down meeting with Los Angeles Mayor Sam Yorty. Rev. J. Raymond Henderson, Rev. Maurice Dawkins, and California Assemblyman Mervyn Dymally held a mass meeting at Second Baptist Church that drew a crowd of three thousand on May 13, 1962. Loren Miller of the NAACP provided legal assistance for the fourteen accused NOI members, while California state CORE leader Celes King III provided $160,000 in bail.[21] Malcolm X attended the trial of the Muslim men charged in the incident, brandishing enlarged photos he considered evidence of police violence (plate 36). Although some African American clergy distanced themselves from the religion advocated by the NOI, the collective efforts of the community highlighted the interconnectedness and solidarity among African Americans on the issue of police brutality.

DIFFERING IDEOLOGIES

While there was relative unity within the Black community on the topic of policing, the ideological rift between Malcolm X and Muhammad was widening. Malcolm X believed in directly confronting injustice and standing up for Black people's right to self-defense, while Muhammad sought to maintain the NOI's organizational stability and avoid direct clashes with authorities. Shortly after the assassination of President John F. Kennedy on November 22, 1963, Malcolm X made an inflammatory statement: "President Kennedy never foresaw that the chickens would come home to roost soon. Being an old farm boy myself, chickens coming home to roost never did make me sad; they always made me glad."[22] His comment, which he issued against Muhammad's orders, only deepened the divide between the two men. Malcolm X's statement on the president's death ultimately led to his suspension and later expulsion from the NOI. His disillusionment with Muhammad and the NOI spurred his founding of Muslim Mosque, Inc., as a spiritual base for himself and former NOI members and for Muslims oriented toward traditional Islam. He created the Organization of Afro-American Unity as a secular political vehicle to unite Black Americans across religious lines, building a broader movement for Black self-determination that transcended the NOI's restrictive requirements. He continued to participate in the fight for Black liberty while promoting Islam and human rights and forging relationships with centrist Black political leaders and organizations.

FREEDOM SUNDAY

Following the attack on Mosque 27, the WCLC and Martin Luther King Jr. joined forces with government and local officials, including Gov. Pat Brown, to organize a day of prayer in Los Angeles scheduled for June 17, 1962. The day was dubbed Freedom Sunday, and King visited the city for three days before delivering the headlining presentation at Ward AME Church and other speeches at Bovard Auditorium and Zion Hill Baptist Church. In anticipation of the events, Brown, L.A. County Supervisor Kenneth Hahn, and Yorty hailed King as "a crusader of the cause of the complete freedom for the darker peoples of the world."[23] In addition, Hahn presented the board of supervisors' "Freedom Sunday" proclamation to Dawkins and fellow WCLC ministers L. Sylvester Odom, G. Mansfield Collins, and John Doggett for "their leadership and for their positive answer to a tense racial situation."[24]

King's speech at Zion Hill, titled "The Dilemma and the Challenge Facing the Negro Today," pushed his vision for racial equality using the slogan "Every Church Member a Registered Voter" to promote the idea that effective use of the ballot could help win freedom. King urged Angelenos to exercise their right to vote and emphasized that there were "powers greater than violence." [25] Although he did not mention the LAPD raid of Mosque 27 directly, he consistently spoke about police brutality and at one point stated: "They tell me you have a problem of police brutality here in Los Angeles. One of the ways this problem will be rectified and dealt with is to go out with a determined effort to get the ballots so that you can say to the political leaders of this city, 'We are determined that this particular chief of police or this particular person will have to go because they have not committed themselves to democracy.'"[26]

In September 1962, the California Advisory Committee to the US Commission on Civil Rights heard testimony about police misconduct in Los Angeles. Wendell Green, representing the Citizens Committee Against Police Brutality, and Morgan Moten, legislative chair of the NAACP, argued that "there is growing hostility in communities against the present police administration" and that "we don't encourage persons to report police brutality to the Bureau of Internal Affairs because such reports are often used as evidence against them," effectively contending that the low complaint numbers masked widespread police misconduct rather than proving departmental fairness. In response, John P. Kennedy, president of the Board of Police Commissioners, said that "most of the minority groups have good relations with officers." LAPD Police

Chief William Parker backed this statement with statistics showing that "only one civil rights complaint out of 187,745 enforcement contacts had been filed against the department since January 1, 1960." Despite the testimony, the hearings did not yield immediate significant police reform.[27]

BIRMINGHAM AND THE RALLY FOR FREEDOM AT WRIGLEY FIELD

In April 1963, King, Rev. Ralph Abernathy, and other protesters were arrested and jailed in Birmingham, Alabama, for violating a state court injunction against public demonstrations. While in solitary confinement, King wrote his renowned "Letter from Birmingham Jail," in which he argued that civil disobedience was necessary to fight unjust laws and that "freedom is never voluntarily given by the oppressor; it must be demanded by the oppressed."[28] The letter had such an impact on Gilbert Lindsay, Los Angeles's first African American city council member, that he sponsored a resolution on April 19, 1963, condemning King's arrest and the actions of Birmingham officials in "allowing dogs to be used to prevent Negroes from using their rights under the Constitution of the United States."[29] Council members Rosalind Wyman and Tom Bradley seconded the resolution. The council also sent a letter to the governor of Alabama and the mayor of Birmingham denouncing "the fact that Dr. Martin Luther King was arrested and placed in jail for the sole reason of attempting to secure these rights by peaceful means for all citizens of the United States of America."[30] Lindsay's resolution demonstrated King's importance in Los Angeles and the growing voices of local African American politicians.

Shocking pictures and television footage of Birmingham police dogs lunging at nonviolent Black Southern protesters and of peaceful protesters being blasted by fire hoses reached millions of viewers on the nightly news and ignited a fresh wave of national condemnation and civil action. Angelenos were quick to make connections between L.A. and Birmingham and demonstrated in support of Southern protesters, while also calling attention to their own experiences of police brutality (plate 37). One Los Angeles protester was photographed holding a sign juxtaposing images of the Mosque 27 shooting and police violence in Alabama (fig. 23). This was an important message, as racial violence in the South was typically seen as unique to that region, and suggestions that Los Angeles might suffer similar injustices were usually dismissed.

On May 26, 1963, a month after his release from the Birmingham jail, King addressed an estimated crowd of forty thousand at Wrigley Field in Los Angeles at the Freedom Rally. He updated supporters on the ongoing campaign to desegregate Birmingham. The rally was also an opportunity to raise funds, which was particularly crucial because the SCLC's emphasis on civil disobedience meant that they were always in need of thousands of dollars for bail charges. According to the *Los Angeles Times*, demonstrations in Birmingham alone cost $300,000 for bail and $6,500 weekly in other expenses.[31]

Attendees crowded into the stands and onto the field of a minor-league baseball stadium meant for a much smaller crowd (plates 38, 39). While the rally emphasized the Birmingham campaign, King and other speakers called for equality throughout the nation, including in Los Angeles. "Birmingham or Los Angeles, the cry is always the same," King said. "We want to be free."[32] Upon arriving in the city on May 25, King's chief of staff, Rev. Wyatt T. Walker, told the *Times* that "Los Angeles has a racial problem potentially as dangerous as the South's.... The major threat here and in other large cities is the tendency to 'ghettoize' Negroes as well as a lack of housing and the scarcity of employment opportunities."[33] The *Times*'s rally coverage appeared on page two, highlighting strong quotes, fundraising success, and notable references to problems in Los Angeles. Surprisingly, though, picture editors ran an image of someone who tried to grab the microphone instead of one of King or of high-profile supporters.[34] By contrast, the *Los Angeles Sentinel* included seven front-page pictures of the event, along with at least five more inside.[35]

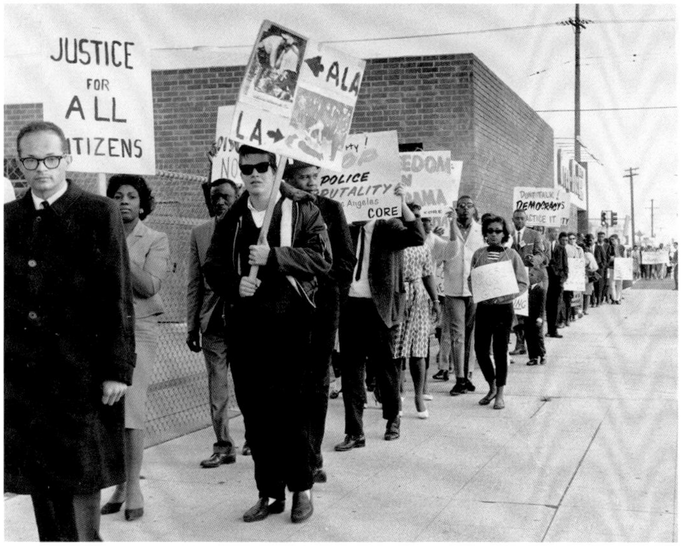

Fig. 23 CHARLES BRITTIN, 1963.
Demonstrators protest against police brutality in Los Angeles and in support of the Birmingham protesters arrested in April 1963.

HOLLYWOOD SPEAKS OUT

The Freedom Rally was a star-studded affair; celebrities present included Sammy Davis Jr. and comedian Dick Gregory, both of whom had attended the 1961 rally, and first-time attendees Paul Newman, Dorothy Dandridge, Rita Moreno, and Tony Franciosa (plates 40, 41). Gregory held the stage longer than any speaker except King, combining his trademark wit with serious political commentary. He joked that the crowd was "looking at a convict" and recalled being chased by white supremacists in Clarksdale, Mississippi. He also discussed broader themes of Black identity and progress.[36] In a personal message, Gregory reminded the crowd that behind the glitz and glamour of Hollywood, Black celebrities were not immune to racial discrimination. Dandridge commented on the rally's significance in Hollywood:

> It really wasn't very long ago that it was considered dangerous for the people in show business to endorse anything more controversial than toothpaste. I don't know how dangerous it is today, but I do know that more and more of us are glad for the opportunity to stand up and be counted. We as actors and actresses should take part in the most important drama that this country has seen.[37]

Dandridge, the first Black woman nominated for an Academy Award for Best Actress, spoke from experience. For years in the 1950s, she and other top Black entertainers such as Lena Horne, Ella Fitzgerald, Count Basie, Nat "King" Cole, and Eartha Kitt could not stay in the very hotels where they performed. In 1952, Dandridge became the first Black performer to stay at the luxury Chase Hotel in St. Louis, Missouri, at her insistence. But she was forbidden to use the hotel's guest elevators and instead was consigned to the service elevator.[38] Her comments in the presence of some of Hollywood's top-rated entertainers signaled a larger shift in Hollywood culture that would later support boycotts, fundraisers, and advocacy campaigns targeting the entertainment industry.

During the rally, World War II veteran, dentist, and local NAACP president Christopher Taylor echoed King's call to fight for civil rights in Los Angeles.[39] Before the rally ended, King called for Angelenos—Hollywood entertainers included—to participate in the upcoming March on Washington for Jobs and Freedom, scheduled for August of that year. After the rally, a CORE-sponsored group marched from the stadium to City Hall, carrying signs reading "L.A. IS Alabama."[40]

The Freedom Rally became the largest civil rights rally to date and the one with the most celebrities in attendance. A total of $75,000 was raised, a considerable amount for that period. Davis alone donated $20,000, and the two-hundred-fifty-person exclusive after-party at actor Burt Lancaster's mansion doubled that amount. Lancaster and friends solicited checks from stars such as Lloyd Bridges, Marlon

Brando, and Paul Newman. Brando, one of the world's highest-paid actors at the time, pledged a day's pay to the SCLC and to visit the South. The party ended with participants joining hands and singing "We Shall Overcome," the movement's anthem (plate 42).[41] Hollywood celebrities drew substantial media attention to the Freedom Rally that might not otherwise have been covered by the mainstream press, expanding the reach of King's message beyond those physically present. Their participation helped legitimize the civil rights movement among white, moderate Americans who may have been hesitant to support what was sometimes portrayed as a radical cause.

THE UNITED CIVIL RIGHTS COMMITTEE

The Freedom Rally's success in fostering unity led to the formation of the Los Angeles–based United Civil Rights Committee (UCRC) in 1963. Comprising seventy-six organizations, including the NAACP and the ACLU, the committee aimed to consolidate the efforts of the Los Angeles civil rights community by focusing on specific policy initiatives. Certainly, amid the trial resulting from the Mosque 27 shooting, frustrations in the Black community were high; segregation and concerns over police brutality weighed heavily on the UCRC's agenda.

Taylor of the NAACP chaired the newly formed UCRC, while Rev. Hamel Hartford (H. H.) Brookins was one of the committee's key leaders (fig. 24). Brookins, a Southerner, began his civil rights career as the first Black president of an interracial ministerial council in Wichita, Kansas, that had been organized to support the desegregation initiative resulting from *Brown v. Board of Education*. In 1960, Brookins moved to Los Angeles and became the pastor of First AME Church. In the aftermath of the shooting at Mosque 27, he was one of the more outspoken civil rights leaders in favor of putting distance between the movement and the NOI. Thanks to the size of his congregation—and his close relationship with Tom Bradley, the newly elected Black councilmember who would go on to become Los Angeles's first Black mayor—Brookins became one of the city's most prominent power brokers and chair of the UCRC in its second year.[42]

Rev. Maurice Dawkins, who was influential within the UCRC, voiced the growing frustration with de facto segregation throughout the city. He warned that continued inaction would spark "Birmingham-style" demonstrations in Los Angeles and that the African American populace was not asking for only minor adjustments.[43] Thomas G. Neusom, a former local NAACP president and a member of the UCRC, echoed Dawkins's concerns and cautioned officials about potential unrest, emphasizing the need for proactive measures to address racial tensions.[44] In response, the Los Angeles County Board of Supervisors pushed for an emergency meeting with industry leaders involved in housing, policing, and education.

"TO MEN OF GOOD WILL"

The emergency UCRC meeting was held at the Statler Hotel on June 6, 1963. Christopher Taylor and local civil rights leader Marnesba Tackett were featured speakers alongside journalist Wendell Green—an *Eagle* and *Sentinel* writer—and businessman Norman O. Houston. Taylor outlined proposals for a citizens' review board of the LAPD, a revision of school district boundaries to achieve integration, and a nondiscrimination clause in all government contracting. The attendees were also encouraged to support the Rumford Fair Housing Act, a bill put forward in 1959 that would eliminate housing discrimination based on race, color, religion, national origin, sex, and familial status in the state of California. Thanks in part to the support garnered at the June meeting, the California legislature would pass the Rumford Fair Housing Act on September 20, 1963. The community's concerns were discussed in different corners of the room by the African American leaders: Houston led a group concerned with jobs, Neusom discussed police relations, Green concentrated on housing, and Tackett focused on education. The group presented a proposal under the title "To Men of Good Will," a statement of the major grievances and immediate demands of the Black community. The proposal began by citing King's influence:[45] "Rev. Martin Luther King has wisely told us: 'You can help us in Birmingham by getting rid of segregation and discrimination in Los Angeles.' Thus, both to help our brothers in Birmingham and to achieve our own birthright in Los Angeles, we now press forward our task."[46] The proposal addressed immediate but attainable policy goals in the four areas of concern, including enacting fair housing legislation at the state and local levels, in part addressed by the Rumford Act; ending racial segregation in schools with a busing plan, redrawing school district lines, and diversifying staff; changing hiring and promotion practices so that Black teachers and students could work and study at predominantly white and less crowded schools; broadening school curriculums to include African American history and culture; creating a "representative, independent, citizens board" to allow victims of police brutality to seek redress; revising recruitment, training, and promotion practices within the police and sheriff's departments; founding a Fair Employment Practices Committee; and adding nondiscrimination clauses to city and state contracts. After presenting the proposal to the city council and board of supervisors, the UCRC gave officials a ten-day grace period to respond before engaging in a Birmingham-style campaign in Los Angeles.[47]

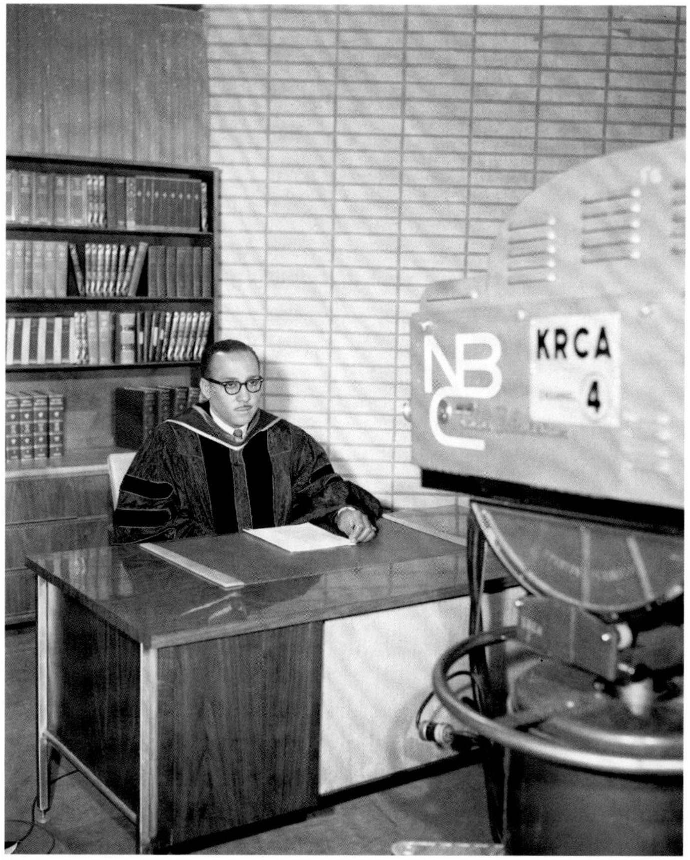

Fig. 24 CHARLES WILLIAMS, 1962. Rev. H. H. Brookins in front of the camera for an interview with NBC.

"BIRMINGHAM-STYLE" CAMPAIGN

The proposals led to introductory discussions and the beginning of "the first real communication between a civil rights group and the LA Police Department,"[48] according to Neusom, but most did not achieve the desired results. For example, the Ad Hoc Committee for Equal Education, founded in 1962, rejected most of the NAACP's and UCRC's proposals and placed responsibility for whatever problems did exist outside its purview.[49] Also, a proposed voluntary student transfer plan that could have addressed de facto segregation was defeated. In response to the board of education's refusal to act, the UCRC engaged in militant protests, confronting the board, district, and city government with a mass march on June 24, 1963 (plate 43). The rally began at First AME Church. The UCRC and its supporters marched to the offices of the board of education, while photographers and TV crews stationed themselves along the route. The LAPD also filmed the event for surveillance purposes (plates 44, 45).

An estimated one thousand Angelenos participated in the direct-action campaign against the board of education throughout the year, which included silent

CHARLES WILLIAMS

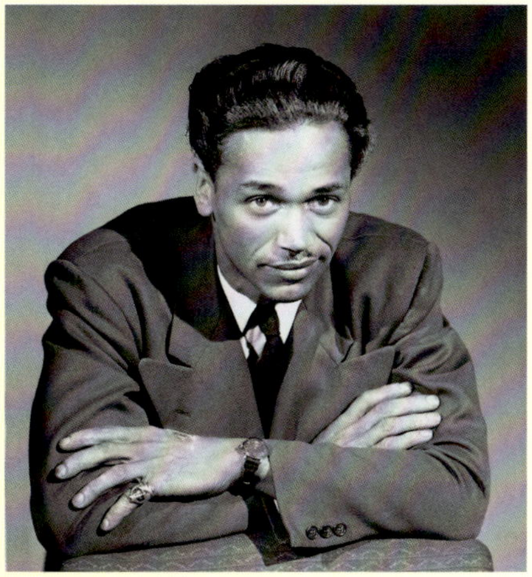

Charles Williams (1908–1986) was an amateur photographer in the mid-1930s when he began selling pictures to leading newspapers (fig. 25). He opened a studio in Los Angeles but moved to Chicago during World War II to prevent his Japanese wife and their young child from being sent to internment camps on the West Coast. When the family returned to L.A., Williams worked at nightclubs taking pictures of patrons and famous entertainers. He later cofounded the California School of Photography and Graphic Design in 1947 to help train young photographers. He also opened the Charm School in 1950, which offered courses to aspiring Black models barred from other training programs. Williams's freelance photography appeared in several local and national Black publications, including the *California Eagle*, the *Los Angles Sentinel*, and the *Pittsburgh Courier*. Williams became L.A. City Council member Gordon Hahn's official photographer in the late 1950s and was appointed his field deputy in 1962.

Fig. 25 Charles Williams, 1946.

boardroom demonstrations and a six-hundred-person march with national leaders (plate 46).[50] In September 1963, in concert with CORE, the UCRC spearheaded sit-ins and hunger strikes for several days at the board of education building (plate 47). Hundreds of youths conducted study-ins by sitting in the corridor during board meetings. In November, CORE held a sing-in that broke up a meeting.[51] Nevertheless, along with its lack of action on education, the local government gave a similar response to demands on the issue of police brutality; the proposals were ignored, and nothing appeared to change.

An all-white jury failed to indict the white police officers involved in the attack on Mosque 27, ignoring the witnesses who reported seeing officers beating people with batons while yelling racial slurs. On the other side, on June 14, 1963, eleven of the fourteen NOI members were found guilty of assault and resisting arrest. To make matters worse, the police shooting was deemed justified as "self-defense."[52] None of the officers faced severe discipline or other consequences for their actions.

Tensions remained high in Los Angeles throughout 1963. On June 12, civil rights leader Medgar Evers, the first NAACP field officer in Mississippi, was murdered by Byron De La Beckwith, a member of the White Citizens Council. The following Sunday, fifteen hundred Angelenos marched in Evers's honor. The mile-long march through a Black neighborhood ended at Wrigley Field, where about a thousand people attended a memorial service.[53]

Housing discrimination and related violence persisted in the growing metropolitan area (plate 48), and the UCRC initiated a new campaign against it in conjunction with CORE. In housing developments by Don C. Wilson Builders in several L.A. suburbs, discrimination against African Americans was blatant and rampant. A photo by Charles Williams of a new Wilson subdivision shows CORE marchers framed by white picket fences and a sidewalk bicyclist (plate 49).

CHARLES BRITTIN

Charles Brittin (1928–2001) first picked up a camera while studying film and photography at UCLA. Brittin's involvement with writers, artists, and other creatives who made up an alternative cultural scene in Venice, California, fueled his art and his photography. In 1962, he and his wife couldn't think of what to give each other for Christmas, so they became members of all the organizations whose work they admired. Both quickly became involved with CORE, and Brittin took photographs at CORE-sponsored demonstrations. He supplied news outlets like the *Los Angeles Sentinel* and the *Los Angeles Free Press* with images to encourage press coverage. The visuals helped shape and amplify CORE's message of racial justice and equality. His photographs covered Non-Violent Action Committee protests, the Black Panther Party, and mass protests against the Vietnam War. His active participation resulted in intimate pictures that revealed the violence that he and other activists frequently faced.

By the end of an eighteen-month campaign of protests and sit-ins, police had arrested two hundred fifty activists, many of whom had suffered beatings. CORE and other groups routinely attracted the ire of the American Nazi Party, the most visible white supremacist counterprotesters (plate 50). The extended protests garnered significant news coverage in the *Times*, reflecting the mainstream media's tendency to sensationalize conflict and violence. Pictures also emphasized heavy police presence and counterdemonstrations. By contrast, Black newspapers published arrest photos to call out police aggression or inspire sympathy. More often, images centered on organizers and activists. Charles Brittin, a well-known activist photographer who documented CORE protests in Los Angeles during much of the 1960s, frequently provided pictures to the *Sentinel*, and CORE circulated Brittin's photographs to sympathetic organizations and press outlets to help shape the visual story in the media.[54]

Notably, sensational pictures from Los Angeles did not translate into national attention. Images from the South dominated the national media, and the concerns of Black Americans living in more progressive regions in the north and west were delegitimatized and remained invisible to the rest of the country.

THE MARCH ON WASHINGTON FOR JOBS AND FREEDOM

Although embattled locally, civil rights activists maintained their commitment to support civil rights initiatives nationwide. In particular, the WCLC mobilized Angelenos to participate in the March on Washington, held on August 28, 1963, in Washington, DC. Rev. Arthur Atlas Peters, now president of the WCLC Los Angeles chapter, wrote a letter to ministers of all denominations stating: "We are so close to getting the basic rights that we must understand that this struggle involves everyone, no matter what their position in life may be. The ministers particularly are involved because our moral and spiritual duty is to lead by example."[55] Over one thousand Southern Californians joined the March on Washington, with some Angelenos flying in chartered planes alongside celebrities (see fig. 2). While in Washington, Harry Belafonte read a statement signed by fifteen hundred actors, demonstrating Hollywood's commitment to equal rights for all.[56]

The March on Washington remains a high point in the civil rights movement. Two hundred fifty-thousand people attended, and King delivered his "I Have a Dream" speech, which became one of his most famous and revered addresses.[57] The gathering was a pivotal moment that helped provide the pressure and support necessary for Congress and President Lyndon B. Johnson to eventually pass the Civil Rights Act of 1964. Among other freedoms, the act prohibited discrimination in public accommodations, banned employment discrimination, and created the Equal Employment Opportunity Commission to enforce federal antidiscrimination laws.

The years 1962 and 1963 were very active for the movement in Los Angeles. The Mosque 27 shooting and the ensuing coverage put a spotlight on the city, its leaders, and its activists. National civil rights figures such as King and Malcolm X used this attention to push their agendas forward and ultimately advance the cause for civil liberty and human rights. Local leaders like Houston, Tackett, Taylor, and Neusom organized activists across the city, while Hollywood stars voiced their support of the movement. In many ways, 1963 was a landmark year for the movement, with both the Los Angeles Freedom Rally and the March on Washington occurring within months of each other. However, despite the progress, simmering tensions still brewed in Los Angeles and would continue to do so over the following years.

3

Plates

The intensity and fervor of the Black freedom struggle nationwide rose steadily as the 1960s progressed. Photographers covered marches and demonstrations in search of dramatic, newsworthy moments, which often included violent reactions. Others found themselves in tense situations, like *Los Angeles Herald Examiner* photographer Howard Ballew, who arrived outside Muhammad's Mosque 27 in April 1962 shortly after LAPD officers shot and killed Nation of Islam member Ronald Stokes.

Activists strategically planned impactful moments to generate coverage and build support for the nonviolent movement. A staggering number of protests were organized throughout Los Angeles in 1962 and 1963, from city hall and board of education offices to housing developments and grocery stores. CORE photographer Charles Brittin stated that "a key reason for staging these demonstrations was to get press coverage" to raise awareness around the issues.[58] Activists witnessed, too, how pictures helped with fundraising and pressured politicians into action. Few leaders were more adept at leveraging imagery than NOI minister Malcolm X, an amateur photographer himself. He wielded newspaper front pages and enlarged pictures of victims of violence in highly publicized settings to reinforce the narrative that Black Americans, not the police, were the ones under attack. *Life* magazine photographer Gordon Parks captured Malcolm X holding up a picture of Stokes in L.A. during the trial of fourteen Muslim men who were arrested amid the violence that led to Stokes's death. In Birmingham, Alabama, Martin Luther King Jr. and protest leaders hoped TV coverage and photography—of such images as police dogs lunging at peaceful protesters—might force the public and city leaders to take notice and enact change.

In Los Angeles, protests continued against school segregation, police abuse, and employment discrimination, but King's Freedom Rally at Wrigley Field in May 1963 attracted the most media coverage. The massive rally drew the attention of dozens of newspapers, and photographers angled for the right shot over one another's shoulders. Julian Wasser captured King's energetic gestures to the crowd; others caught the glamour of movie stars who attended the event and the exclusive fundraiser that followed. The huge turnout and multiracial celebrity support generated unprecedented media interest.

Scattered among the archives of L.A. civil rights–era photography are significant reminders of the resistance that activists encountered at every step: ministers being told that police abuse was a nonissue, and protesters marching through city streets while being surveilled and filmed by law enforcement. Less subtly, a white neighbor's shotgun blast through a Black family's window was documented by Charles Williams, and in another contested neighborhood, the American Nazi Party carried signs claiming "Hitler Was Right" and banners with swastikas urging "White Men Unite!" Instances of white resistance were not isolated occurrences. The delays and foot-dragging among city leaders and school boards, and the courtroom decisions and legal mechanisms that underpinned systemic racism, could not be caught on camera. Decades of agitation and demonstrations made it clear that the city's response to racial injustice was slow and insufficient. The inaction and disregard from those in power generated a response that would shake the city to its core.

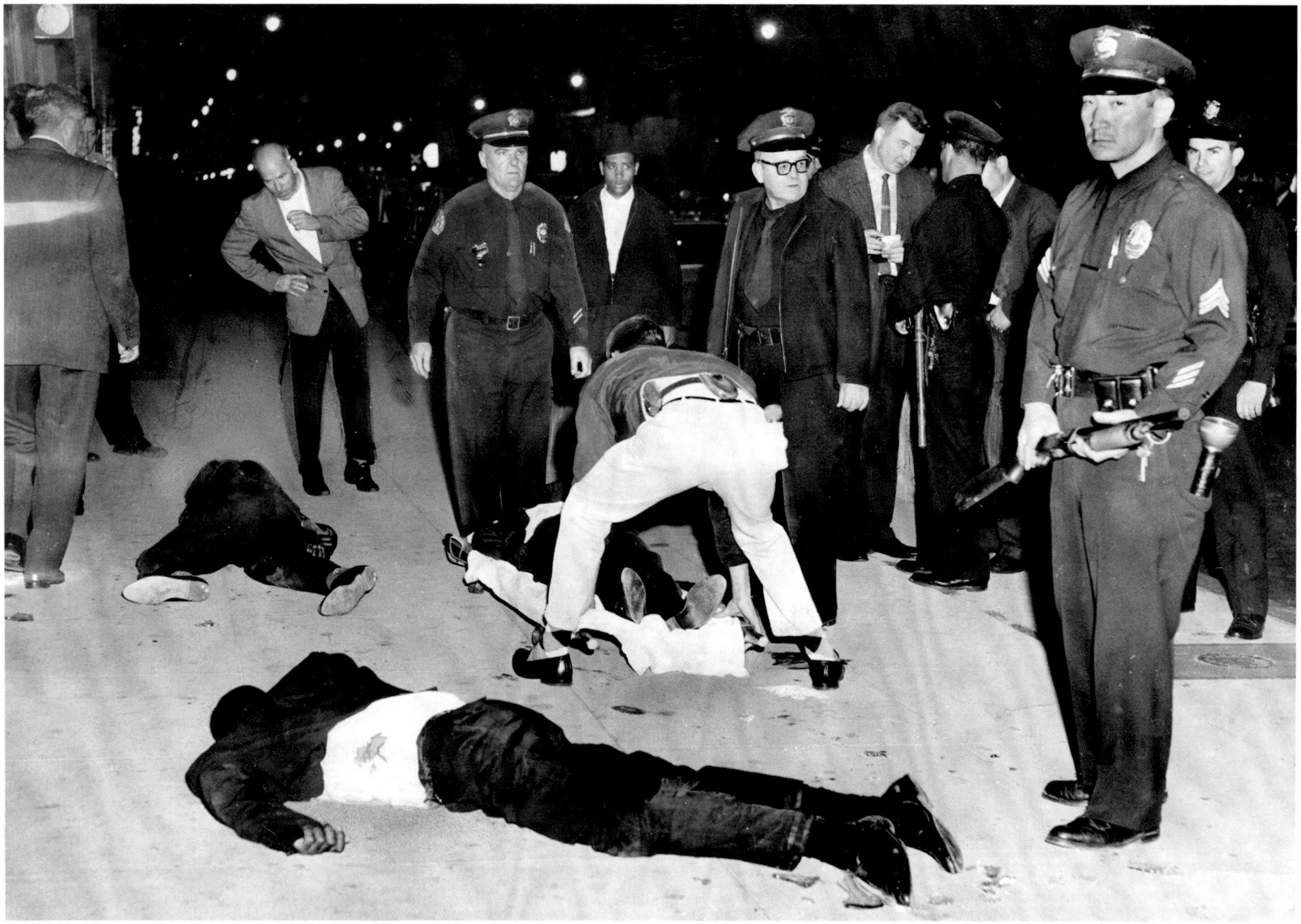

Plate 33 HOWARD BALLEW, 1962

LAPD Sgt. Stanley Uno (*far right*) looks toward news photographer Howard Ballew following the shooting of Ronald Stokes and others outside Mosque no. 27. The two handcuffed men on the ground were severely injured. Stokes, in the foreground, was killed. Ballew's picture ran on the front page of the *Los Angeles Herald Examiner*'s Saturday Pictorial and on the cover of the Nation of Islam's newspaper, *Muhammad Speaks.* NOI leader Malcolm X repurposed the powerful photograph to support the organization's narrative of the altercation.

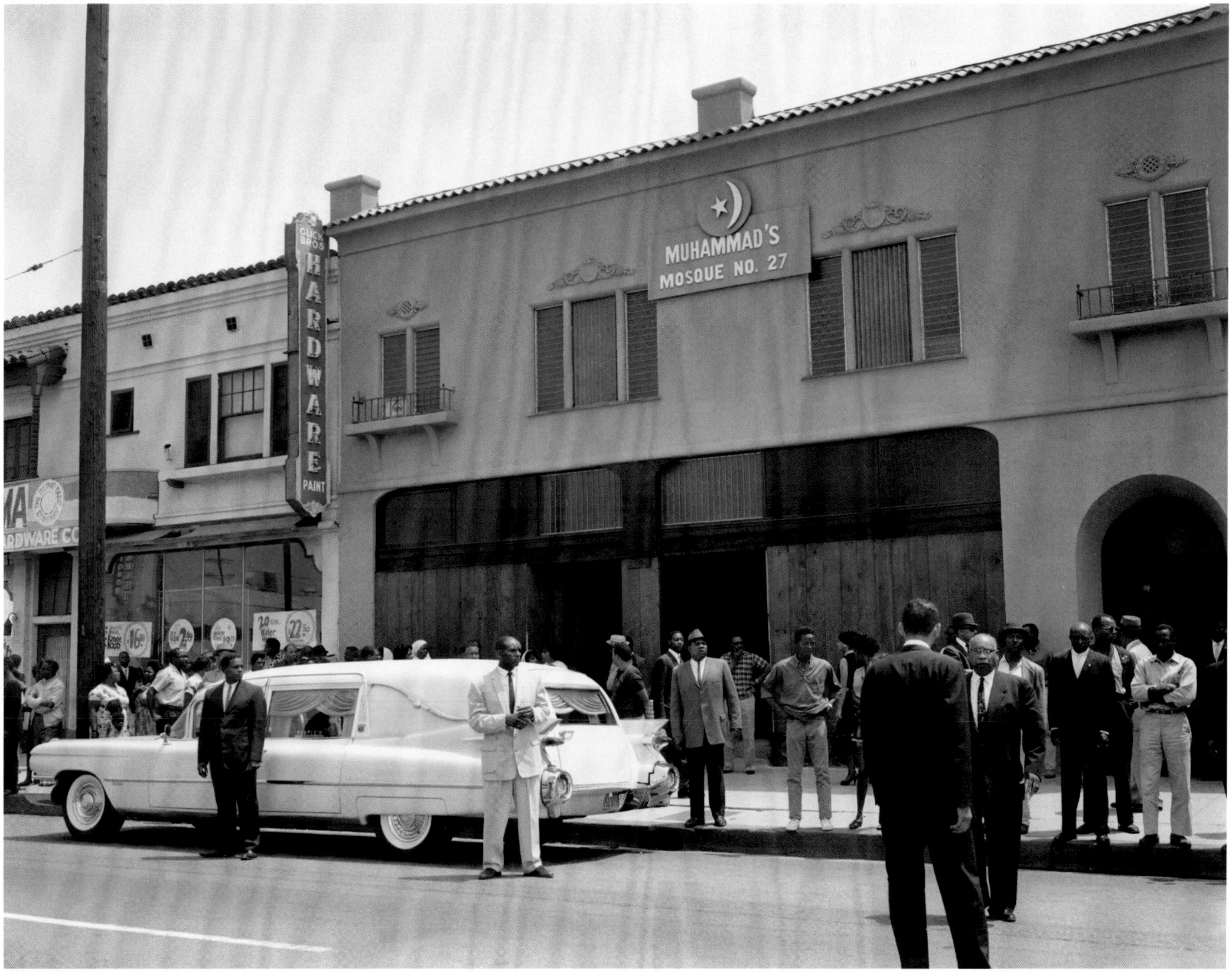

Plate 34 HARRY ADAMS, 1962

Mosque No. 27 members and community residents wait near a white hearse outside the mosque, where the funeral service for Ronald Stokes took place. Harry Adams documented the somber occasion for the *California Eagle.*

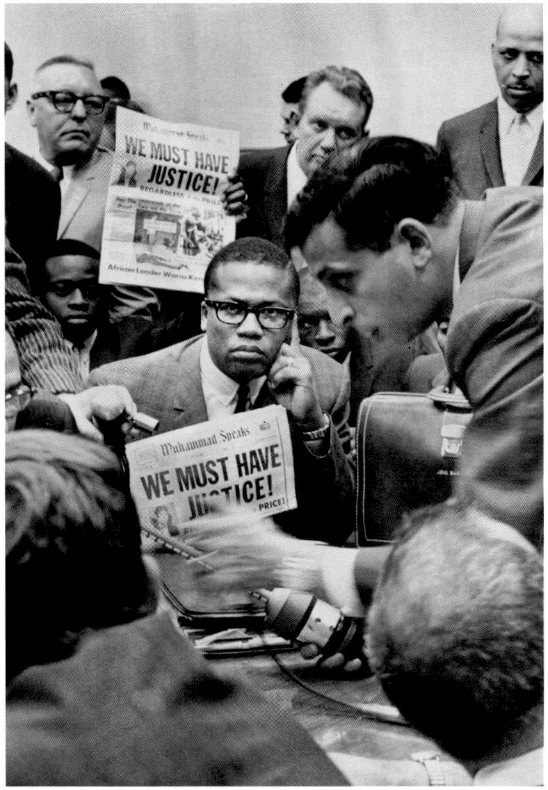

Plate 35 ROBERT FLORA, 1963

John Henry Morris (*center*), minister of Mosque no. 27, speaks to the press amid supporters holding up copies of *Muhammad Speaks* after the conclusion of the trial of fourteen Nation of Islam members in June 1963, in which eleven were found guilty. The headline "We Must Have Justice!" provides a counternarrative to the courtroom injustice.

Plate 36 GORDON PARKS, 1963

Malcolm X looks at the camera outside the courtroom during the trial of fourteen NOI members. Gordon Parks made this photograph, which appeared in a May 31, 1963, *Life* magazine essay with the caption "In Anger: With picture of Muslim killed by Los Angeles cop, Malcolm X tells story to foreign newsmen." The image that Malcolm X repurposed here was originally published on the front page of the *California Eagle.*

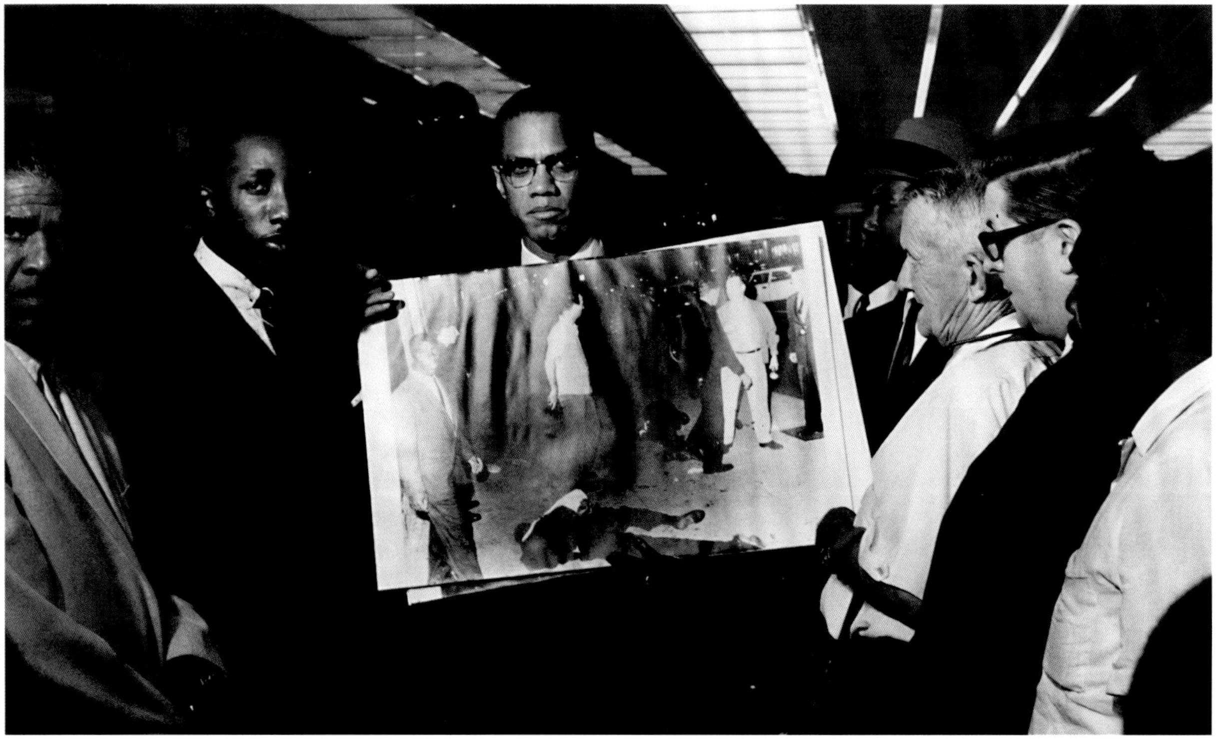

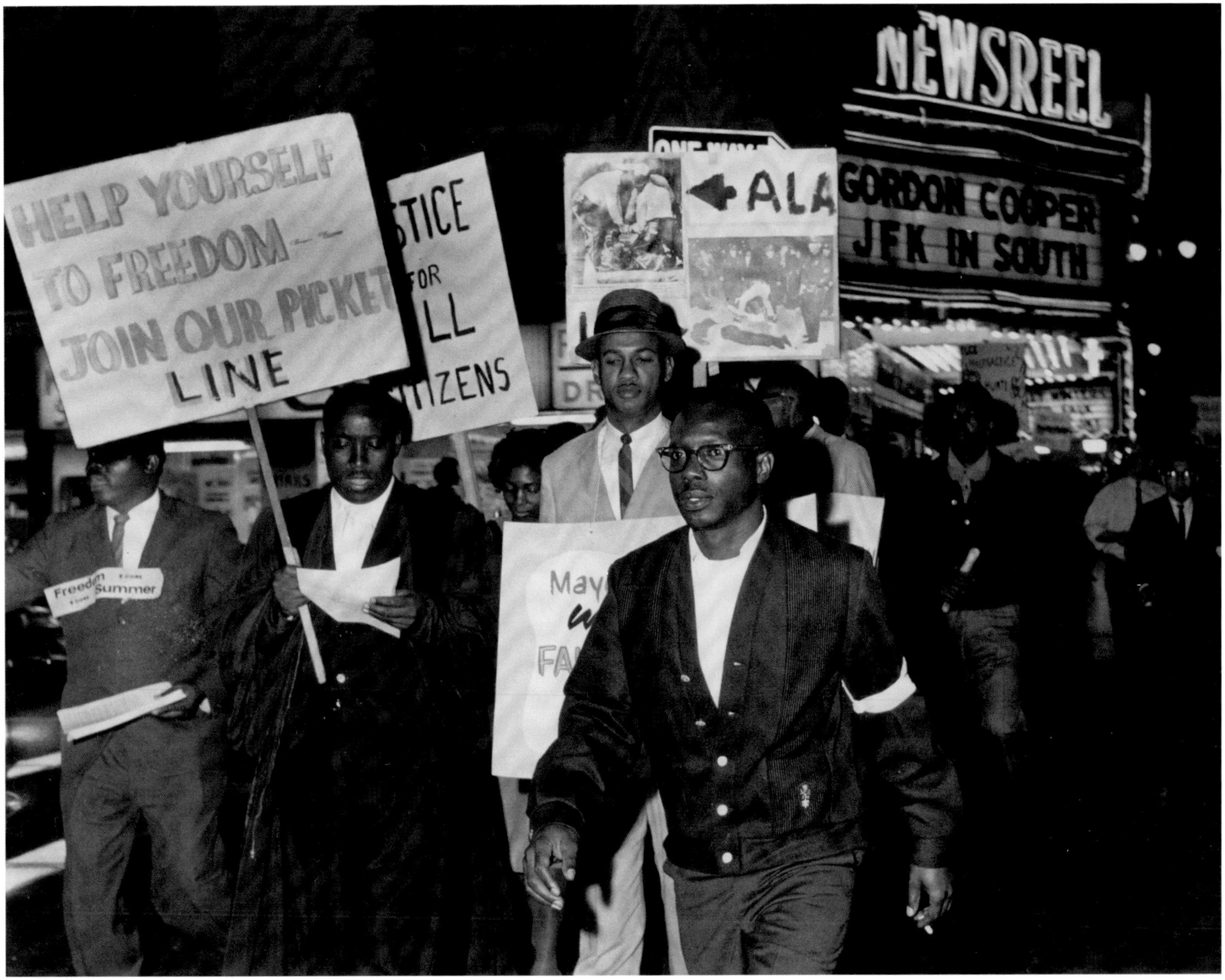

Plate 37 CHARLES BRITTIN, 1963
Rev. Maurice Dawkins (*center left*) leads a nighttime march against racist violence, wearing his religious robes to project the moral authority of the church. Behind him, a marcher's placard juxtaposes a photo of the murder of Ronald Stokes outside Mosque 27 with an image of a Birmingham police officer pressing his knee on a woman's neck. The marchers used photographic evidence to share their message with onlookers and the camera that civil rights action is needed as much in Los Angeles as in Alabama.

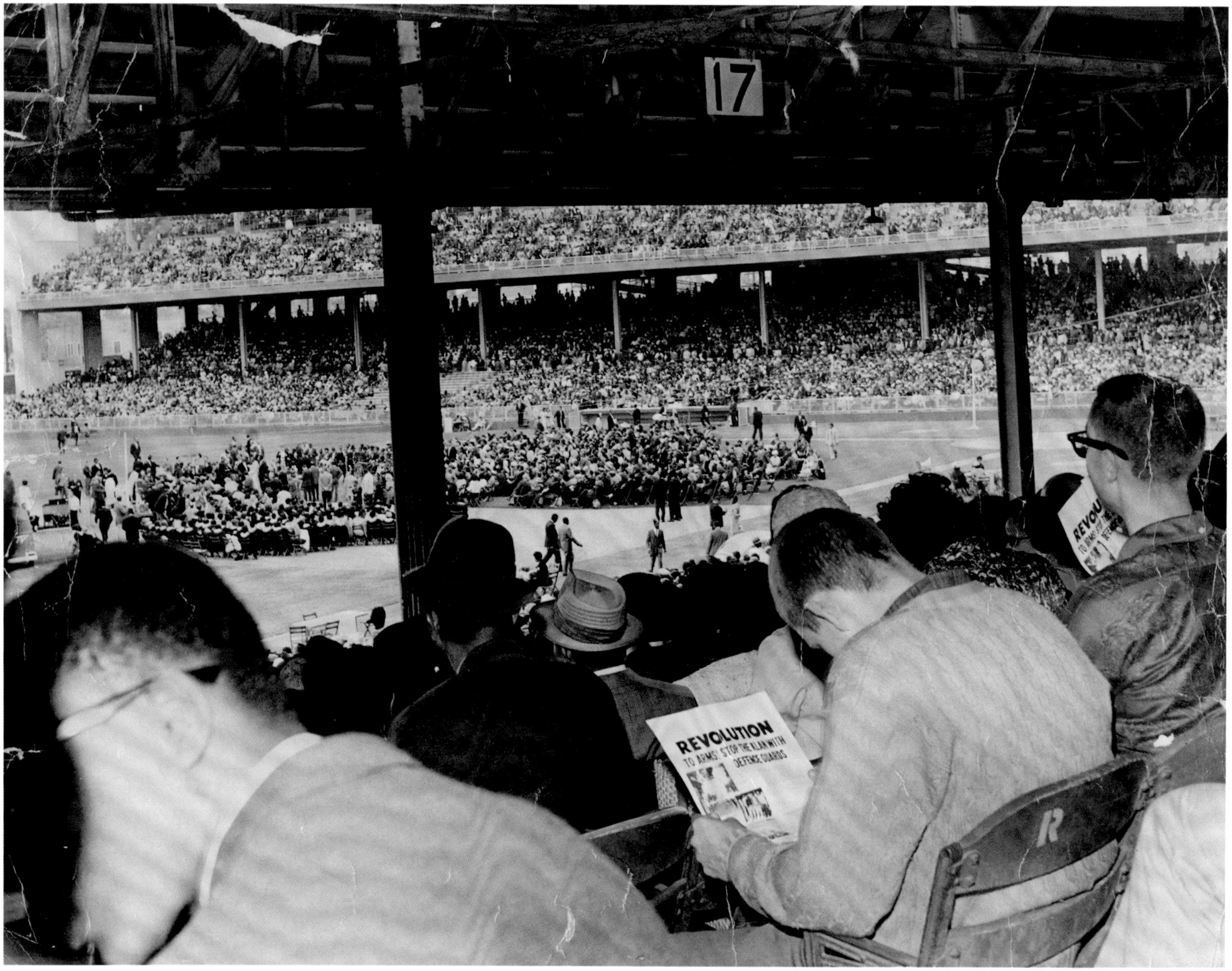

Plate 38 UNKNOWN PHOTOGRAPHER, 1963

Spectators view the stage as well as the special guests seated in the infield at the May 26 Freedom Rally at Wrigley Field. This *Los Angeles Herald Examiner* picture conveys a sense of scale and perspective at the stadium, where an estimated forty thousand attendees gathered to hear Martin Luther King Jr. One participant studies a pamphlet with the headline "Revolution to Arms! Stop the Klan with Defense Guards."

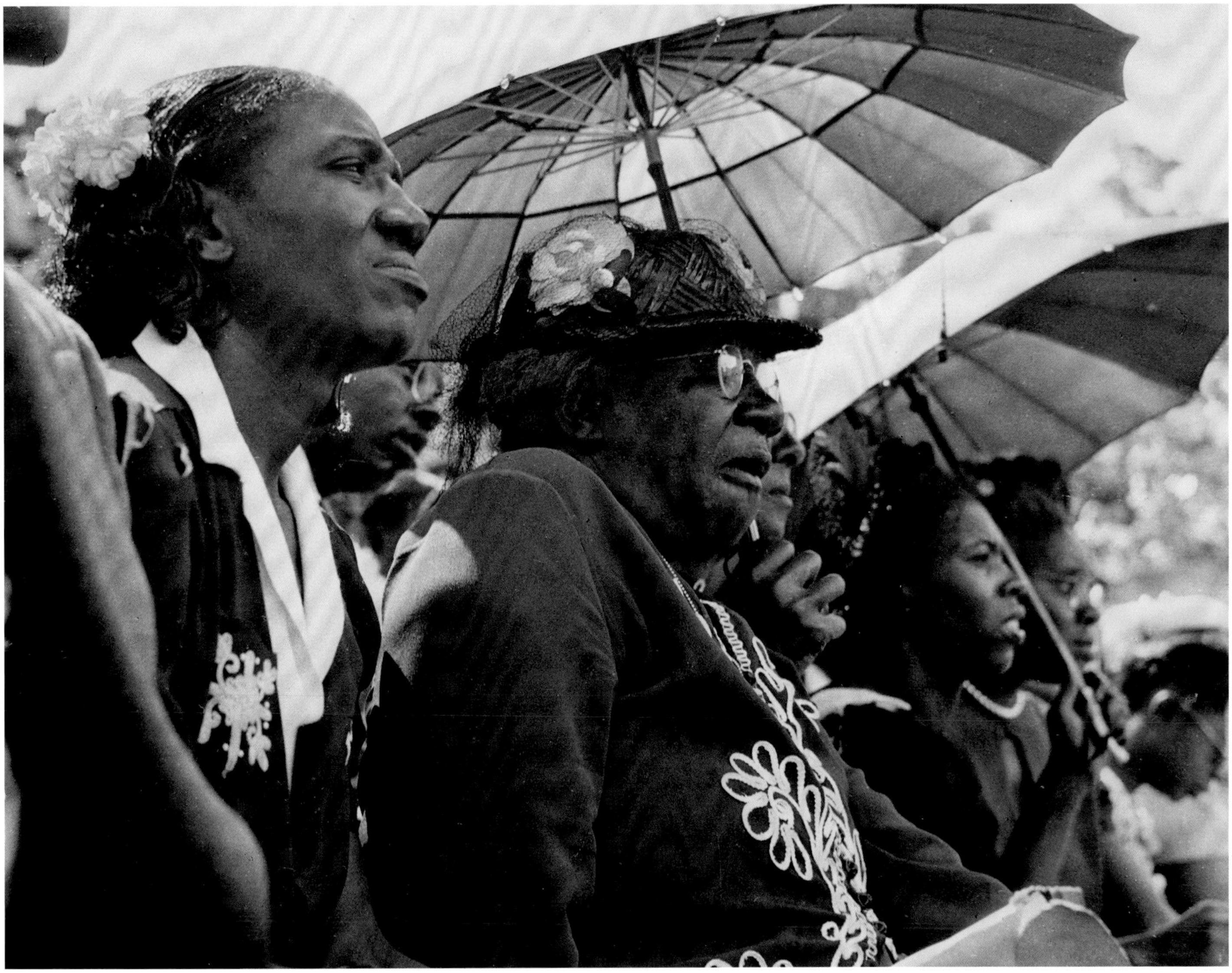

Plate 39 JOSEPH SCHWARTZ, 1963

Women listen intently to speakers at the Freedom Rally at Wrigley Field, featuring Martin Luther King Jr., Hollywood stars, and local civil rights leaders. Many civil rights advocates intentionally wore smart suits and dresses at such events to project dignity and counter negative stereotypes about African Americans.

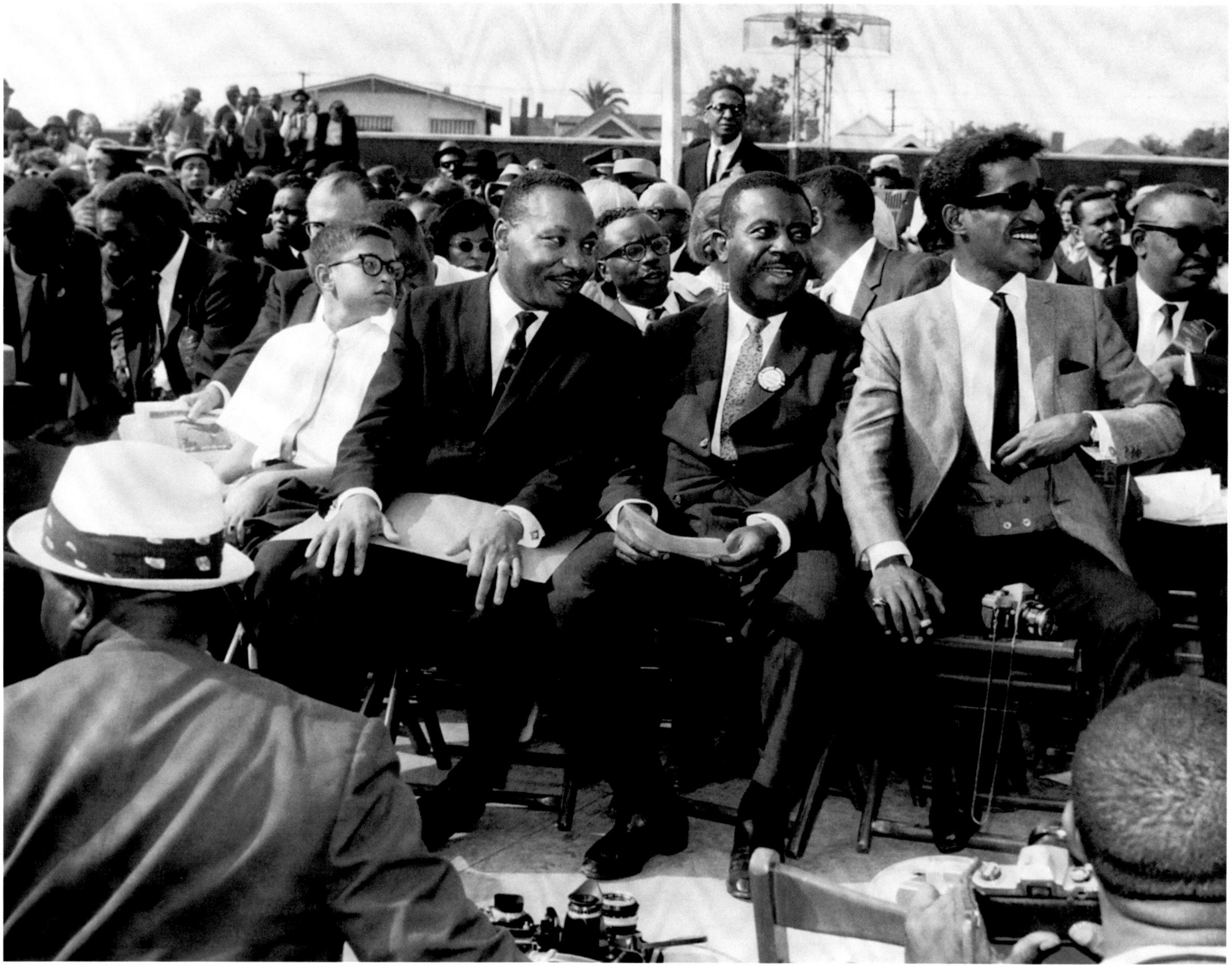

Plate 40 JACK DAVIS, 1963

Martin Luther King Jr., Rev. Ralph Abernathy, and Sammy Davis Jr. smile as they look toward the speaker's podium during the Freedom Rally at Wrigley Field. Freelancer Jack Davis snapped this view over the shoulders of two other photographers, pulling viewers into the scene. Sammy Davis Jr. brought star power as well as his own camera to the event.

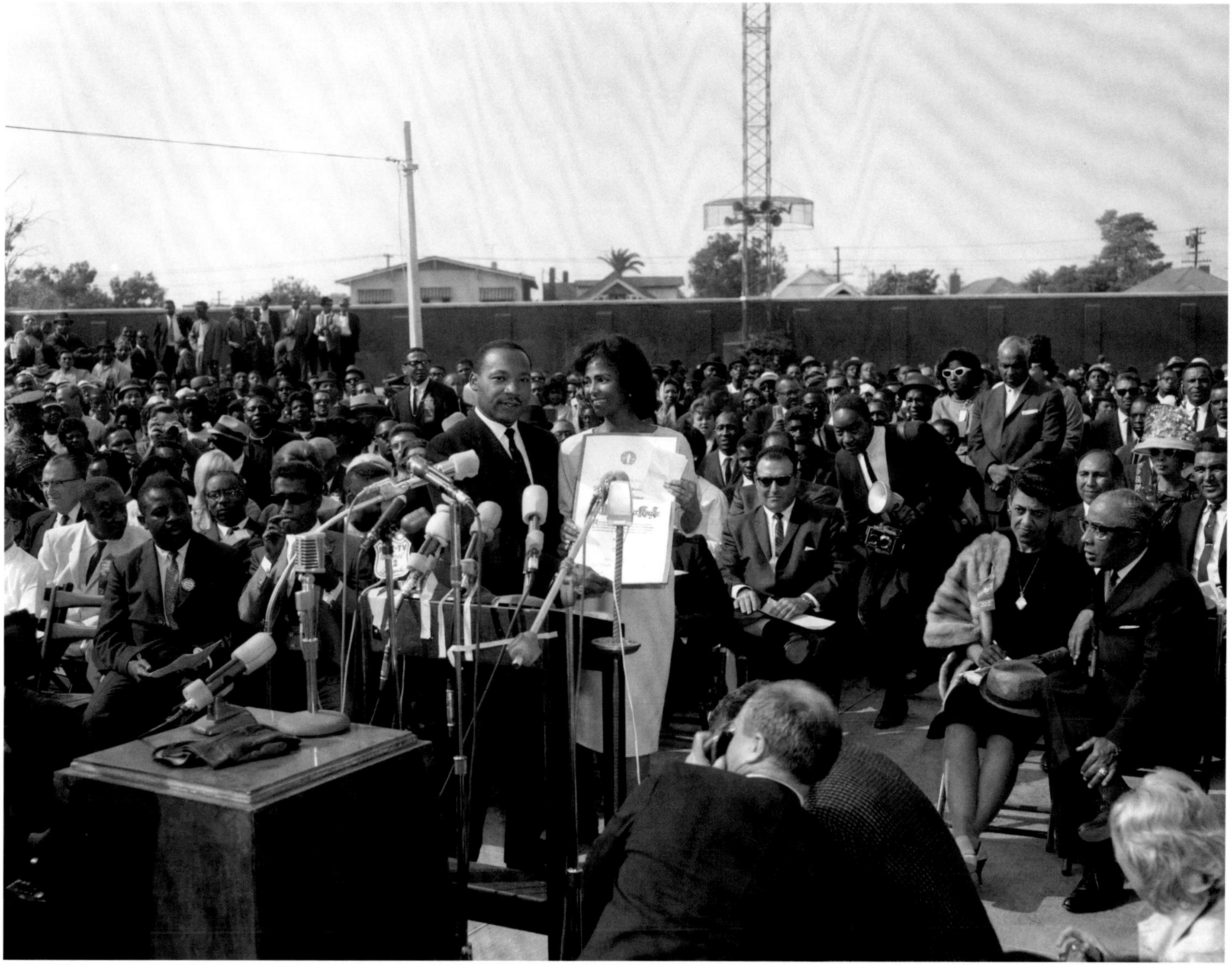

Plate 41 HARRY ADAMS, 1963

One of many Hollywood stars in attendance, Dorothy Dandridge (*center*) presents Martin Luther King Jr. with a citation on behalf of the board of supervisors. Harry Adams covered the rally for the *California Eagle*, landing three pictures on the front page of the May 30 issue.

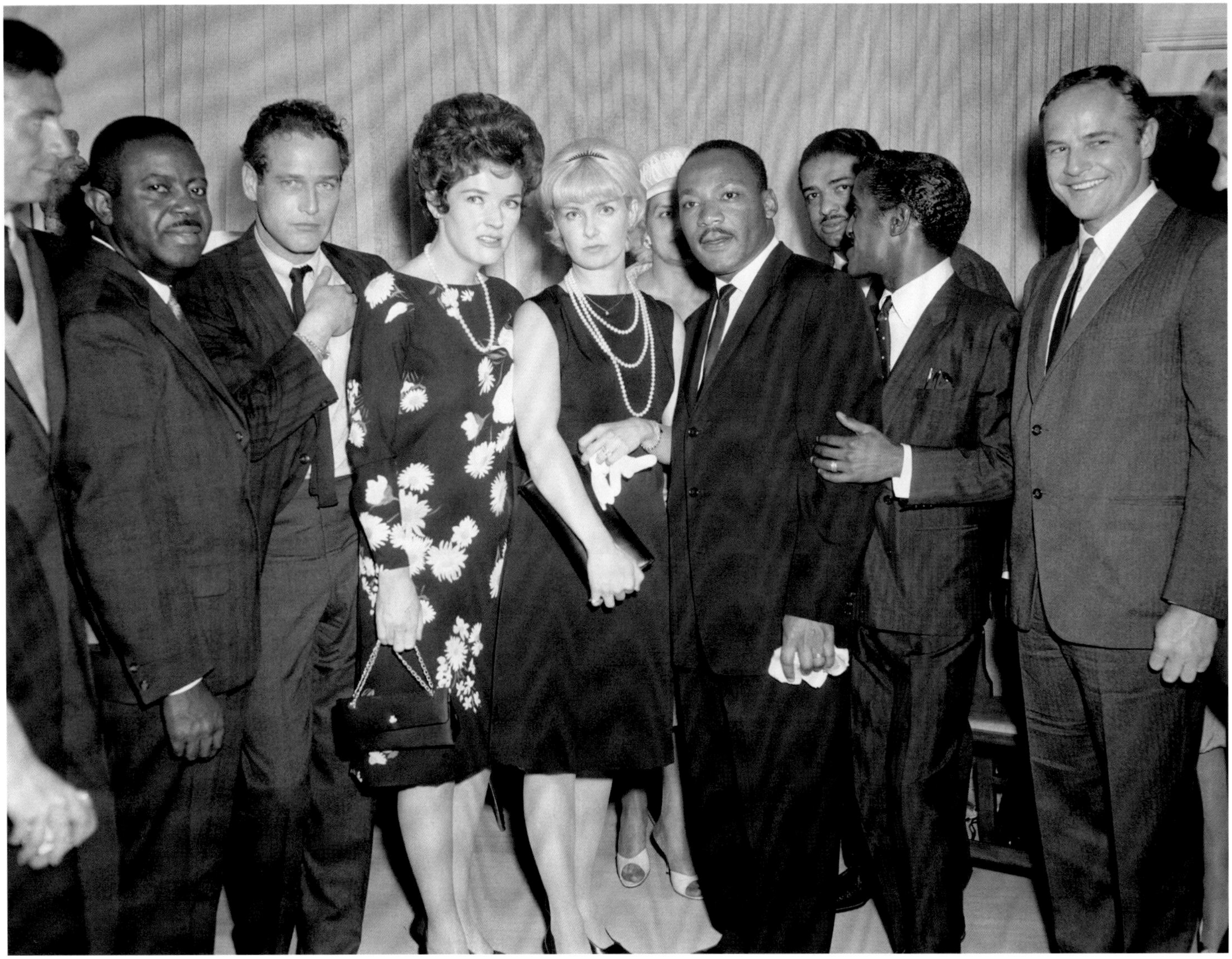

Plate 42 HARRY ADAMS, 1963

Hollywood stars Paul Newman (*third from left*), Polly Bergen, Joanne Woodward, Sammy Davis Jr. (*with head turned*), and Marlon Brando pose with Martin Luther King Jr. and Rev. Ralph Abernathy (*left, next to Newman*) during a fundraiser at Burt Lancaster's home after the Freedom Rally in May.

Plate 43 GORDON DEAN, 1963

In June, marchers packed along the sidewalk demand an end to police brutality and ongoing segregation in education, employment, and housing. The *Valley Times* article in which this picture ran quoted civil rights leaders saying they would continue protesting the board of education until their demands for school integration were met.

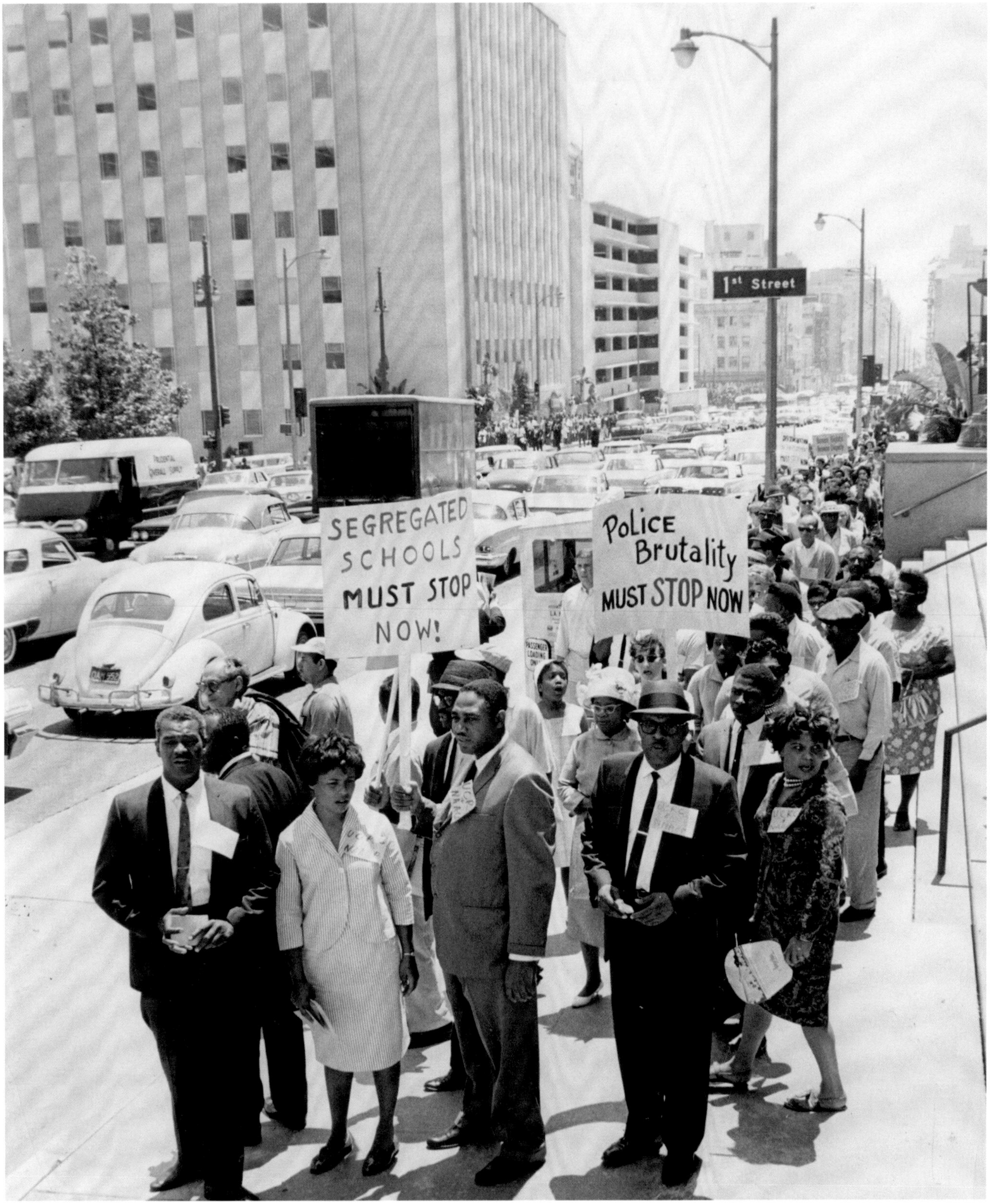
1st Street
SEGREGATED SCHOOLS MUST STOP NOW!
Police Brutality MUST STOP NOW

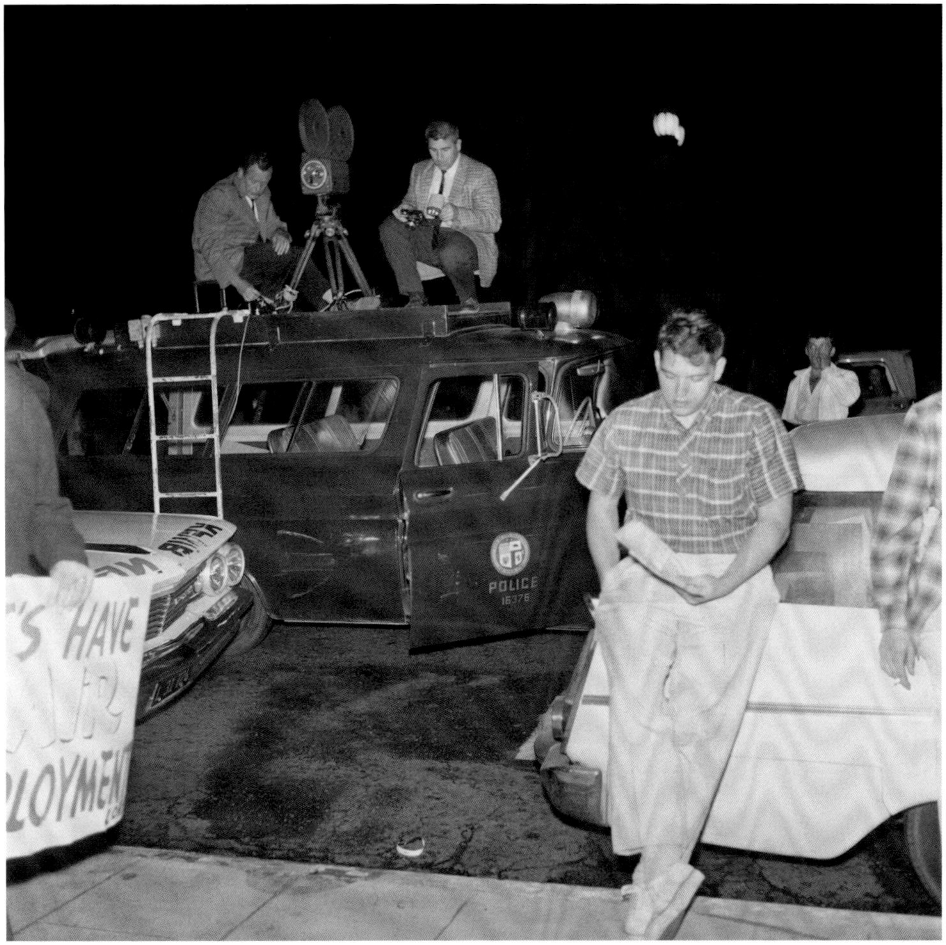

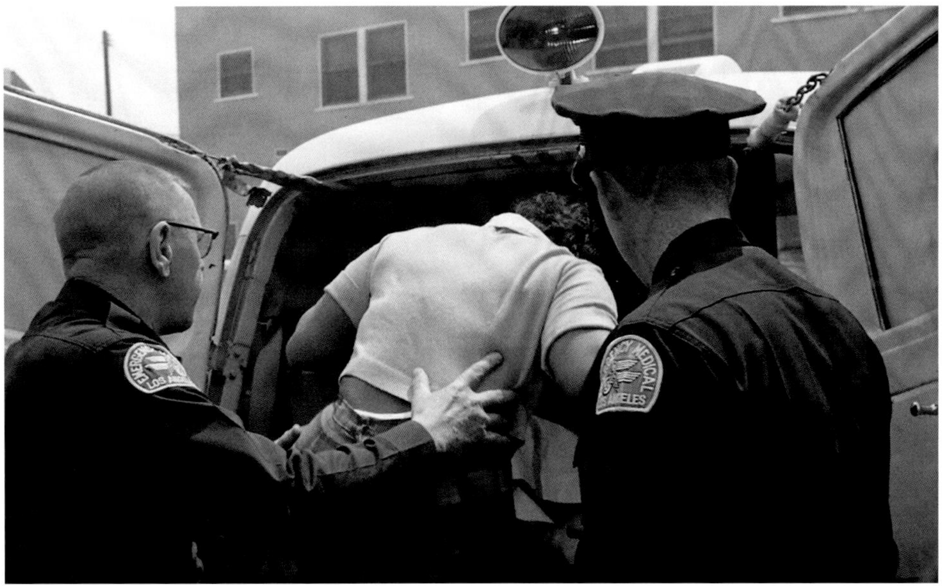

Plate 44 JACK DAVIS, 1963

Plainclothes LAPD officers film marchers from atop a police wagon. Jack Davis's picture was never published, but it documents a familiar sight at many civil rights rallies in Los Angeles and nationwide: police using cameras as weapons of surveillance. Police monitored activists for many reasons, including to track them and to deter parolees or those in trouble with authorities from participating in demonstrations.

Plate 45 JACK DAVIS, 1963

Activists determined to march against discrimination in Los Angeles faced a host of hazards along the way. Counterprotesters often threatened demonstrators and threw objects at them. LAPD officers harassed or arrested protesters of all ages and backgrounds, sometimes causing injuries.

Plate 46 UNKNOWN PHOTOGRAPHER, 1963

On August 8, more than six hundred people marched against discrimination in schools, including California Assemblyman Mervyn Dymally (*front row, far left*); UCRC chair Christopher Taylor (*front row, third from left*); CORE national director James Farmer (*front row, fourth from left*); actors Rita Moreno (*front row, third from right*) and Tony Franciosa (*second row, behind Moreno at left*); and UCRC education chair Marnesba Tackett (*front row, far right*).

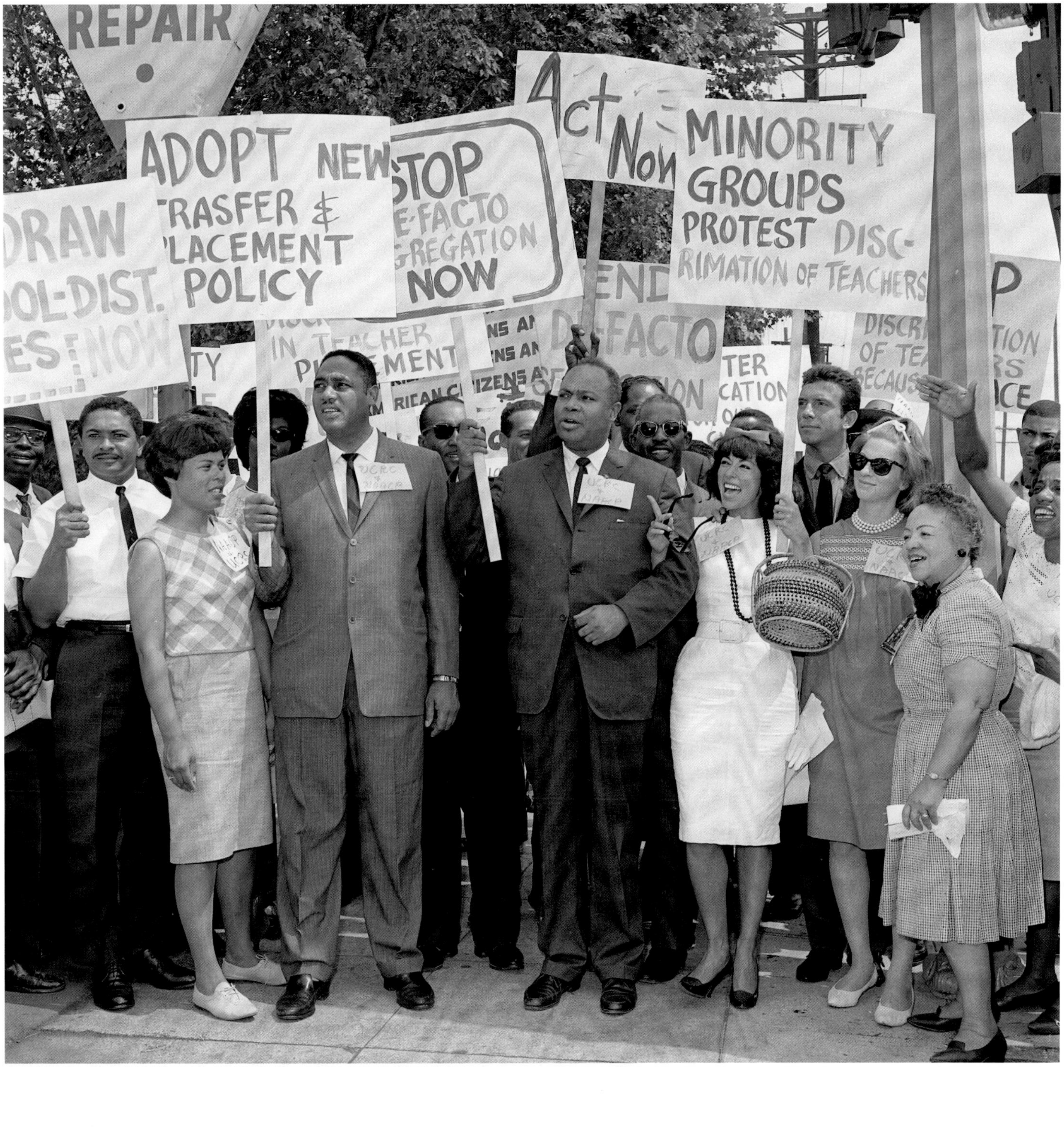
REPAIR
ADOPT NEW
TRASFER &
PLACEMENT
POLICY
STOP
E-FACTO
GREGATION
NOW
Act Now
MINORITY
GROUPS
PROTEST DISC-
RIMATION OF TEACHERS
DRAW
OOL-DIST.
NOW
IN TEACHER
DE-FACTO

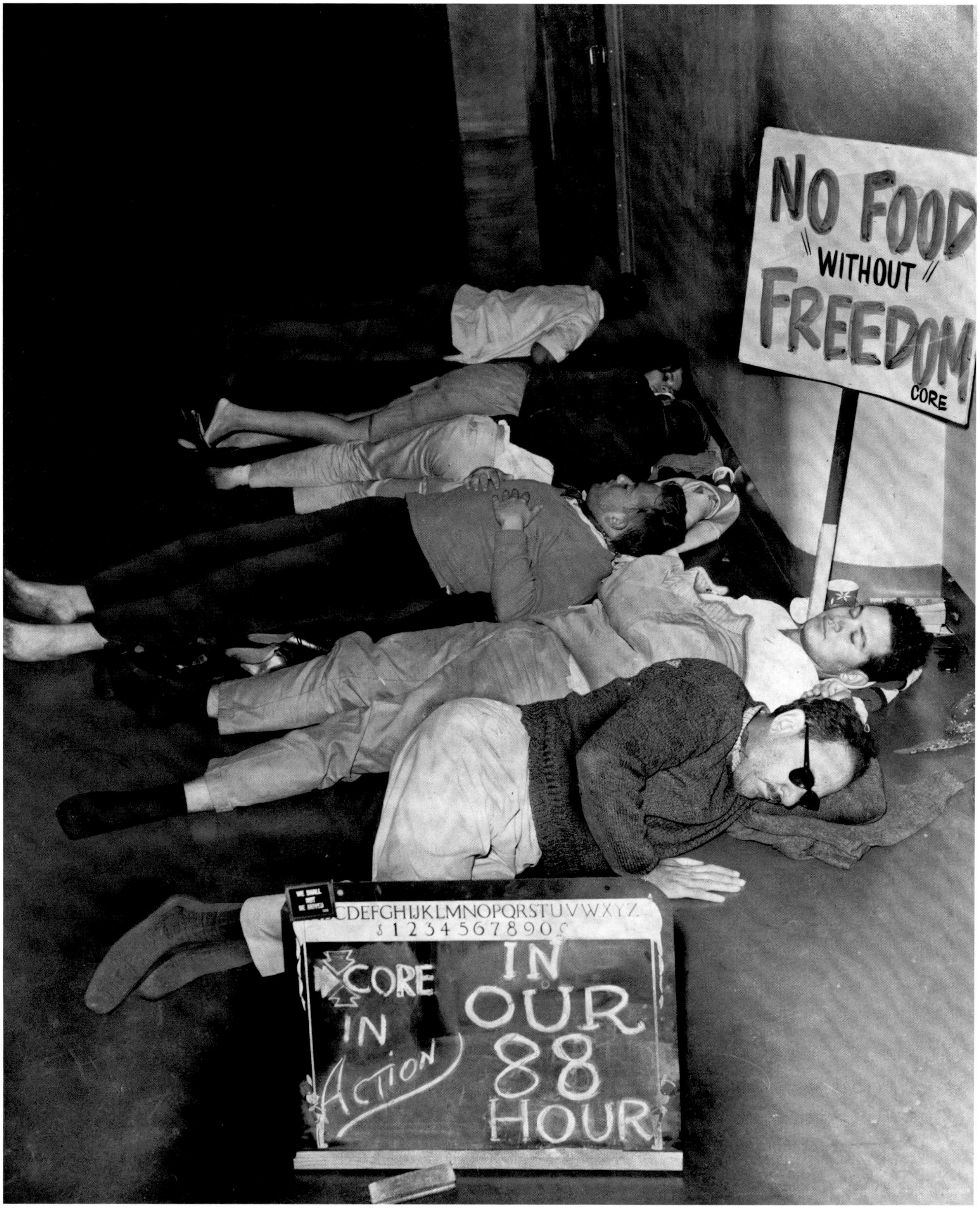
NO FOOD
"WITHOUT"
FREEDOM
CORE
CORE
IN
Action
IN
OUR
88
HOUR

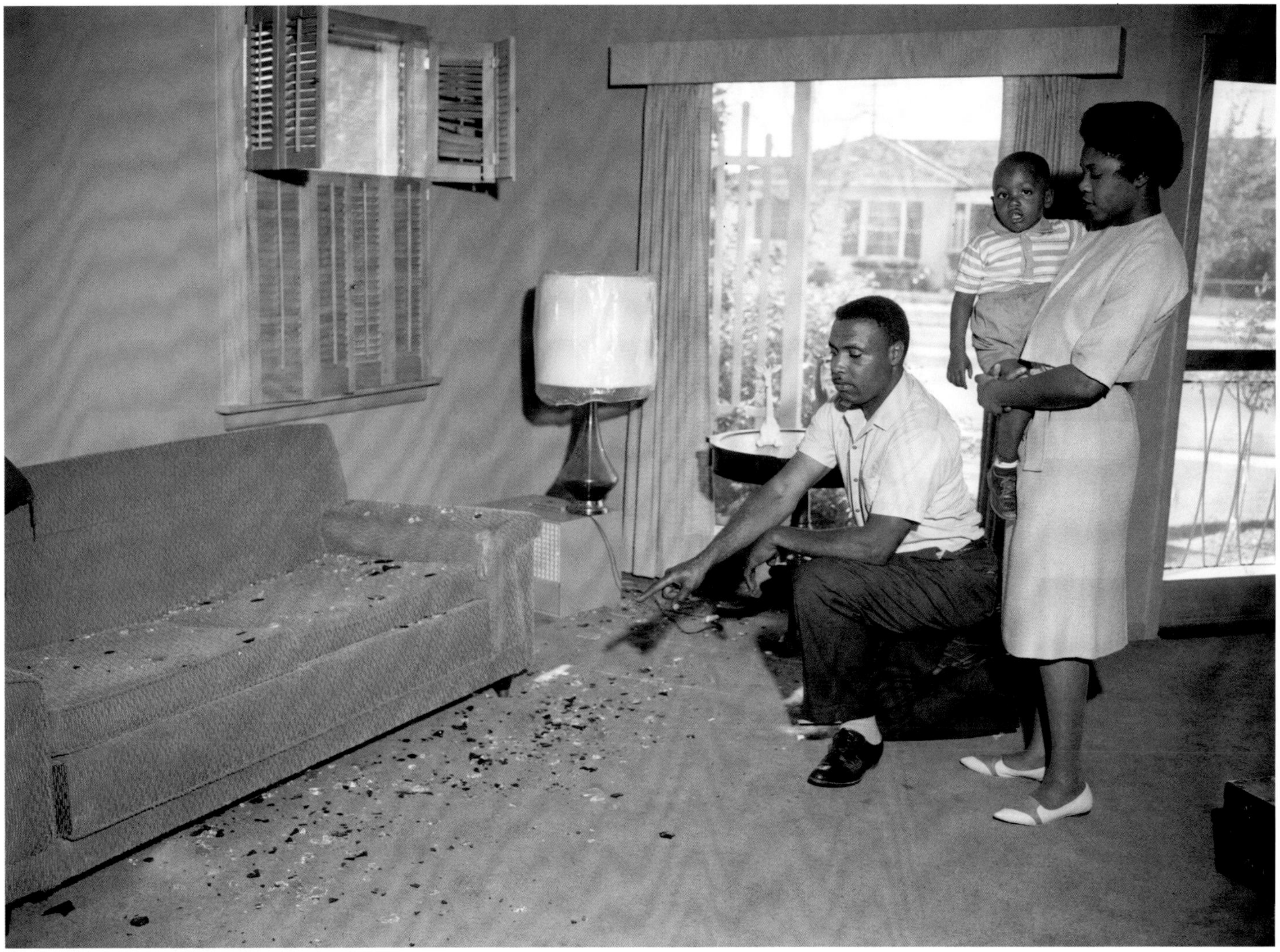

Plate 47 UNKNOWN PHOTOGRAPHER, 1963

Six CORE activists sleep at the offices of the board of education during a sit-in hunger strike demanding school integration. According to a *Los Angeles Sentinel* article, three protesters fasted ten and a half days, drinking only water, and were ordered by their physicians to break the fast or suffer severe health consequences.

Plate 48 CHARLES WILLIAMS, 1962

Thomas Wells, alongside his wife, Eleanor, and their young nephew, points to debris and damage after a shotgun blast and beer bottles broke their front window the night before. The family had moved into this home just three weeks earlier. A front-page *California Eagle* article noted Wells borrowed a gun afterward from a neighbor to protect his family.

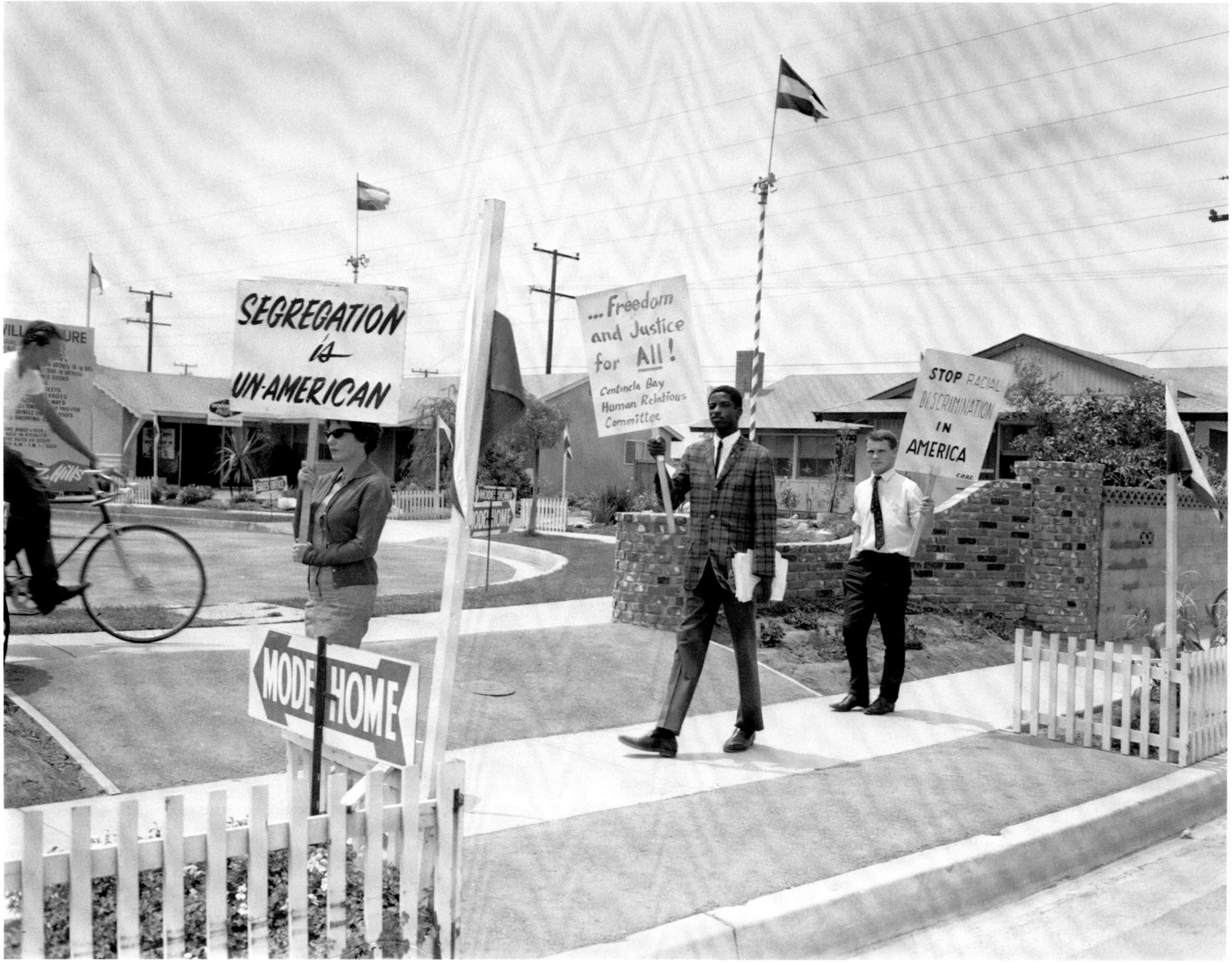

Plate 49 CHARLES WILLIAMS, 1962

CORE protesters picket at a Dominguez Hills housing tract. The developer, Don C. Wilson Builders, was a familiar target for peaceful protests because of its long-standing refusal to sell houses to Black Angelenos.

Plate 50 CHARLES BRITTIN, ca. 1963

Members of the American Nazi Party interrupt a protest by CORE members against housing discrimination in Los Angeles. Throughout the 1960s, Nazis staged counterdemonstrations across the country, wearing their uniforms and swastika armbands and displaying racist signage.

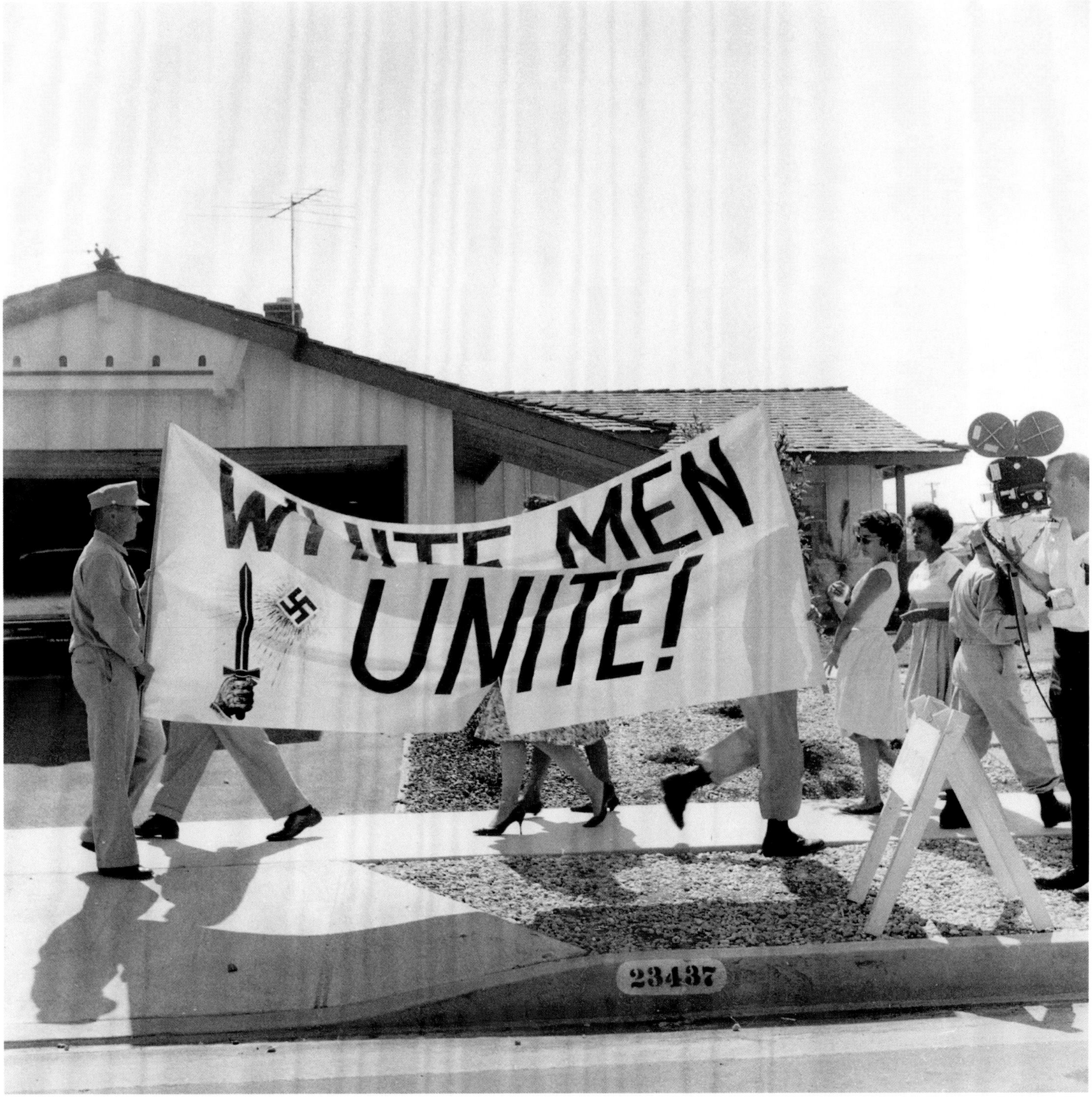
MEN
UNITE!
23437

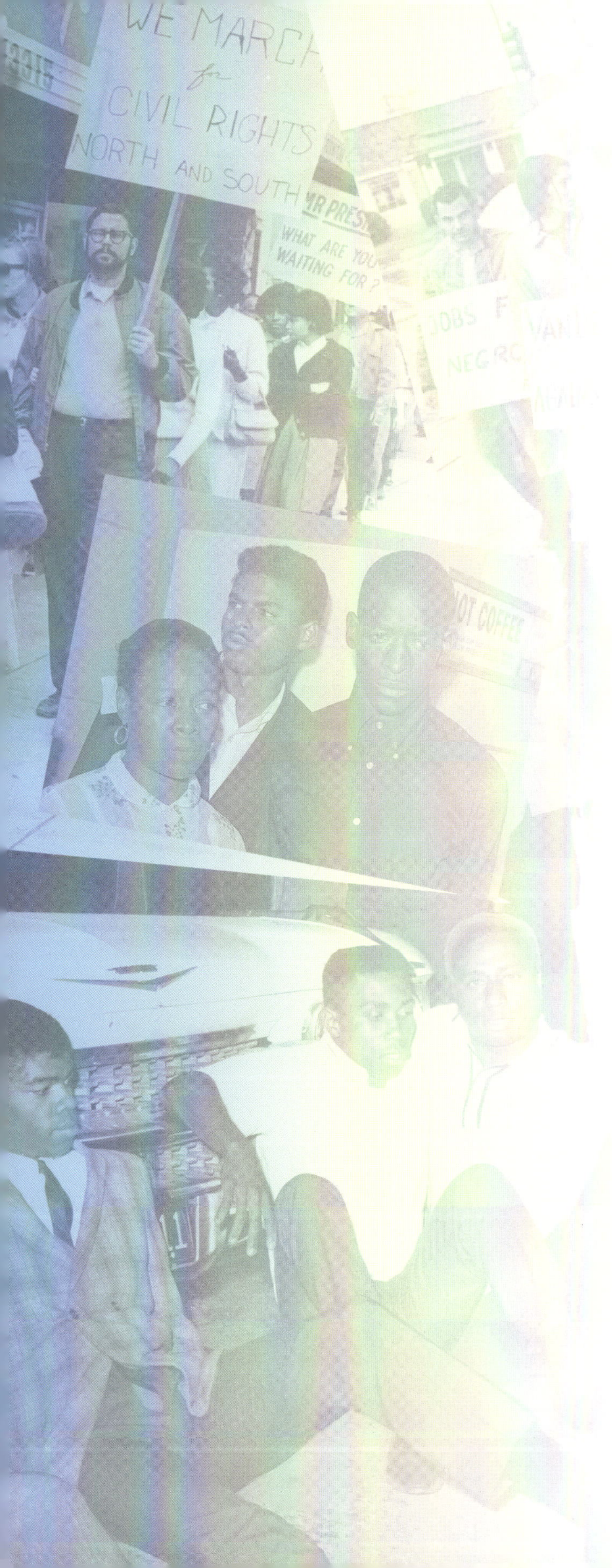

4

“The Violence of Poverty and Humiliation”

DEFENDING FAIR HOUSING

The triumphant March on Washington for Jobs and Freedom in August 1963 drew international attention to racial, economic, and political injustice in the United States and contributed to the passage of the Civil Rights Act of 1964 and the Voting Rights Act of 1965. Photographic and television coverage of the event raised hopes and spirits throughout pro–civil rights America. However, the historic gathering and landmark legislation did not end the widespread poverty, high unemployment, stubborn segregation, unchecked police brutality, and rampant disenfranchisement affecting Black communities across the country. From New York to California, newspapers and magazines published stories and images of the ongoing battle for basic human rights (fig. 26; plates 51, 52).

In Los Angeles, the third most populous city in the United States in 1963, housing discrimination continued to weigh heavily on the Black community. The Rumford Fair Housing Act, introduced by William Byron Rumford, a Black lawmaker in the California legislature, had passed in September of 1963, but it triggered an aggressive backlash from the powerful California Real Estate Association, whose predominantly white membership had opposed open housing and integrated neighborhoods since the 1920s. The association helped draft Proposition 14, a constitutional amendment on the November 1964 ballot that would effectively repeal the Rumford Act.

Working in conjunction with the UCRC, the NAACP, and CORE, and under the guidance of Rev. Thomas Kilgore of Second Baptist Church, the WCLC appealed to churches and local organizations, leveraging grassroots support to combat Proposition 14. City council member Tom Bradley and other local politicians also mobilized to defeat the proposition (plate 53). Kilgore succeeded Rev. J. Raymond Henderson as pastor of Second Baptist Church in 1963. He originally hailed from Woodruff, South Carolina. As a young man, he had been a member of Ebenezer Baptist Church in Atlanta, where Martin Luther King Jr.'s grandfather Pastor A. D. Williams had served as minister, giving Kilgore a personal connection to King and the civil rights movement. Prior to his move to Los Angeles, Kilgore led Friendship Baptist Church in New York City. During his time in New York, he also oversaw the local office of the SCLC.[1]

A pivotal moment in the anti–Proposition 14 campaign occurred at a banquet at the Hollywood Palladium in February 1964 that featured an address by King. "The true test of liberalism is whether the white person who says he is committed to justice is willing to allow Negroes to live in his neighborhood, and even next door," King said. As he urged the audience to use political power through the ballot to defeat Proposition 14, he also stated: "If the Rumford Fair Housing bill is repealed, California, the nation, and democracy will be set back in one of the most shameful developments of recent times."[2] Sharing the stage with King were key figures in California politics, including State Controller Alan Cranston, Rumford, and Rev. H. H. Brookins. Together, they urged citizens to "rise up and save" the Rumford Act.[3] The *Los Angeles Sentinel* devoted a full page of photos to the well-dressed attendees, and it ran a banner along the bottom of the paper: "Register NOW to be Eligible to Vote Nov. 3. Vote NO on Prop. 14—It's Your Right to Live Where You Choose—Don't Let Them Kill that Right!"[4]

During King's repeated trips to California, he fervently challenged the contradiction inherent in a "liberal state" whose residents opposed fair housing laws and warned of broader implications for America if Proposition 14 passed. "If the voters do not save the housing bill," King said, "it will be a tragic setback."[5] On May 31, 1964, the WCLC and a broad coalition of religious groups co-hosted the Religious Witness for Human Dignity event at the Los Angeles Memorial Coliseum. Among the fifteen thousand attendees were several Hollywood celebrities and two hundred religious leaders representing various faiths, including Catholic, Protestant, and Jewish. As the keynote speaker, King addressed a diverse audience, framing the issue of open housing as a matter of moral responsibility: "Now is the time to make real the promises of

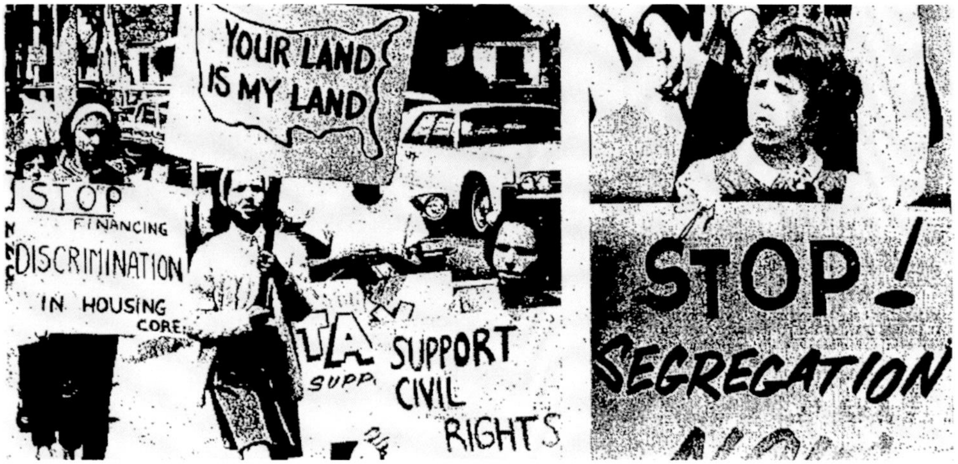

Fig. 26 Civil rights activists march from Alhambra to Monterey Park, in hopes of ending segregation and housing discrimination. *Independent Star-News*, 1964.

democracy. Now is the time to open the floodgates of opportunity and allow now an avalanche of justice to pour upon us. Now is the time to get rid of segregation and discrimination. Now is the time to make justice a reality for all of God's children. This is the challenge of the hour."[6]

King's involvement in the California housing controversy drew sharp criticism, particularly from members of the Association for the Protection of American Rights (APAR), who picketed the speech with signs that equated fair housing policies with communism and treason. The conflict escalated in May when King officiated at the opening of the WCLC West Coast bureau in L.A. APAR protesters carried signs that read "King Has Hate, Does Travel," "Thank God for Chief Parker," and "Stop Brutality Against Police." APAR blamed conflicts between police and African Americans on "radical socialists" and the "arrogant defiance of lawful authority by self-styled civil rights leaders."[7]

In addition to the real estate industry, conservative groups such as the John Birch Society and the American Nazi Party supported Proposition 14. They framed the issue not as racial discrimination but as the protection of property rights, free market principles, and personal liberty.[8] In agreement, the *Los Angeles Times* wrote two editorials supporting the initiative. The August 31 editorial criticized Gov. Pat Brown's "inflammatory" rhetoric, specifically his charge that "shock troops of bigotry" had moved behind the California Real Estate Association. The *Times* also charged the governor with denying the "good will" of those who supported the proposition.[9] By October 1964, the *Times* openly recommended that its readers vote "yes" on Proposition 14, emphasizing that "owners should have absolute discretion in the choice of a buyer or renter of their real property.... We seriously question whether social, as distinct from civil, justice can properly be achieved at the expense of still another basic right."[10] In both editorials, the *Times* framed its support as protecting fundamental property rights while opposing housing discrimination based on color. Brown maintained his alliance with civil rights groups and argued that passage of the initiative would place a provision into California's constitution "for discrimination of which not even Mississippi or Alabama can boast."[11]

Ultimately, Proposition 14 passed with 65 percent of the vote. Expressing disappointment, King would later write in the *Saturday Review*: "California ... was the first major state in the country to take away gains Negroes had won at a time when progress was visible and substantial elsewhere.... California, by passing this callous act, voted for ghettos."[12]

The conservative victory was not a complete surprise, considering that Republican Barry Goldwater, an anti–social welfare and anti-integration candidate, won the 1964 California presidential primary. What made the results significant was the split-ticket voting, which revealed a sharp divide between national and state issues. While President Lyndon B. Johnson won California in the general election with 59.11 percent of the popular vote compared to Goldwater's 40.79 percent, many white Californians who supported Johnson for president simultaneously backed Proposition 14.[13]

Proposition 14 remained California law for only a short period. In 1966, the California Supreme Court declared it unconstitutional under the Fourteenth Amendment's Equal Protection Clause. The US Supreme Court upheld that ruling in *Reitman v. Mulkey* (1967), allowing the Rumford Fair Housing Act to remain in effect.[14] This legal battle culminated with the passage of the Federal Fair Housing Act and Title VIII of the Civil Rights Act of 1968, which prohibited housing discrimination nationwide and superseded state laws. While its victory was short, Proposition 14 still managed to have a long-term, negative impact on low-income Black communities in Los Angeles, particularly in the South Central neighborhood of Watts.

MISSISSIPPI FREEDOM SUMMER

In the summer of 1964, the Student Nonviolent Coordinating Committee (SNCC) and CORE called on young people from various backgrounds to participate in Freedom Summer, a civil rights initiative focused on increasing African American voter registration in the South. In response, hundreds of young white and Black activists, including fifty-seven students from Southern California, traveled to Mississippi to participate. Their mission included engaging in voter registration drives, spearheading community organizing, and promoting public education.

The initial cohort of Freedom Summer volunteers began training on June 14, 1964, at the Western College for Women in Oxford, Ohio, before their planned trip to Mississippi. Merely a week later, the disappearance of three young men, all civil rights workers affiliated with CORE, shook the nation. James Chaney, a Black Mississippian, and Michael Schwerner and Andrew Goodman, both white Jewish New Yorkers, went missing in Philadelphia, Mississippi, after investigating the bombing of a Black church. Six weeks later, their bodies were discovered buried in an earthen dam on a farm in Longdale, Mississippi, murdered by the Ku Klux Klan.[15]

Angelenos reacted in force to the murders.[16] There were rallies and fundraising efforts, and Los Angeles City Council member Tom Bradley and other officials introduced a resolution to support a memorial service for the martyrs. The resolution was accepted unanimously. During the event, Brookins preached to a crowd of seven hundred and raised funds for a Freedom Community Center in Meridian, Mississippi, in the slain men's honor. Prominent Black Angelenos—including baseball legend Jackie Robinson and architect Paul Williams—brought in an additional $25,000.[17] Los Angeles newspapers maintained a steady stream of coverage but included few visuals. The *Times* reported almost daily on the ongoing search, while the *Sentinel* spoke with Angelenos who had been in Mississippi recently and reported on local marches demanding federal protection. After Freedom Summer came to an end, the *Sentinel* interviewed nine of the fifty-seven Angelenos, including Watts resident James Garrett, who had spent several hours with Chaney just days before his disappearance.[18]

LEGISLATIVE WINS AND LOSSES

On July 2, 1964, President Johnson signed the Civil Rights Act into law, marking one of the largest national victories for the civil rights movement. The bill prohibited discrimination based on race, color, religion, sex, or national origin. About a month later, the president signed the Economic Opportunity Act (EOA), a cornerstone of his War on Poverty program. The EOA allocated nearly $1 billion in federal funds to provide job training, employment, education, and other assistance to reduce poverty nationwide. It established programs such as Upward Bound for college readiness aimed at low-income high school students; Job Corps for job training; the Neighborhood Youth Corps for providing work experience for urban youths; and numerous other community initiatives. The two legislative victories proved that political participation could have a direct impact on the lives of African Americans. In response to these wins, the WCLC continued its work—partnering with the NAACP, the UCRC, and CORE—to support voter turnout for the November presidential election to reelect Johnson.[19]

Passage of the EOA allowed local service organizations to distribute the allotted federal funds, thereby empowering people experiencing poverty to address their own needs. Additionally, the EOA aligned with the UCRC's goal of eradicating poverty, especially during a time when the decline of manufacturing jobs and factory closures in African American neighborhoods like South Central Los Angeles had intensified. Class disparities soared as white-collar opportunities grew, while blue-collar workers faced increasing unemployment and underemployment, reflecting a process favoring suburban areas over urban neighborhoods.[20]

A FIGHT OVER FUNDING

While an excellent idea in theory, in practice the local disbursement of EOA funds became a contentious issue in Los Angeles. Mayor Sam Yorty and other prominent politicians favored a Youth Opportunities Board (YOB) composed of city and county officials and board of education members to oversee the multimillion-dollar program. The Equal Opportunities Federation and Community Anti-Poverty Committee—a coalition of labor, African American, and Mexican American community groups—opposed the mayor's efforts. They criticized the YOB as a paternalistic political organization and a mechanism for the mayor to control federal funds.[21] Instead, they proposed a more democratic, thirty-two-member board, half of whom would come from twelve designated communities. The conflict generated mass protests at the civic center, which included community leaders such as *Sentinel* publisher Leon Washington. In disgust, Brookins compared liberal Los Angeles to the Jim Crow South. "I'm appalled," he said. "People who protest the actions of segregation in the South are sitting by while local politicians swindle them out of millions in poverty programs."[22] Meanwhile, Yorty condemned the federal anti-poverty Office of Economic Opportunity for "fostering class struggle."[23]

King supported the coalition's position and the community's critiques that the YOB excluded poor people from policymaking by assuming they lacked intelligence and responsibility. "It's not making progress to make the rich richer while the poor smother in the air-tight cage of poverty," he said. "And the decision-making power must rest with the people who are subjected to poverty."[24] To present the clergy's position, the WCLC sponsored a four-day conference called "The Church Speaks on Poverty, Housing, and De Facto Segregation" in July 1965.[25] Many impoverished Angelenos felt they were being used as political pawns rather than empowered to improve their communities. The conflict surrounding the structure of the poverty board was one of the sparks that would set the city ablaze during the Watts Uprising in August 1965.

THE "OUTRAGE OF SELMA"

Voting rights became a national focus in 1965, spurred by the tragic events of Freedom Summer and ongoing barriers such as literacy tests and poll taxes used against Black voters in the South.

On February 1, 1965, King led more than two hundred fifty activists to the Dallas County Courthouse in Selma, Alabama, to register to vote and to highlight widespread voting discrimination. All of them, including King, were arrested during the peaceful demonstration and charged with parading without a permit. Selma was chosen for its low African American voter registration—only 2 percent—and the likelihood that Sheriff Jim Clark's notorious brutality would draw national attention to the plight of Black voters. This strategy was in the same vein as that practiced by CORE members who had strategically set up their hunger strike in the Los Angeles Board of Education hallway in September 1963, where officials and media could not miss them.[26]

While her husband was incarcerated, Coretta Scott King met with Malcolm X, who had been invited by SNCC members to speak at Brown Chapel in Selma. Malcolm X told her directly: "I didn't come to Selma to make his job difficult. I really did come thinking that I could make it easier. If the white people realize what the alternative is, perhaps they will be more willing to hear Dr. King."[27] She later recalled being surprised by the former NOI leader's demeanor. "I didn't expect him to say that.... He had such a gentle manner, and he seemed very sincere."[28] Just weeks later, on February 21, 1965, Malcolm X was assassinated in New York City. Coretta Scott King called his death a "great tragedy" that occurred at a time when Malcolm X was "moving toward a greater understanding of the nonviolent movement."[29]

Martin Luther King Jr. returned to Los Angeles from February 24 to 28, 1965, to speak at Jewish synagogues and Baptist churches, attend a benefit screening of the film *The Greatest Story Ever Told*, participate in a civic luncheon organized by the City of Los Angeles and the Los Angeles World Affairs Council, and conduct fundraising activities. His return occurred under the cloud of Malcolm X's assassination and amid extraordinary security measures following credible threats against his own life. An anonymous telephone threat to "blow up that nigger" gained credibility after police discovered that more than a thousand pounds of dynamite had been stolen from a Sylmar storage shed just days before King's arrival. The police searched buildings throughout Los Angeles while maintaining heavy protection for King. They found dynamite inside the Cinerama Dome, where King was scheduled to attend the benefit screening.[30]

The police dedicated fifteen hundred man-hours, "the largest amount of man-hours ever devoted to a private person in the history of the LAPD," to protect King, according to Inspector Ed Walker. When King spoke at Temple Israel of Hollywood on February 26, sharpshooters were positioned on the apartment building across the street and two large bodyguards stood directly behind him as he addressed an audience of fourteen hundred.[31]

Coretta Scott King acknowledged the constant danger they faced, telling reporters that while she tried to help their children understand that "their daddy is trying to help people," she admitted, "We all realize that something could happen, but I don't worry to the extent that I can't sleep.... If it does happen, I think it would be the will of God." She discussed this as she prepared for her own visit to Los Angeles to perform a "Freedom Concert" at Second Baptist Church on Friday night, March 5. Her lifelong dedication to justice began well before her role as a national civil rights leader. As an undergraduate at Antioch College in Ohio, she joined the campus NAACP chapter and served on the Race Relations and Civil Liberties Committees. She earned a bachelor of arts degree in music and education in 1951, then received a scholarship to the New England Conservatory of Music in Boston to study vocal performance, where she met King in 1952.[32]

Coretta Scott King toured widely across the United States and internationally. Her March 1965 concert in Los Angeles featured her as soprano soloist in what was described by the *Sentinel* as "a moving, sensitive story of the freedom struggle told in song and narration." The event aimed to raise funds for her husband's work with the SCLC, to educate and inspire the Los Angeles community, and to strengthen ties between local supporters and the national movement, building on the momentum of King's recent, highly secured visit to the city.[33]

A few days after the L.A. fundraiser, on March 8, 1965, SCLC leader Hosea Williams and SNCC leader John Lewis led a peaceful march from Selma to the courthouse in Montgomery, Alabama. The demonstration was held in response to the murder of Jimmie Lee Jackson, a Black church deacon killed by state troopers during a peaceful voting rights march a month earlier. After an extremely violent confrontation with police at the Edmund Pettus Bridge in which six hundred marchers were brutally attacked, the day came to be known as Bloody Sunday. The violence led to the hospitalization of more than fifty demonstrators and triggered national outrage after it was televised.[34] The events of Bloody Sunday demonstrated to President Johnson that the civil rights movement could not wait any longer for the Voting Rights Act. On March 17, 1965, Congress introduced a bill to strengthen the Fifteenth Amendment by outlawing implicitly racist barriers to voting.

Although Black Angelenos were uninhibited in the right to vote, the local civil rights community closely monitored the events in Selma and organized to support the effort (plate 54). Marchers implored Johnson and the federal government to act, carrying signs including one that read: "Mr. President What Are You Waiting For?" The Council of Churches of Southern California and the UCRC demonstrated outside the Federal Building in Los Angeles against police brutality in Selma. James Garrett, a leader in SNCC, led a sit-in at the US Marshals office in Los Angeles while singing "Freedom Now."[35] Brookins was among those who spoke to a crowd of six hundred protesters outside. A CORE spokesman who was arrested described the urgency of the action: "I've been to Mississippi, and I know that while we go home peaceably here, they'll be using cattle prods on Negroes down there tonight."[36]

In describing the events to the *Sentinel*, board of education candidate Rev. James Jones, who participated in the Selma march, quoted King's explanation about why he violated a court order to march. "I would rather be dead on the streets of Alabama than to butcher my conscience ... so I have to march," he said.[37] Los Angeles CORE and other participating groups garnered massive press and photographic coverage as they engaged in direct action. Police officers and federal marshals dragged well-attired protesters, including women in dresses, across the floor of the Federal Building (plate 55). As previous protests had demonstrated, the mainstream media's obsession with images of brutalized young white people galvanized support for the movement. From photos of white hunger strikers to protesters being thrown into paddy wagons, the visibility of white supporters of the civil rights movement fascinated certain segments of the population. Photographers and television news crews documented dramatic arrests, inspiring more supporters to join what would become a multiday campaign. CORE photographer Charles Brittin wrote in the *Los Angeles Free Press*, a provocative underground newspaper launched in 1964, that "one government employee tried to smash the camera of the photographer representing the *Free Press*."[38]

The Selma marches culminated on March 21, 1965, in a five-day, fifty-four-mile march from Selma to Montgomery, with thousands of protesters—led by King and escorted by National Guardsmen and FBI agents—walking to advocate for equal voting rights. Angelenos were mobilized and flown to Alabama to participate.[39] Three planes with nearly three hundred passengers from Los Angeles, including clergy, civic leaders, and labor, traveled to Selma for the march. Local activist Bruce Hartford was among those who made the journey (plate 56). Camera slung over his shoulder, he collected a series of unique snapshots that conveyed a participant's perspective of the historic event (plate 57).[40]

The *Sentinel* ran a photo of several L.A. ministers, including Peters, Jones, and Kilgore, and others on their way to Selma, with full coverage of the Selma-to-Montgomery march two weeks later. The April 1 front page featured King, Coretta Scott King, and other leaders nearing the end of the historic march. A separate image highlighted actor and singer Harry Belafonte, just one of several Hollywood celebrities present. Other pictures emphasized the long and tiring journey with King changing socks, marchers resting alongside a road, and bedraggled activists trudging through the driving rain.[41] A wide range of entertainers—including Joan Baez, Nina Simone, Mahalia Jackson, and the group Peter, Paul and Mary—used their music and celebrity presence to raise spirits and attract national media attention.

PROJECT SCOPE

After Selma, while the Voting Rights Act was pending in Congress, the SCLC launched the Summer Community Organization and Political Education (SCOPE) project to maintain momentum. King and Hosea Williams initiated this voter registration project, believing Southern communities still needed activists to help register voters and protect against violence. Drawing inspiration from Freedom Summer, they recruited college students to lead the potentially dangerous effort. King visited the UCLA campus and introduced SCOPE to a rapt crowd of forty-five hundred students, alumni, faculty, and staff who filled the lawn and the spaces between the academic buildings (plate 58).[42]

King appointed local civil rights activist Gwen Green as Williams's assistant director. While her appointment to SCOPE vaulted her to national prominence, she already held the distinction of being the first female executive director of the WCLC. A lifelong activist born to NAACP leaders, Green started an NAACP chapter in Boulder, Colorado, when her husband was denied a haircut as a law student. As a thirty-five-year-old mother of two, she joined the WCLC in 1960, fought for her title and pay, and contributed hard work and political expertise to the organization, which at that point had only been led by men (fig. 27).[43]

Working under the tutelage of Williams, Green implemented a plan to register Southern African Americans who had experienced discriminatory voting practices. She supervised the program and led thousands of predominantly white college students from Los Angeles and other cities to six Southern states and one hundred twenty counties. Green arranged for their lodging and helped acclimate them to living in the homes of African Americans, emphasizing the importance of working alongside members of the local community. The SCOPE volunteers faced significant risks to their safety, since leaders in Southern counties resented outside meddling.

In addition to offering students her political expertise, Green supported students emotionally, earning the nickname "Mama."[44] She ensured fair treatment for the young volunteers and arranged bail when necessary following arrests. Jewish students like Hartford and Willy Leventhal rose to official field staff positions under Green's guidance.[45] Hartford, called the "skinny kid" by the staff, worked on voter registration and conducted door-to-door canvassing in Crenshaw County, Alabama, chronicling his work through photographs.[46] His involvement with CORE and SCOPE began with recorded images he had seen of peaceful demonstrators being abused by uniformed members of the Nazi Party in Torrance.[47] "I was very angry at the people who allowed the Holocaust to happen, as well as the Germans who did it. I learned that the American Nazi Party was attacking the Congress of Racial Equality picket lines.... My feeling was, if the Nazis were against CORE, then I am going to go support CORE," Hartford said.[48]

Overall, the cross-country alliance benefited Angelenos and Southerners in innumerable ways. White students in particular learned critical organizing skills, witnessed the reality of Black life in the South, and brought new ideas informed by firsthand experience to the movements that shaped American life throughout the next decade. By the end of the summer, the students, staff, and other activists involved in the SCOPE project registered forty-nine thousand new voters.[49]

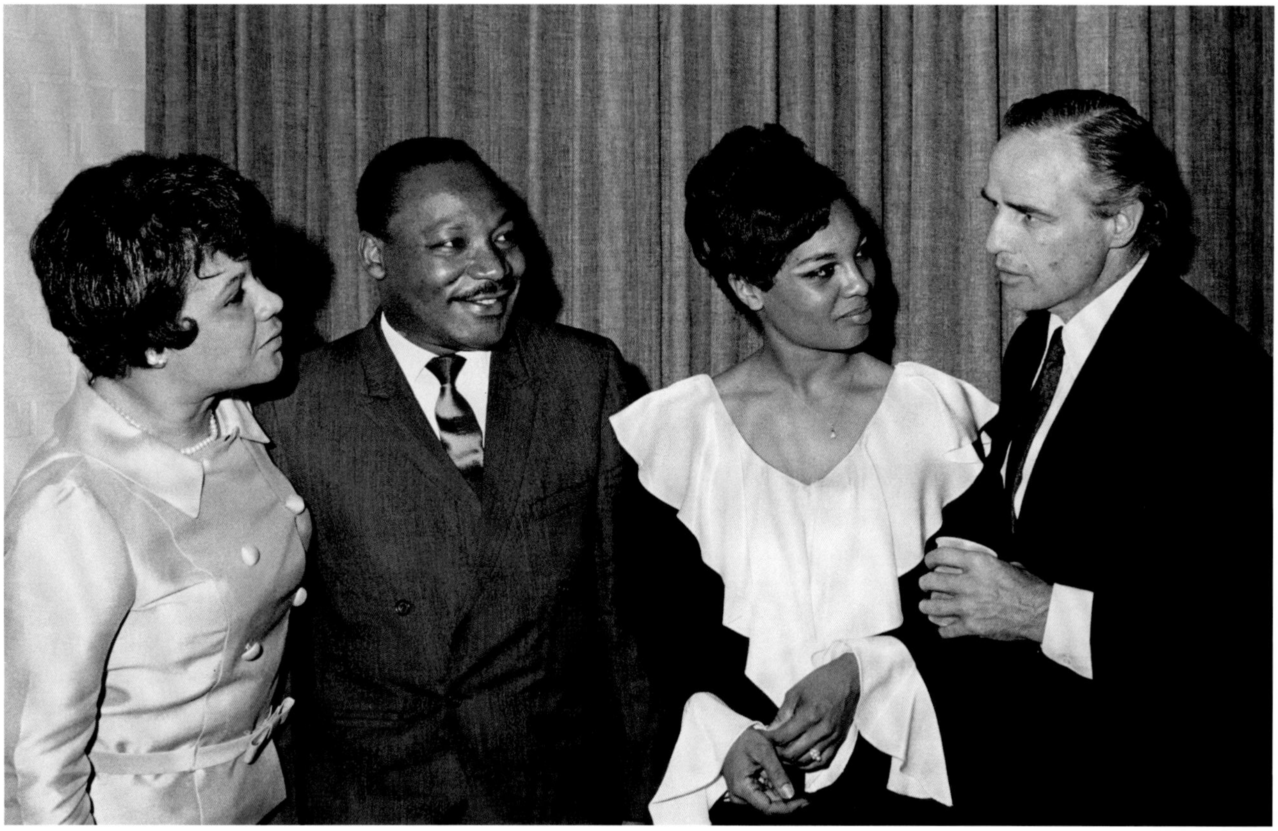

Fig. 27 HOWARD BINGHAM, 1968. *From left*: Gwen Green, Martin Luther King Jr., Claudia Green (daughter of Gwen Green), and Marlon Brando engage in conversation during King's last visit to Los Angeles before his assassination on April 4.

THE VOTING RIGHTS ACT

The attention garnered from the Selma campaign and SCOPE contributed to the passage of the Voting Rights Act on August 6, 1965. The landmark legislation guaranteed all citizens, regardless of race, the right to vote without interference. Johnson and King both recognized that, in the president's words, the "outrage of Selma" was responsible for the law.[50] In his address to the SCLC on August 11, King spoke about the movement's power: "Montgomery led to the Civil Rights Act of 1957 and 1960; Birmingham inspired the Civil Rights Act of 1964; and Selma produced the voting rights legislation of 1965."[51] The power of solidarity and the desire for change among Angelenos would reemerge as common threads throughout the tumultuous year of 1965.

RACE AND REBELLION IN WATTS

By late summer 1965, Black Angelenos had already spent decades resisting police brutality in their communities, while the city government failed to confront its root causes.[52] In addition to police violence,

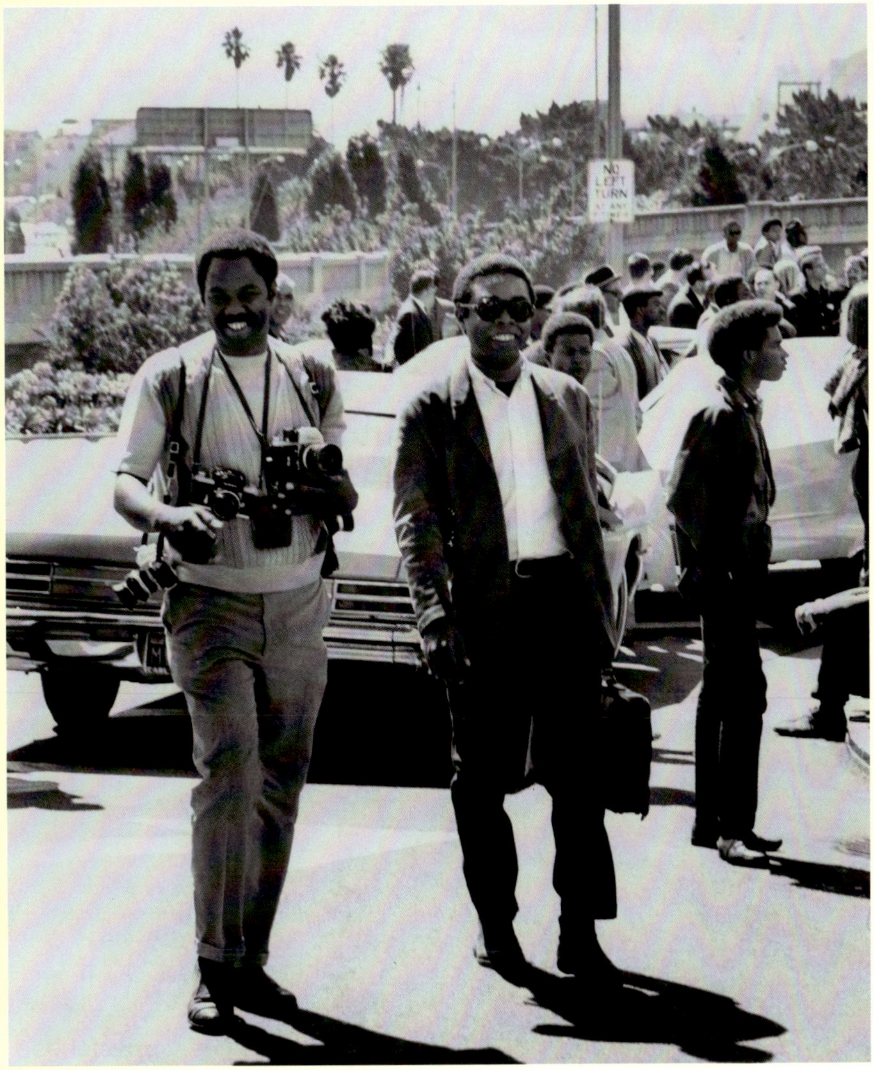

HOWARD BINGHAM

Howard Bingham (1939–2016) moved from Jackson, Mississippi, to Los Angeles as a boy and became one of the city's best-known photographers (fig. 28). Bingham attended Compton Community College but failed his photography class. He started his career at the *Los Angeles Sentinel* in the early 1960s and was trained by photographer Cliff Hall. He was later fired for spending too much time on his own studio work. Bingham's fortuitous encounter with Cassius Clay during a 1962 *Sentinel* assignment began a lifelong friendship with the boxing icon, who later changed his name to Muhammad Ali. Bingham's coverage of the Watts Uprising in 1965 led to a commission from *Life* magazine to cover the Black Panther Party, though his months-long assignment went unpublished. His other work appeared in *Ebony, Time, Newsweek,* and *Sports Illustrated*, as well as *Life*.

Fig. 28 Howard Bingham (*left*), with *Life* magazine writer Gilbert Moore, 1968.

residents in the former railroad town of Watts suffered the economic and social consequences of discrimination and inaction, from failed poverty programs to housing restrictions and overcrowding. Between 1960 and 1965, the proportion of habitable housing in Watts dropped from 82 percent to 67 percent, a trend intensified by the passage of Proposition 14. Meanwhile, subsidized freeway construction and "slum clearance" programs enabled industries and jobs to move to inaccessible suburbs, resulting in double-digit unemployment by 1965.[53] In the same period, median family income fell by 7.5 percent, while over 40 percent of Watts residents lived in poverty.[54]

On Wednesday, August 11, an urban rebellion began in Watts. The spark that ignited the uprising happened when California Highway Patrol officer Lee Minikus observed twenty-one-year-old Marquette Frye driving recklessly in a 1955 gray Buick on Avalon Boulevard at around 7 p.m. and pulled him over. Riding with Marquette was his brother, Ronald Frye, who had recently been discharged from the US Air Force. After Marquette failed a field sobriety test, he was arrested, and the car was set to be impounded. Their mother, Rena Frye, arrived at the scene and asked to take her car home rather than see it towed. As the situation unfolded, a crowd began to gather, and additional police units arrived as reinforcements. In the growing commotion, one officer clubbed Marquette with a baton. The atmosphere quickly became volatile, and Rena and Ronald joined the struggle to protect Marquette. As a result, both were also arrested (fig. 29).[55] The violence outraged bystanders and was the final straw for residents fed up with years of social inequities. What followed was a six-day revolt against not only police brutality but also poverty, poor housing conditions, and unemployment (plate 59).

Los Angeles officials declared a curfew on Friday, August 13, 1965. As noted by political scientist Jeanne Theoharis, it "only covered Black LA—an area that the media then began calling 'Watts,' although it covered the neighborhoods of Watts, Central, Avalon, Florence, Green Meadow, Exposition, and Willowbrook. That this swatch of two hundred fifty thousand residents could be effectively cordoned off from the rest of the city is a testament to the degree of segregation in LA."[56] The curfew prohibited residents from being outside their homes after 8 p.m., leading to approximately thirty-five hundred arrests, most for curfew violations.

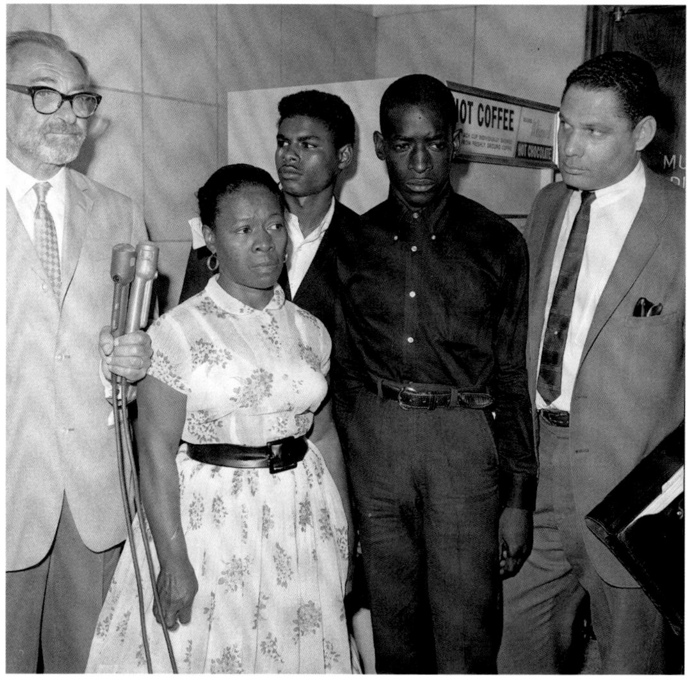

Fig. 29 *From left,* an unidentified reporter, Rena Frye, Ronald Frye, Marquette Frye, and attorney A. L. Wirin in a Los Angeles courthouse, 1965.

At least thirty-four people died as a result of the uprising, and thousands were arrested. An estimated $40 million in property was destroyed (plate 60). About fourteen thousand members of the National Guard had been deployed to help the LAPD quell the unrest.[57] On the second night, Robert Richardson, who grew up in the area and worked in

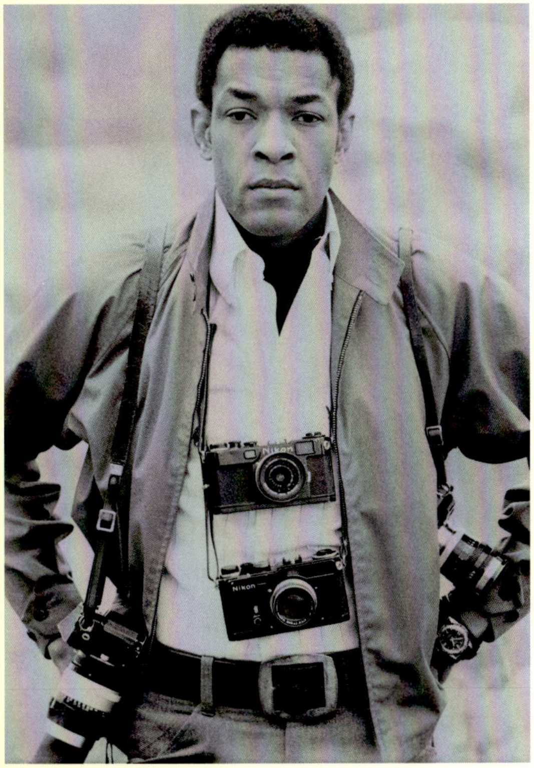

JOE FLOWERS

Joe Flowers (1927–1996) built an impressive career in Los Angeles after arriving in the city in 1957 (fig. 30). He published his freelance work in major publications through his association with the prestigious Black Star photo agency, the first privately owned photo agency in the country. As a result, his pictures and those of other photographers reached a national audience in several magazines, including *Time*, *Life*, *Paris Match*, *Ebony*, and *Sepia*. Flowers's pictures documenting the 1965 Watts Uprising, which Black Star president Howard Chapnick emphasized were taken "without regard for his personal safety," were included in a special display devoted to the revolt at the 1968 Watts Summer Festival. Flowers produced significant corporate work for Motown Records, IBM, and Miller Brewing Company and was chief photographer for the television show *Soul Train* from 1984 to 1994.

Fig. 30 Joe Flowers.

sales in the advertising department at the *Times*, was caught in the tumult. He phoned in eyewitness accounts to *Times* editors, making him unofficially the paper's first Black reporter.[58] The *Times* provided daily coverage throughout the violence and received the Pulitzer Prize for its reporting the following year.

Capturing the unrest as it unfolded was dangerous. *Jet* magazine's cover photo by Robert Flora conveyed the tense and risky work "inside a riot zone" (plate 61).[59] The news media relied on a mix of brave reporters and intrepid picture makers. A *Jet* article referenced *Time*, *Life*, *Newsweek*, the Associated Press, and CBS as just a few of the outlets quickly hiring local Black newsmen, at least temporarily, who could navigate Watts. Being Black did not guarantee safety, however, and many photographers were hurt. *Jet*'s Bill Gillohm was chased by a mob, while two freelance photographers found occasional acceptance, he said. "They would talk to us for a little while, and then they'd tell us to get the hell out of there."[60] Some, like freelancer Howard Bingham, gained exposure and opportunities to work during the uprising. Photographers captured a wide range of scenes, and their impact depended upon how the images were framed or edited. The vast majority of pictures were complicated and layered with meaning and remain so nearly six decades later. The broader view of the rebellion, as seen on the pages of mainstream newspapers and on television newscasts, resembled a war zone complete with National Guard troops, Army Jeeps, and machine guns. Text alongside the images described tactics and destruction along with enemies and injuries, not unlike scenes of the Vietnam War appearing more regularly in the news. Pictures of beaten or dead Watts residents were not printed, however.[61]

The slogan "Burn, baby, burn," said on live radio by local disc jockey Nathaniel "Magnificient" Montague, transformed from an already popular phrase about achieving goals into a rallying cry as insurgents repeated it.[62] Despite the widespread destruction of property, the young protesters largely sought to spare churches, homes, libraries, and African American businesses while targeting companies notorious for high prices and racial discrimination, which demonstrated the inherently political nature of the uprising (plate 62).[63] The highly destructive form of protest in a movement that had been largely nonviolent represented a sign of desperation (plate 63). Those who cheered, "Now they've heard about us, now they know about Watts," had been ignored until the uprising broke out.[64]

REBUILDING WATTS

After the Watts Uprising, local churches and nonprofit organizations collaborated with city and county officials and civil rights organizations to restore peace and plan for the future. As early as August 15, 1965, Brookins and fifty other local leaders met with Governor Brown to discuss extending curfew laws.[65] The Los Angeles County Board of Supervisors directed its Commission on Human Relations, led by civil rights advocate John Buggs, to develop a plan to end the violence and align community views on preserving public order.[66] One of the first meetings was held at Athens Park, about a mile from Watts. Other preexisting organizations played crucial roles in rebuilding the community. The Westminster Neighborhood Association (WNA), under Rev. Archie Hardwick's leadership, became a pivotal force in the area's recovery. Hardwick organized and distributed emergency supplies, food, and clothing to impacted residents. Collaborating with the County Human Relations Commission, the WNA organized the inaugural Watts Summer Festival in 1966, a significant event in the community's healing process. The WNA also provided a safe space for residents and community groups to convene and housed the Watts Happening Cultural Center, a vital hub and conservatory for local Black artists.

The Watts Labor Community Action Committee (WLCAC) was established a few months before the Watts Uprising and quickly became essential to the community's recovery. The organization emerged as a significant local employer, addressing one of the area's critical needs. The WLCAC also offered affordable housing options to residents. Perhaps one of its most significant achievements was the construction of the Martin Luther King Jr. Community Hospital, a vital addition to the area's infrastructure and health care services, which opened on March 27, 1972.

Assigning blame for the unrest entered rebuilding discussions and revealed deep-seated tensions among city leaders. The Black community, in general, placed the blame squarely on government officials who ignored their long-standing complaints about police abuse. White officials accused Black clergy and civil rights leadership of failing to maintain peace within their areas of influence.[67] Some of these officials argued that the Black leaders' advocacy for civil disobedience had contributed to an aggressive atmosphere that ultimately turned violent. Interestingly, Black residents also criticized clergy and civil rights leaders for focusing more on pacifying the Black community than on using their power to engage in fruitful policy negotiations with city officials.[68] These varied perspectives revealed not only the uneasiness between racial groups but also the divisions within communities.

POLITICAL DEMANDS

To bring national attention to the demands and concerns of local civil rights leaders, a coalition of prominent figures invited King to help mediate between the community and government officials. He had initially planned to visit Los Angeles in 1965 to support the WCLC's anti-poverty efforts; however, upon his arrival on August 17—just as the Watts Uprising was winding down—he made a last-minute change of plans. Despite SCLC advisers such as Bayard Rustin urging caution, King insisted on visiting the neighborhoods at the center of the conflict (plate 64).

The alliance of local leaders arranged a tour and a meeting at the WNA, in the burned-out heart of Watts, drawing an impressive crowd of five hundred. But the gathering did not proceed without incident. As King addressed the audience with his characteristic call for unity, stating, "All over America, the Negroes must join hands," he was interrupted by a heckler who added, "and burn."[69] Another man, perhaps impatient with King's philosophy of nonviolence, shouted: "We up here in Los Angeles will not turn the other cheek."[70] Others, however, treated King with respect. One woman shouted to a heckler: "You're talking to Dr. Martin Luther King. Get out, psycho."[71] In the end, Black Angelenos requested that King ask Mayor Sam Yorty and Police Chief William H. Parker to visit their community. Although King promised to do what he could, the mayor and police chief refused the invitation.

At the WNA, King met with local community members and Black ministers to assess the situation firsthand.[72] In his autobiography, King described the climate of the meeting at the WNA: "The people of Watts were hostile to nonviolence, but when we actually went to them and emphasized the dangers of hatred and violence, the same people cheered. Only minutes before, the air had been thick with tension, but when they were reminded of the Rev. James Reeb and Viola Liuzzo, the martyrs of the Selma campaign, they cheered the thought that white people can and do cooperate with us in our search for jobs and dignity."[73]

While on the ground, King also sought to mediate between Watts locals and government officials to find systemic solutions that would provide "dignity and work" while preempting more violence.[74] In his carefully crafted rhetoric, King condemned both the violence of the riots and "the violence of poverty and humiliation" that produced them.[75] He emphasized the urgency of unblocking anti-poverty programs and implementing reforms to end police terror.

During his trip, King visited the headquarters of the Los Angeles Council of Churches and had lunch with about fifty clergy. Additionally, he met with city leaders, including *Times* publisher Otis Chandler, with Kilgore participating.[76] He held press conferences and met with Governor Brown. He and Rustin held a three-hour meeting with Yorty and Parker on August 20 to convey the Black community's long-standing demands for Parker's resignation, the creation of a community-controlled police review panel, and to give legitimacy to the community's grievances. Although Yorty and the city council had officially lauded King's activism in the South, they proved unreceptive to his efforts in Los Angeles, as evidenced by the mayor's refusal to relinquish control of federal anti-poverty funds and allow community oversight. These actions revealed the contradiction between Los Angeles's public image as a land of freedom and opportunity and the reality faced by many of its residents. Rustin, who was incensed by the dismissive posture of the two L.A. officials, later recounted that his and King's discussions with Parker and Yorty "left us completely nonplussed."[77] King told reporters after the meeting that the officials "didn't agree with most of the things we said." Yorty claimed that charges of police brutality were unfounded, and that the white community would not stand for Parker's resignation. Both Yorty and Parker denied "that there was any prejudice in Los Angeles."[78] Tellingly, when King and Rustin mentioned the overwhelming vote for Proposition 14, the mayor and police chief countered, "That's no indication of prejudice. That's a personal choice."[79]

Demonstrating his dislike of King's attempt to mediate, Yorty denied the civil rights leader's request to access Lincoln Heights Jail, where many arrested during the uprising were incarcerated, claiming a visit would set off a riot. In the end, King warned Yorty and Parker that ignoring police terror and portraying Watts's youth as criminals were dangerous delusions that could provoke an urban "Holocaust." As historian Thomas F. Jackson points out, "These were among the strongest words King had ever directed toward a public official."[80]

In addition to attempting to work with city officials, local ministers asked King to appeal to the federal government to take action on unemployment, decaying housing, and police brutality in the city.[81] King offered his findings directly to President Johnson and ultimately recommended the immediate implementation of the poverty program and increased government efforts "toward obtaining full employment for both the Negro and white poor."[82] That same month, Johnson authorized $25 million for the city's poverty program.

STEERING THE NARRATIVE

The causes, events, and consequences of the Watts Uprising became the subject of significant debate and media attention. The mainstream media's approach was evident in *Life* magazine's August 1965 issue, which largely failed to discuss the conditions that led to the uprising but instead sensationalized it, claiming that the rallying cry of African Americans was "Get Whitey!" and characterizing the rebellion as a "Wild Plundering–Grab It and Run." [83] The photographic narrative mirrored the sensational emphasis on fires, violence, and looting. Black residents were shown throwing rocks and running with stolen goods, and the largest photograph—save the article's opening two-page spread—featured young brothers, ages nine and twelve, getting their mug shots taken. Pictures of injured soldiers, endangered firefighters, and law enforcement officers represented law and order, the visual opposite of a "Cauldron of Hate," "War Cry," and "Rock Throwers on a Rampage." *Life*'s readers numbered nearly fifty million in the mid-1960s, and they were witnessing a significant visual shift on the magazine's pages. For nearly a decade, nonviolent protesters were portrayed being clubbed, hosed, or spit on as they took on long-festering issues and injustice. Now, readers were seeing activists eschew peaceful tactics and engage in open rebellion.[84]

Locally, *Los Angeles Times* picture editors highlighted warlike scenes, injured officers, and a slow return to order. Sensational headlines and reporting without adequate context stoked the fears of white Angelenos, and photographs made their fears visible. The coverage of the *Times* and *Life* was not entirely unexpected. Spokespeople in the Black community who were contacted by the mainstream media did not typically represent those suffering from the worst effects of poverty; thus, those in Los Angeles's most desperate neighborhoods and communities remained largely unheard. Scholars and press veterans writing shortly after the urban unrest stated that the "Negro areas have not been considered newsworthy. Reporters rarely ventured into the Negro ghetto, rarely wrote of its problems." [85]

The *Sentinel*'s Watts coverage went to press on August 19, a week after the uprising began. The weekly newspaper's August 12 issue was ready for newsstands when the trouble broke out. Though unable to provide breaking news coverage, the *Sentinel* offered a variety of reports and perspectives. Articles expressed regret and dismay over the destruction but also took Parker and the LAPD to task and called out Yorty for held-up poverty funds. The August 19 issue included eighteen photographs, including some of looting and fires, visually similar to the *Times.* Notably different, however, was that the *Sentinel* printed several arrest photos, including one titled "Brute Force" and two with police batons around the necks of Black residents. The harsh tactics were made visible, as was a throng of Watts residents outside the offices of the Non-Violent Action Committee (N-VAC) in search of bread and milk. There were also pictures of Black-owned businesses that had been spared. Several reporters and photographers provided firsthand accounts of the dangerous conditions, including an Air Force veteran, Howard Morehead, who said that, in Watts, "I saw a city under siege as if in the eye of a wartime battle." [86]

MCCONE REPORT: VIOLENCE IN THE CITY

A week after the uprising, Governor Brown sponsored an investigation to identify its causes, propose solutions, and prevent future violence. The resulting McCone Commission report cited unemployment, substandard education, and poor living conditions as potential causes. On the issue of police brutality, the commission recommended strengthening the oversight capabilities of the Police Commissioners Board and called for "a better understanding by the law enforcement agencies of Negro community attitudes and, on the other hand, a more widespread understanding within the Negro community of the value of the police and the extent to which the law enforcement agencies provide it with security."[87]

Adding insult to injury, the report minimized Black poverty by pathologizing Black families as "matriarchal" and blaming violence on Black men's wounded masculinity. This "culture of poverty" theory, made famous in 1965 by the Moynihan Report and echoed in the McCone Commission's report, according to Rustin, "steers clear of confronting the thorny issues of Negro unemployment as such" and deflected socioeconomic problems of educational achievement, hiring discrimination, and police brutality onto the Black community.[88]

Later that fall, an article that King wrote for the *Saturday Review* intimated that Los Angeles should have anticipated the violent consequences "when its officials tied up federal aid in political manipulation; when the rate of Negro unemployment soared above the depression levels of the 1930s; when the population density of Watts became the worst in the nation; and when the state of California repealed a law that prevented discrimination in housing."[89] The local media also warranted some of the blame. Authors of the 426-page report by the Kerner Commission, produced in 1967 after nationwide urban unrest, faulted the national media for failing to communicate the harsh realities, along with the successes, of being Black.[90] Recognizing the dearth of mainstream news coverage of the Black community, the Kerner Commission, appointed by President Johnson, recommended that the media "integrate Negroes and Negro activities into all aspects of coverage and content, including newspaper articles and television programming. The news media must publish newspapers and produce programs that recognize the existence and activities of Negroes as a group within the community and as a part of the larger community."[91] Thirteen years after the US Supreme Court struck down the "separate but equal" doctrine in *Brown v. Board of Education*, the commission issued a dire warning: "Our nation is running toward two societies, one Black, one white—separate and unequal."[92]

4

Plates

As the fight for equality gained momentum around the country, it rose to a boiling point in Los Angeles in 1965. Students, community leaders, ministers, and Hollywood stars like Harry Belafonte and Marlon Brando joined local protests or traveled to support major campaigns in the South. Everyday Angelenos marched for miles, proudly raising protest signs high. Some were dragged, hoisted, and wrestled from the downtown Federal Building as they demanded federal protection for activists in Selma. Others blocked vehicles, determined to protest for fair housing in their city. The Non-Violent Action Committee (N-VAC) attacked discriminatory hiring practices by picketing Van de Kamp's Holland Dutch Bakery. N-VAC disrupted business inside Van de Kamp's with sit-ins and sip-ins and picketed outside, even in the rain. Bruce Hartford was among the committed N-VAC activists who developed an interest in taking pictures that were sometimes used for leaflets and publicity. When Hartford traveled to Selma in 1965 after seeing footage of beatings at the Edmund Pettus Bridge, he documented the experience from a participant's point of view.[93] He was just one of many Angelenos who risked their lives far from home.

The Watts Uprising in August turned the nation's attention to Los Angeles. Sparked by an incident of police violence following a traffic stop, the six-day revolt also showed the community's yearslong frustration with poverty, poor housing, and unemployment. Images of rioting and burning buildings became etched into America's consciousness as newscasts, newspapers, and magazines reached millions of viewers and readers nationwide. The range of visuals featured plumes of smoke billowing high above commercial districts. Pictures of heavily armed police officers and African Americans under arrest quickly followed. Then came an overwhelming focus on residents looting property amid the chaos. This tenor was set in motion by the *Los Angeles Times* and its picture editors as the organization delivered fast-breaking coverage. Dramatic scenes, such as Robert Flora's shot of LAPD officers positioned behind a street sign along Vernon Avenue, landed on magazine covers.

The heavy police presence and military Jeeps reinforced the idea of the LAPD as an occupying force in Black neighborhoods. Angry residents targeted retailers and looted or burned shops known to discriminate against local residents. The subsequent McCone Commission, which investigated the causes of the uprising, noted with interest that "no residences were deliberately burned, that damage to schools, libraries, public buildings were minimal, and that certain types of business establishments, notably service stations and automobile dealers, were for the most part unharmed."[94] Photographer Joe Flowers documented a sidewalk strewn with shards of glass, and Dick Stone pictured a barbershop that remained undamaged with a sign taped to its window to signal Black ownership.

City leaders and authorities feigned surprise at the unrest in Watts despite decades of warnings. Black newspapers and photographers worked hard to make activism visible, but the *Times* largely ignored the festering issues. Concerns about underfunded and segregated schools or police brutality were often buried. Employment discrimination was brushed aside. Editorials questioned calls for decisive action or second-guessed local Black leaders. The absence of a single Black reporter on the *Times* staff when Watts exploded seems unthinkable in retrospect.[95] The *Times*, like so many US media sources, failed to communicate the Black experience to its readers. Few Black Angelenos were asked for their perspectives over the years, and few were surprised by the outburst in 1965.

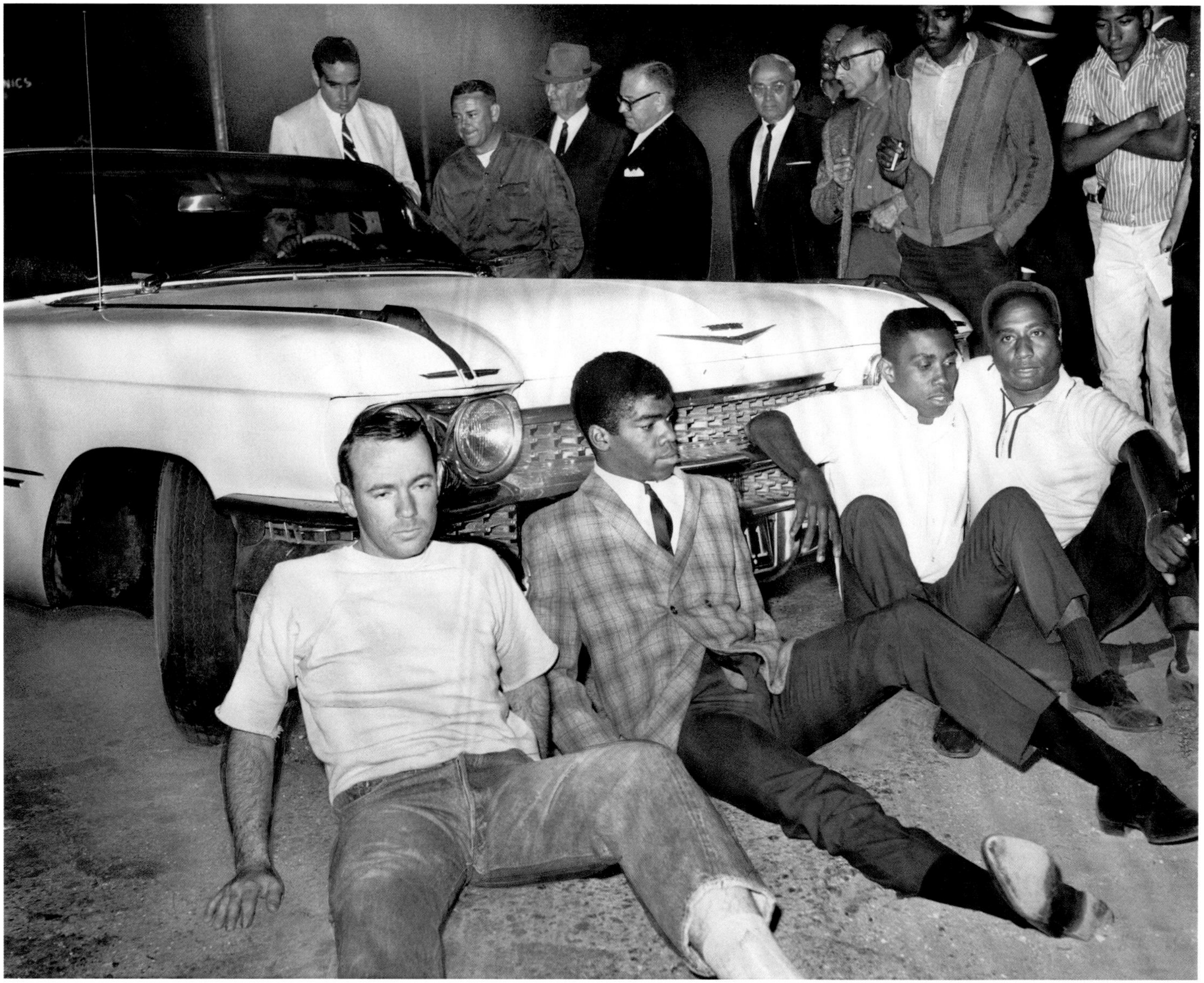

Plate 51 UNKNOWN PHOTOGRAPHER, 1964

Four CORE activists block a car driven by a real estate agent trying to leave a Southwest Realty Board meeting. CORE picketers lay down in the parking lot and blocked exits to call attention to ongoing housing discrimination citywide. This picture was part of the May 26 *Los Angeles Herald Examiner* coverage of fourteen arrests at the demonstration.

Plate 52 BOB MARTIN, 1964

N-VAC picketers march in the rain against discriminatory hiring practices at a Van de Kamp's Holland Dutch Bakery on Laurel Canyon Boulevard in North Hollywood. Bob Martin's picture ran on the front page of the March 23 *Valley Times,* a daily San Fernando Valley newspaper.

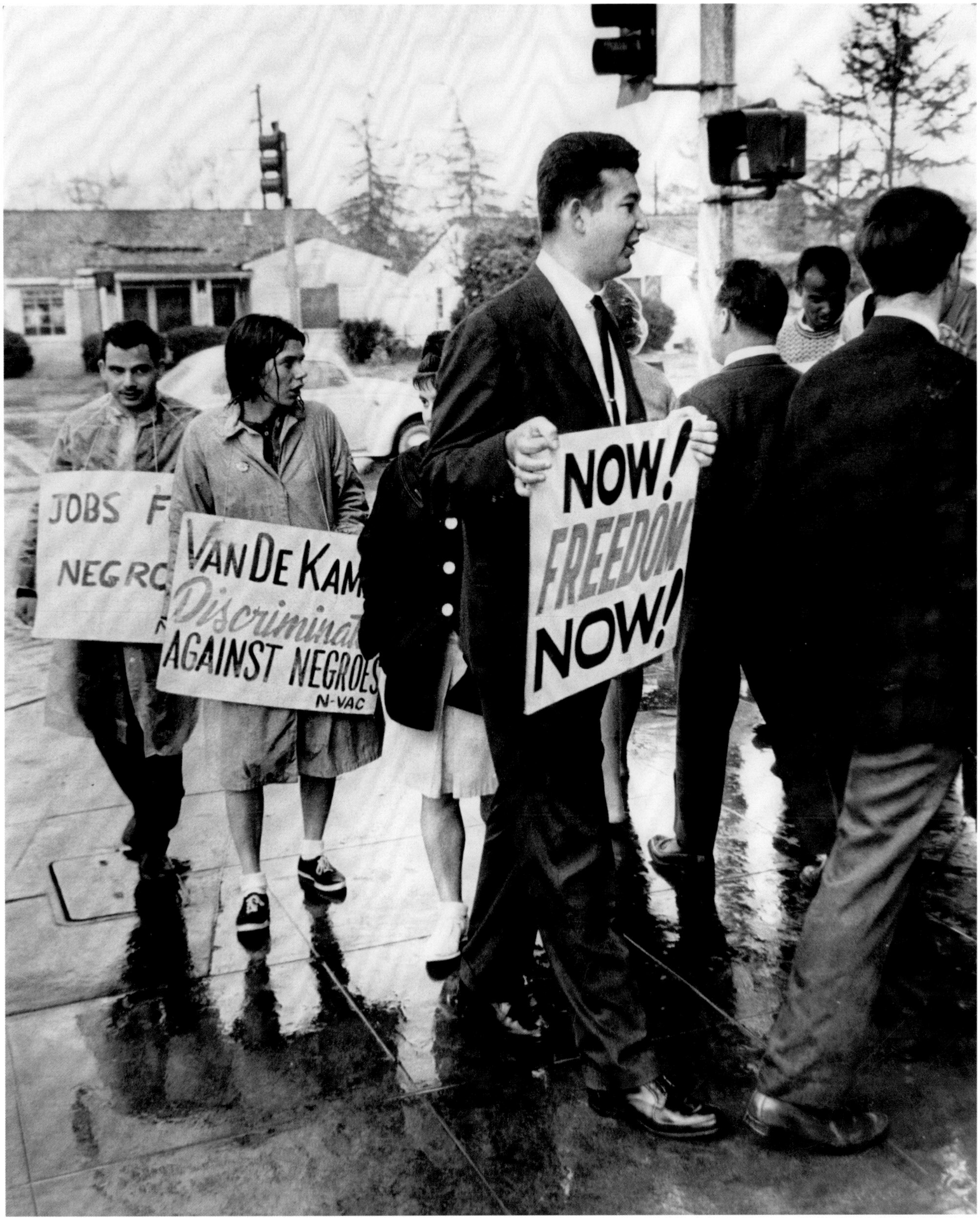
JOBS F
NEGRO
VAN DE KAM
Discriminat
AGAINST NEGROES
N-VAC
NOW!
FREEDOM
NOW!

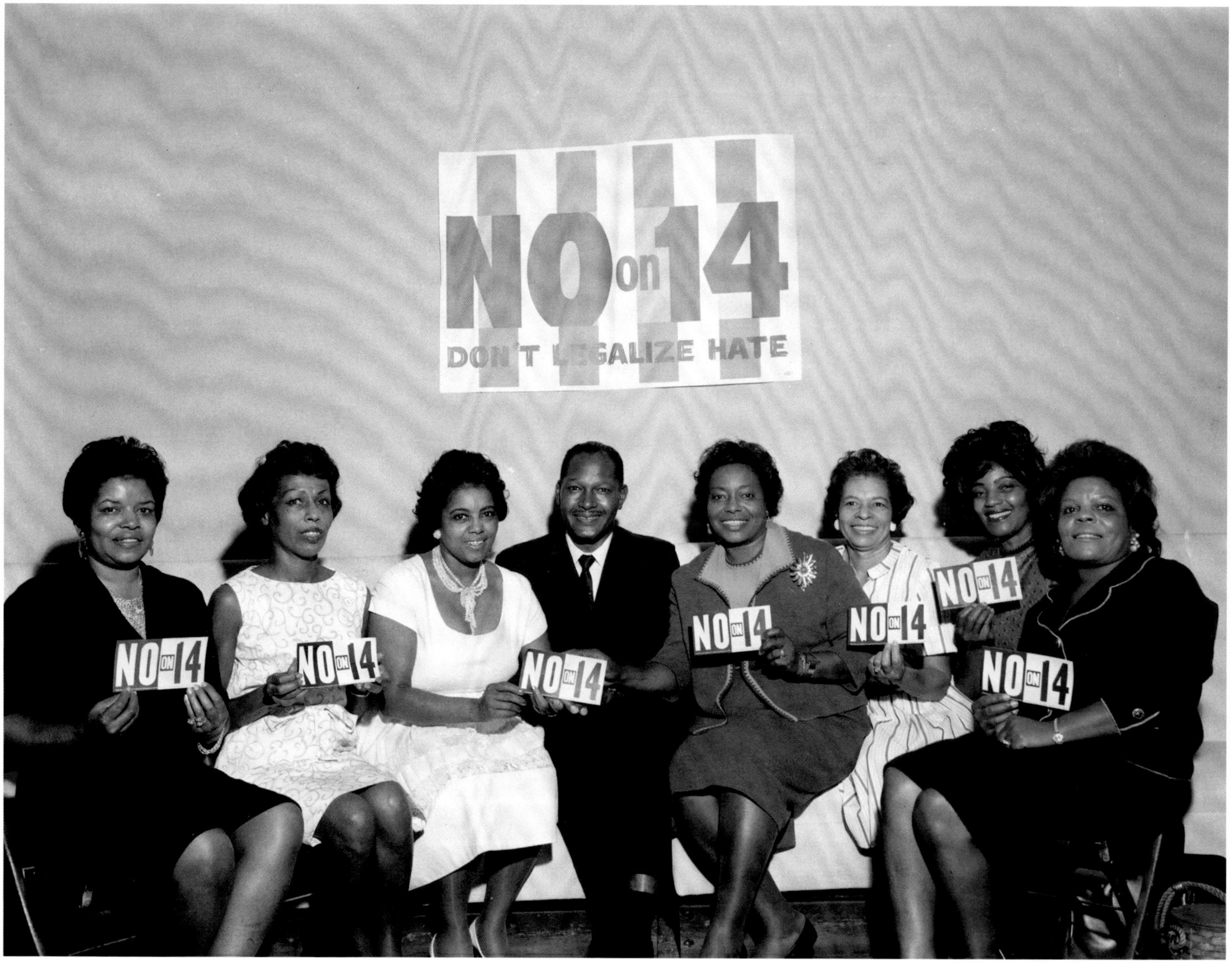

Plate 53 UNKNOWN PHOTOGRAPHER, 1964
City council member Tom Bradley (*center*), who in 1973 would become the first Black mayor of Los Angeles, is flanked by members of the Long Beach Fair Housing Foundation at a fundraiser in October against Proposition 14. The divisive measure, led by the California Real Estate Association, sought to repeal a state law called the Rumford Fair Housing Act, which prohibited housing discrimination.

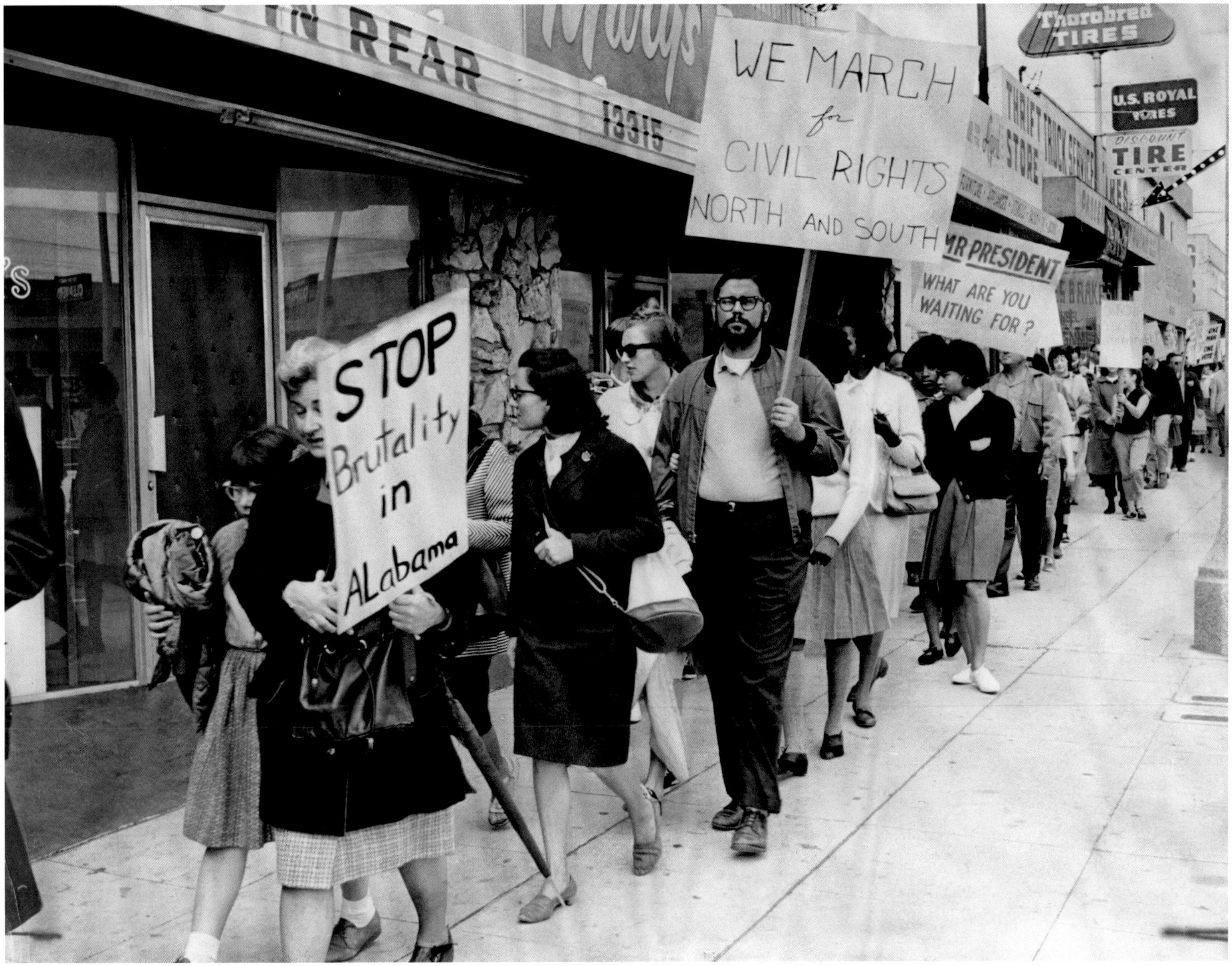

Plate 54 STEVE YOUNG, 1965

Interracial marchers protest the brutal repression of voting rights demonstrators in Selma. Sympathy protests like this twelve-mile trek from Pacoima to Van Nuys on March 13 broke out nationwide, with signs imploring President Lyndon B. Johnson to act.

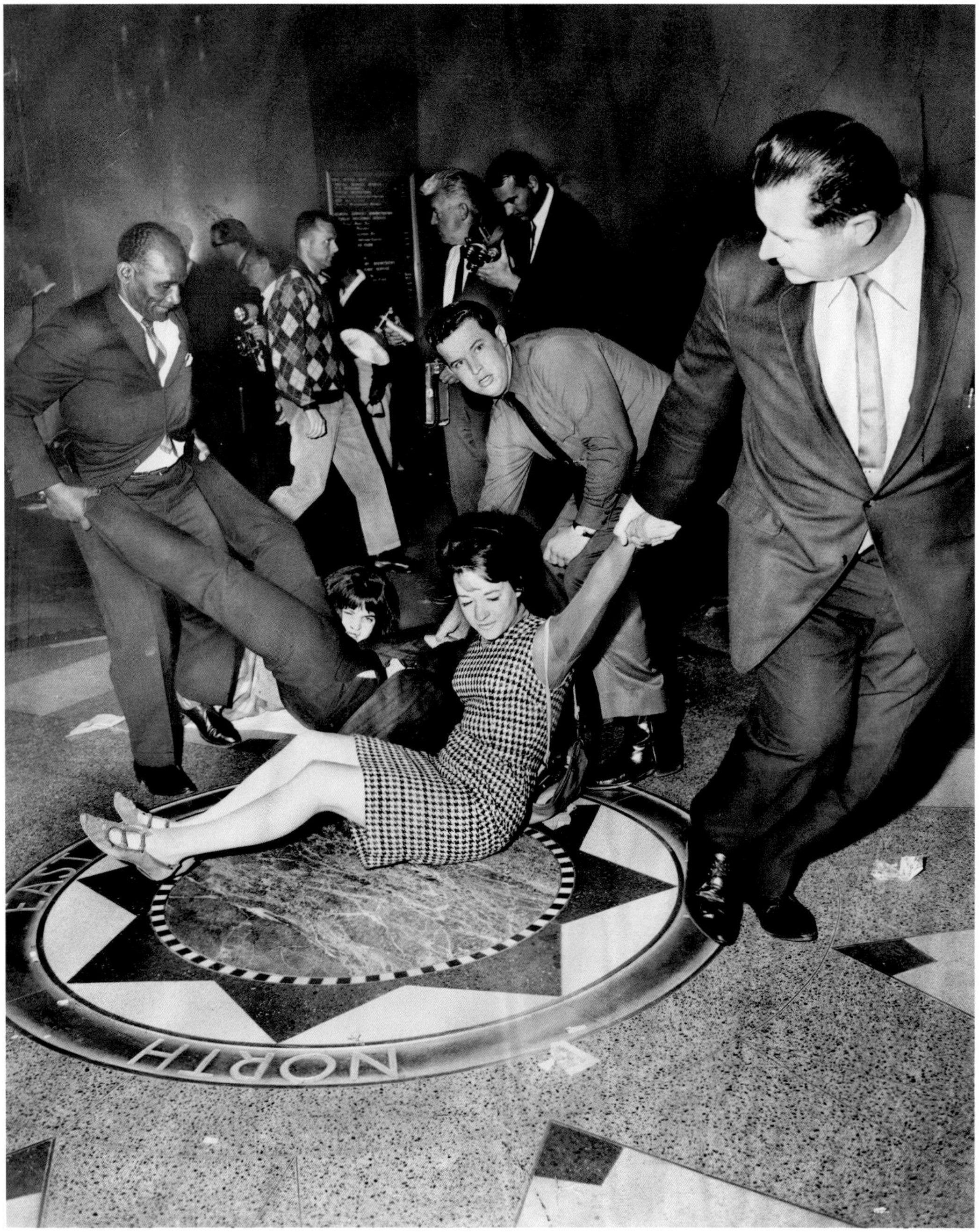

Plate 55 CLIFF WESSELMANN, 1965

Protesters hold a demonstration inside the Federal Building in downtown Los Angeles in reaction to brutality in Selma. The three protesters visible here went limp and were dragged across the floor on their way to being arrested. Cliff Wesselmann captured this view for the *Los Angeles Herald Examiner*.

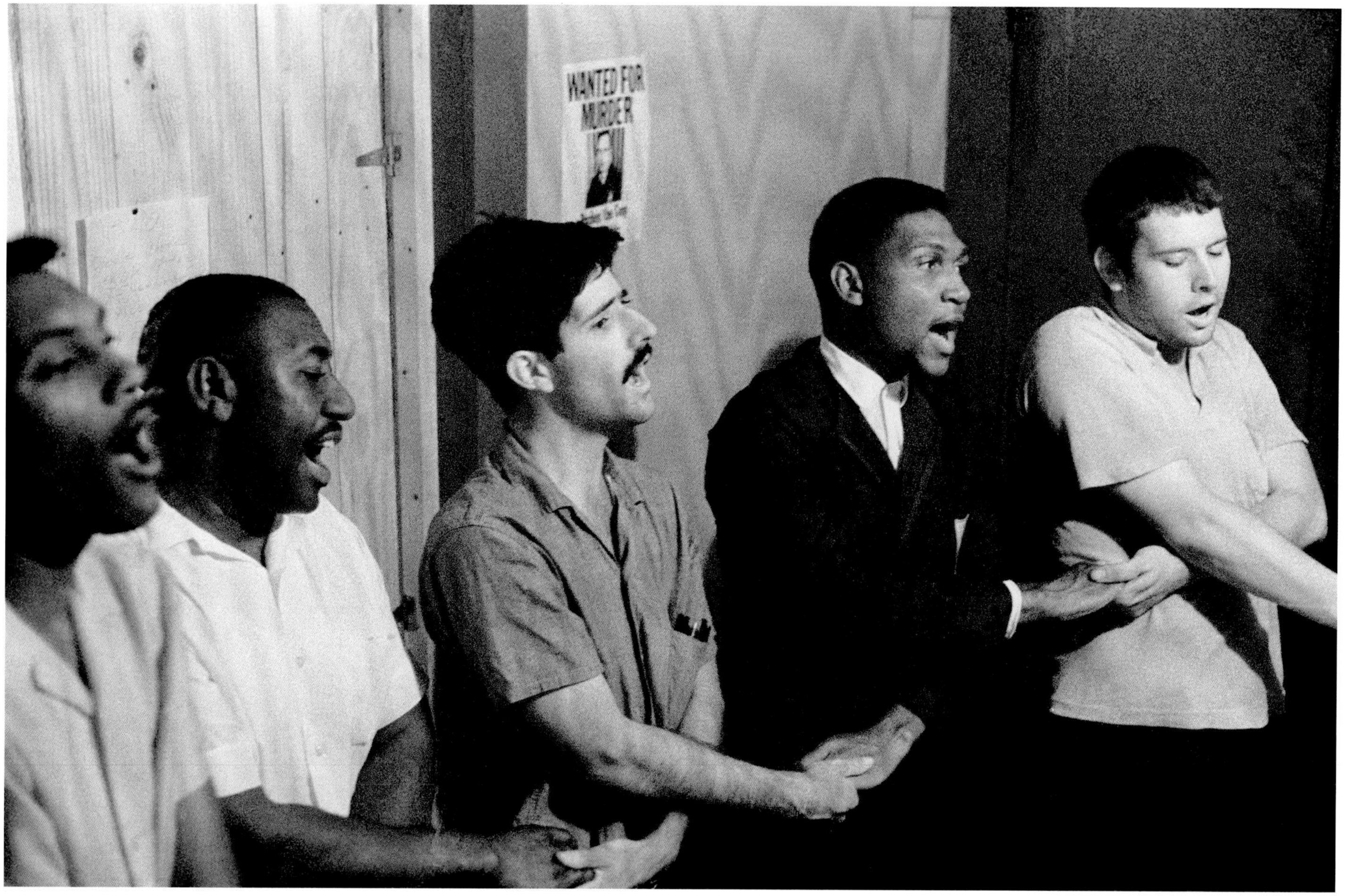

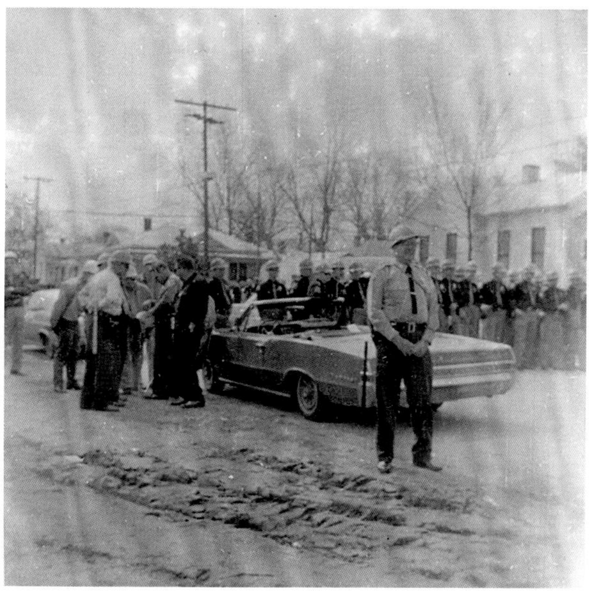

Plate 56 JOHN PHILLIPS, 1965

Los Angeles activist Bruce Hartford (*center*) links arms and sings freedom songs at the SCLC Freedom House in Selma before the Selma to Montgomery march. *Life* magazine photographer John Phillips took this picture of Hartford, who volunteered on the security crew to protect hundreds of marchers as they slept along the route. Hartford joined more than twenty-five thousand others on the final march in Montgomery to the Capitol steps to hear Martin Luther King Jr. speak.

Plate 57 BRUCE HARTFORD, 1965

Bruce Hartford documented his experiences in Selma with a borrowed camera and a single roll of film. He captured this formation of Alabama troopers and police officers, known for their unprovoked brutality against demonstrators. His casual images represent the perspective of an ordinary citizen during a pivotal moment in the country's history.

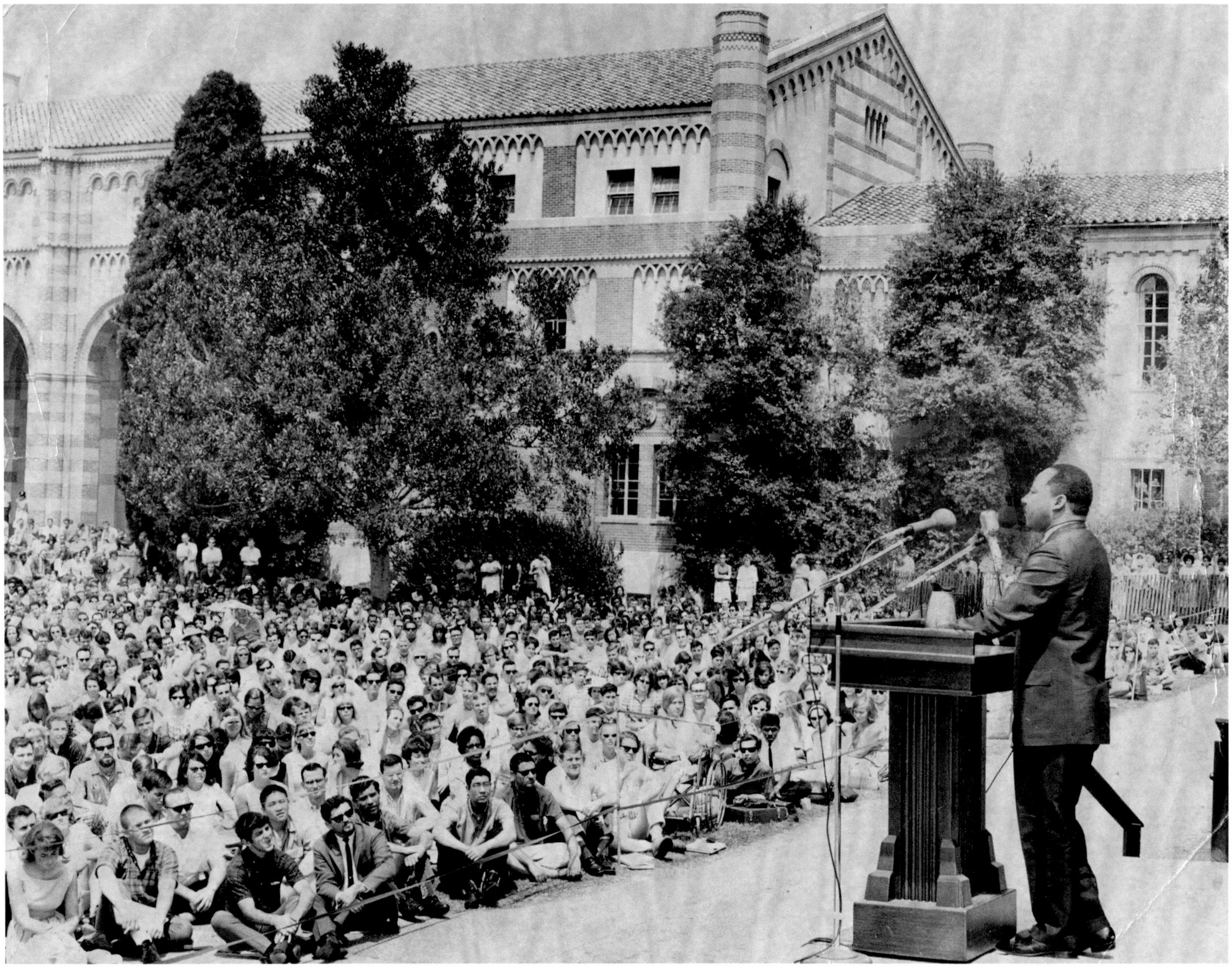

Plate 58 UNKNOWN PHOTOGRAPHER, 1965
Martin Luther King Jr. speaks to a massive crowd at UCLA about the SCLC's initiative to increase voter registration in Black communities in more than one hundred Southern counties. King continued to draw significant crowds and inspire hope among young people in Los Angeles and beyond.

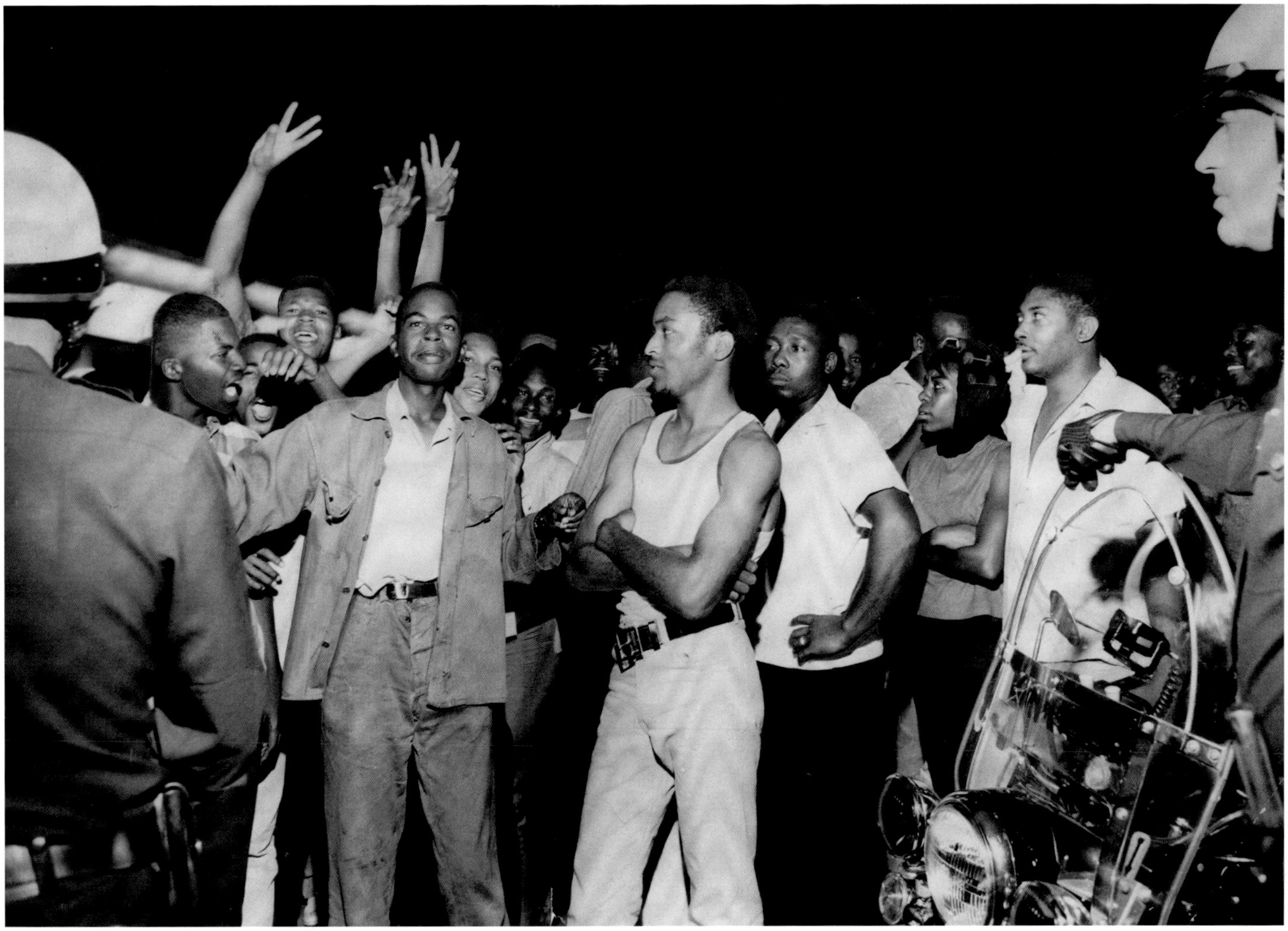

Plate 59 DON CORMIER, 1965

Cormier, a *Los Angeles Times* photographer, captured the tension and energy of a growing crowd of residents near Imperial Highway and Avalon Boulevard, close to the location where Marquette Frye had been arrested. Violence would soon erupt in Watts and last six days.

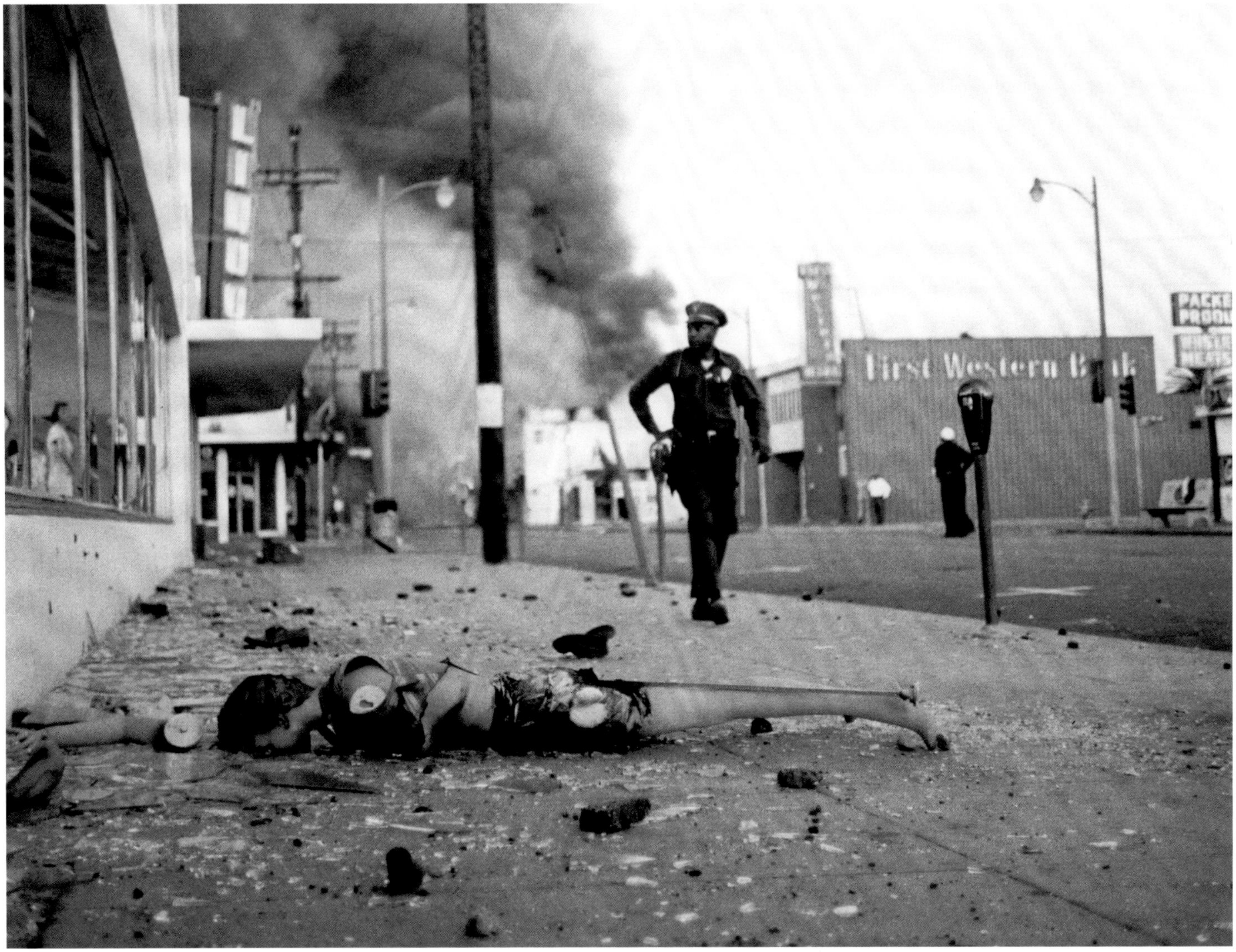

Plate 60 JOE FLOWERS, 1965

An LAPD officer patrols a debris-strewn sidewalk outside storefronts in Watts. A charred store mannequin missing most of its limbs lies facedown as smoke billows from distant buildings. This picture by freelance photographer Joe Flowers focuses on the destruction caused by the Watts Uprising rather than on individual looters.

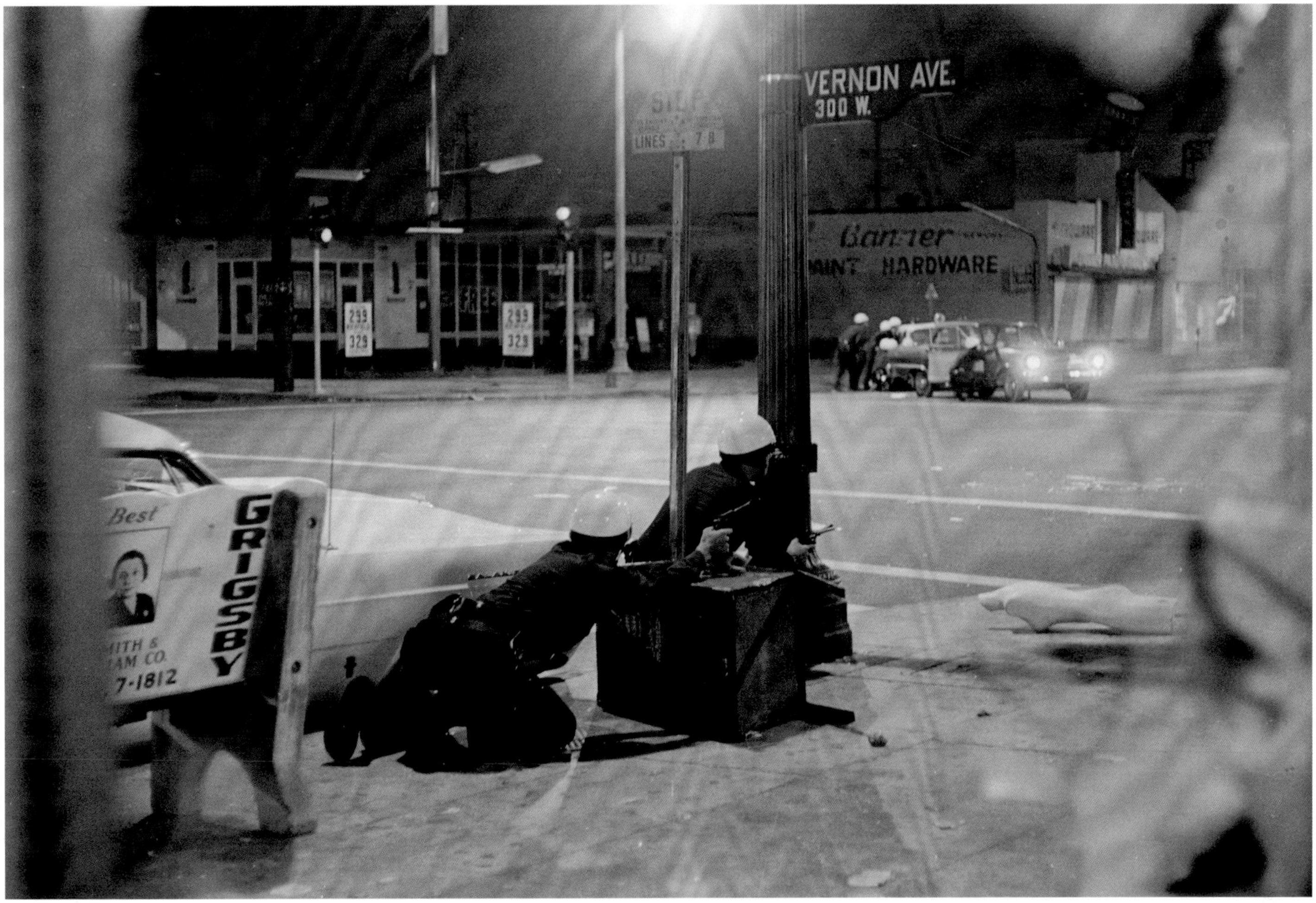

Plate 61 ROBERT FLORA, 1965

Police officers seek cover along Vernon Avenue during the Watts Uprising. Robert Flora's picture provides an up-close look at the situation and the perspective of officers fearful of snipers. *Jet* magazine published the UPI photographer's image on its September 2 cover, promising a special report on "Life Inside a Riot Zone."

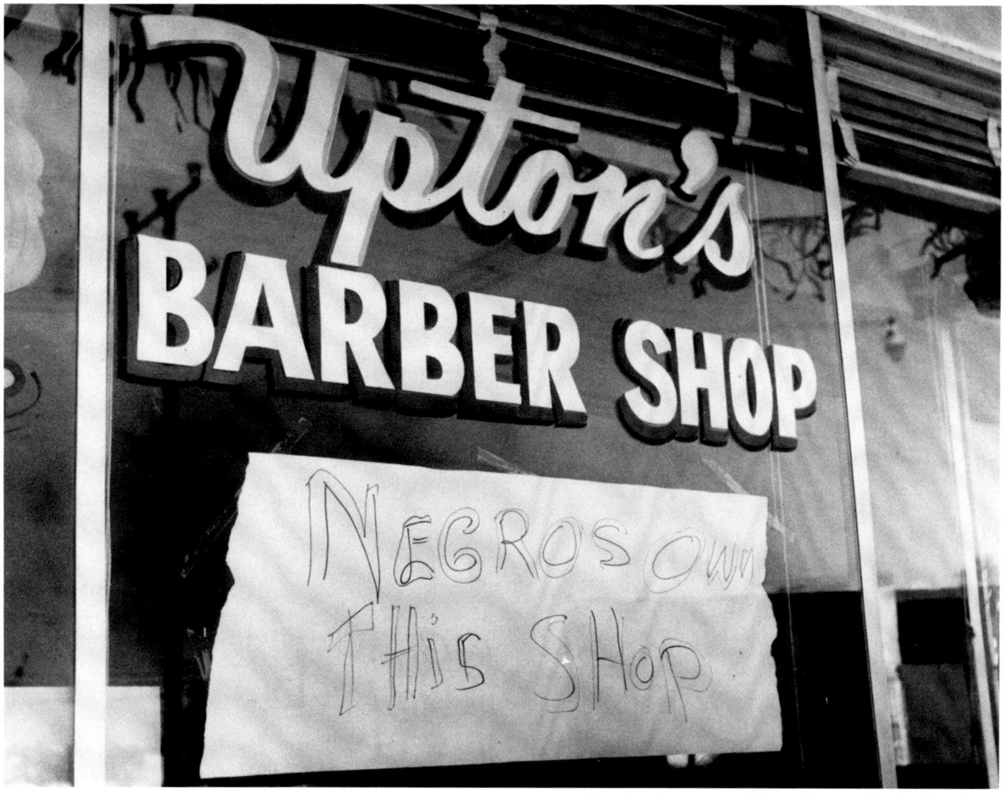

Plate 62 DICK STONE, 1965

A Black-owned barbershop at 106th and Avalon survived the destruction of the Watts Uprising. Many small-business owners scrawled messages or posted hastily made signs on their windows to deter looters. This image was printed in the August 19 issue of the *Los Angeles Sentinel*.

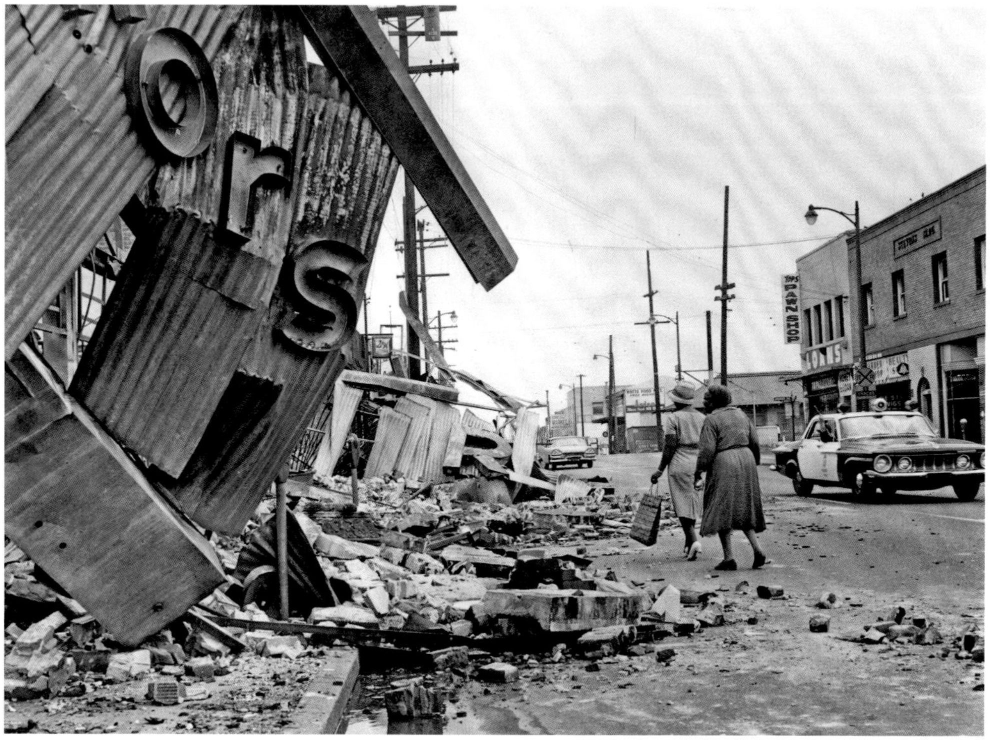

Plate 63 R. L. OLIVER, 1965

Two women pass a destroyed store on 103rd Street. The calm scene, perhaps meant to suggest a return of safety and access, appeared on the front page of the *Los Angeles Times* on August 17th below the headline, “Riot Is Over.”

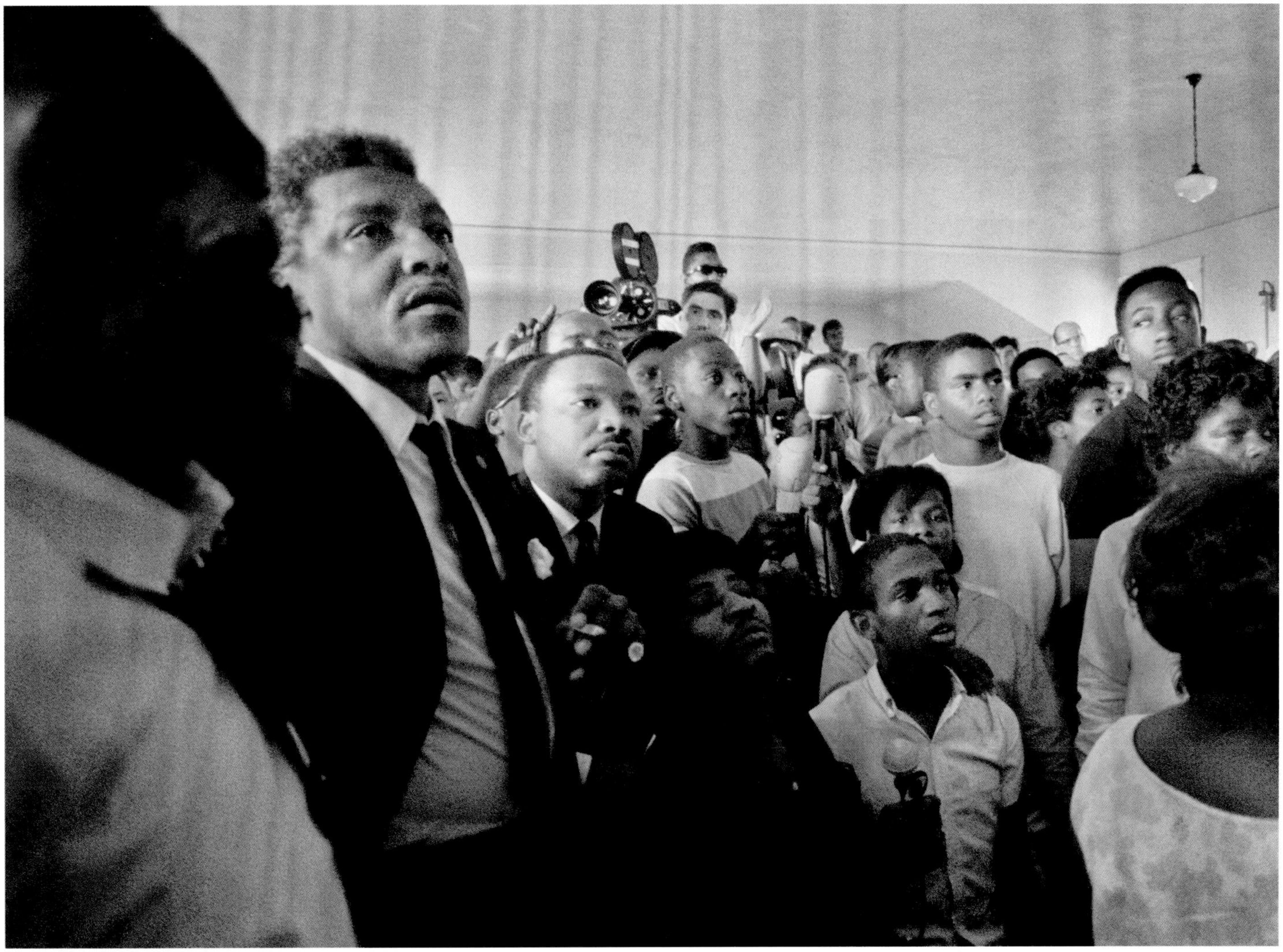

Plate 64 LAWRENCE SCHILLER, 1965

Martin Luther King Jr. (*third from left*) and activist Bayard Rustin (*second from left*) listen intently during a meeting at the Westminster Neighborhood Association in Watts. Though Rustin tried to dissuade him, King insisted on visiting the community at the center of the recent uprising. Schiller covered the Watts Rebellion and its aftermath for *Newsweek* magazine.

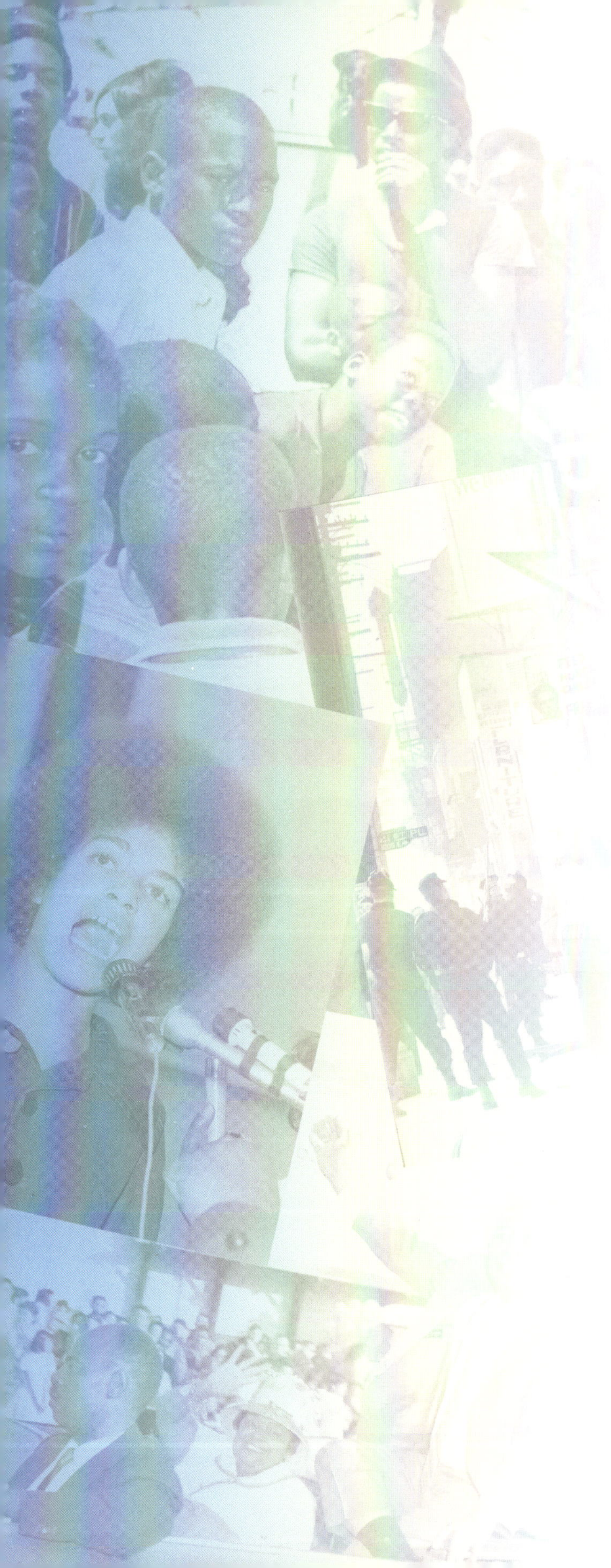

5

Still Strong

On the night of June 16, 1966, twenty-four-year-old SNCC chair Stokely Carmichael—just hours after being released from jail for trespassing—stood in front of a crowd of fifteen hundred at Broad Street Park in Greenwood, Mississippi, and made a declaration that would change the course of the civil rights movement. "This is the twenty-seventh time I have been arrested," he said. "I ain't going to jail no more. We been saying freedom for six years, and we ain't got nothing. What we got to start saying now is Black Power! We want Black Power."[1] With that bold pronouncement, the civil rights movement took a generational turn from peaceful disobedience to direct rebellion. Young activists began raising both their voices and their clenched fists, demanding immediate justice. This evolving movement, inspired by the Black nationalism of Malcolm X, slain in 1965, resonated with young African Americans who were more concerned about self-determination and self-defense than integration and nonviolence. Carmichael became the face of Black Power and the subject of numerous books, newspapers, and magazine stories seeking to explain the movement's new tone and changing tactics.

In Los Angeles, where the embers of the Watts Uprising a year earlier were still smoldering, the move toward Black Power picked up steam. A rally featuring Carmichael was organized by the fledgling Black Congress, an umbrella organization representing South Central Los Angeles's fervent mix of civil rights organizations, community service entities, and Black nationalist groups, including the Black Panther Party and the US Organization. On November 26, 1966, at Will Rogers Memorial Park (now Ted Watkins Memorial Park) in Watts, a crowd of more than three thousand roared in response to Carmichael's rhetoric explaining Black Power ideology and advocating for its practice (plate 65). In his fiery style, he took on President Lyndon B. Johnson, recalling how the president declared, "We shall overcome," when he announced the Civil Rights Act of 1964. "But you will not hear him yell 'Black Power,'" Carmichael said, according to the *Los Angeles Sentinel*. Carmichael also called for Black Americans to redefine themselves. "We've got to say we are Black and beautiful."[2] Carmichael's visit coincided with his meteoric rise and was covered extensively in the *Los Angeles Times*.[3] Notably, both the *Times* and *Sentinel* remarked on the calm and orderly crowd. Carmichael would return to appreciative Los Angeles audiences as he became the leading voice in the growing movement. Howard Bingham photographed Carmichael alongside leading Black Power advocates in 1968 (plate 66). The civil rights leader faced significant challenges from politicians and the mainstream media who would cast Black Power advocates as divisive and a force to be feared.[4]

By 1966, profound changes had occurred in the broader landscape of the freedom movement, evidenced by a clear geographic shift. "Whereas 71 percent of all movement-initiated events in the years 1961 to 1965 occurred in the South, the comparable proportion for the succeeding five-year period was less than half (34 percent) the earlier figure," reported sociologist Doug McAdam.[5] Exciting news and images of the Black Power movement inspired young African Americans all over the country to engage in more assertive action.

The mainstream media were also transformed. The absence of a single Black reporter on the *Times* staff in a city with roughly three hundred fifty thousand Black residents when Watts exploded seems unthinkable in retrospect.[6] In the weeks after the uprising, new recruits added more diverse perspectives. An October 10, 1965, article—one in a seven-part series in the *Times*—included a photo of Jack Jones, a Black reporter, interviewing a twenty-year-old man who talked about taking part in civil rights demonstrations but needing work to survive (fig. 31). The Pulitzer Prize–winning series gathered the perspectives of residents, especially young people, to better understand the underlying causes of the desperate situation in Watts. Not surprisingly, the status of Black photographers at the paper was similar to that of reporters. Over the years, countless photographers had applied unsuccessfully for jobs there. Guy Crowder, who became the

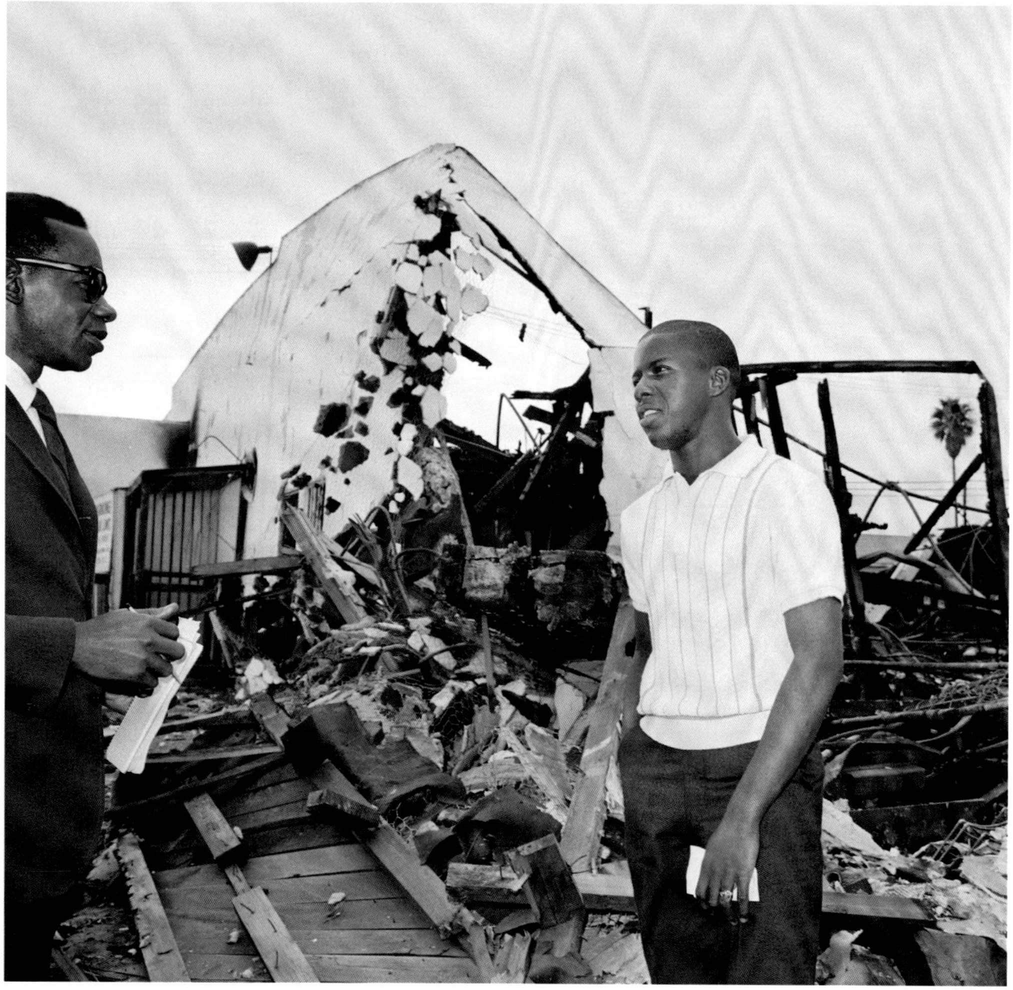

Fig. 31 Watts resident Charles Steppes speaks with *Los Angeles Times* reporter Jack Jones (*left*) for a seven-part series that ran in the newspaper in October 1965.

first Black photographer for the Los Angeles County Board of Supervisors, was among those rejected. The *Times* did not hire its first Black photographer, Fitzgerald Whitney, until 1968.[7] Whitney's photographs of the unfolding drama in South Central were an important stepping stone to his three-decade career as a staff photographer.

While the *Times* was slow to change, Watts pushed the newspaper toward more inclusivity. Still, it remained "the least trusted news medium in Los Angeles among Black residents," according to a book published in 1977, which reported that even the *Times*'s management recognized that "all the media in Los Angeles, including the *Times*, were derelict in not exposing conditions in Watts."[8] Although more media attention would be paid to Black Angelenos, the subtle shifts could not change how Watts coverage had frightened the white population, justifying added repression in the eyes of many. The uprising seemingly lent credence to white fears of a rebellious Black population, and the call for Black Power carried a strong message. Public attention to Black Power was perhaps one of the most significant outcomes of the Watts Uprising.

By 1966, Black nationalism had been embraced by the racially mixed groups SNCC and CORE, and some chapters removed white activists from leadership positions and advised them to organize for social justice within their own communities. Locally, Black Power ideology and initiatives from older organizations, such as the Universal Negro Improvement Association and the Nation of Islam, were reinvigorated. Undoubtedly, the uprising led to a dramatic transformation of the social landscape as organizations that emerged from the ashes of Watts gained traction for their diverse beliefs and strategies. These groups adopted a distinctly militant character, representing a qualitative change in the Black freedom movement from 1965 to 1975. Scholars Sundiata Keita Cha-Jua and Clarence Lang emphasize this distinction, asserting that Black Power activism possesses its own history, characteristics, ideologies, and culture. Elements of Black radicalism, Pan-Africanism, and Black feminism are accepted in this shifting environment.[9]

FREEDOM CITY

This new orientation was evident in a proposal advocated by several Black organizations for Watts and its surrounding unincorporated areas to secede from Los Angeles and become a "Freedom City."[10] Although clearly rooted in the self-determination aspect of Black Power, secession gained backing from mainstream organizations and even some Black political leaders who believed the proposed Freedom City—bounded by the Harbor Freeway, Vernon Avenue, Alameda Street, and El Segundo Boulevard—could be economically viable with federal government support. In the end, the proposal failed due to bureaucratic obstacles to placing the measure on ballots and a lack of support from NAACP national leadership.[11]

WATTS SUMMER FESTIVAL

One idea brought to fruition was the Watts Summer Festival. Initially conceived as a dance, it expanded into a cultural celebration commemorating the uprising, fostering community pride, and supporting local development efforts. Local leader Tommy Jacquette, head of Self-Leadership for All Nationalities Today (SLANT), was hired by the Westminster Neighborhood Association (WNA) to recruit Black youth to work in programs serving the community. Jacquette became a Watts Summer Festival committee member and its executive director.[12] Billy Tidwell, a social worker and another founder of the Watts Summer Festival, recruited and organized young people under the banner of "Sons of Watts," an anti-riot, activist peace organization he had begun earlier. The average age of its members was twenty-five, and most were unemployed. Some had participated in the uprising or were former gang members.[13]

The first Watts Summer Festival took place August 12–14, 1966, with the Sons of Watts serving as crowd control. Approximately ten thousand people attended the event at Will Rogers Memorial Park on the first day. Photographs of dancing, rides, booths, and a parade captured the joyful community roots of the now iconic festival (plate 67). Its primary focus was the celebration of Black heritage, and it offered informational booths showcasing services from public and private programs. Entertainment featured various dance and musical acts, including Zulu dancers and renowned trumpeter Hugh Masekela. Arts and crafts were displayed and African jewelry and clothing were sold. The festival's pinnacle was its parade, in which R. Sargent Shriver, architect of the War on Poverty programs, served as marshal. The parade also featured the winner of the Miss Watts beauty contest, twenty-one-year-old Tamu Harper (plate 68).[14] The *Sentinel* featured Harper on its front page and eighteen pictures of the festival inside. All were taken by Harry Adams. The *Times* covered the event on its front page and placed one picture of Miss Watts and two of the parade inside. This was notable because prior to the uprising, the *Times* gave little to no attention to Black community events.[15]

The festival embodied what scholars labeled the "Black aesthetic," a form of self-representation

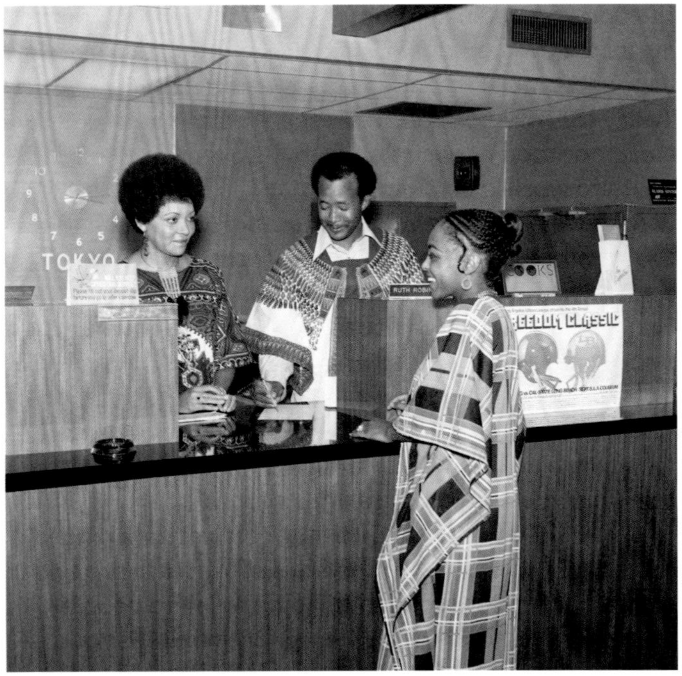

Fig. 32 GUY CROWDER, 1973. Employees greet a customer at the Watts branch of California Federal Bank.

popularized during the mid-1960s and 1970s in which African Americans transformed their outward appearance and cultural expressions to reflect their values and beliefs (fig. 32).[16] The Black aesthetic was formalized within the Black Arts Movement (BAM) and appeared in various aspects of Black life, including hairstyles, fashion, clothing, and language.

BLACK ARTS MOVEMENT

Writer and poet Larry Neal called BAM the sister of the Black Power movement, given its alignment with Black nationalism and expressions against oppression. He argued that the difference between BAM and the Harlem Renaissance of the 1920s was that the Harlem Renaissance was an "emergent" exploration of Blackness, while BAM spoke clearly about the power of Black self-identity and loudly expressed pride and self-respect in its slogan, "Black Is Beautiful."[17] Other leading voices in BAM included Sonia Sanchez and Nikki Giovanni, who wrote politically charged poems and essays while acknowledging gendered experiences.

One of BAM's most well-known founders was writer and poet Amiri Baraka (formerly known as LeRoi Jones), who created the Black Arts Repertory Theatre/School and a cultural center called the Spirit House in Newark, New Jersey. After visiting Los Angeles in 1967, Baraka formed a close relationship with Maulana Karenga, a prominent advocate of cultural nationalism. In 1965, Karenga, along with Jacquette, Hakim Jamal—a cousin of Malcolm X's—and others, established the US Organization. The organization's name refers to "Us, Black people, African people,"[18] and its ideas were rooted in African principles. It became one of the leading national and local political organizations during the Black Power era in theory and practice.

Karenga developed the philosophy of Kawaida (a Swahili word meaning "tradition") that incorporated African thought and practice as a framework for the future. He also led the creation of Kwanzaa, a Pan-African celebration of African people that occurs annually from December 26 to January 1. At the heart of Kwanzaa is the Nguzo Saba, or seven principles of an African-centered value system, to strengthen African communities. Today, millions of Black people throughout the world celebrate Kwanzaa.

In September 1965, Academy Award–winning screenwriter Budd Schulberg established the Watts Writers Workshop (fig. 34). Participants in this Black writers' collective wrote novels, plays, films, and poems about urban life and social justice. *From the Ashes: Voices of Watts* (1967) was a landmark anthology edited by Schulberg, featuring local writers and unfiltered reflections on life in 1960s South Los Angeles. The workshop published literary works and amplified voices in film and television. Eventually, the Watts Repertory Theater Company, founded by poet and activist Jayne Cortez, became an essential part of the group's work.

GUY CROWDER

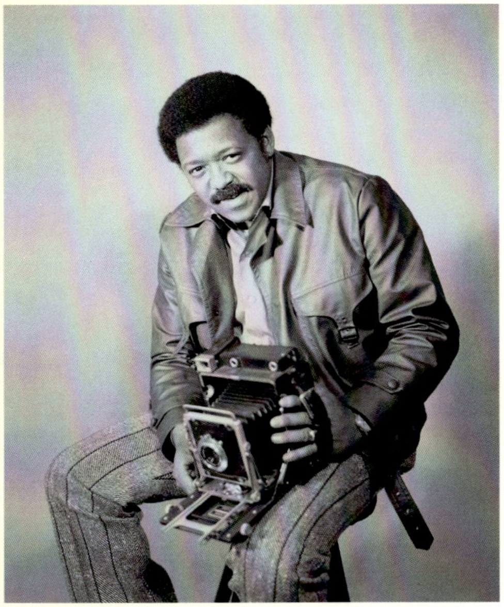

Guy Crowder (1940–2011) arrived in Los Angeles at the age of five and graduated from high school in Compton (fig. 33). During his time in the Marine Corps Reserves, Crowder became interested in photography. He took classes at trade schools, built a photo lab in his garage, and worked at his father-in-law's photo studio. He freelanced for the *Los Angeles Sentinel*, the *L.A. Metropolitan Gazette*, and the *Los Angeles Times* during his nearly forty years behind the lens. Crowder shot everything from political rallies and community events to sporting games and touring Motown acts. He amassed a significant corporate clientele and employed several photographers at his own studio. In 1974, he became the first Black employee of the board of supervisors when L.A. County Supervisor Kenneth Hahn hired him as staff photographer, a role he held for twenty-plus years before retiring.

Fig. 33 Guy Crowder.

Los Angeles's early racial segregation underpinned this concentrated Black Arts community, primarily centered in South Central Los Angeles and the Central Avenue corridor. Music was essential to L.A. BAM. Jazz musician Horace Tapscott and his Pan Afrikan Peoples Arkestra gained prominence as a multigenerational music collective and service organization that fought for employment for African American artists. Other institutions that played significant roles in BAM included the Mafundi Institute, a cultural center and hub for artists, the Watts Towers Arts Center (plate 69), and the Watts Happening Coffee House, a community space and performance venue that was designated an L.A. Historic-Cultural Monument in 2021. The Watts Towers Arts Center, cofounded by sculptor Noah Purifoy, nurtured professional and community artists of all ages. In response to the Watts Uprising, Purifoy and other artists used debris from the affected neighborhoods to create *66 Signs of Neon*, a series of assemblages that toured museums and community centers nationwide (plate 70). John Outterbridge, who taught at the Watts Towers Arts Center in the mid-1960s, also found inspiration in transforming wreckage into positive creative expressions. He would become director of the center in 1975. The Watts Towers are a set of seventeen interconnected sculptures built by Italian immigrant Simon Rodia from 1921 to 1954. He used steel, wire mesh, mortar, broken glass, and pottery to create the one-hundred-foot-high structure without any formal plans or architectural training. The towers are internationally renowned for their blend of artistic sculpture

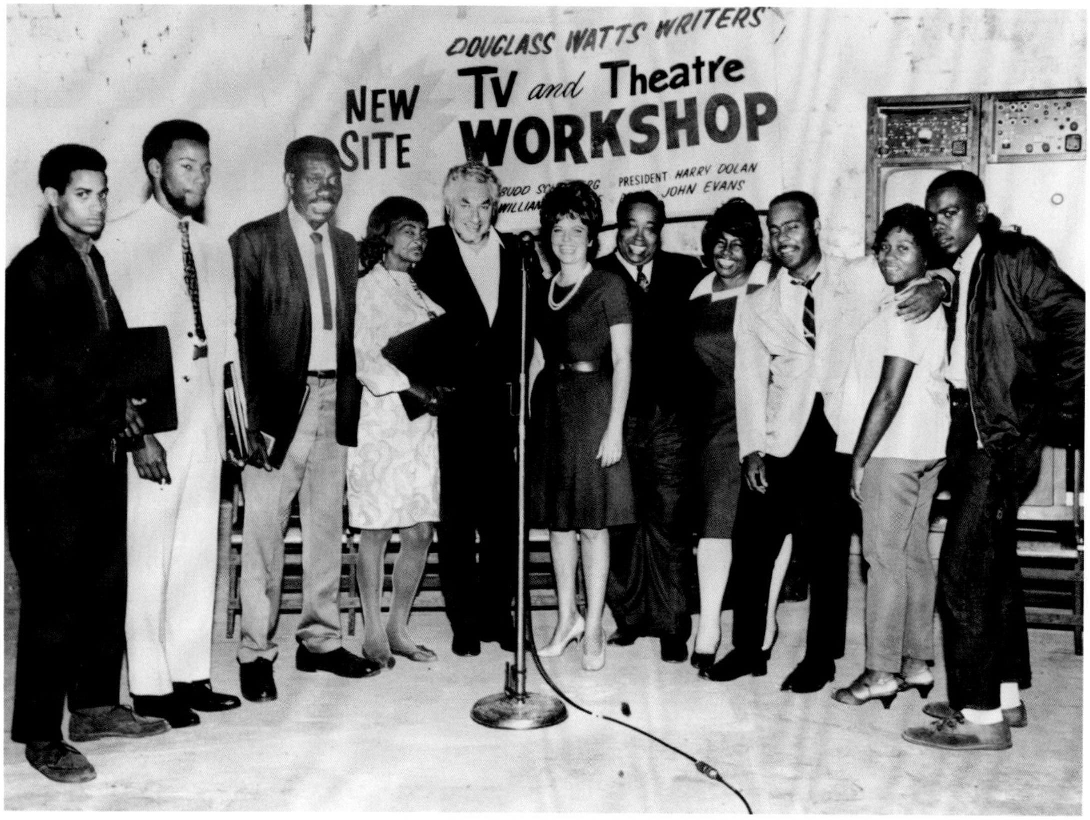

Fig. 34 Budd Schulberg (*center, left of microphone*) and members of the Douglass Watts Writers TV and Theatre Workshop, ca. 1965–73.

Fig 35 Front cover of L.A.-based *SOUL* magazine, the first nationally distributed Black music magazine, featuring Little Richard in a photo by Howard Bingham, 1966.

and architecture;[19] their preservation was championed in 1992 by Mayor Tom Bradley, who considered them a symbol of hope for the community.[20]

A critical voice within the West Coast Black Arts Movement was *SOUL* magazine, founded by Ken and Regina Jones, a husband-and-wife team from Watts. Ken, a TV news reporter, had covered the Watts Uprising, while Regina, granddaughter of Golden State Mutual Life Insurance cofounder William Nickerson, had been working as a dispatcher for the LAPD when she took one of the first emergency calls reporting the rebellion. Their experiences underscored the need for a platform to celebrate Black life and address the social and political issues facing their community. The couple launched *SOUL*—the first nationally distributed African American music publication—in April 1966. The magazine grew into a vital cultural outlet, spotlighting soul music as well as Black art, film, and the wider African American experience. The April 21, 1966, cover featured singer Little Richard in a bold black-and-white photograph by Howard Bingham. The image highlights the artist's electrifying presence and the magazine's mission "to spotlight the cultural power of Black entertainers during a transformative era" (fig. 35).[21]

Another development was the founding in 1967 of the Brockman Gallery by brothers Dale and Alonzo Davis. It exhibited the artwork of Romare Bearden, David Hammons, John Outterbridge, Noah Purifoy, Betye Saar, and Charles White, among others. It also displayed the work of Helen Singleton, a former

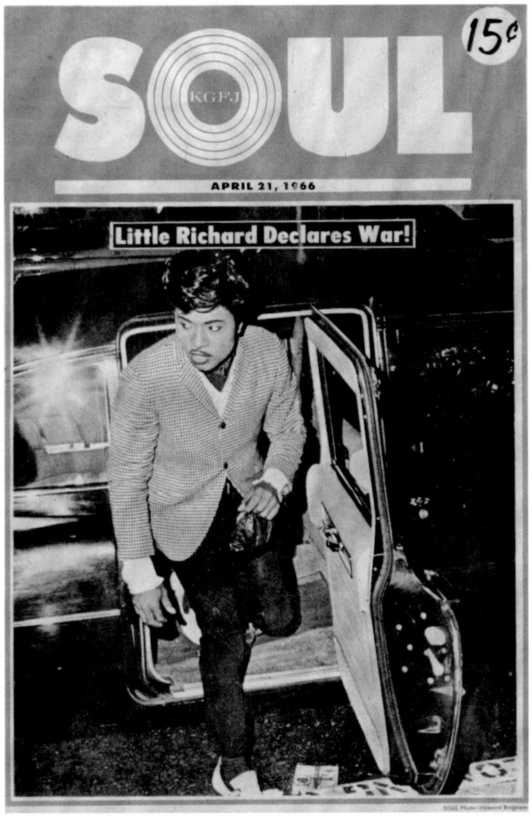

Freedom Rider who later served as the gallery's deputy director and acting executive director.

FIGHTING FOR SOCIAL PROGRESS

Several revolutionary Black nationalist organizations worked in concert with the arts community in the post-revolt era. The United Front, the Che-Lumumba Club, and the Black Panther Party were three organizations that combined Black nationalism with socialism. The United Front was a South Central–based multiracial communist group that centered its work in the fight for economic justice and prisoners' rights. Organized as a commune, it was led by Robaire Nyjuky, a former teacher, and Raymond "Masai" Hewitt, who later became a noted theorist for the local and national Black Panther Party. The Che-Lumumba Club—named after Cuban revolutionary leader Che Guevara and Congolese independence leader Patrice Lumumba—was formed at the behest of Communist Party leader Charlene Mitchell. When Mitchell received the Communist Party USA's presidential nomination in 1968, she became the first African American woman to achieve this historic milestone.[22] Angela Davis, Valerie "Tamu" McFalls, and Joseph Johnson were among the club's notable members. The historic Southwest College became an important organizing and meeting place for the Che-Lumumba Club. Spearheaded by Odessa Cox, Southwest was established in 1967 as the first public community college in South Central Los Angeles after two decades of organizing.[23]

The Southern California chapter of the Black Panther Party was formally established in 1968. After Alprentice "Bunchy" Carter was released from Soledad Prison in 1967, Eldridge Cleaver recruited him to establish the chapter. The party's L.A. branch played a crucial role in implementing the national party's community programs, self-defense strategies, and political work.

The Black Congress was formed in 1966 but formalized in 1967. Its primary founder was Walter Bremond, a social worker who received a grant from the Cummins Engine Foundation to establish a federation of organizations (fig. 36).[24] In his book *Fire This Time*, Gerald Horne argues that the "Black Congress led to a focus away from integration and toward community control."[25] The group adopted the US Organization's philosophy of operational unity, meaning that the Black Congress collaborated on areas of common interest. The same group transformed the US newspaper *Harambee* into a news organ for the Black Congress. John Floyd, a cofounder of the Black Panther Political Party, became the paper's editor. Elaine Brown of the Black Student Alliance was a reporter.[26] The Black Panther Political Party was a splinter group of Alabama's Lowndes County Freedom Organization (LCFO), an independent political organization that featured a black panther as its emblem and emphasized voter registration and Black electoral power. Gordon Parks photographed Maulana Karenga and other leaders at Black Congress organizational meetings as they helped plan a 1966 Black Power rally with Stokely Carmichael (plate 71).

"TO PROTECT AND OBSERVE"

The Temporary Alliance of Local Organizations (TALO) was the second federation of organizations that developed in the post-revolt era. TALO's formation was prompted by a tragic incident on May 7, 1966, involving Leonard Deadwyler, a twenty-five-year-old Black mechanic. Deadwyler was rushing his pregnant wife, who was in labor, to the hospital. A white flag was tied to his car's antenna to signal that he was experiencing an emergency and might run through red lights. Police officer Jerold Bova approached Deadwyler's stopped vehicle with his gun drawn and put the "whole upper part of his body" into the car. Deadwyler was shot and killed in the presence of his wife.[27] Local activists organized a rally of about four hundred people at Will Rogers Memorial Park to protest the killing, which city leaders feared would trigger another revolt (plate 72). But TALO worked to maintain peace. Johnnie L. Cochran Jr., who would become a leading Black attorney in the United States, joined with the NAACP and filed a wrongful death and emotional distress suit on behalf of Deadwyler's widow, Barbara Deadwyler (plate 73). Although she testified during the coroner's inquest that her husband was shot deliberately, the jury accepted the officer's claim that the car had lurched forward, causing his gun to fire involuntarily, and the case was ruled an accidental homicide.

Led by reparations advocate Robert Brock, TALO played a crucial role in establishing the Community Alert Patrol (CAP), which monitored neighborhoods to prevent police brutality and de-escalate confrontations between the police and the local Black residents (plates 74, 75).[28] CAP was composed of volunteers who posted signs on their cars with the slogan "To protect and observe," a deliberate modification of the LAPD's motto "To protect and to serve" (plate 76).[29] In mid-June, just one week after CAP launched, the *Sentinel* featured two front-page pictures along with a lengthy account from a ride-along reporter. One picture was taken of a crowd outside a taco stand. The other showed a discussion with police officers. The coverage provided the Black community with a broader understanding of CAP's purpose. CAP volunteers knew the power of recording images and carried still and motion-picture cameras in their cars. Images carry a perceived truth, seemingly proof or evidence of an event, and the tactic irked police officers. According to the ride-along reporter, annoyed officers would shine their spotlights at the cameras.[30]

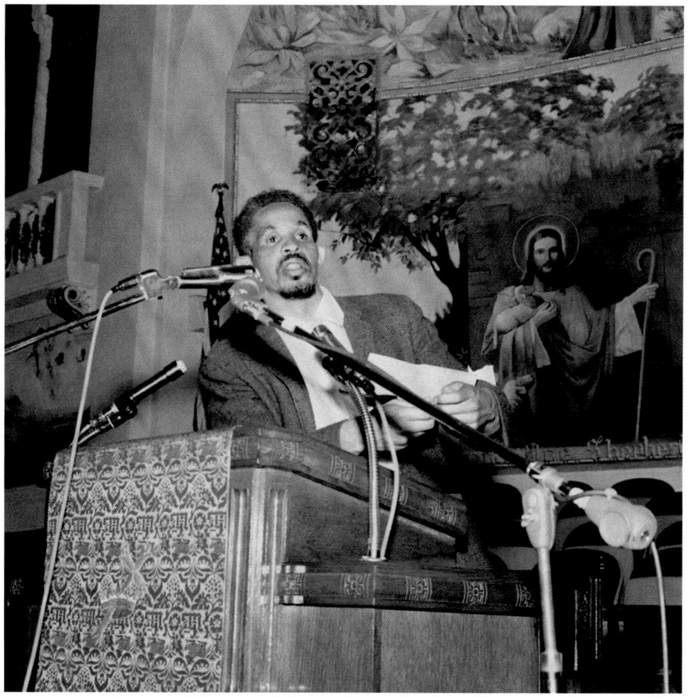

Fig. 36 HARRY ADAMS, 1968. Walter Bremond speaking at the Black Congress Recognition Awards.

Although several volunteers had prior gang affiliations, involvement in the group fostered a sense of unity. Led by Lenier Eggleston (Brother Lenny) and Ron

Wilkins (Brother Crook), CAP eventually gained nonprofit status and received grants to sustain its efforts. Groups like CAP and the Sons of Watts contributed to a decline in gang activity in Los Angeles as they united in opposition to systemic oppression. Although CAP originated in Los Angeles, it gained national attention when the Black Panther Party for Self-Defense adopted a similar model. But the Panthers took a more daring approach by arming their patrols, leading to greater notoriety.[31]

One month after the Deadwyler case closed, the *New York Times Magazine* published an article by Thomas Pynchon, "A Journey into the Minds of Watts." Pynchon explored schools, neighborhoods, bars, and vacant lots still marked by the 1965 riots. Despite various humanitarian efforts following the revolt, Pynchon observed that fundamental conditions had not changed. Pynchon called out L.A.'s "racial sickness," marked by two separate, disconnected worlds. He wrote, "While the white culture is concerned with various forms of systematized folly—the economy of the area in fact depending on it—the Black culture is stuck pretty much with basic realities like disease, failure, violence and death," which white individuals "have mostly chosen—and can afford—to ignore."[32]

Recognizing that reliance on white society to relinquish its privilege was unlikely, the Black community persisted in advancing its own interests. One important local effort for welfare rights came out of the Nickerson Gardens housing projects in Watts, led by Johnnie Tillmon, a mother who relied on a government welfare program. She resented the heavy-handed treatment and indignities she and others faced from welfare workers. Channeling the self-determination of the Black Power era, Tillmon demanded "welfare power." She insisted that poor Black women who were welfare recipients should run their own organizations. Tillmon influenced Martin Luther King Jr. and spoke at the Mother's Day March led by Coretta Scott King in 1968 that officially launched the Poor People's Campaign (plate 77).[33] Also attending the event was Catherine Jermany, president of the Los Angeles County Welfare Rights Organization, who championed reproductive rights along with the alleviation of poverty.

Civil rights organizations in Los Angeles remained deeply engaged in addressing the issues of housing, employment, policing, and poverty. CORE's Los Angeles chapter joined the statewide boycott of See's Candy Company because only 1 percent of its employees were Black, and it established its own CAP to monitor police activities. The new patrol was announced following a federal government threat to withdraw funds from CAP.[34] The WCLC coalesced with new organizations by joining the Black Congress, working on poverty-related issues, and continuing to organize fundraisers for King and the work of the national movement. On October 16, 1967, King addressed a packed audience in Bovard Auditorium at the University of Southern California (USC). His powerful message about the need for a more forceful nonviolent movement resonated with the crowd of over eighteen hundred. At the time of this speech, however, King was under siege by the media, the White House, and even some of his allies for "breaking silence" and denouncing the escalating Vietnam War.[35] Polls showed that 73 percent of Americans disagreed with King's antiwar stance, in which he called America "the greatest purveyor of violence in the world today."[36] King's nonviolence movement was losing ground and media attention to Carmichael and Black Power, and the cracks were beginning to show. A few months after his speech, King was approached by CBS News correspondent Daniel Schorr following a press conference in Washington, DC, at which King had announced the upcoming Poor People's Campaign. Schorr asked the civil rights leader why he looked so troubled. "It's because of what you people in television are doing," King replied. "You keep driving people like me, who are nonviolent, into saying more and more militant things. And if we don't say things militantly enough for you, we don't get on the evening news. And who does? Stokely Carmichael and [former Black Panther Party leader] H. Rap Brown."[37]

BLACK ELECTORAL POWER

In addition to civil rights organizations, a relatively new group of Black elected officials used their power base to challenge discriminatory public policies and support local equity initiatives. Until 1963, Los Angeles had no Black public officials. When city council member Edward Roybal vacated his 9th District seat following his 1962 election to Congress, L.A. County Supervisor Kenneth Hahn appointed Gilbert Lindsay as the city's first Black officeholder in that district (plate 78). That same year, two Black candidates won their races for city council. Tom Bradley, a retired police officer turned lawyer (and future mayor), won in the 10th District, and newcomer Billy Mills, a graduate of Compton College and UCLA, won in the 8th District. Remarkably, three of the fifteen Los Angeles City Council districts now had African American representatives; before 1963, each of those districts held significant Black populations, but non-Black people had represented them.

Throughout their tenure, the three Black councilmembers worked to provide more access to city services for their districts and pressed the city council to support the civil rights movement. They also participated in the Watts recovery effort alongside civil rights and nationalist Black power groups. In one case, demonstrating allegiance to TALO, several Black elected officials picketed a hearing in June 1966 hosted by the city police commission after individuals considered Black nationalists were excluded from the meeting. Some civil rights leaders also refused to enter the room and stood in the hallway as a form of protest.[38]

In November 1966, Assemblyman Mervyn Dymally became the first African American to serve in California's state Senate. Perhaps the most outspoken of the city's Black elected officials, Dymally was not invited to the Athens Park meeting in 1965, "nor was he invited to meet with Governor Brown during the revolt."[39] Dymally's advocacy and legislative accomplishments, including passing legislation that created the Charles R. Drew Postgraduate Medical School in partnership with UCLA, led to his election as the forty-first lieutenant governor of California in 1975, the first African American in the state to hold the position.

MASS PROTEST AND HIGH SCHOOL WALKOUTS

While Dymally's rise reflected growing political representation for African Americans at the state level, grassroots activism continued to play a crucial role in advancing civil rights locally, particularly among youth and parents demanding educational equity. During the late 1960s, inspired by the Watts Uprising, favorable court decisions, and the broader movement for racial justice, students, parents, and community leaders organized mass demonstrations and walkouts at Los Angeles public secondary schools. Manual Arts High School became the catalyst, with protests against its administration during fall 1967.

Located in South Central, the school was by that year 95 percent Black, dramatically overcrowded, and underresourced.[40] When students' and parents' concerns were not taken seriously despite letters and petitions, the United Parents Council (UPC)—led by President Margaret Wright, Walter Bremond, and Maulana Karenga of the Black Congress, with Los Angeles NAACP President Celes King III—launched demonstrations at the start of the school year.

The protests targeted Manual Arts' principal, Robert Denahy, who was accused of suspending students for minor infractions while refusing to adequately stop drug and alcohol trafficking. Other grievances included the school's discriminatory enforcement of dress codes, particularly targeting Black students wearing natural hairstyles.[41] Alongside the students, UPC organized rallies and led daily picketing. Demonstrations escalated, with rocks and bottles thrown and small fires ignited. In response, Los Angeles Superior Court Judge Ralph H. Nutter issued a temporary restraining order against Wright and fifty other "John Does," prohibiting them from entering school grounds without invitation and from "interfering with the conduct of school administration."[42]

Black elected officials sought to amplify the voices of students and parents who felt ignored, ensure their grievances reached appropriate authorities, and serve as crucial intermediaries. Democratic Congressman Augustus Hawkins, who joined the picket line, wrote in the *Sentinel*: "The only satisfactory plan for resolving the Manual Arts problem and to keep the same situation from occurring in other schools is to make tremendous changes to the school system's approach to the Negro's educational needs."[43] Assemblyman Bill Greene also picketed alongside the students and argued that Denahy's proposed ouster "was not a matter of race."[44] While speaking at a board of education meeting, Greene urged members to investigate conditions at Manual Arts and to turn the controversy into something positive by finding solutions to the problems. The board voted to conduct a citywide investigation into narcotics and liquor trafficking upon Greene's insistence. Dymally and Mills also supported the protesters' grassroots action and advocated for an immediate investigation. But they were jeered and shouted down during their attempts to speak at the board meeting.[45] Eventually, the campaign succeeded: Denahy went on sick leave in November 1967 and was reassigned, additional teachers were transferred to Manual Arts, and the Los Angeles Board of Education established task forces to address school–community relations. In addition, the board promised to notify all teachers that students were allowed to wear their hair "natural" as long as it was clean.[46]

The following year, four hundred African American students at Jefferson High School and between fifteen thousand and twenty thousand students from five predominantly Chicano high schools in East Los Angeles—Wilson, Garfield, Roosevelt, Lincoln, and Belmont—staged coordinated walkouts during the first week of March 1968. These interconnected protests challenged educational inequities and demanded college preparatory courses, more Black and Latino administrators, adequate resources, and increased community input in school governance.[47] Despite Jefferson High School's significant participation, the overwhelming scale of the Chicano protests overshadowed its involvement. At Jefferson, students protested poor cafeteria conditions, lack of a Black history curriculum, teacher insensitivity, and inadequate guidance counseling. The Los Angeles County Conference of Negro Elected Officials announced it had "set up two committees to investigate student unrest" at Jefferson. Democratic Assemblyman Leon D. Ralph served as conference chair to address the grievances.[48]

The sustained pressure achieved concrete results. Three Black administrators were assigned to Jefferson as principal, vice principal, and guidance counselor. The *Sentinel* called the appointments of Lewis J. Johnson Jr. as principal and Dave Stewart as third vice principal a "Black Boycott Victory," stating that "virtually all their demands based on 'Black awareness' had been met."[49] The activism grew beyond individual campuses to include Fremont High, which was 95 percent Black, fueling a broader generational movement that reshaped civil rights and educational equity in Los Angeles.[50]

The seeds of the transformative 1968 East L.A. student walkouts were planted in an unlikely setting: Camp Hess Kramer, a Jewish youth facility in Malibu. From 1963 onward, Rabbi Alfred Wolf's dedication to social justice enabled the camp to host the Chicano Youth Leadership Conference (CYLC). With backing from allies like philanthropist Tobias Kotzin, this initiative cultivated leadership capabilities and political engagement among Mexican American youth. The program produced numerous future walkout leaders—Sal Castro, Moctesuma Esparza, Gloria Arellanes, Carlos Montes, and other emerging Chicano youth—who found community, critical dialogue, and a sense of purpose at the camp.[51]

The Chicano student protests began with an unplanned walkout at Wilson High School on March 1, 1968, and escalated into what became popularly known as a blowout, describing the larger coordinated

Chicano protests involving ten thousand students. The organized protests at Garfield High School on March 5 quickly spread across East L.A. Sal Castro, a Mexican American social studies teacher at Lincoln High School, helped organize hundreds of students to walk out of classes, supported by crucial Chicano organizations including the Brown Berets, United Mexican American Students (UMAS), and United Chicano Students.[52] Chicano students' list of demands focused on community control of schools, bilingual education, hiring more Mexican American teachers, establishing citizen review boards, and creating parent councils. When the Los Angeles Board of Education rejected all thirty-nine demands on March 28 and arrested thirteen organizers, including Castro, on March 31, the movement appeared to have failed. Castro also lost his teaching position but was reinstated after two thousand people protested, and students organized round-the-clock sit-ins at the board of education offices.[53] Despite initial setbacks, the walkouts succeeded beyond their specific demands, catalyzing the broader Chicano civil rights movement. One year later, local schools increased the number of Mexican American faculty members, adopted bilingual classes, and reduced class sizes, illustrating the increasing momentum of the Chicano movement that spread throughout the Southwest.[54]

KING IS ASSASSINATED

On April 4, 1968, a month after his final visit to Los Angeles, Dr. Martin Luther King Jr. was murdered in Memphis, Tennessee, where he had been supporting Black sanitation workers who were striking for better pay and working conditions. When he died, the WCLC was organizing local components of two SCLC national programs: Operation Breadbasket and the Poor People's Campaign. Operation Breadbasket was an economic development program that sought to bring more jobs and profits to the Black community by boycotting corporations that refused to do business with and support Black customers. Los Angeles ministers met with the national director of the program, Rev. Jesse Jackson, to consider the feasibility of launching the program in Los Angeles.[55] The Poor People's Campaign was aimed at highlighting poverty, unemployment, and the need for fair wages by demanding federal legislation to help alleviate economic disparities. During King's final visits to Los Angeles, he addressed the California Democratic Council, a progressive caucus in Orange County, on March 17, 1968, and spoke at Holman Methodist Church in Los Angeles to fundraise for the fight against poverty.[56] His presentation emphasized the interconnected nature of economic justice and peace, linking the Poor People's Campaign and his position against the Vietnam War to the broader fight for racial equality.

King's local and national work on behalf of civil rights was honored throughout Los Angeles. On the day he was assassinated, Supervisor Hahn directed that flags fly at half-staff. The next day, the Los Angeles City Council passed a resolution eulogizing King, which was presented and signed by councilmembers Lindsay, Mills, and Bradley. On April 7, a memorial service was held at the Los Angeles Memorial Coliseum. Rev. Lanneau L. White, minister of Holman Methodist, led the memorial for twenty thousand attendees. The somber event brought together various entertainers and civil rights activists, including jazz singer Oscar Brown Jr. and labor leader Cesar Chavez, who spoke about King's inspiration for their respective movements. Jewish temples and Catholic churches also publicly honored King. A notable memorial occurred when two hundred clergy members in their religious vestments led a procession of eighteen hundred people to the historic First Methodist Church (plate 79).

King's assassination sparked civil unrest in 188 cities. President Johnson declared a state of emergency and called in seventy thousand federal troops to clamp down on the turmoil. During a live television broadcast, he urged Americans to reject the blind violence that had struck King, who had lived by nonviolence.[57] Leaders of the Black Congress were also devastated when they learned of King's death but spoke openly against a violent uprising and effectively maintained peace in Los Angeles by providing a constructive alternative for mourners. The Los Angeles activist community organized a shopping boycott of Easter, thereby turning Black anger into a protest against the discriminatory practices of merchants (plate 80). The *Sentinel* editorialized that Los Angeles should be proud of the many people who contributed to maintaining peace and calm in the city. It published a special memorial edition on April 11 honoring King, featuring forty-four pages of photographs and stories paying respect to Coretta Scott King and to King's legacy. The paper ran special reports from those who traveled to Atlanta for the funeral, including Rev. Thomas Kilgore, and reflections from Bradley, local ministers, and the broader community. The issue included heartfelt contributions from entertainers Lena Horne and Sidney Poitier, and published a story of Marlon Brando bursting into tears while sharing the horrific news over the telephone.[58]

King's death signaled the end of the modern civil rights movement for many reasons. Some considered even nonviolent direct action as too risky, while others believed that the passage of legislation that ended legal segregation, protected voting rights, and ensured fair housing meant the movement was no longer necessary. Still, the legacy of direct action and community organizing did not stop in Los Angeles. Work began on a proposal to build Martin Luther King Jr. Hospital to provide health services to people in marginalized communities. Coretta Scott King spoke at the dedication of the hospital in 1972.

BLACK POWER PEAKS AND PERSECUTION

The Black Congress held its first annual Recognition Awards presentation night on August 2, 1968, at Second Baptist Church and continued organizing community service programs to support Black Student Unions (BSUs) on college campuses and fighting police brutality and other forms of discrimination. However, by the early 1970s, the Black Power movement was losing momentum. First, it suffered from a political backlash fueled by white and conservative resentment of civil rights laws and practices designed to promote racial equality. The election of Ronald Reagan as California's governor in 1966 marked a turning point that negatively affected civil rights–related public policies and poverty programs. For example, Reagan's conservative platform led to cuts in welfare programs and state funding for education. He had opposed the Rumford Fair Housing Act and engaged in anti-communist witch hunts, bringing national attention to Angela Davis at UCLA, whose firing he engineered (plate 81). When asked about the causes of the Watts Uprising, Reagan responded: "The mass influx of Negroes from Southern states, who expect to find streets paved with gold, promises in the War on Poverty program that can't be kept, and other elements with an axe to grind."[59] Still, Reagan received 58 percent of the vote—more than half of the state's citizens—ousting Pat Brown, whose policies were comparatively liberal.[60]

Another factor in the movement's decline was intense political repression. Sociologist Doug McAdam identifies three critical factors for successful social movements: favorable conditions, strong support structures, and activists' belief in success, collectively known as cognitive liberation. However, political repression can undermine these factors by weakening opportunities, damaging support networks, and demoralizing activists. This repression can also alienate external supporters, potentially causing a loss of credibility and resources and ultimately limiting the movement's effectiveness and access to political opportunities.[61] The Black Power movement in Los Angeles faced significant repression, as coordinated efforts by local law enforcement agencies undermined and disrupted its core organizational functions and activities.

Similar actions occurred at the federal level, as the FBI's Counterintelligence Program, or COINTELPRO—launched in 1956 and exposed in 1971—revealed a wide-ranging set of covert tactics aimed at neutralizing political organizations deemed

ROLLAND J. CURTIS

Rolland J. Curtis (1922–1979) settled in Los Angeles in 1946 after serving in the Marines during World War II. He worked as an LAPD officer before playing football at USC, where he earned the nickname "Speedy" on the field. He also received a master's degree in public administration. Curtis's interest in photography led to his appointment in the mid-1960s as field deputy to L.A. City Council member Tom Bradley. In addition to doing constituent work, Curtis photographed political meetings, community events, and office-related activities. He continued in this role with councilmember Billy Mills from 1967 until 1973. Curtis's most important photographic contribution lies in documenting the vital community and political work of the council's first two Black members as they represented their districts during a turbulent era.

threatening. The FBI's strategies included extensive and illegal surveillance, harassment, infiltration, and the deliberate exacerbation of tensions between civil rights and Black Power groups and their leaders, including King and the SCLC, Malcolm X and the NOI, Carmichael and SNCC and the Black Panther Party for Self-Defense. In the case of CAP volunteers, the local police response to their monitoring efforts was consistently hostile as they endured harassment, tailing, and excessive ticketing.[62] A Los Angeles member of SNCC complained that the organization was under constant surveillance and their phones were tapped. Because of the harassment and repression, the group eventually changed its organizational structure to include paramilitary defense measures. This also occurred in the case of the Black Student Alliance (BSA). Led by Harry Truly, an instructor at California State University, Los Angeles, the BSA was established in 1968 to ensure that educational institutions met the needs of Black people by engaging in political education and intensifying the fight against racism and capitalism. Given the security concerns around mass organizing during the Black Power era, the BSA instituted a six-week probation period for those seeking to join and adopted a paramilitary structure. BSA members played an important role in fostering collaboration with BSUs at Historically Black Colleges and Universities (HBCUs) and at predominantly white institutions. They also extended their educational and organizing work to BSUs at junior high and high school levels.

RAID AT BLACK PANTHER HEADQUARTERS

The Black Panther Party's armed bravado and bold tactics generated immense attention during its formative years, yet the early publicity largely focused on the group's confrontational tactics and overshadowed positive coverage of its community programs, including its free breakfast program for children. The party largely relied on its newspaper, the *Black Panther* (est. 1967), to tell its own story. The newspaper was best known for Emory Douglas's art and its coverage of Panther activism, and its sales went toward fundraising.

Photographers including Howard Bingham, Charles Brittin, Guy Crowder, Stephen Shames, and others documented the local Black Panther Party's rise and eventual repression in L.A. (plates 82, 83). The organization's focus on self-defense drew repressive action from law enforcement.[63] Infiltration and using agent provocateurs to intentionally cause conflict and heighten mistrust and tensions between Black Power organizations were frequent tactics used by the FBI. According to party cofounder Bobby Seale, FBI Director J. Edgar Hoover ordered FBI offices to "exploit all avenues of creating dissension within the ranks of the Black Panther Party" and weaken the organization, especially the breakfast program, which Hoover said represented the most influential activity of the Black Panthers.[64] The breakfast program in Los Angeles, the Alprentice "Bunchy" Carter Free Clinic, and other programs were frequently attacked.

Those methods led to a January 17, 1969, shooting at UCLA that claimed the lives of two Black Panther Party members and led to the incarceration of two US Organization members for murder. Evidence suggests that both organizations had been infiltrated by individuals tasked with sowing discord. This tragic incident prompted Bremond to step down as head of the Black Congress, contributing to the organization's decline and ultimately fragmenting the movement's solidarity.[65]

Similarly, the LAPD/SWAT's five-hour shootout at the Black Panther Party headquarters on 41st Street and Central Avenue on December 8, 1969, became another pivotal moment of repression, leaving three party members and three officers wounded. Eventually, LAPD/SWAT used explosives to blow the roof, forcing eleven Black Panthers to surrender and abandon their headquarters (plate 84).[66] Notably, the raid appeared on the front pages of the *Times* and the *Sentinel*. The next week's *Sentinel* included pictures of massive protests, a young boy selling *Black Panther* newspapers, raised fists, and a box full of money collected to help raise bail. The incident sparked widespread protests at a rally involving thousands of young activists, including Angela Davis and elected officials such as Dymally and Mills. Overall, other Black elected officials in attendance expressed resentment that the police had not consulted them before the raid. Dymally stated he was present at the raid of the Black Panther Party's headquarters and that a police officer assaulted him.[67]

THE MARCH CONTINUES

Despite the decline of organizational power, Black newspapers and photography remained relevant and continued to make Black life and racist violence visible while other media ignored it. Pictures of determined activists and massive rallies raised awareness of the ongoing movement. Most importantly, photography bore witness to decades of civil rights activism among those determined to make Los Angeles a better place for all.

More than seventy years after the start of the civil rights movement, many of the issues that launched it—police brutality, unfair housing, education inequity, and economic and criminal injustice—continue. But the quest for civil rights is ongoing. In recent years, Black Lives Matter, Movement for Black Lives, Color of Change, and other more contemporary formations have been at the forefront of grassroots organizing in the twenty-first century, utilizing digital technologies to mobilize supporters and demand change (plate 85). Though distinct in their approaches and immediate goals, the social justice groups today represent a continuous thread in the long-standing freedom movement for racial equality and justice in America.

5

Plates

The destruction in Watts in August 1965 gradually gave way to recovery efforts. As civil rights legislation proved insufficient in impacting communities far from the South, a new generation of activists imagined bolder approaches to achieving racial equality. Because change was slow and racial discrimination was immediate and pervasive, the emergence of Black nationalist ideas fostered a sense of urgency in Los Angeles.

Stokely Carmichael, the new chair of SNCC, championed Black Power as the media questioned the movement's changing tenor. *Life* magazine's Gordon Parks spent four months traveling with Carmichael. The article "Whip of Black Power" showed the political activist galvanizing supporters at a 1966 rally in Watts. An unpublished picture caught leaders behind the scenes planning a Black nationalist rally. Carmichael understood L.A.'s fervent mix of energy and tension, commenting to Parks: "People think *I'm* militant. Wait until those kids grow up! There are young cats around here who make me look like a dove of peace."[68]

One of the newer groups included the Black Panther Party for Self-Defense, to which Carmichael devoted his time. L.A.-based photographer Howard Bingham, who spent several months covering the Black Panthers for *Life*, took a picture of Carmichael in February 1968 at a fundraiser for party leader Huey Newton's legal defense. Speakers at that event included party cofounder Bobby Seale and SNCC's H. Rap Brown. Bingham snapped the picture and hundreds of others, but *Life* ultimately decided against publishing the commissioned article.[69]

In 1967, the *Black Panther* newspaper was published to craft the party's narrative. Stephen Shames's picture of a young female Panther selling newspapers reminds viewers that by 1969, women made up over half the party's membership.[70] The group's focus on survival and uplift was overshadowed by the mainstream media's fascination with their guns, berets, and militarism. A "Feed Hungry Children Free Breakfast" sign outside the party's office on Central Avenue signifies this stark contrast following the LAPD's attack on the premises in December 1969.

The dramatic post-Watts shift from civil rights integrationism to Black nationalist self-determination was accompanied by a significant visual change in what was shown in America's media. Early imagery of white supremacists and police mistreating passive Black protesters differed dramatically from young Black activists boldly resisting white racism. A decrease in support and public opinion of the broader freedom movement accompanied the changing visuals. A special section in the July issue of *Life*, "Watts: '65–'66. Still Hell to Pay," opened with pictures of fire, Molotov cocktails, and the words "Burn, Baby, Burn." The images sent the message that Watts was dangerously close to erupting again before the section transitioned to a staid mix of portraits of leaders seeking change. The sensationalized imagery seemed intended to shatter hope for a more optimistic future.

Photographs of the Community Alert Patrol (CAP) exemplified the Black community's ongoing mistrust of the LAPD. Ron Wilkins, a CAP leader, is pictured in his car with a CAP sign affixed to the door. The group sought "to protect and observe" the LAPD to help diffuse tension. CAP volunteers understood that their presence, along with still and movie cameras, created a form of surveillance that could deter police violence. Local photographer Jack Davis documented a scene not unlike what CAP sought to observe.

The emerging Black Arts Movement drew on Black identity and lived experiences to breathe life into Watts and South Los Angeles. The exhibition *66 Signs of Neon*, built with repurposed materials pulled from the rubble, interpreted the uprising through assemblage art. Harry Drinkwater documented the works, first shown at the inaugural Watts Summer Festival. One featured charred metal circles as sunflowers, with the Watts Towers in the distance. The first Watts festival was an exuberant success.

Many of the Black photographers who bravely bore witness to the civil rights movement in Los Angeles were honored by photographer/curator Roland Charles in the groundbreaking 1983 exhibition *The Tradition Continues: California Black Photographers* at the California Museum of Afro-American History and Culture (now the California African American Museum) in L.A.'s Exposition Park. The show's success led Charles to found the nonprofit organization Black Photographers of California, which recognized the fine art and documentary work of Harry Adams, Howard Bingham, Jack Davis, Fitzgerald Whitney, Vera Jackson and many others who trained their cameras consistently on Black life in Los Angeles.

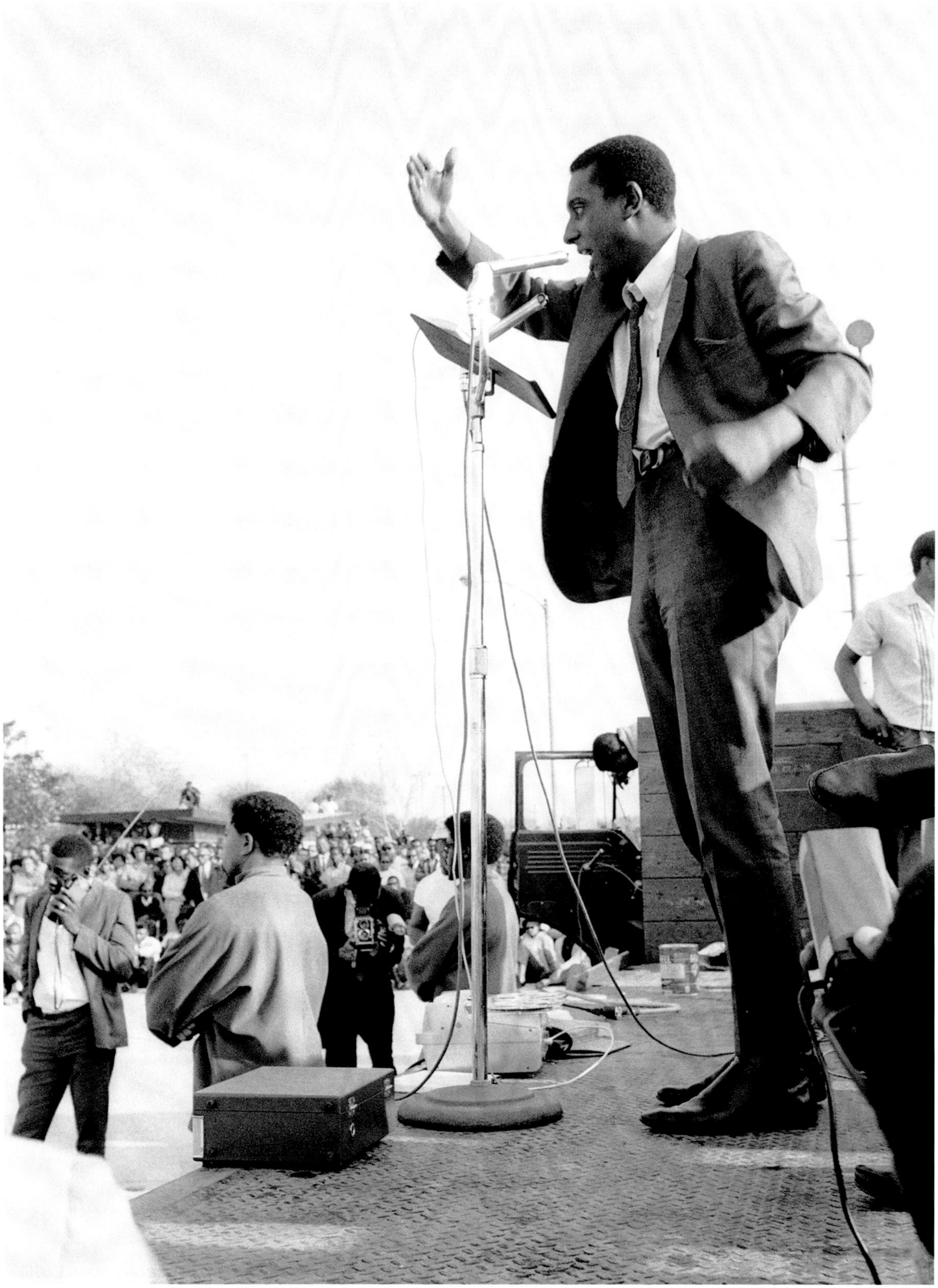

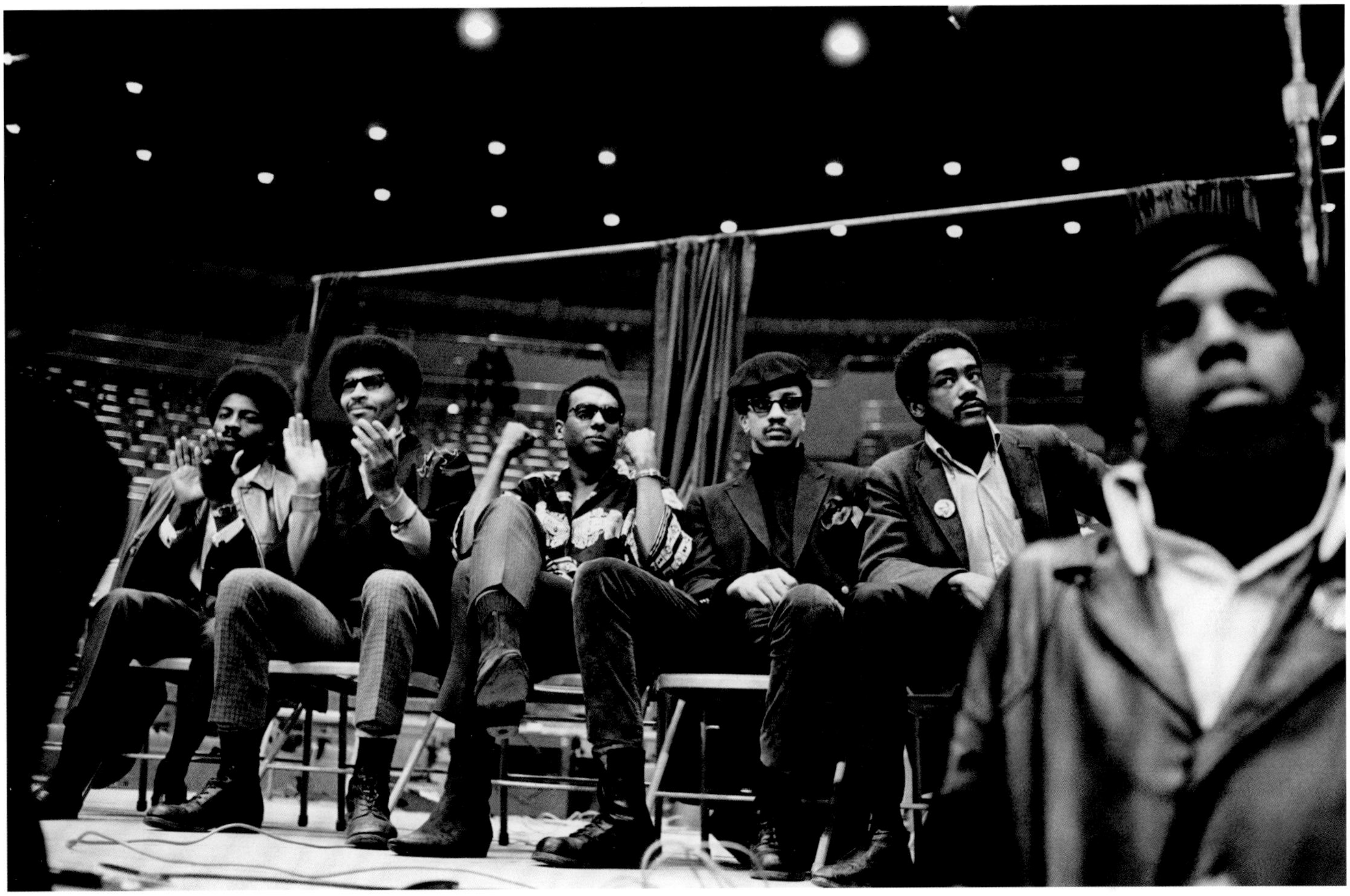

Plate 65 GORDON PARKS, 1966

Stokely Carmichael delivers his fiery rhetoric to a receptive crowd of thousands at a Watts rally. This picture of the dynamic SNCC leader opened the groundbreaking *Life* magazine essay "Whip of Black Power," written and illustrated by Gordon Parks, the magazine's first African American staff photographer.

Plate 66 HOWARD BINGHAM, 1968

Leaders of Black nationalist groups appear on stage at the Huey P. Newton Defense Fund rally at the L.A. Memorial Sports Arena on February 18. Seated (*from left*) are local Black Panther Party leader Alprentice "Bunchy" Carter, Black Panther Party member Carver Chico Nesbitt, Stokely Carmichael, SNCC leader H. Rap Brown, and Black Panther Party cofounder Bobby Seale. Howard Bingham took this photograph on assignment for *Life* magazine and also documented free breakfast programs, Free Huey rallies, and Newton's courtroom trial.

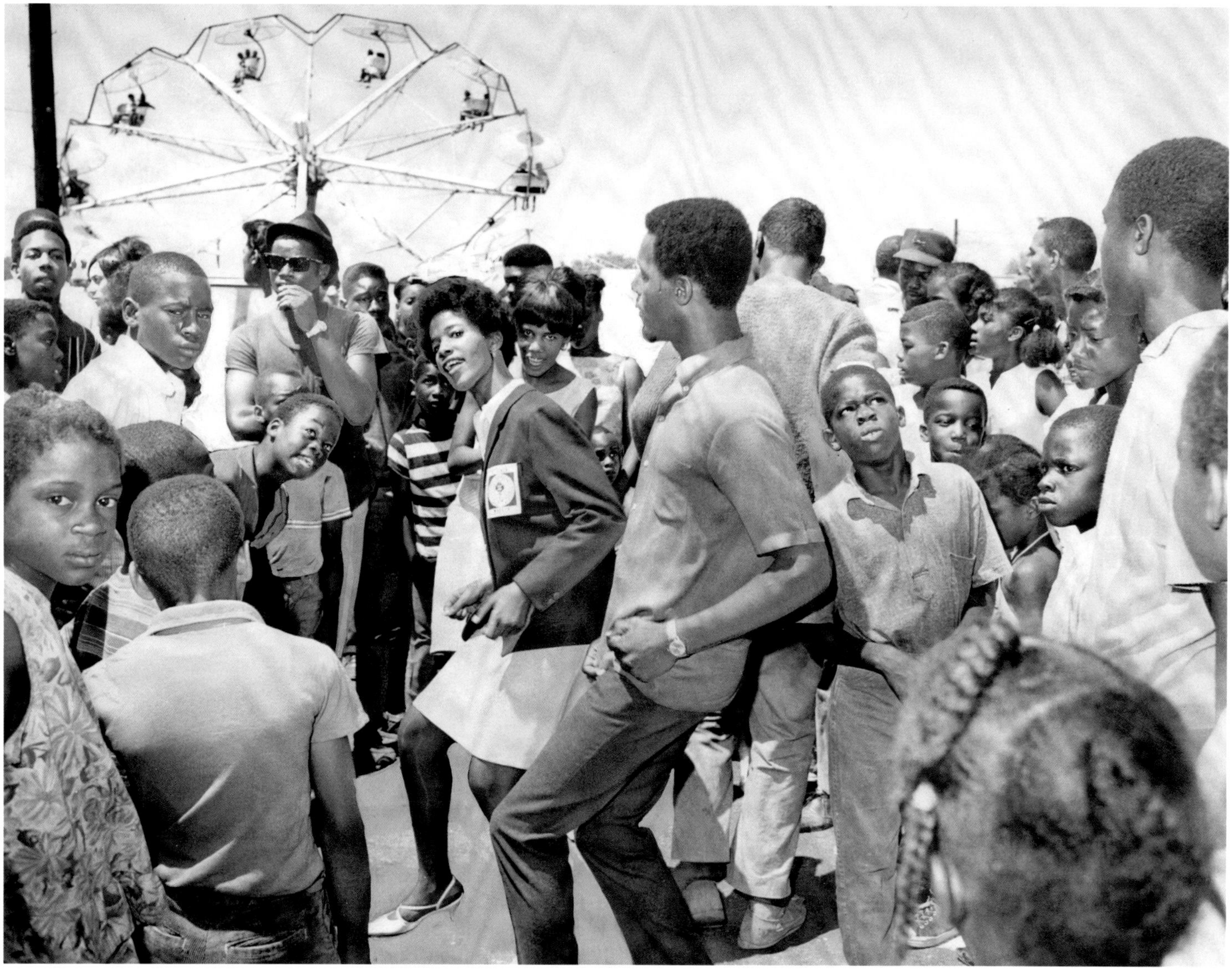

Plate 67 UNKNOWN PHOTOGRAPHER, 1966

A young couple dances in the street during the Watts Summer Festival, part of the healing process for the riot-stricken neighborhood. Thousands of Angelenos took part in the multiday gathering that featured a parade, jazz festival, art exhibits, and carnival rides, among dozens of other attractions.

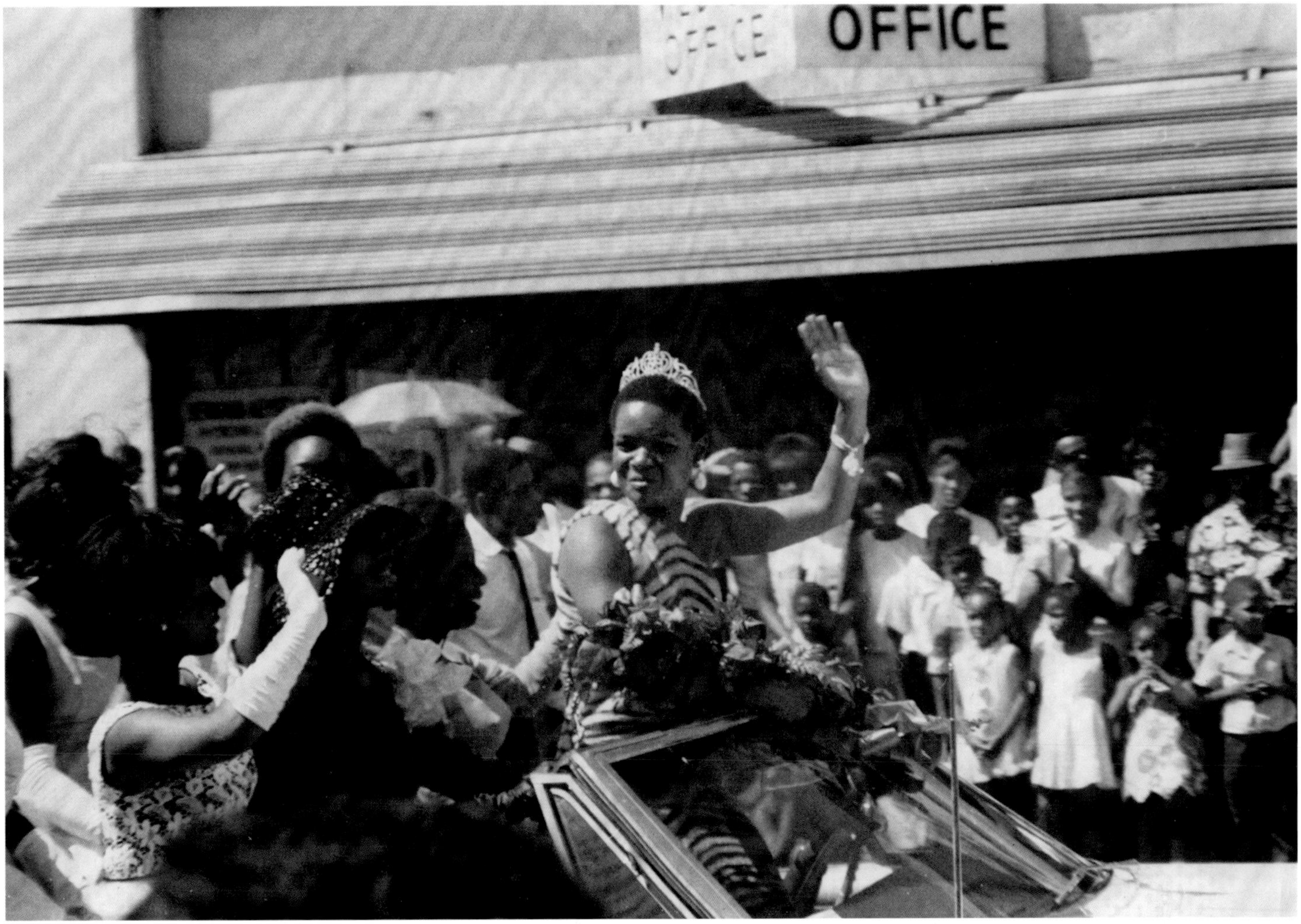

Plate 68 MELVIN EDWARDS, 1966

Newly crowned Miss Watts Tamu Harper rides in a convertible during the Watts Summer Festival parade. The twenty-one-year-old aspiring actress was one of three hundred contestants. Her image appeared in numerous local newspapers.

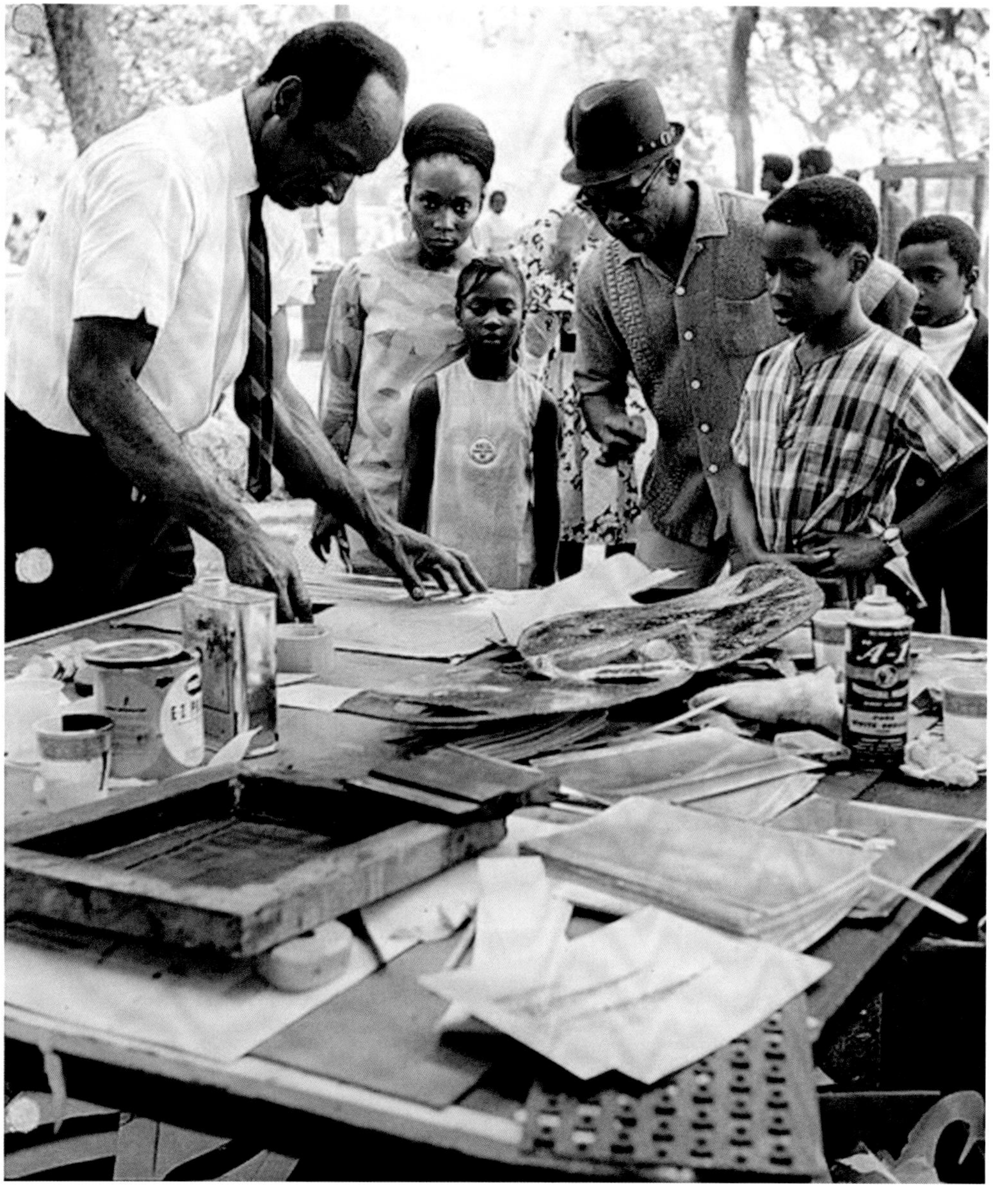

Plate 69 UNKNOWN PHOTOGRAPHER, 1968
Artist Judson Powell (*far left*) demonstrates art techniques at the Watts Towers Art Center, where he worked closely with other Watts artists, including Noah Purifoy, to connect youth to art, culture, and community. Powell remains best known as an assemblage artist, musician, and community activist.

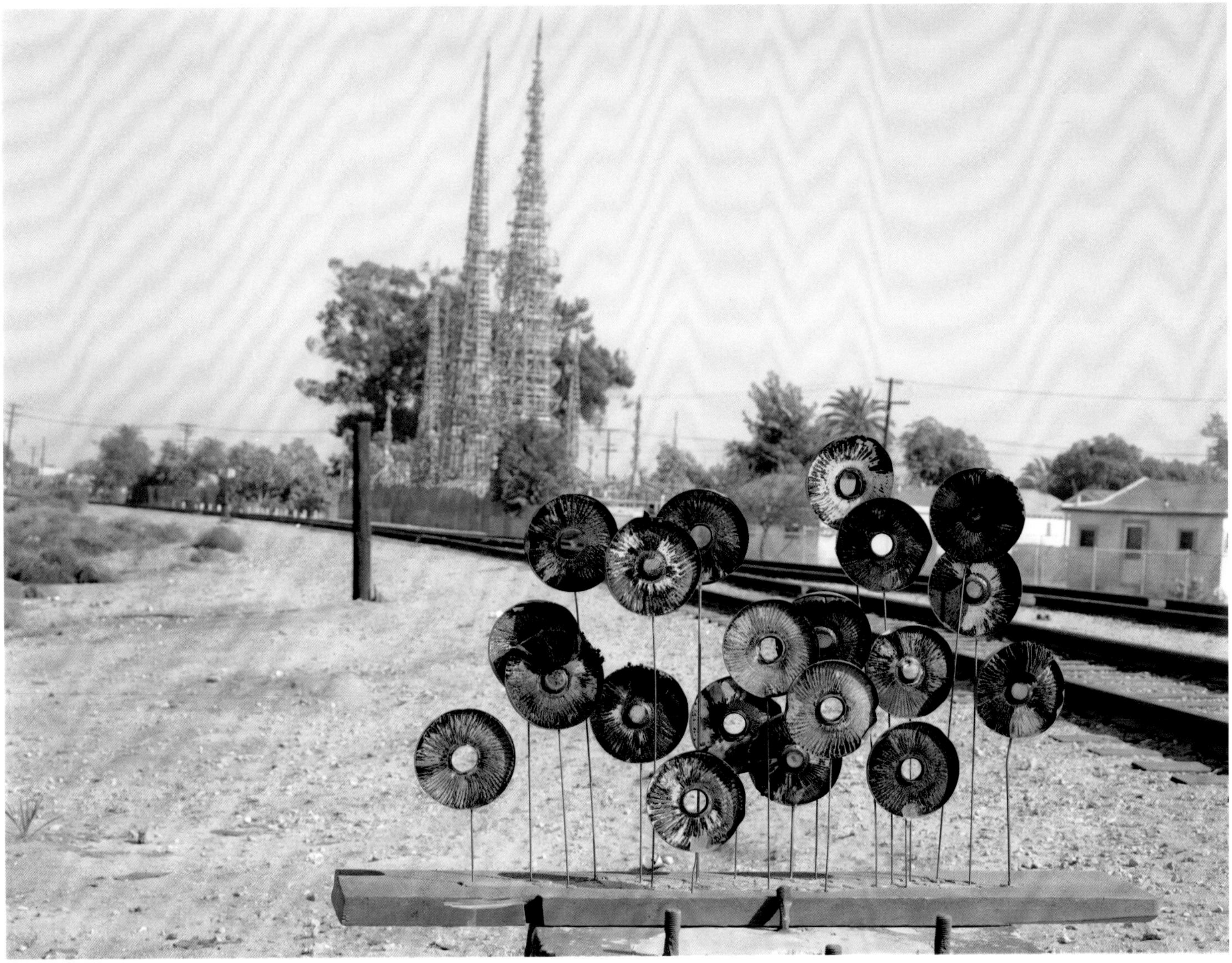

Plate 70 HARRY DRINKWATER, 1966

Artist Debby Brewer assembled this sculpture, titled *Sunflowers,* with materials gathered from the ruins of the Watts Uprising. Mounted atop thin metal rods of differing lengths, the sculpture re-creates the presence of blooming sunflowers. The sculpture was included in the *66 Signs of Neon* exhibition, which was mounted in response to the uprising and photographed by Harry Drinkwater for the exhibition catalog *Junk Art: 66 Signs of Neon*. The iconic Watts Towers are visible in the background.

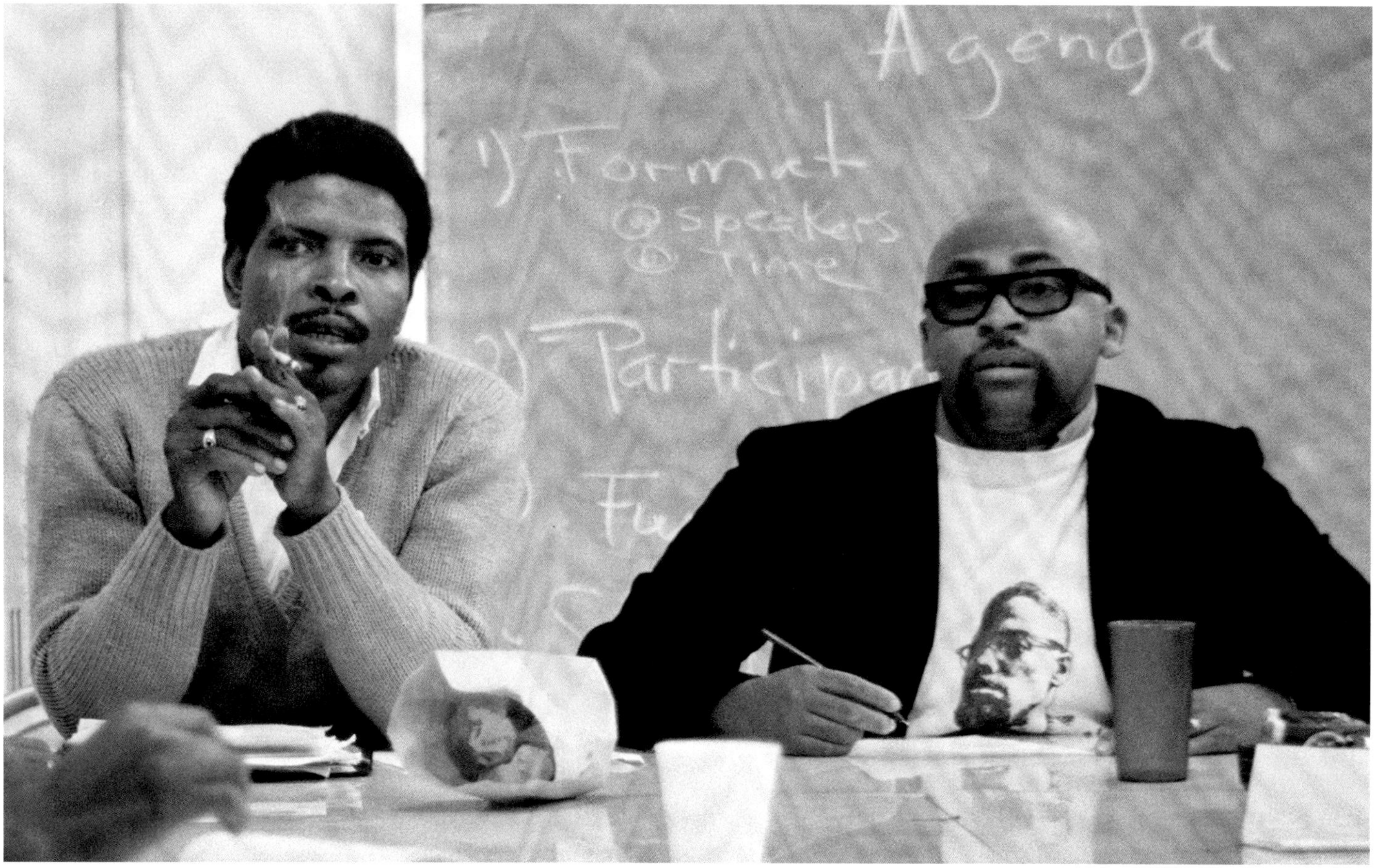

Plate 71 GORDON PARKS, 1966

Local leaders Robert Hall (*left*) and Maulana Karenga discuss the upcoming 1966 Watts rally during a Black Congress planning meeting. Gordon Parks documented this behind-the-scenes conversation for *Life* magazine, though this image was not selected for publication.

Plate 72 ROBERT FLORA, 1966

A teenager wears a leaflet promoting a protest organized in the aftermath of the killing of motorist Leonard Deadwyler in Los Angeles. Activists rallied at Will Rogers Memorial Park as tensions threatened to boil over in Watts once again. Deadwyler's unprovoked shooting death by an LAPD officer infuriated the community. This picture and others by UPI photographer Robert Flora were often made available by newswire for publication well beyond Los Angeles.

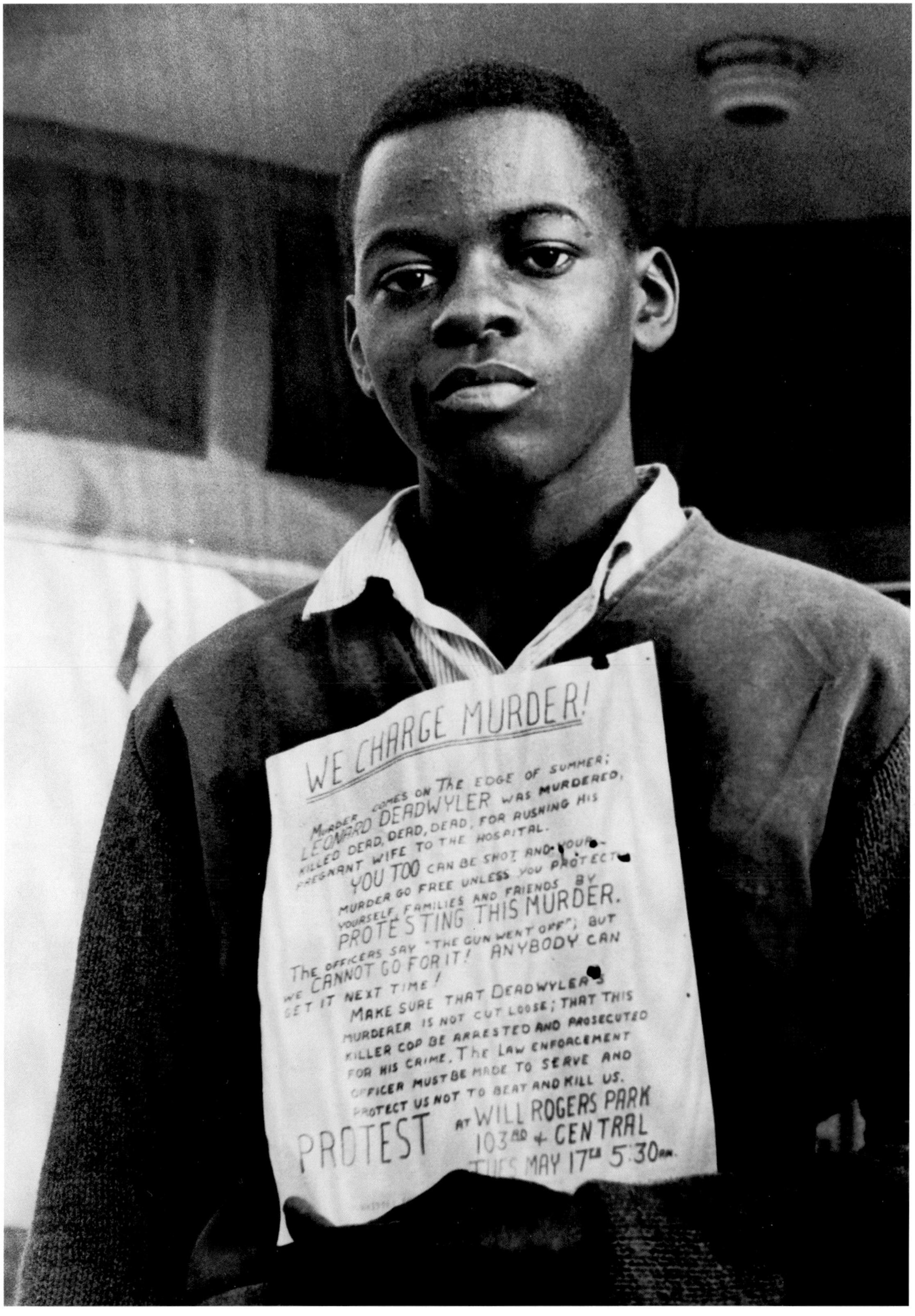
WE CHARGE MURDER!
MURDER COMES ON THE EDGE OF SUMMER; LEONARD DEADWYLER WAS MURDERED, KILLED DEAD, DEAD, DEAD, FOR RUSHING HIS PREGNANT WIFE TO THE HOSPITAL.
YOU TOO CAN BE SHOT AND YOUR MURDER GO FREE UNLESS YOU PROTECT YOURSELF, FAMILIES AND FRIENDS BY PROTESTING THIS MURDER.
The OFFICERS SAY "THE GUN WENT OFF"; BUT WE CANNOT GO FOR IT! ANYBODY CAN GET IT NEXT TIME!
MAKE SURE THAT DEADWYLER'S MURDERER IS NOT CUT LOOSE; THAT THIS KILLER COP BE ARRESTED AND PROSECUTED FOR HIS CRIME. The LAW ENFORCEMENT OFFICER MUST BE MADE TO SERVE AND PROTECT US NOT TO BEAT AND KILL US.
PROTEST
AT WILL ROGERS PARK
103RD + CENTRAL
TUES MAY 17TH 5:30PM.

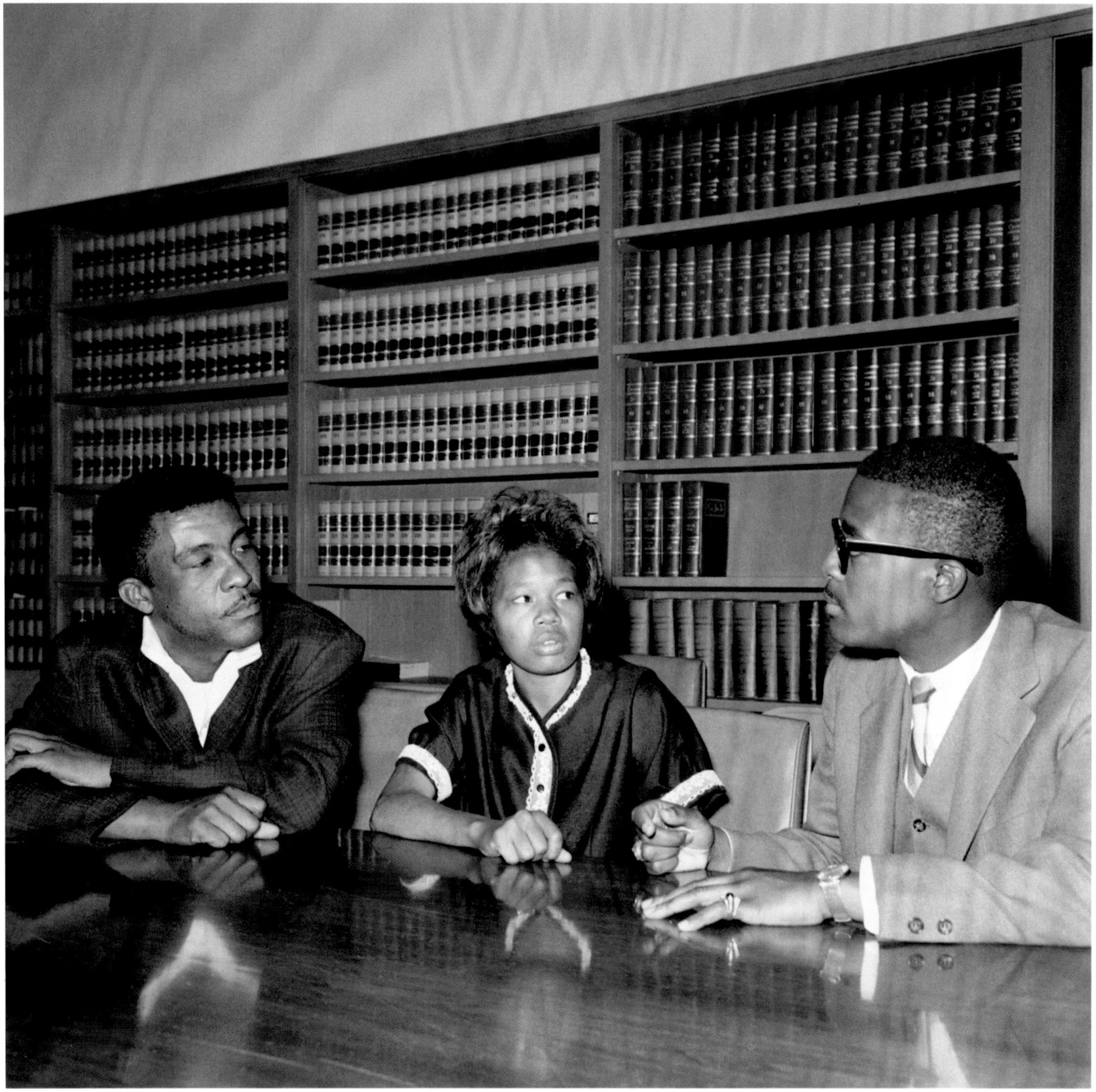

Plate 73 HARRY ADAMS, 1966

Attorney Johnnie L. Cochran Jr. (*right*) meets with Barbara Deadwyler, widow of Leonard Deadwyler, who was killed by an LAPD officer in May 1966. This was one of Cochran's first high-profile cases.

Plates 74, 75 JACK DAVIS, 1966

Positioning himself over the hood of a police car, freelance photographer Jack Davis documents a half dozen officers outside Caldonia's food stand. Another picture, taken much closer to the interaction, captures the frustration and indignation of two young women whose purses are being searched.

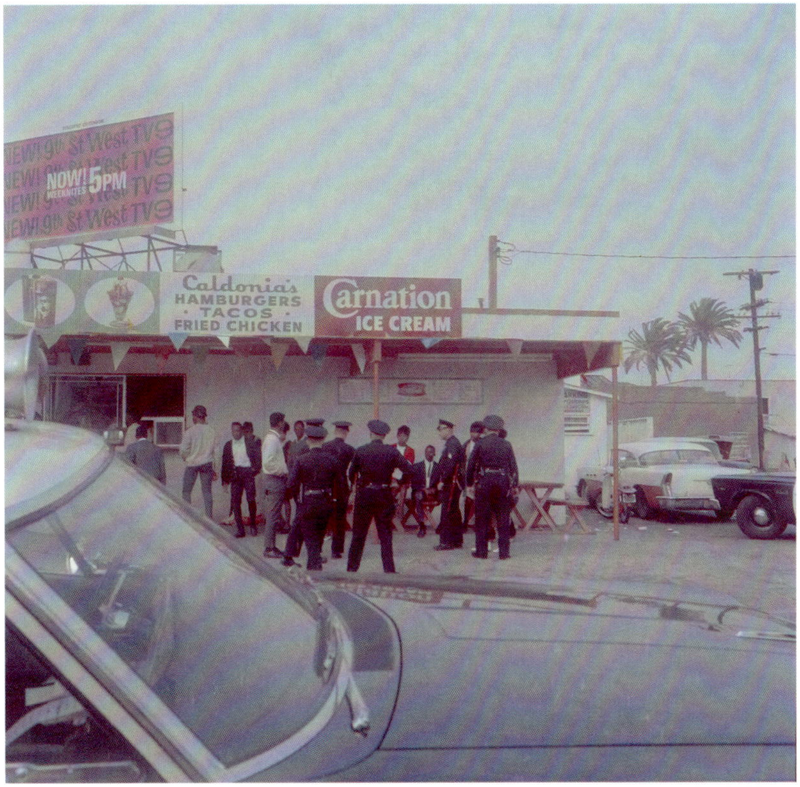
NOW! 5PM
Caldonia's
HAMBURGERS
TACOS
FRIED CHICKEN
Carnation
ICE CREAM

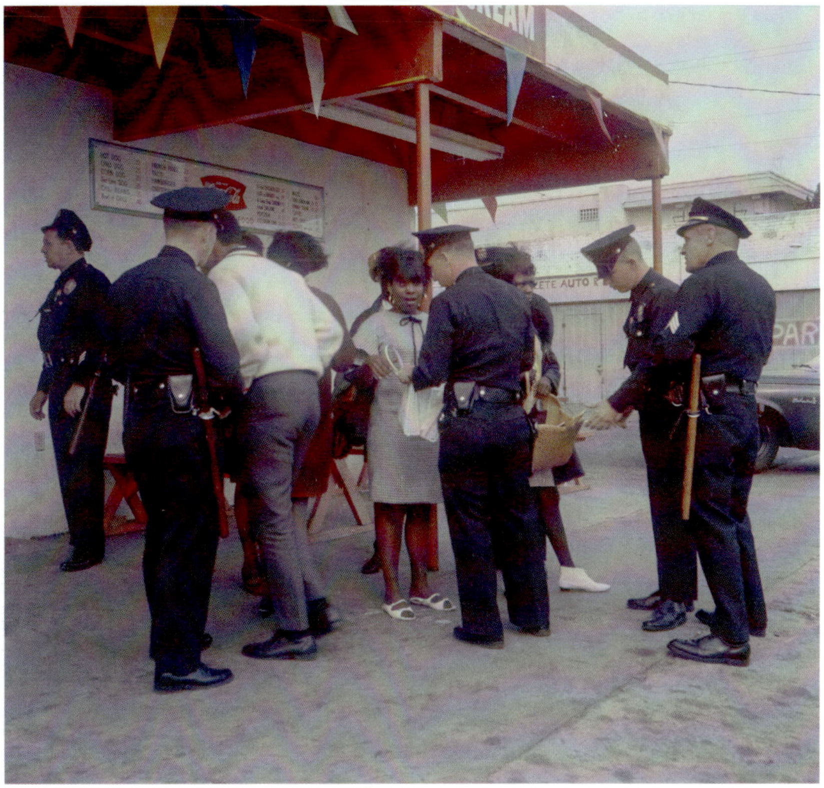

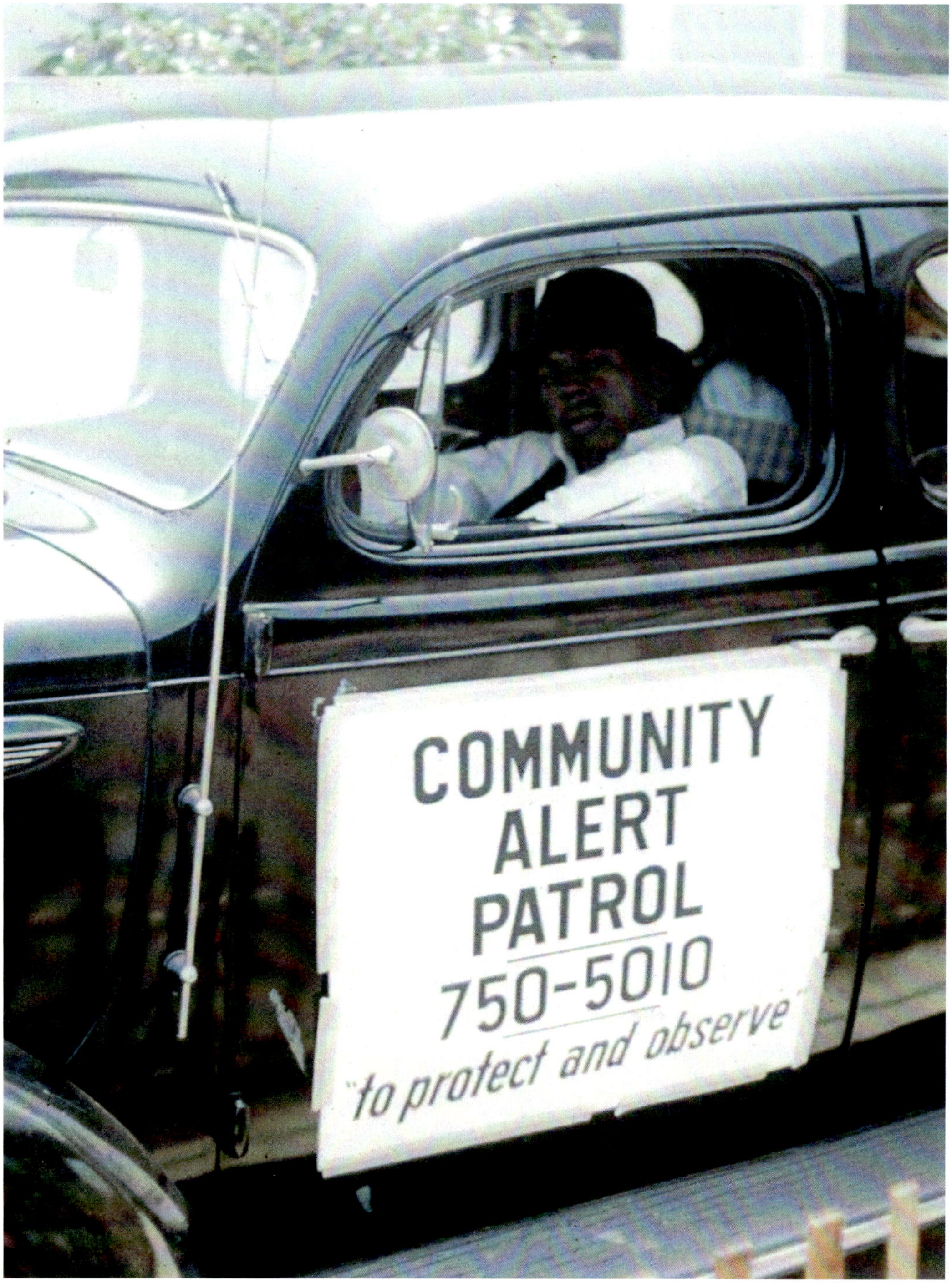
COMMUNITY
ALERT
PATROL
750-5010
"to protect and observe"

Plate 76 UNKNOWN PHOTOGRAPHER, 1966

Activist Ron "Brother Crook" Wilkins sits in an automobile emblazoned with a Community Alert Patrol sign, announcing the organization's role in monitoring the police. When the *Los Angeles Sentinel* profiled CAP in mid-June, it called attention to Brother Crook's dressy attire: "Regardless to what piece of police action Crook stops to observe, all action stops and police and citizens alike cast an observing eye on Crook."[71]

Plate 77 UNKNOWN PHOTOGRAPHER, 1968

Local and national welfare-rights leader Johnnie Tillmon speaks at the 1968 Mother's Day March on Washington coordinated by Coretta Scott King. As board chair of the influential National Welfare Rights Organization, Tillmon had been instrumental in helping Martin Luther King Jr. understand the challenges facing female wage-earners and those on welfare.

Plate 78 CHARLES WILLIAMS, 1966

Los Angeles City Council member Gilbert Lindsay and wife Theresa wave to onlookers during the Nisei Parade celebration in Little Tokyo. Lindsay became the city's first Black council member in 1963.

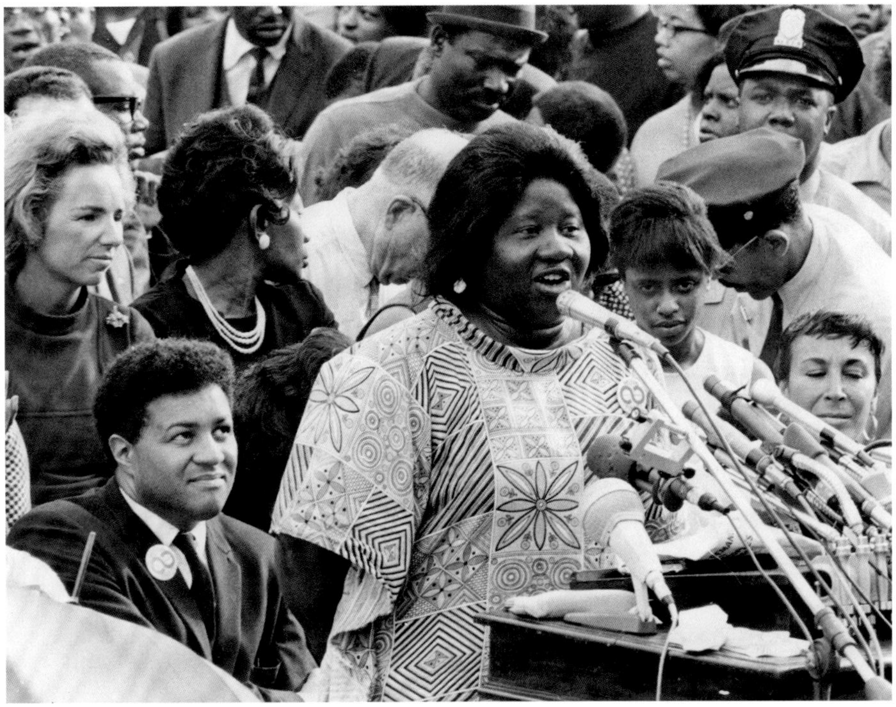

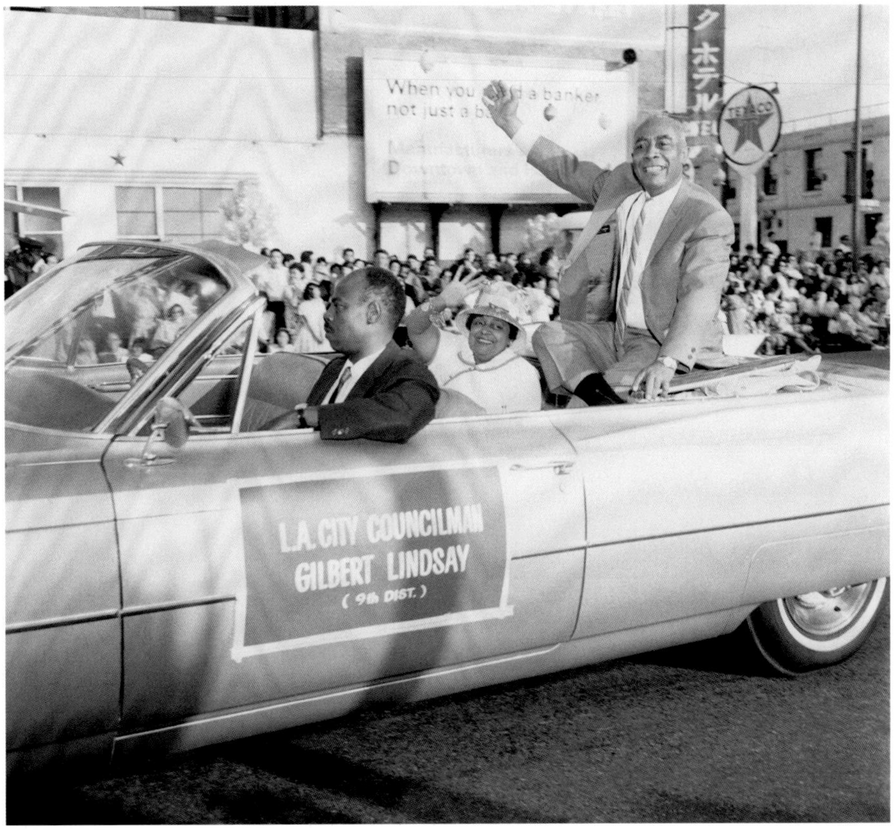

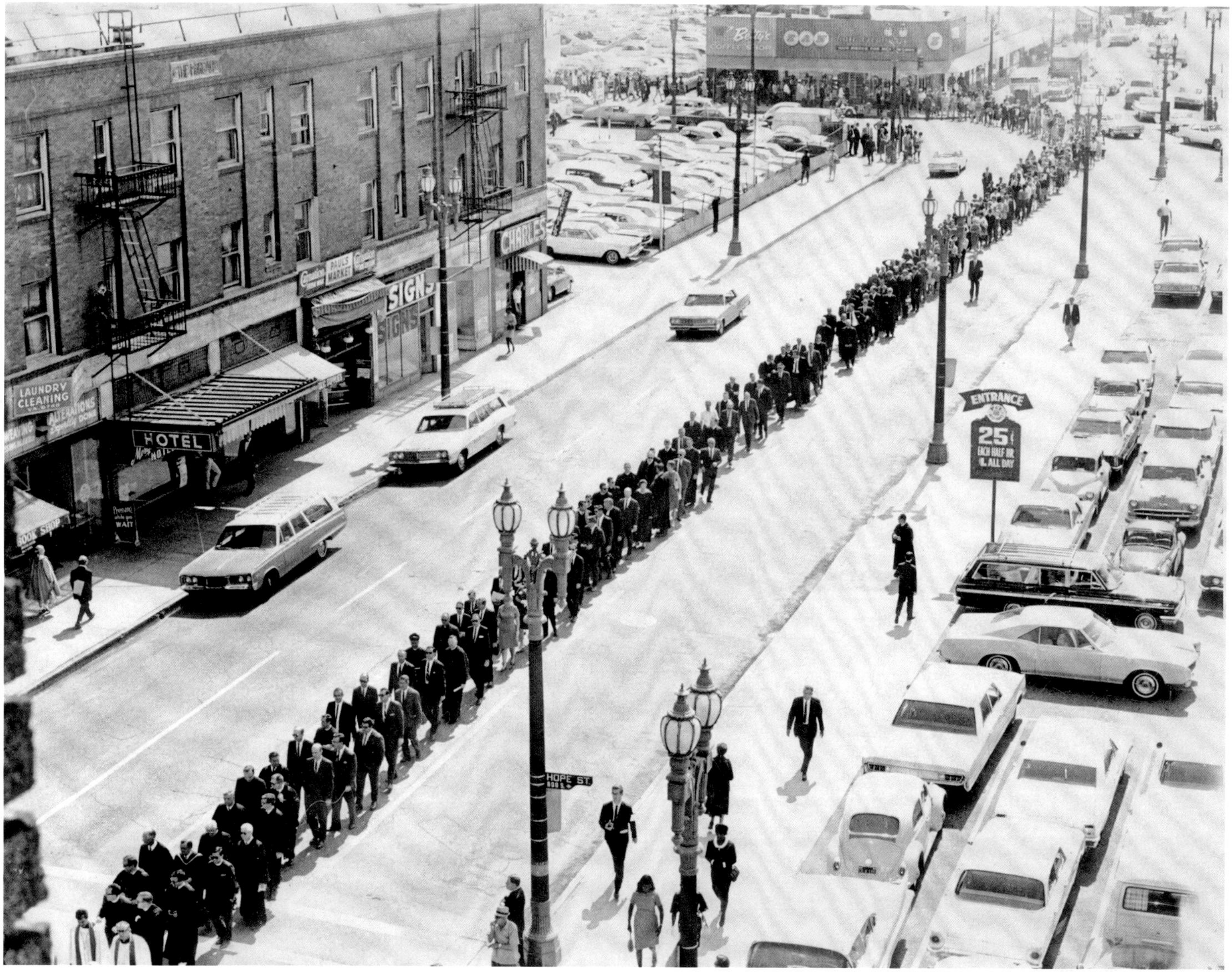

Plate 79 UNKNOWN PHOTOGRAPHER, 1968

An interfaith procession of two hundred ministers, priests, and rabbis, along with about eighteen hundred other mourners, march to First Methodist Church for a memorial service in honor of Martin Luther King Jr. A *Los Angeles Herald Examiner* photographer snapped this view from the roof of the church.

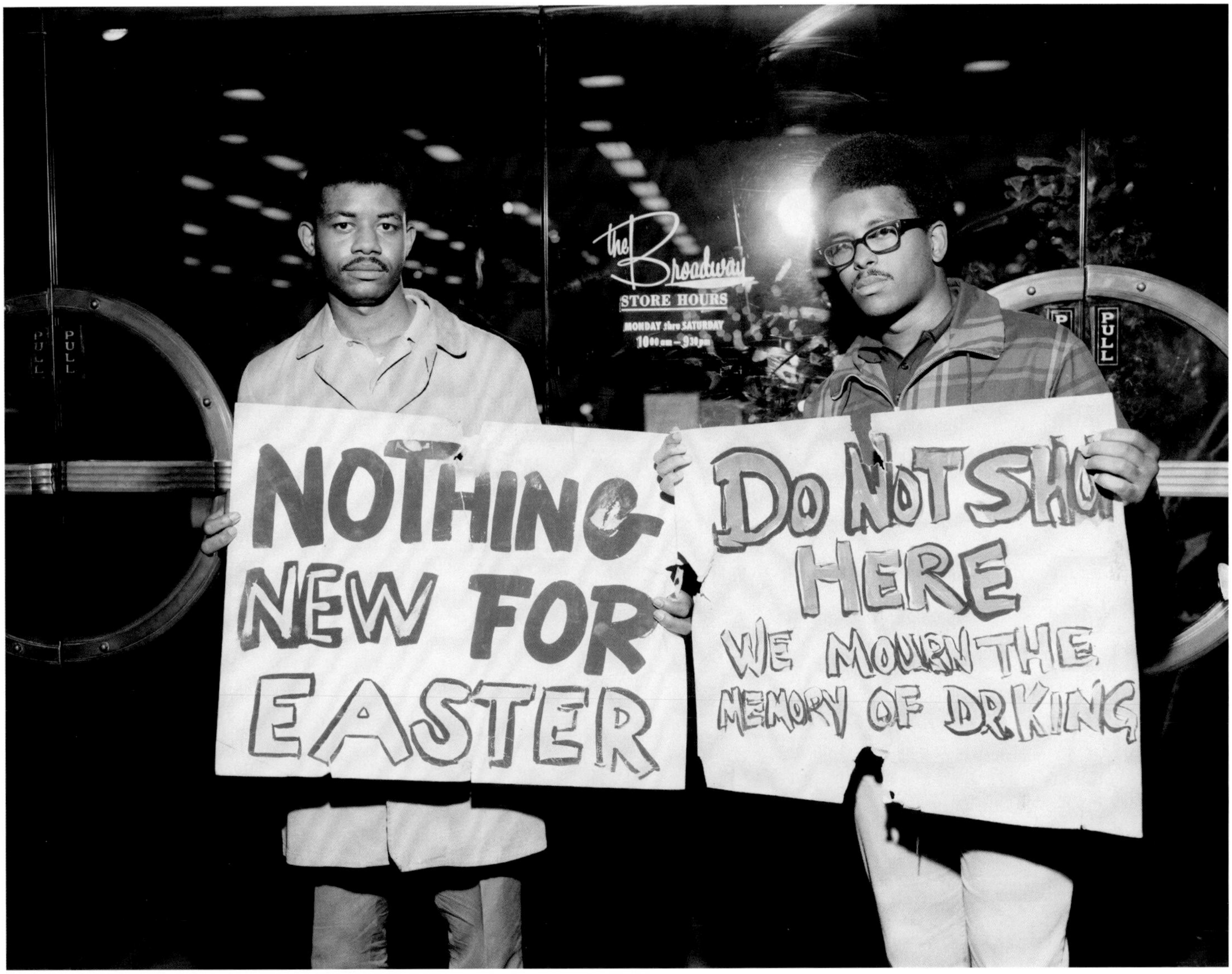

Plate 80 ROLLAND J. CURTIS, 1968

Two men demonstrate outside the Broadway department store at the Baldwin Hills Crenshaw Plaza, which refused to close during citywide mourning after Martin Luther King Jr.'s assassination in April. Picketers encouraged an economic boycott in Los Angeles in honor of King's commitment to racial and economic justice.

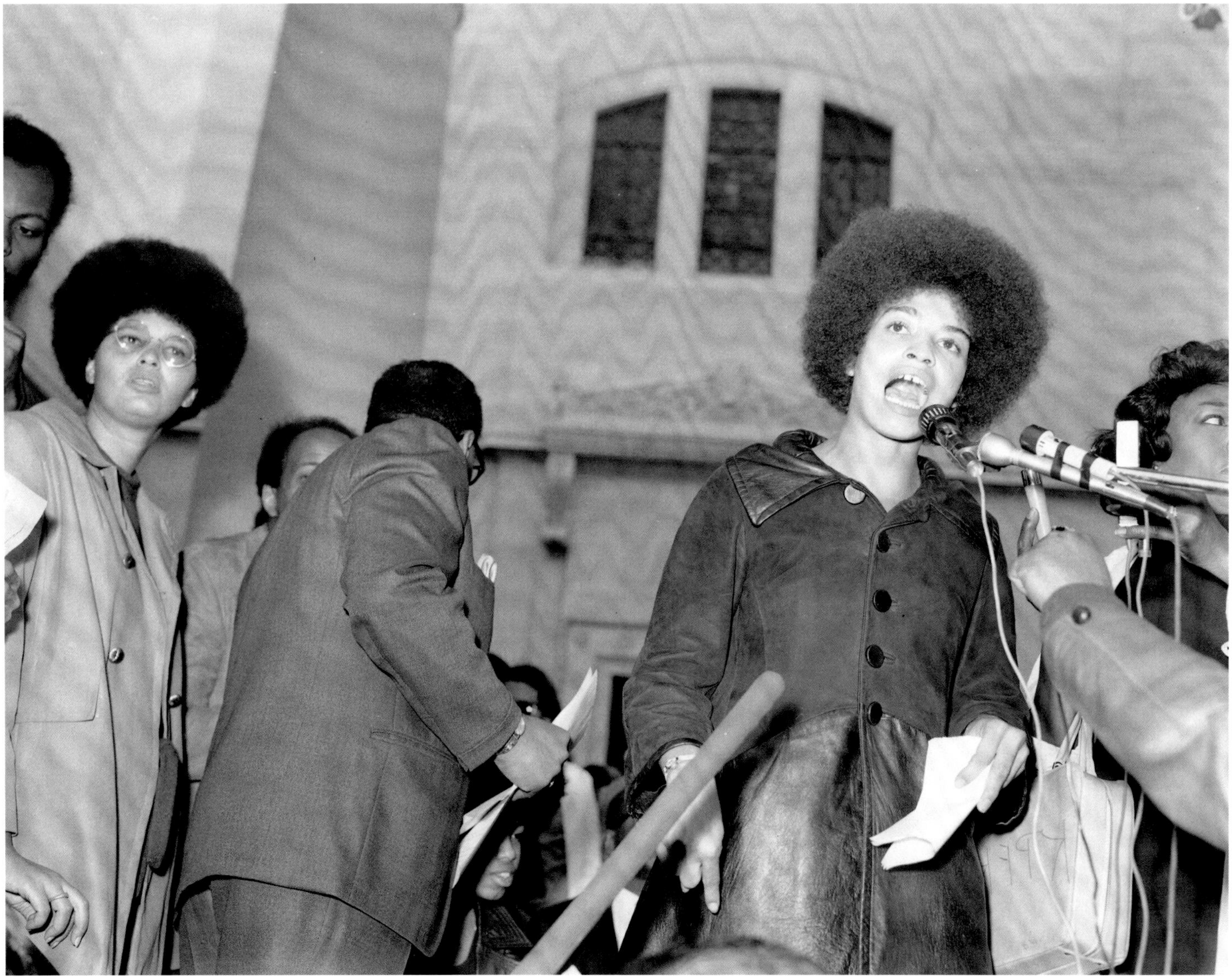

Plate 81 ROLLAND J. CURTIS, 1969

Activist Angela Davis speaks on the steps of City Hall during a December 11 protest. The SWAT/LAPD's dramatic raid three days earlier on the Black Panther Party's L.A. headquarters inspired a massive community rally of more than five thousand attendees. Leaders from a coalition of groups spoke amid raised fists and chants of "All Power to the People."[72]

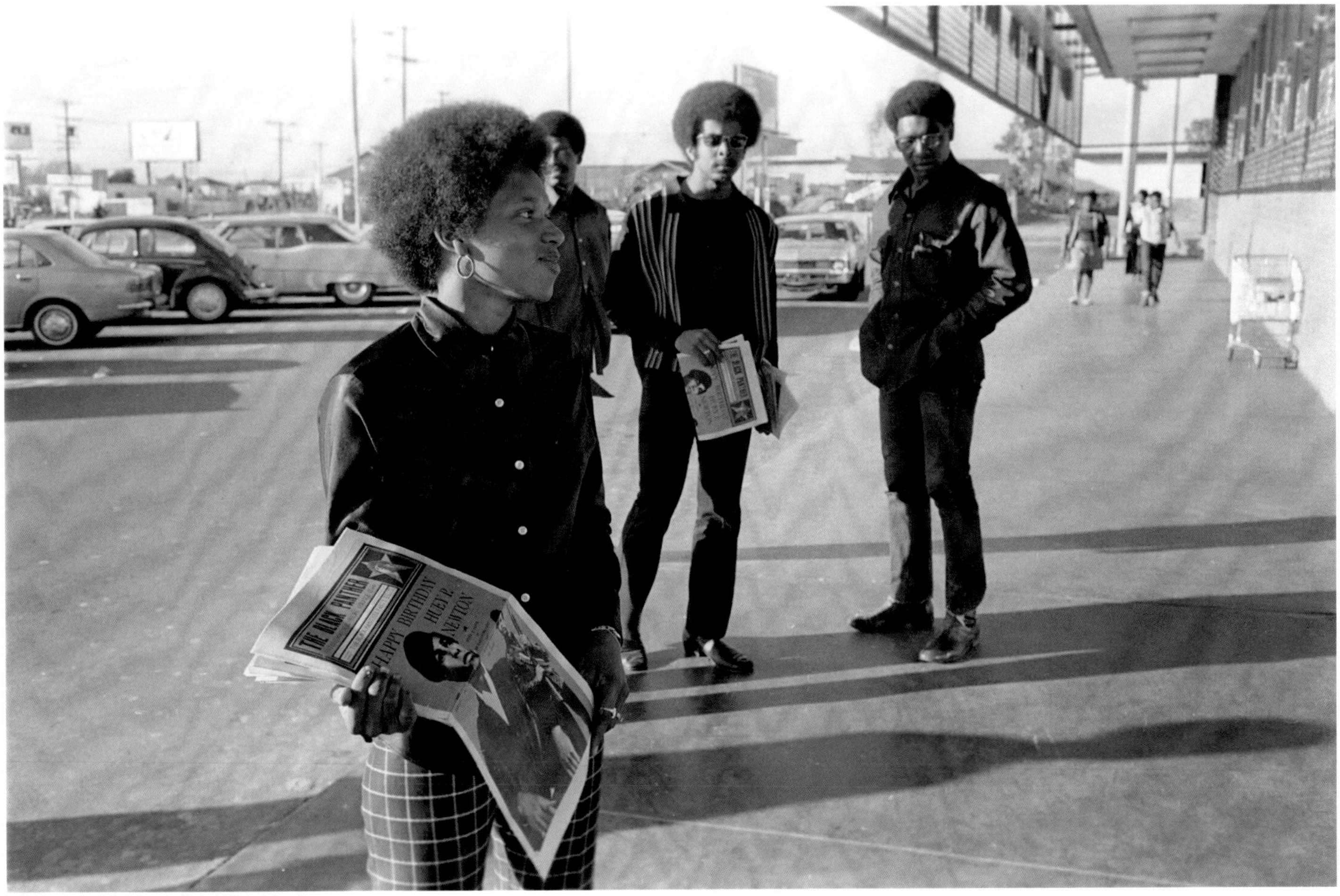

Plate 82 STEPHEN SHAMES, 1970

A woman sells *Black Panther* newspapers outside a grocery store. Photographer Stephen Shames met Black Panther Party cofounder Bobby Seale in 1967 and closely documented rallies, community programs, and political campaigns until 1973. Community-centered pictures like this one countered the Panthers' violent reputation, which the mainstream media often amplified.

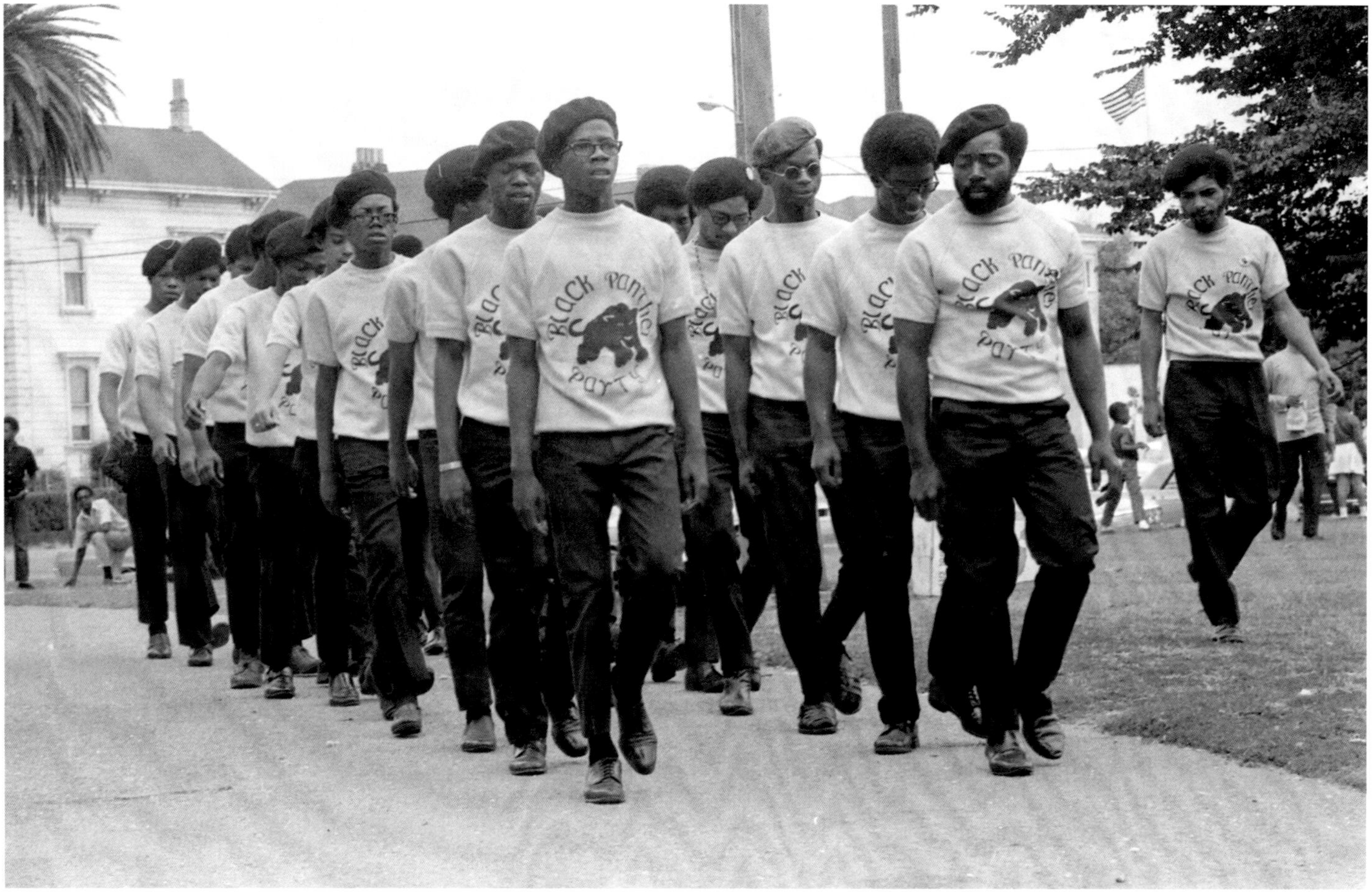

Plate 83 JEFFREY BLANKFORT, 1968

Dressed in matching shirts and berets, members of the Los Angeles chapter of the Black Panther Party march under the direction of Deputy Minister of Information John Huggins (*far right*). The group traveled to Oakland to participate in a Free Huey Rally.

Plate 84 GUY CROWDER, 1969

LAPD officers stand outside Black Panther Party headquarters at 41st Street and Central Avenue after an early morning raid and five-hour shootout. An assault force of 350 officers raked the building with gunfire and dynamited a hole in the roof into which they dropped canisters of tear gas. The FBI and local police considered the party a threat to national security. Similar sieges occurred at Panther chapters nationwide.

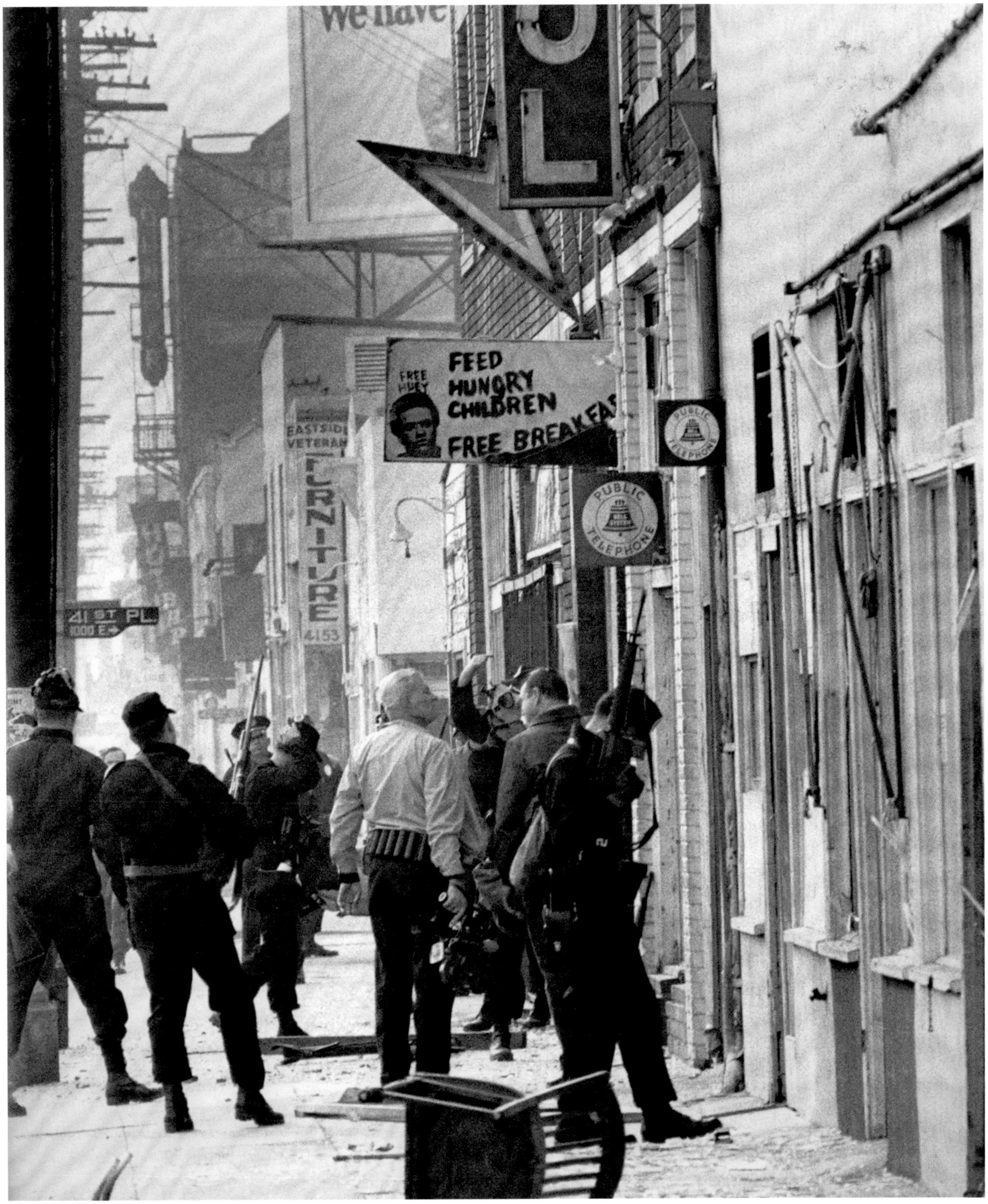

We have
FEED
HUNGRY
CHILDREN
FREE BREAKFAS
PUBLIC TELEPHONE
PUBLIC TELEPHONE
EASTSIDE
VETERAN
FURNITURE
4153
41 ST PL.
1000 E

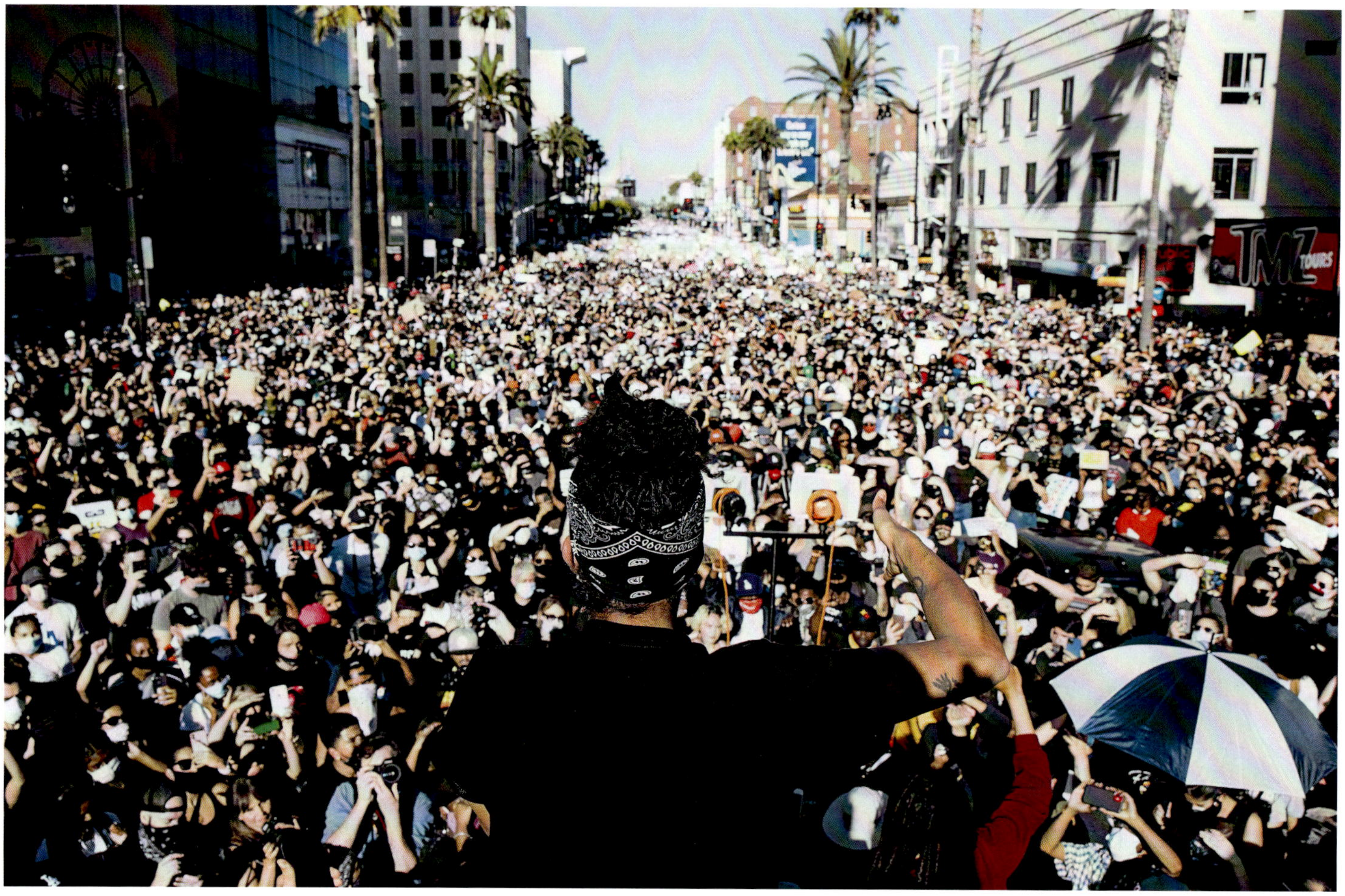

Plate 85 TOMMY OLIVER, 2020

Protesters fill Hollywood Boulevard during a Black Lives Matter rally in the summer of 2020. Black filmmaker Oliver took this widely shared photograph of a massive crowd united in solidarity.

Timeline: The Modern Civil Rights Era in Los Angeles

This timeline includes selected milestones in the struggle for African American civil rights in Los Angeles from 1954 through 1968. It also lists some significant national events that affected Black Angelenos during the period.

1954

MAY

In *Brown v. Board of Education*, the US Supreme Court unanimously ends segregation in public schools, declaring it unconstitutional and a violation of the Equal Protection Clause of the Fourteenth Amendment.

1955

MARCH

The Sears, Roebuck and Co. store in Santa Monica hires its first Black store clerk after years of protests against its discriminatory hiring practices.

AUGUST

Emmett Till, a fourteen-year-old African American boy, is lynched by two white men in Mississippi for allegedly offending a white woman. His mother, Mamie Till-Mobley, holds an open-casket funeral to draw attention to the tragedy, sparking public outrage.

DECEMBER

NAACP activist Rosa Parks refuses to give up her bus seat to a white man in Montgomery, Alabama, igniting a legal challenge against segregation nationwide.

1956

MARCH

Seven thousand people attend a fundraising rally at Olympic Auditorium to support the eighteen-week Montgomery Bus Boycott. Rev. Ralph Abernathy of the Montgomery Improvement Association gives a speech on the boycott's progress.

APRIL

Approximately three thousand people gather at Second Baptist Church to hear Rosa Parks speak about her pivotal role in the Montgomery Bus Boycott.

The Los Angeles NAACP kicks off a membership drive at Second Baptist Church during Parks's visit, which is led by chapter president Thomas Neusom and membership chair Marnesba Tillmon Tackett. Singer Sammy Davis Jr. serves as honorary chair. The drive brings in over eleven thousand new members, making the L.A. chapter one of the largest in the country with over twenty thousand members.

JUNE

Martin Luther King Jr. delivers the first of several guest sermons at Second Baptist Church.

NOVEMBER

The US Supreme Court declares segregation on public buses unconstitutional.

1957

JANUARY

The Southern Christian Leadership Conference (SCLC) is founded in Atlanta. Martin Luther King Jr. leads the organization in advocating for civil rights through nonviolent resistance.

MAY

L.A. ministers Maurice Dawkins, J. Raymond Henderson, and Arthur Atlas Peters join twenty-five thousand in Washington, DC, for the SCLC's Prayer Pilgrimage for Freedom. Participants urge the federal government to enforce *Brown v. Board of Education*.

NOVEMBER

The NAACP launches a "No Job, No Bud" boycott against Anheuser-Busch brewery, organizing pickets at the company's location in the San Fernando Valley.

1958

FEBRUARY

Martin Luther King Jr. completes a three-day residency at California Institute of Technology in Pasadena. He delivers three speeches and a keynote address titled "Progress in Race Relations," engaging with students and religious leaders on civil rights issues.

1960

JANUARY

Los Angeles Police Chief William H. Parker testifies before the US Civil Rights Commission that "there is no segregation or integration problem in this community," despite widespread racial tensions and discriminatory practices.

FEBRUARY

Four African American students from North Carolina Agricultural and Technical State University stage a sit-in at a whites-only lunch counter in a Greensboro F. W. Woolworth store, marking the beginning of the Southern sit-in movement.

Martin Luther King Jr. delivers a sermon at Temple Isaiah, showcasing the involvement of Westside and Jewish community members in the local civil rights movement.

MARCH

Students from UCLA boycott local Woolworth stores, including those in Compton and Santa Monica.

Members of the local Congress of Racial Equality (CORE) picket S. H. Kress and Woolworth stores in Los Angeles to end the companies' discriminatory practices nationwide.

APRIL

Activists form the Student Nonviolent Coordinating Committee (SNCC) in response to widespread student-led sit-ins at segregated Southern lunch counters. SNCC quickly becomes a key force for nationwide student involvement in the civil rights movement.

JULY

A march of five thousand protesters, led by local and national civil rights leaders including Martin Luther King Jr., A. Phillip Randolph, and Bayard Rustin, is held at the Los Angeles Memorial Sports Arena, site of the Democratic National Convention attended by presidential nominee John F. Kennedy.

1961

JANUARY

The founding conference of the Western Christian Leadership Conference (WCLC) is attended by more than one hundred ministers. Rev. L. Sylvester Odom of Ward AME Church and Rev. Edward Stovall of Progressive Baptist Church in Berkeley are selected for leadership positions.

JUNE

Los Angeles CORE organizes Freedom Rides to help integrate interstate travel. UCLA students and local activists join Freedom Riders in places such as Jackson, Mississippi, and Houston, Texas, where they face arrest. Their actions pressure federal enforcement of the Supreme Court's *Boynton v. Virginia* (1960) ruling, which declared racial segregation in interstate travel facilities illegal.

The WCLC hosts a Freedom Rally at the Los Angeles Memorial Sports Arena, drawing an estimated twenty-eight thousand attendees, including Gov. Edmund G. "Pat" Brown. Headliner Martin Luther King Jr. calls the gathering the greatest civil rights rally ever and helps raise funds to support the Freedom Rides.

King appears with Rev. John Doggett at USC's Bovard Auditorium, where Doggett, a Pasadena pastor and chair of two Freedom Rallies, presents him with a check to support the nationwide movement.

Musician Horace Tapscott founds the Pan Afrikan Peoples Arkestra in Los Angeles to preserve African American music and culture and to provide educational opportunities and community services. He will go on to create the Union of God's Musicians and Artists Ascension (UGMAA), which is also closely aligned with civil rights and Black Power organizations.

1962

APRIL

LAPD officers raid the Nation of Islam's Mosque No. 27, injuring six members and fatally shooting Ronald Stokes. William Rogers is left paralyzed. In response, Nation of Islam (NOI) leader Malcolm X travels to Los Angeles and condemns the attack at a press conference. He organizes protests against police brutality and racial injustice.

CORE campaigns against housing discrimination in Monterey Park. The activists organize sit-ins and picket tract offices, which leads the city council to condemn racial discrimination in housing.

AUGUST

CORE's Operation Windowshop arranges for African American families to visit model homes in suburban Los Angeles to expose housing discrimination. "Dwell-ins" citywide draw media attention and help spur the passage of California's Rumford Fair Housing Act the following year.

NOVEMBER

Edward Roybal is elected to the US House of Representatives, the first Mexican American from California to serve in Congress since 1879.

1963

Johnnie Tillmon, a single mother of six, founds Aid to Needy Children–Mothers Anonymous in Los Angeles, organizing welfare recipients at Nickerson Gardens, the housing development where she lives. Her grassroots activism will lead to the formation of the National Welfare Rights Organization in 1966, on which she will serve as first chair and later executive director.

JANUARY

Gilbert Lindsay is appointed the first Black city council member. The elections of Tom Bradley and Billy Mills to the council in April and July, respectively, mark a historic shift in Black political representation in Los Angeles.

MAY

An estimated forty thousand people, including Hollywood celebrities, gather at Wrigley Field to hear Martin Luther King Jr. speak at a Freedom Rally. The rally is organized by the WCLC with support from the Southern California Baptist Ministers Conference and other local groups to fund civil rights efforts.

JUNE

The United Civil Rights Committee (UCRC) is founded as a multiracial coalition of seventy-six organizations to combat segregation and discrimination through nonviolent mass actions. Rev. H. H. Brookins and Marnesba Tackett are some of the organization's key leaders.

Facing threats of Birmingham-style campaigns, L.A. County supervisors meet with UCRC activists. The UCRC releases "To Men of Good Will," a proposal demanding concrete action against racial injustices in housing, policing, and education.

Eighteen-year-old twin sisters Bobbie and Renee Hodges lead weekly protests against Don Wilson Builders' discriminatory housing practices in Torrance. The college students are arrested three times while picketing the whites-only Southwood Riviera Royale development and become prominent figures in the thirteen-month CORE-organized boycott.

Led by the NAACP, fifteen hundred Angelenos march to honor slain civil rights leader Medgar Evers. The mile-long march through a Black neighborhood ends at Wrigley Field, where five hundred people attend a memorial service for Evers.

CORE and UCRC lead sit-ins and hunger strikes at the L.A. Board of Education offices. Youths stage study-ins during board meetings. In November, CORE members will disrupt a meeting with a sing-in.

AUGUST

The American Civil Liberties Union (ACLU) files a class-action lawsuit against the Los Angeles Unified School District to end racial segregation. The case of *Crawford v. Board of Education* will not be resolved until two decades later.

UCRC holds weekly protest marches against segregation in Los Angeles schools. James Farmer, James Forman,

Martin Luther King Jr., and Roy Wilkins each join one of the marches.

Over one thousand Southern Californians, including members of the NAACP, CORE, and the WCLC, join the March on Washington for Jobs and Freedom in Washington, DC. Simultaneously, three thousand march in Los Angeles in support of the event.

SEPTEMBER

The Rumford Fair Housing Act is passed. The law, named after its author, Assemblyman William Byron Rumford, prohibits housing discrimination in California.

1964

FEBRUARY

During a banquet at the Hollywood Palladium sponsored by the Consolidated Realty Board, Martin Luther King Jr., alongside State Controller Alan Cranston, Assemblyman William Byron Rumford, and Rev. H. H. Brookins, discusses the dangers of Proposition 14.

MAY

An estimated two hundred religious leaders gather at the Los Angeles Memorial Coliseum for the Religious Witness for Human Dignity event, where Martin Luther King Jr. addresses a crowd of fifteen thousand on civil rights and his opposition to Proposition 14.

Members of the Association for the Protection of American Rights (APAR) picket King's appearances at WCLC events, including the opening of the WCLC's West Coast bureau. They display signs equating fair housing with communism.

Police seize the picket signs of CORE protesters who are in Ocean Park as part of a statewide initiative challenging Bank of America's unfair hiring practices. Twenty-five-year-old Woodrow Coleman is arrested after lying in front of a truck to prevent confiscated picket signs from being taken away.

JUNE

At a press conference, Father William DuBay, a civil rights supporter, reads a cable he transmitted to Pope Paul VI calling for the removal of Cardinal James Francis McIntyre for failing to provide moral leadership on the issue of racial discrimination.

JULY

President Lyndon B. Johnson signs the Civil Rights Act, which prohibits discrimination in public accommodations based on race, color, religion, or national origin.

AUGUST

Sixteen CORE members are arrested in the Los Feliz neighborhood for stretching themselves across the driveway at the Los Angeles Breakfast Club and preventing cars from leaving a White Citizens' Council meeting.

In response to the murders of three civil rights workers in Mississippi, city council member Tom Bradley introduces a memorial resolution, and Rev. H. H. Brookins preaches to seven hundred people, raising funds for a Freedom Community Center in Mississippi.

NOVEMBER

California voters overwhelmingly pass Proposition 14, allowing property owners to discriminate in housing sales and rentals based on race.

1965

FEBRUARY

Malcolm X, also known as El-Hajj Malik El-Shabazz, is assassinated while giving a speech at the Audubon Ballroom in Harlem, New York.

Following death threats and reports of stolen dynamite, police discover explosives planted at the Cinerama Dome, where Martin Luther King Jr. is scheduled to attend a screening.

MARCH

The WCLC presents Coretta Scott King as a soprano soloist in a successful fundraiser at Second Baptist Church. Her performance combines music and narration about the civil rights movement.

L.A. civil rights groups demonstrate outside the downtown Federal Building to protest the harsh treatment of marchers in Selma, Alabama.

Los Angeles activists fly to Alabama and join the five-day, fifty-four-mile march from Selma to Montgomery alongside thousands of other protesters advocating for equal voting rights.

John Floyd of SNCC travels to Alabama to support voter registration drives with the Lowndes County Freedom Organization. This experience inspires him to focus on electoral politics in Los Angeles.

Political adviser Daniel Patrick Moynihan writes the internal memo "The Negro Family: The Case for National Action," in which he describes the breakdown of the Black family as a "tangle of pathology." The controversial report's public release is condemned by liberals as "blaming the victim."

APRIL

Martin Luther King Jr. addresses a crowd of forty-five hundred at UCLA to encourage students to join the Summer Community Organization and Political Education (SCOPE) project.

Gwen Green, executive director of the WCLC, is appointed assistant director of SCOPE and transfers to Atlanta. The project deploys over twelve hundred people across six Southern states to register African Americans to vote and to train student activists. The program bridges Los Angeles and Southern civil rights efforts.

JUNE

Ted Watkins leads the establishment of the Watts Labor Community Action Committee as an anti-poverty coalition for Watts residents.

JULY

The WCLC sponsors the four-day conference "Church Speaks on Poverty, Housing, and De Facto Segregation," addressing discriminatory housing, economic inequality, and urban segregation.

A study group that meets regularly at Aquarium Bookstore establishes the US Organization. Led by Maulana Karenga and Hakim Jamal, the organization aims to create an African American revolution through the celebration of African culture and traditions.

AUGUST

President Johnson signs and Congress enacts the Voting Rights Act to combat discrimination against African Americans and other marginalized groups in the voting process.

The arrest of Marquette Frye by L.A. police officers in Watts sets off a six-day uprising that leaves thirty-four dead, over one thousand injured, and thousands arrested. The racial unrest draws national attention to police brutality, inequality, and discrimination against African Americans. *Los Angeles Times* advertising salesman Robert Richardson is hastily drafted into a reporter's role during the Watts Uprising, marking the *Times*'s belated recognition of its lack of coverage of residents in its own city.

Martin Luther King Jr. and aides meet with Gov. Edmund G. "Pat" Brown, Los Angeles Mayor Sam Yorty, and Los Angeles Police Chief William Parker regarding the Watts Uprising. King and Rev. Thomas Kilgore also meet with *Los Angeles Times* publisher Otis Chandler and address community members at the Westminster Neighborhood Association (WNA) in Watts.

Celes King III, owner of King Bail Bond Agency, posts bonds for people arrested during the Watts Uprising, helping secure their release.

The Sons of Watts, previously founded by Billy J. Tidwell, a University of California, Berkeley, graduate from Watts, helps to maintain peace following the unrest. The group promotes nonviolence and launches a pioneering employment training program that attracts funding from the private sector and the government.

Governor Brown forms the McCone Commission to investigate the Watts Uprising. The report identifies high unemployment, inadequate education, poor police–community relations, substandard housing, and limited transportation as key factors contributing to the unrest.

SEPTEMBER

Screenwriter Budd Schulberg establishes the Watts Writers Workshop to give young people an outlet to express social justice concerns through literature and poetry.

1966

The Black Congress is formed under the leadership of Walter Bremond as a federation of Black organizations, adopting the philosophy of operational unity to coordinate efforts between diverse Black organizations.

Black leaders and community advocates propose that Watts secede from Los Angeles to form a "Freedom City," encompassing the area bordered by the Harbor Freeway, Vernon Avenue, Alameda Street, and El Segundo Boulevard. Rooted in the principle of self-determination, the proposal fails due to bureaucratic obstacles.

The Los Angeles chapter of CORE joins a statewide mass picket of See's Candy Company to end racial discrimination inside the corporation.

APRIL

Regina and Ken Jones launch *SOUL* magazine to amplify the African American perspective on life and culture.

MAY

An LAPD officer fatally shoots Leonard Deadwyler, who was rushing his pregnant wife to the hospital. The incident fuels community outrage, and lawyer Johnnie L. Cochran Jr. represents the Deadwyler family. The jury rules the death an "accidental homicide."

Stirred by Leonard Deadwyler's death, the Temporary Alliance of Local Organizations (TALO) is formed at the behest of reparations activist Robert Brock, becoming the second federation of organizations in the post–Watts Uprising era.

JUNE

The Community Alert Patrol (CAP) is founded as a civilian-led group dedicated to monitoring police conduct in Los Angeles. Countering LAPD's "To Protect and to Serve" motto with "To Protect and Observe," CAP conducts nonviolent patrols to defend Black communities from police brutality and systemic abuse.

AUGUST

The inaugural Watts Summer Festival is held. Tommy Jacquette, a community activist who becomes the festival's executive director, helps transform the multiday event into a celebration of Black culture and community resilience.

OCTOBER

Among the wave of new Black activist groups that includes the Black Student Alliance, United Front, and the Che-Lumumba Club, John Floyd and Ayuko Babu form the Black Panther Political Party, emphasizing electoral power. Following a naming dispute with Huey Newton and Bobby Seale's Black Panther Party, it becomes a local SNCC chapter.

NOVEMBER

SNCC chair Stokely Carmichael advocates for Black Power at Will Rogers Memorial Park before a crowd of three thousand.

DECEMBER

The US Organization establishes Kwanzaa as a seven-day holiday (December 26 to January 1) rooted in African harvest festivals. The holiday celebrates family, community, and culture through seven core principles, including unity and self-determination. Kwanzaa will grow to be celebrated worldwide.

Hakim Jamal founds the Malcolm X Foundation in Compton to advance Black empowerment. Grounded in Malcolm X's philosophy, its strategy focuses on providing free Montessori education for Black children that teaches early learning in math, science, and cultural identity as tools for self-reliance, liberation, and community transformation.

1967

Brothers Dale and Alonzo Davis open the Brockman Gallery in Leimert Park, one of the first Black-owned art galleries in the United States. The gallery exhibits emerging and established African American artists such as Betye Saar, David Hammons, and Romare Bearden and serves as a vital cultural hub.

OCTOBER

Martin Luther King Jr. speaks to eighteen hundred people at USC's Bovard Auditorium during the university's Great Issues Forum. A bomb threat interrupts the speech, forcing an evacuation, but King returns to finish his address.

NOVEMBER

The Western Regional Black Youth Conference features keynote speaker James Foreman of SNCC, who delivers the speech "Liberation Will Come from a Black Thing." Among the two hundred attendees are Olympic athletes Tommie Smith and John Carlos, as well as Lew Alcindor (later known as Kareem Abdul-Jabbar), who strategize about an Olympic boycott, thereby advancing Black Power organizing.

1968

FEBRUARY

More than ten thousand gather at a rally and fundraiser at the Los Angeles Memorial Sports Arena to support incarcerated Black Panther Party leader Huey Newton. Speakers include party cofounder Bobby Seale, James Forman, Eldridge Cleaver, Alprentice "Bunchy" Carter, H. Rap Brown, Stokely Carmichael, Maulana Karenga, Reies Tijerina, and others.

MARCH

African American and Chicano high school students stage coordinated walkouts protesting educational inequities, overcrowding, and discriminatory practices.

Several Los Angeles ministers meet with Rev. Jesse Jackson, national director of Operation Breadbasket, at Second Baptist Church to discuss expanding the program nationwide.

APRIL

Martin Luther King Jr. is assassinated on April 4. Just three weeks earlier, he spoke at Holman Methodist Church and the California Democratic Council in Orange County on various issues, including voting rights, the Poor People's Campaign, the Vietnam War, and civil rights.

Several memorial services are held across Los Angeles to honor King, including one attended by two hundred clergymen from various denominations.

In response to the news of King's death, the Black Congress speaks out against destructive unrest. The organization maintains peace in Los Angeles by organizing an Easter shopping boycott, channeling Black anger into protest against discriminatory merchant practices.

The *Los Angeles Sentinel* publishes a special memorial edition featuring forty-four pages of photographs and stories about the slain civil rights leader. The issue includes reflections from local ministers, elected officials, and community organizers, as well as heartfelt contributions from entertainers Lena Horne, Sidney Poitier, and Marlon Brando.

MAY

Activist Johnnie Tillmon helps lead the Mother's Day March and Rally with Coretta Scott King, drawing six thousand participants to officially launch the Poor People's Campaign. The marchers protested welfare cuts and the stigmatizing treatment experienced by mothers on public aid.

The Black Student Alliance (BSA), established at California State University, Los Angeles, serves as a key connector in building collaborative networks between Black Student Unions (BSUs) at Historically Black Colleges and Universities (HBCUs), predominantly white colleges, and secondary schools.

AUGUST

Three young Black Panther Party members—Tommy Lewis, Steve Bartholomew, and Robert Lawrence—are shot and killed by Los Angeles police officers at a Crenshaw District service station during what the officers call a routine check. A fourth, Anthony Bartholomew, survives the encounter.

DECEMBER

Catherine Jermany, president of the Los Angeles County Welfare Rights Organization, leads two hundred fifty welfare recipients in a two-hour confrontation at the Hall of Administration, demanding Christmas bonuses of $35 per child and $40 per adult from county officials.

Acknowledgments

My earliest memory of electoral politics involves playing among voting booths at my grandparents' South L.A. home, which served as a polling station. It was an early lesson in civic engagement that would shape my personal and professional path. Later, as a professor at California State University, Northridge (CSUN), interested in weaving local civil rights history into my teaching, I discovered that while substantial records of African American civic engagement and activism existed, they remained buried in collections with limited public access. A discussion with CSUN provost Harry Hellenbrand changed my approach completely, as he connected me to the Institute of Arts and Media (now the Tom & Ethel Bradley Center at CSUN), which houses a remarkable collection of images documenting Black life in L.A. With Harry's support, I collaborated with students on the book *African Americans in Los Angeles*, highlighting the grassroots resilience that is often hidden in plain sight.

My inspiration deepened when I discovered the volume *North of Dixie* by historian Mark Speltz—a powerful photo collection of civil rights activism outside the South. I knew that the Bradley Center's vast archive of images by African American photographers presented an opportunity to fill a gap with a focused visual history of the civil rights era in Los Angeles. Elizabeth Nicholson, senior editor at Getty Publications, responded to my book idea with unexpected enthusiasm, and I connected with Mark, who generously agreed to join as coauthor and contribute his skills, time, and partnership. I am deeply grateful to both for bringing invaluable wisdom to this project.

The groundbreaking research and writing of distinguished professors Jeanne Theoharis and Clayborne Carson, and of curator Susan D. Anderson of the California African American Museum (CAAM), are forerunners to this work. Mark and I extend our heartfelt thanks to them for taking leave of their demanding schedules to provide feedback that supported and strengthened this book in myriad ways. At CSUN, Mark Stover, dean of the University Library, championed this project, and I was fortunate to have served as special projects director at the Tom & Ethel Bradley Center during his tenure. The College of Arts and Sciences provided a sabbatical and funded the digital map "The Enduring Spirit of Martin Luther King in Los Angeles."

I am grateful to the activist-intellectuals whose memories and expertise have given this project a human dimension, bringing this history to life. They include but are not limited to former city council member Robert Farrell, Lorraine Bradley, John Floyd, Robert Johnson, Delores Jardan-Stokes, Ron Wilkins, Norma Mtume, Harry Carey, Kicheko Davis, Byron Booth, Kumasi and Ayuko Babu, and Akil S. Batani-Khalfani. I am forever indebted to Gwendolyn Green, the former executive director of the Western Christian Leadership Conference and a friend with whom I share a special bond.

Many archivists at research institutions supported this project with their time and expertise. Mark and I extend deep gratitude to Bradley Center historian/archivist Keith Rice, archivist Beth Peattie, and licensing manager Kendra Gonzalez for providing access and insights into the rich collections there. Sincerest thanks to Michelle Welsing at the Southern California Library for Social Studies and Research, and to CAAM, UCLA Special Collections, USC Special Collections, UC Berkeley Bancroft Library, Los Angeles Public Library, and Peter Kunhardt and staff at the Gordon Parks Foundation.

We are grateful to the photographers, activists, and scholars who provided insights and ideas and graciously aided our efforts, including Jeffrey Blankfort, Bruce Hartford, Lawrence Schiller, Stephen Shames, and Deborah Willis. Special thanks go to Mazie Harris, associate curator of photographs at the J. Paul Getty Museum, for her helpful discussions and assistance. To manuscript editor Sharon Shahid and the staff at Getty Publications, including associate editor Darryl Oliver, designer Jon Grizzle, production coordinator Molly McGeehan, rights coordinator Nancy Rivera, and editorial assistant Molly Stevens, we offer our deepest respect and appreciation.

For me, this project required a deeply personal foundation and would not have been possible without the support of family members who became true collaborators: Connie and Christopher Whitlock, Rafiki Cai, and my daughter, Ashley Jackson, who served as technologist, researcher, and chapter editor.

This work is grounded in my inherited responsibility. I hold special reverence for my great-grandparents, Isaiah and Minnie Smith, who raised my grandmother, Lucinda Hunt, who spoke softly but acted with remarkable courage. My cousin Daisy McNealy, one of our family's earliest migrants from Mississippi to Los Angeles in 1912, now holds a place of honor in a stained-glass window at First African Methodist Episcopal Church. I carry the memory of my mother, Maudestine Stanford, who dared to vote when others challenged her right to and remained active in service well into her senior years; my aunts Alna Pearl Brown and Myrtle Joan Gibson; my uncles Hebron, Herbert, and Alfred Hunt; and my cousins Beverly Porter and Donald Bronson, all of whom encouraged my educational pursuits and strengthened my commitment to family and community. I salute those who still carry the torch—cousins Bobbe Akalonu, Thomas Persons, and Lorna Nash—and are preserving our story.

Karin L. Stanford

Americans are more likely to see pictures of Los Angeles engulfed in the flames of the Watts Uprising than images of the decades of peaceful civil rights activism that preceded 1965. Then and now, the city's persistent racial inequities are often hidden, forgotten, or overshadowed by more dire conditions elsewhere, especially in the South. *Marching West* represents an effort to reveal the full history of the civil rights struggle in Los Angeles and to broaden the visual narrative of that urgent and compelling story.

The opportunity to collaborate on a book like this one is rare, and the chance to explore the rich archives of the Black photographers and newspapers that chronicled the Los Angeles community and its activism is truly a gift. I would like to extend my deep gratitude to Karin Stanford for inviting me to collaborate with her on this work and for sharing her expertise in the L.A. movement's history. In addition to reiterating my thanks to all the curators, scholars, photographers, and Getty Publications leadership and staff who contributed to this project, I want to thank Elizabeth Nicholson, senior editor, for her unwavering support.

None of this would have been possible without the friends and family who encouraged and sustained me through all the challenges. Immense gratitude and love to Heather Beaton, whose curious and warm spirit brings more joy than one can imagine. I dedicate this book to my daughter, Marie Speltz, whose generous heart, sense of humor, and smile brighten every day.

Mark Speltz

Notes

INTRODUCTION

1. Arthur Berman, "30,000 at Rally Hear Plea for Civil Rights," *Los Angeles Times*, May 27, 1963.
2. Martin Luther King Jr., "The Rising Tide of Racial Consciousness," September 6, 1960, The Martin Luther King, Jr. Research and Education Institute, Stanford University, transcript, https://kinginstitute.stanford.edu/king-papers/documents/rising-tide-racial-consciousness-address-golden-anniversary-conference.
3. Douglas Flamming, *Bound for Freedom: Black Los Angeles in Jim Crow America* (University of California Press, 2006), 2.

CHAPTER ONE

1. Deborah Willis, *Reflections in Black: A History of Black Photographers 1840 to the Present* (W. W. Norton & Company, 2002), xvi.
2. Laura Wexler, "'A More Perfect Likeness,' Frederick Douglass and the Image of the Nation," in *Pictures and Progress: Early Photography and the Making of African American Identity*, ed. Maurice O. Wallace and Shawn Michelle Smith (Duke University Press, 2012), 21.
3. "Bridget 'Biddy' Mason," National Park Service, last modified February 7, 2021, https://www.nps.gov/people/biddymason.htm; "Santa Monica Mountains, Ballard Family," National Park Service, last modified September 22, 2022, https://www.nps.gov/samo/learn/historyculture/ballard-family.htm; "Heads and tails–and odds and ends," Notable Kentucky African Americans Database, accessed July 23, 2024, https://nkaa.uky.edu/nkaa/items/show/300001795; and Karin Stanford, *African Americans in Los Angeles* (Arcadia Press, 2010), 12–13.
4. John S. Portlock, "'Fabled Land of Make-Believe': Charlotta Bass and Jim Crow Los Angeles," in *The Strange Careers of the Jim Crow North: Segregation and Struggle Outside of the South*, ed. Brian Purnell and Jeanne Theoharis (New York University Press, 2019), 67–68.
5. "Building a Community: A Look at African American Institutions in Early Los Angeles," Los Angeles Public Library, February 1, 2021, https://www.lapl.org/collections-resources/blogs/lapl/building-community-look-african-american-institutions-early-los; U.S. Census Bureau, *Twelfth Census of the United States*, 1900 (Population by Race for Cities over 25,000), summarized in *African American Citywide Historic Context Statement* (San Francisco Planning Department, 2015).
6. E. Frederick Anderson, *The Development of Leadership and Organization Building in the Black Community of Los Angeles from 1900 Through World War II* (Century Twenty One Publishing, 1980), 116–17.
7. Max Bennett Thrasher, "An Account of Booker T. Washington's California Tour," in *The Booker T. Washington Papers, Vol. 7: 1903–4*, ed. Louis R. Harlan and Raymond W. Smock (University of Illinois Press, 1977), 167–69; Marne L. Campbell, *Making Black Los Angeles: Class, Gender, and Community, 1850–1917* (University of North Carolina Press, 2016), 192–93.
8. W. E. B. Du Bois, "Colored California," *The Crisis: A Record of the Darker Race*, August 1913, 192–95, https://www.marxists.org/history/usa/workers/civil-rights/crisis/0800-crisis-v06n04-w034.pdf.
9. Eleanor Mason Ramsey, "Allensworth: A Study in Social Change" (PhD diss., University of California, Berkeley, 1977), 15.
10. Anderson, quoted in Lynell George, "'Allensworth: 100 Years of the California Dream' at the California African American Museum," *Los Angeles Times*, May 26, 2008, https://www.latimes.com/entertainment/arts/la-et-allensworth26-2008may26-story.html.
11. Louis R. Harlan and Raymond W. Smock, eds., *The Booker T. Washington Papers, Vol. 13: 1914–15* (University of Illinois Press, 1984).
12. Alice C. Royal, *Allensworth, the Freedom Colony: A California African American Township* (Heyday Books, 2008), 84–88.
13. Emory J. Tolbert, *The UNIA and Black Los Angeles: Ideology and Community in the American Garvey Movement* (Center for Afro-American Studies, University of California, Los Angeles, 1980), 53.
14. W. E. B. Du Bois to Walter White, undated, file C, container 301, NAACP Papers, Library of Congress, cited in Beth Hayslett, "In the Shadows of 'History Written with Lightning': The NAACP's Protest Against *The Birth of a Nation*" (master's thesis, Dartmouth College, 2000), 1.
15. Charlotta Bass, *Forty Years: Memoirs from the Pages of a Newspaper* (pub. by author, 1960), cited in Hayslett, "In the Shadows," 39.
16. Flamming, *Bound for Freedom*, 34.
17. Ibid., 242–247, 357–58.
18. Tolbert, *UNIA and Black Los Angeles*, 143.
19. Ibid., 72.
20. Holly Roose, "Multicultural Garveyism in the Far West," in *The Racial Frontier: African Americans in the West from the Great Migration to the Twenty-First Century, 1915–2015*, eds. Dwayne Mack and Herb Ruffin II (University of Oklahoma Press, 2016), 167.
21. Tolbert, *UNIA and Black Los Angeles*, 137–59.
22. Hadley Meares, "Betty Hill's 'Bath House' Battle," *Curbed Los Angeles*, https://la.curbed.com/2019/8/19/20757888/betty-hill-segregation-pools.
23. Flamming, *Bound for Freedom*, 286–91.
24. Ibid., 287.
25. Ibid., 289.
26. *California Eagle* editorial, August 26, 1927, https://www.newspapers.com/article/california-eagle-pullman-porters-brother/131794818/.
27. Edward Berman, "The Pullman Porters Win," *The Nation*, August 21, 1935, https://socialwelfare.library.vcu.edu/eras/great-depression/brotherhood-of-sleeping-car-porters-win-over-pullman-company/.
28. Flamming, *Bound for Freedom*, 357–58.
29. Douglas Flamming, *African Americans in the West* (ABC-CLIO, 2009); Josh Sides, *L.A. City Limits: African American Los Angeles from the Great Depression to the Present* (University of California Press, 2003), 57–94; and James v. Marinship, 25 Cal. 2d 721 (1944).
30. *James*, 25 Cal. 2d 721.
31. Transcript of interview with Vera Jackson, "The Black Press: Soldiers Without Swords," https://www.pbs.org/blackpress/film/fulltranscript.html.
32. Alison Jefferson et al., "African American History of Los Angeles," *Survey LA* (2018), 88, https://planning.lacity.org/odocument/7db8747f-87fb-4c6f-bb95-5482be050683/SurveyLA_AfricanAmericanHCS_05242019.pdf; and Kevin Allen Leonard, "In the Interest of All Races: African Americans and Interracial Cooperation in Los Angeles During and After World War II," in *Seeking El Dorado: African Americans in California*, ed. Kevin Mulroy et al. (University of Washington Press, 2001), 323–24, 328.
33. Buddy Collette with Steven Isoardi, *Jazz Generations: A Life in American Music and Society* (Continuum, 2000).
34. Marl Young, "The Amalgamation of Locals 47 and 767," *Overture Magazine*, December 1988.
35. Buddy Collette, William Douglass, and Marl Young, interviews by Steven L. Isoardi, Central Avenue Sounds Oral History Project, UCLA Oral History Program, 1989–1990.
36. "Marl Young: The Groundbreaking Legacy of a Civil Rights Leader," AFM Local 47, last modified February 7, 2018, https://www.afm47.org/press/marl-young/.
37. Bass, *Forty Years*, 128.
38. *Los Angeles Sentinel* editorial, January 3, 1946, https://libproxy.csun.edu/login?url=https://www.proquest.com/historical-newspapers/violence-threat-against-short-must-not-go/docview/562095430/se-2.
39. Lynn M. Hudson, *West of Jim Crow: The Fight Against California's Color Line* (University of Illinois Press, 2020), 167–68, https://csu-un.primo.exlibrisgroup.com/permalink/01CALS_UNO

/1uh4jr6/alma991012541207202914; and *Los Angeles Sentinel* editorial, January 3, 1946.

40. Commodore Wynn, ed., *Negro Who's Who in California* (Negro Who's Who in California Publishing Co., 1948), 54.

41. Hadley Meares, "The Thrill of Sugar Hill," *Curbed Los Angeles*, February 22, 2018, https://la.curbed.com/2018/2/22/16979700/west-adams-history-segregation-housing-covenants.

42. Amina Hassan, *Loren Miller: Civil Rights Attorney and Journalist*, vol. 10 (University of Oklahoma Press, 2015).

43. *Los Angeles Sentinel* editorial, August 26, 1948.

44. Brad Pye Jr., interview by R. Kent Kirkton, July 31, 1991, transcript, Center for Photojournalism and Visual History, California State University, Northridge, 20.

45. Scott Kurashige, *The Shifting Ground of Race: Black and Japanese Americans in the Making of Multiethnic Los Angeles* (Princeton University Press, 2008), 1–3.

46. "Little Tokyo Historic District," National Park Service, last modified October 12, 2023, https://www.nps.gov/places/little-tokyo-historic-district.htm.

47. Kurashige, *Shifting Ground of Race*, 165.

48. Ibid., 105, 158, 172.

49. Stephanie Hinnershitz, "Zoot Suit Riots and Wartime Los Angeles," National WWII Museum New Orleans, June 1, 2023, https://www.nationalww2museum.org/war/articles/zoot-suit-riots-and-wartime-los-angeles.

50. "Zoot Suiters Learn Lesson in Fights with Servicemen," *Los Angeles Times*, June 7, 1943; and "City-Wide Youth Meet to Hit Bias Tomorrow," *California Eagle*, June 7, 1943.

51. "Zoot Suiters Learn Lesson"; and "City-Wide Youth."

52. "Sleepy Lagoon Murder and the Zoot Suit Riots," L.A. Law Library, https://www.lalawlibrary.org/pdfs/grants/Sleepy_Lagoon_Murder.pdf.

53. Kenneth Burt, "The Power of a Mobilized Citizenry and Coalition Politics: The 1949 Election of Edward R. Roybal to the Los Angeles City Council," *Southern California Quarterly* 85, no. 4 (2003): 413–38.

54. *Los Angeles Times* editorial, April 17, 2016, https://www.latimes.com/socal/daily-pilot/tn-wknd-et-0417-sylvia-mendez-70-anniversary-20160417-story.html.

55. "Los Angeles Unified School District Historic Context, 1870–1969," prepared by Sapphos Environmental, Inc., for the Los Angeles Unified School District, Office of Environmental Health and Safety (2014), 109, https://planning.lacity.gov/odocument/5a14c032-614e-4cd2-b58a-9507df31fbd1/Los%20Angeles%20Unified%20School%20District%20Historic%20Context%2C%201870-1969.pdf.

56. Jeanne Theoharis, "WALKOUT!: High School Students and the Development of Black Power in LA," in *Neighborhood Rebels: Black Power at the Local Level*, ed. Peniel E. Joseph (Palgrave Macmillan US, 2010), 107–29.

57. Ibid., 163.

58. Grace E. Simons, "School Board President Ducks Issue in Fremont High Race Baiting Outbreak," *Los Angeles Sentinel*, March 20, 1947.

59. Shana Bernstein, *Bridges of Reform: Interracial Civil Rights Activism in Twentieth-Century Los Angeles* (Oxford University Press, 2011), 88–89.

60. Ibid.

CHAPTER 2

1. Timothy B. Tyson, *The Blood of Emmett Till* (Simon and Schuster, 2017), 2.

2. "100,000 View Mutilated Body," *California Eagle*, September 8, 1955.

3. Joseph M. Rose, "Of Images and History: Five African-American Photographers in Los Angeles" (master's thesis, California State University, Northridge, June 1999), 76.

4. "100,000 View Mutilated Body"; and "Our People Have No Protection, Says Till's Uncle," *California Eagle*, November 17, 1955.

5. "Truckloads of Gifts Speeding to Mississippi," *California Eagle*, December 22, 1955; and "Open Season on Negroes," *California Eagle*, December 22, 1955.

6. "7000 Attend 'Bama Protest Rally: Leader Sparks Meeting," *Los Angeles Sentinel*, March 29, 1956.

7. Ibid.

8. Marnesba Tackett, "Black Leadership in Los Angeles: Marnesba Tackett," interview by Michael Balter, Online Archive of California, 1982, transcript, https://oac.cdlib.org/view?docId=hb8n39p5jk;NAAN=13030&doc.view=frames&chunk.id=div00004&toc.depth=1&toc.id=&brand=oac4.

9. "Local NAACP Rolls Up Big Membership," *Los Angeles Sentinel*, April 12, 1956.

10. Ibid.

11. Donzaleigh Abernathy, *Partners to History: Martin Luther King, Jr., Ralph David Abernathy, and the Civil Rights Movement* (Crown, 2003), 33.

12. Velva Henderson, "Velva Henderson to King Papers Project," July 3, 1990, Martin Luther King, Jr. Research and Education Institute, Stanford University.

13. David Neumann, "A Respectable Militancy: Reverend J. Raymond Henderson and the Civil Rights Struggle in Los Angeles, 1941–1963," *Southern California Quarterly* 100, no. 4 (2018): 471–504.

14. "Candidate: Maurice A. Dawkins," Our Campaigns, accessed August 19, 2019, https://www.ourcampaigns.com/CandidateDetail.html?CandidateID=8430.

15. "Leader Here to Get Pilgrimage Off the Ground," *Los Angeles Sentinel*, April 18, 1957.

16. "Los Angeles Branch Operations, 1957," Selected Branch Files, 1956–1957, 204, NAACP Papers; and "Governor to Declare May 17 'Prayer' Day," *Los Angeles Sentinel*, May 9, 1957.

17. Martin Luther King Jr., "Give Us the Ballot," speech, May 17, 1957, Martin Luther King, Jr. Research and Education Institute, transcript; and Clayborne Carson et al., eds., *The Papers of Martin Luther King, Jr., Volume IV: Symbol of the Movement, January 1957–December 1958* (University of California Press, 1957).

18. "Negroes Rally and Pray for Desegregation," *Los Angeles Times*, May 18, 1957.

19. "'Don't Get Weary,' Rev. King Advises Overflow Audience," *California Eagle*, February 27, 1958.

20. Neumann, "Respectable Militancy," 499.

21. August Meier and Elliott Rudwick, *CORE: A Study in the Civil Rights Movement* (University of Illinois Press, 1975).

22. Mike Davis and Jon Wiener, *Set the Night on Fire: LA in the Sixties* (Verso Books, 2020), 51–52.

23. John R. Vile, "Talley v. California," Free Speech Center, last modified March 31, 2025, https://www.mtsu.edu/first-amendment/article/34/talley-v-california.

24. "57 Spotlights 3 Phases of Race Battle," *California Eagle*, January 2, 1958.

25. Meier and Rudwick, *CORE*, 95.

26. *Los Angeles Times* editorial, March 26, 1960.

27. Robert Singleton, interview by Elston L. Carr, UCLA Center for African American Studies Oral History Program, 1996–1997, transcript, https://static.library.ucla.edu/oralhistory/pdf/submasters/21198-zz00099pt5-1-submaster.pdf.

28. Robert Singleton, "Helen and Robert Singleton – UCLA 100 – Our Stories, Our Impact," UCLA, October 2, 2019, video, 00:49, https://ourstoriesourimpact.irle.ucla.edu/robert-singleton/.

29. Ibid.

30. Singleton, interview by Carr.

31. Ibid., 155–56.

32. Martin Luther King Jr. and A. Philip Randolph, "Statement Announcing the March on the Conventions Movement for Freedom Now," address, June 9, 1960, Martin Luther King, Jr. Research and Education Institute, transcript.

33. "King, Powell to Address Prayer Rally," *Los Angeles Sentinel*, June 30, 1960; and "Adam Clayton Powell to Speak at Independent," July 7, 1960.

34. Maurice Berger, *For All the World to See: Visual Culture and the Struggle for Civil Rights* (Yale University Press, 2010), 125.

35. John F. Kennedy, "Acceptance of the Democratic Nomination for President," speech, July 15, 1960, John F. Kennedy Presidential Library and Museum; "1960 Democratic Party Platform," Democratic Party, Democratic National Convention, Los Angeles, July 11, 1960; and Taylor Branch, *Parting the Waters: America in the King Years, 1954–63* (Simon and Schuster, 1988), 318.

36. Rose, "Of Images and History," 184.

37. "Affiliate Action," SCLC newsletter, May 1961.

38. "Rev. Peters Heads Group," *Los Angeles Sentinel*, July 4, 1963.

39. Elliott Rudwick, *Race Riot at East St. Louis, July 2, 1917* (University of Illinois Press, 1982), 135–37.

40. Davis and Wiener, *Set the Night on Fire*, 59.

41. "Second Baptist Church Freedom Riders Heading into Mississippi," *Los Angeles Sentinel*, July 13, 1961.

42. Sandy Banks, "Taking a Trip into Civil Rights History," *Los Angeles Times*, January 8, 2011, https://www.latimes.com/archives/la-xpm-2011-jan-08-la-me-banks-20110108-story.html.

43. "From the Freedom Rides to the L.A. City Council," UCLA Newsroom, May 10, 2011, https://newsroom.ucla.edu/stories/from-the-freedom-rides-to-the-l-a-city-council.

44. Ibid.

45. *Los Angeles Times* editorial, June 19, 1961.

46. Wanda Joyner Dorsey, "Staffer Impressed by Dr. King Speech," *Los Angeles Sentinel*, July 13, 1961.

47. Jim Goodrich, "Rally Success," *Los Angeles Times*, July 16, 1961.

48. Dorsey, "Staffer Impressed."

49. Ibid.

50. "40,000 at Greatest Rally," *California Eagle*, June 22, 1961.

51. Singleton, interview by Carr.

52. Martin Luther King Jr., "Temple Isaiah Speech," February 1960, audio, 0:39:37, https://templeisaiah.com/mlk/.

53. King, "Temple Isaiah Speech," 0:12:43.

54. Joyce Antler, "Emma Lazarus Federation of Jewish Women's Clubs," February 27, 2009, Jewish Women's Archive, https://jwa.org/encyclopedia/article/emma-lazarus-federation-of-jewish-womens-clubs.

55. "Three Pray for Dr. King at City Hall," *Los Angeles Times*, August 1, 1962.

56. Charles E. Brown, "The Epic of Ashton Jones," *Ebony*, October 1965, 45–56.

57. Martin Luther King Jr., "Canoga Park High School Speech," Canoga Park High School, video, January 1961, 00:18, https://canogaparkhs.lausd.org/apps/pages/index.jsp?uREC_ID=4203783&type=d&pREC_ID=2508491.

58. Esther B. Jones, "Sympathy March in Pasadena," *Los Angeles Sentinel*, April 7, 1960.

59. Eric Etheridge, *Breach of Peace: Portraits of the 1961 Mississippi Freedom Riders* (Atlas & Co. Publishers, 2008).

60. Mamie Till-Mobley and Christopher Benson, *Death of Innocence: The Story of the Hate Crime That Changed America* (Random House, 2003), 139.

61. "Dont Get Weary."

62. Helen Singleton, "Helen and Robert Singleton – UCLA 100 – Our Stories, Our Impact," UCLA, October 2, 2019, video, 00:49, https://ourstoriesourimpact.irle.ucla.edu/robert-singleton/

63. "Equality Demand by King," *Los Angeles Herald & Express,* June 19, 1961.

CHAPTER 3

1. "Seven Unarmed Negroes Shot in Cold Blood by Los Angeles Police," *Muhammad Speaks*, August 1962, https://drive.google.com/file/d/1mPCSDqob3NBf08jcLkh2K012TfUwutHD/view.

2. Frederick Knight, "Justifiable Homicide," *Journal of Negro History*, vol. 79, no. 2 (1994): 188.

3. Delores Jardan-Stokes, transcript, 26; Delores Daaimah Jardan, *Etched into My Soul: Expressing My Memories and Gratitude over Eight Decades* (Book Power Publishing, 2023), 88.

4. Monroe Jones, interview by Keith Rice and Karin Stanford, November 15, 2021, video, Tom & Ethel Bradley Center, California State University, Northridge, https://www.youtube.com/watch?v=t2X27duTYlg.

5. *California Eagle* editorial, May 23, 1963; and Malcolm X, "Malcolm X Los Angeles Press Conference," May 4, 1962, UCLA Film & Television Archive, https://www.youtube.com/watch?v=EPsFihYdD6g.

6. Malcolm X, "Malcolm X Los Angeles Press Conference."

7. Ibid.

8. Afrii Diaspora Dialogue, "*Malcolm X, May 05, 1962, in Los Angeles Mosque No. 27,*" accessed September 2, 2025, https://afrii.forum/articles/historia/speeches/malcolm-x-may-05-1962-in-los-angeles-mosque-no-27/.

9. Robert Farrell, "Thousands Mourn Death of Local Muslim Leader," *California Eagle*, May 10, 1962.

10. Maurice Berger, "Malcolm X as Visual Strategist," *New York Times*, September 19, 2012, https://archive.nytimes.com/lens.blogs.nytimes.com/2012/09/19/malcolm-x-as-visual-strategist/, and Thulani Davis, *Malcolm X: The Great Photographs* (Stewart, Tabori, and Chang, 1993), 7–27.

11. Berger, "Malcolm X as Visual Strategist"; and "Top New York Muslim says L.A. is on Trial," *Los Angeles Times*, May 4, 1963, 8.

12. Berger, "Malcolm X as Visual Strategist."

13. Claude Andrew Clegg III, *An Original Man: The Life and Times of Elijah Muhammad* (St. Martin's Press, 1997), 20.

14. Manning Marable, *Malcolm X: A Life of Reinvention* (Penguin UK, 2011), 319–20.

15. Knight, "Justifiable Homicide," 185; and Garrett Felber, *Those Who Know Don't Say: The Nation of Islam, the Black Freedom Movement, and the Carceral State* (UNC Press Books, 2019), 7.

16. Knight, "Justifiable Homicide," 192.

17. Marable, *Malcolm X*, 351.

18. Hakim Jamal, *From the Dead Level: Malcolm X and Me* (Random House, 1972), 221.

19. Ibid., 222–23.

20. Malcolm X, "Malcolm X Los Angeles Press Conference."

21. Jeanne Theoharis, "'Alabama on Avalon,' Rethinking the Watts Uprising and the Character of Black Protest in Los Angeles," in *The Black Power Movement: Rethinking the Civil Rights–Black Power Era*, ed. Peniel E. Joseph (Routledge, 2013), 39; and Celes King III, interview by Bruce M. Tyler and Robin D. G. Kelley, April 27, 1985, Black Leadership in Los Angeles, UCLA Library, Center for Oral History Research, 154–55.

22. *New York Times* editorial, December 2, 1963, https://www.nytimes.com/1963/12/02/archives/malcolm-x-scores-us-and-kennedy-likens-slaying-to-chickens-coming.html.

23. "Rev. King in Rallies Sunday," *Los Angeles Sentinel*, June 14, 1962; and "Draft Plans for Freedom Day," *Los Angeles Sentinel*, June 7, 1962.

24. "Rev. King in Rallies Sunday."

25. Ibid.

26. Martin Luther King Jr., "The Dilemma and the Challenge Facing the Negro Today," speech, June

17, 1962, audio, 43.7 minutes, Martin Luther King Jr. Estate Collection.

27. "Charges of Racial Discrimination Against Police Hearing," *Los Angeles Times*, September 14, 1962.
28. Martin Luther King Jr., "Letter from Birmingham Jail," *UC Davis Law Review* 26 (1992): 835.
29. Meeting minutes from the Los Angeles City Council, vol. 470, April 19, 1963, Los Angeles City Archives, 734.
30. Ibid., 735
31. "Negro 'Ghetto' Termed Major Threat to L.A.," *Los Angeles Times*, May 25, 1963.
32. Berman, "30,000 at Rally Hear Plea."
33. "Negro 'Ghetto'," *Los Angeles Times*.
34. Berman, "30,000 at Rally Hear Plea."
35. "Greatest Freedom Rally Here Nets Heroes over $75,000," *Los Angeles Sentinel*, May 30, 1963; and Berman, "30,000 at Rally Hear Plea."
36. Emilie Raymond, *Stars for Freedom: Hollywood, Black Celebrities, and the Civil Rights Movement* (University of Washington Press, 2015), 117–20.
37. Dorothy Dandridge, "The Power of African American Women Disc 1," speech, Pacifica Radio Archives, Internet Archive, https://archive.org/details/pra_powerofafricanamericanwomen_1/02_We_Want_To_Be_Free.wav.
38. Donald Bogle, *Dorothy Dandridge: A Biography* (Amistad Press, 1997); and "Let Me In: Jackie Robinson Busted Barriers at Chase Hotel," Retro Simba, last modified February 13, 2023, https://retrosimba.com/2023/01/30/let-me-in-jackie-robinson-busted-barriers-at-chase-hotel/.
39. Berman, "30,000 at Rally Hear Plea."
40. "Greatest Freedom Rally."
41. Raymond, *Stars for Freedom,* 119.
42. "Rights Group Selects Dr. Brookins as Head," *Los Angeles Times*, June 17, 1964.
43. "L.A. Meeting Proposed to Avert Racial Strife: Businessmen, Negro Leaders, City, County Officials Would Participate in Conference," *Los Angeles Times*, June 4, 1963.
44. Paul Weeks, "Law Enforcement Hit by Negroes," *Los Angeles Times*, June 25, 1963.
45. Christopher Taylor et al., "To Men of Good Will: A Statement of Major Grievances and Immediate Requirements of the Negro Community," June 3, 1963, Tim Sampson Papers, Box 12, Labor Archives and Research Center, San Francisco State University, 2.
46. Taylor et al., "To Men of Good Will," 1–2.
47. Paul Weeks, "Negro Reactions Mixed on Rights Response: 10-Day Wait-and-See Attitude Agreed On by New United Civil Rights Committee," *Los Angeles Times*, June 8, 1963.
48. "What Leaders Said About Right's Week," *Los Angeles Sentinel*, June 15, 1963.
49. Theoharis, "Alabama on Avalon," 39–66.
50. Ibid., 42
51. August Meier and Elliott Rudwick, *CORE: A Study in the Civil Rights Movement, 1942–1968* (Oxford University Press, 1973), 246–47.
52. Garrett A. Felber, "Those Who Say Don't Know and Those Who Know Don't Say: The Nation of Islam and the Politics of Black Nationalism, 1930–1975" (PhD diss., University of Michigan, 2017); "Prison for the Innocent," *Muhammad Speaks*, August 30, 1963.
53. "1,500 Parade in Memory of Evers Here," *Los Angeles Times*, June 17, 1963.
54. "Picketing for Justice," *Los Angeles Sentinel*, August 1, 1963; and "Two for Freedom," *Los Angeles Sentinel*, August 8, 1963.
55. "Mobilization of Groups for March on Washington," *Los Angeles Sentinel*, August 29, 1963.
56. Raymond, *Stars for Freedom*, 117–18.
57. "March on Washington for Jobs and Freedom," National Park Service, https://www.nps.gov/articles/march-on-washington.htm.
58. Charles Brittin, *West and South* (Foggy Notion Books, 2011), 9.

CHAPTER 4

1. Thomas Kilgore, interview by Robin D. G. Kelley, 1998, Black Leadership in Los Angeles, UCLA Library, Center for Oral History Research.
2. Marie Hughes, "Housing Foes Picket King, CRB Banquet," *California Eagle*, February 20, 1964.
3. "Picket Dr. King: Housing Foes Hit Banquet," *Los Angeles Sentinel*, February 20, 1964.
4. "Leaders Join Rev. King at CRB Banquet," *Los Angeles Sentinel*, February 20, 1964; and *Los Angeles Sentinel*, August 27, 1964.
5. "Dr. King Urges Initiative Defeat," *Los Angeles Sentinel*, April 30, 1964, A4.
6. "Martin Luther King Jr. Speaks at Human Dignity Event," L.A. Memorial Coliseum Timeline, 2023, https://www.lacoliseum.com/timeline/human-dignity-event-to-have-dr-king-at-coliseum/#:~:text=On%20May%2031%2C%201964%2C%20less,Dyke%2C%20pictured)%2C%20Dr.
7. "Hate Pickets Thank God for Chief Parker," *California Eagle*, May 7, 1964.
8. Kurashige, *Shifting Grounds of Race*.
9. "Inflammatory Talk on Prop. 14," *Los Angeles Times*, August 31, 1964.
10. "Why Prop. 14 Deserves a YES Vote," *Los Angeles Times*, October 18, 1964.
11. "Brown Assails Prop. 14," *Los Angeles Times*, October 8, 1964.
12. Martin Luther King Jr., "Beyond the Los Angeles Riots: Next Step, the North," *Saturday Review*, November 13, 1965, 33–35.
13. "Electing the President," California Secretary of State, *California Statement of Vote*, November 2, 2004, xv, https://elections.cdn.sos.ca.gov/sov/2004-general/sov_preface_docs_11_2004.pdf.
14. Reitman v. Mulkey, 387 US 369 (1967).
15. Alison Martin, "Bodies of James Earl Chaney, Andrew Goodman and Michael Schwerner Found in Philadelphia, Mississippi," *Chicago Sun-Times*, August 5, 2022, https://chicago.suntimes.com/2022/8/5/23289169/james-earl-chaney-andrew-goodman-michael-schwerner-bodies-found-philadelphia-mississippi
16. "Watts Rally Aids Mississippi Summer Project," *Los Angeles Sentinel*, August 20, 1964; and "Watts Action Group Holds Rally for Miss.," *Los Angeles Sentinel*, July 16, 1964.
17. "Co-worker of Missing Trio Reveals Mississippi Terror," *Los Angeles Sentinel*, July 2, 1964; "Marchers Demand US Protection," *Los Angeles Sentinel,* July 2, 1964; and "57 Students Home from Mississippi," *Los Angeles Sentinel*, August 27, 1964.
18. "Memorial Service Honors Slain Trio," *Los Angeles Sentinel*, August 27, 1964; and "Watts Youth Comes Home," *Los Angeles Sentinel*, August 27, 1964.
19. "Leaders Map New Strategy to Defeat Racist Legislation," *Los Angeles Sentinel*, September 10, 1964.
20. Sides, *L.A. City Limits*, 176.
21. "War on Poverty Status Pointed Out by Hawkins," *Los Angeles Sentinel*, July 22, 1965.
22. "Brookins Predicts Mass Poverty Demonstrations," *Los Angeles Sentinel*, July 15, 1965.
23. Sides, *L.A. City Limits*.
24. "32 Member Poverty Board Backed by King," *Los Angeles Sentinel*, July 15, 1965.
25. "WCLC to Open 4-Day Session," *Los Angeles Times*, July 6, 1965.
26. George Goodman, "Selma Crisis Shakes Nation; Johnson Acts: Locals Demonstrate," *Los Angeles Sentinel*, March 11, 1965; and *Los Angeles Sentinel* editorial, April 1, 1965.
27. Clayborne Carson, ed., *The Autobiography of Martin Luther King Jr.* (Warner Books, 1998), https://kinginstitute.stanford.edu/publications/autobiography-martin-luther-king-jr/chapter-25-malcolm-x; and Liv Brinkley, "The Only Meeting Between Coretta Scott King and Malcolm X," Grunge, April 29, 2022, https://www

.grunge.com/847689/the-only-meeting-between -coretta-scott-king-and-malcolm-x/.

28. Brinkley, "Only Meeting Between Coretta Scott King and Malcolm X."

29. Carson, *Autobiography of Martin Luther King Jr.*, 285–90; Coretta Scott King, *My Life with Martin Luther King, Jr.* (Holt, Rinehart and Winston, 1969), 256; and Brinkley, "Only Meeting Between Coretta Scott King and Malcolm X."

30. "Martin Luther King Jr. Had Strong Relationship with LA During Civil Rights Movement," CBS Los Angeles, May 7, 2021, https://www.cbsnews.com/losangeles/news/martin-luther-king-jr-had-strong-relationship-with-la-during-civil-rights-movement; and Theoharis, *King of the North*, 140.

31. "Police Pull Out Stops for King," *Los Angeles Sentinel*, March 4, 1965; and Patrick Lombard, "MLK Address at Temple Israel of Hollywood," Larchmont Buzz, January 21, 2019, https://larchmontbuzz.com/larchmont-village-people/mlk-address-at-temple-israel-of-hollywood/.

32. "How Coretta Scott King Forged Her Own Legacy," History, January 18, 2024, https://www.history.com/articles/coretta-scott-king-civil-rights-leader.

33. "Mrs. King to Sing at Second Baptist," *Los Angeles Sentinel*, March 4, 1965; and Vergie W. Murray, "Mrs. King's Concern Very Successful," *Los Angeles Sentinel*, March 11, 1965.

34. David J. Garrow, *Protest at Selma: Martin Luther King, Jr., and the Voting Rights Act of 1965* (Yale University Press, 2015).

35. George Goodman, "Selma Crisis Shakes Nation," *Los Angeles Sentinel*, March 11, 1965.

36. Ibid.

37. Ibid.

38. "Massive Climax to a Week of Civil Rights Protests in Los Angeles," *Free Press*, March 19, 1965.

39. "Mansfield Collins—Tuskegee Airman, Confidante to Dr. Martin Luther King Jr, Co-organizer of the West Coast's Largest Civil Rights Rallies, Dies at 101," *L.A. Focus on the Word*, October 6, 2022, https://www.lafocusnews.com/mansfield-collins-tuskegee-airman-confidante-to-dr-martin-luther-king-jr-co-organizer-of-the-west-coasts-largest-civil-rights-rallies-dies-at-101/.

40. Bruce Hartford, *"Troublemaker": Memories of the Freedom Movement* (Westwind Writers, 2019), 143–56.

41. "Photo Standalone 36–No Title," *Los Angeles Sentinel*, April 1, 1965.

42. "Veterans of the Civil Rights Movement: Summer Community Organization and Political Education (SCOPE) Project," Civil Rights Movement Archive, accessed December 26, 2018, https://www.crmvet.org/info/scope65.htm; and "Dr. King Boosts SCOPE Project at UCLA Rally," *Chicago Defender*, May 1, 1965.

43. Gwen Green, interview by Kent Kirtkon and Keith Rice, February 19, 2014, video, Tom & Ethel Bradley Center, California State University, Northridge, https://www.youtube.com/watch?v=kfjntByO9KQ&list=PLK5L1RQvapAUOhYYaPFsCL0j-eD68qG9p&index=1

44. Green, interview by Kirkton and Rice; "Los Angeles' Gwen Green Recalls Role in Historic Voting Rights Campaign 50 Years Later," *Daily News*, August 5, 2015, http://www.dailynews.com/social-affairs/20150805/los-angeles-gwen-green-recalls-role-in-historic-voting-rights-campaign-50-years-later; and "Veterans of the Civil Rights Movement," Civil Rights Movement Archive.

45. "Gwen Green Recalls Role"; and "Veterans of the Civil Rights Movement," Civil Rights Movement Archive.

46. Bruce Hartford, "CORE, SCLC 1963–67, California, Alabama, Mississippi," Civil Rights Movement Archive, https://www.crmvet.org/vet/hartford.htm.

47. Bruce Hartford, interview by students of the Everest system, 2012, Civil Rights Movement Archive, https://www.crmvet.org/nars/bruce12.htm.

48. Ibid.

49. William S. Leventhal, interview by David P. Cline, Library of Congress, April 13, 2013.

50. Lyndon B. Johnson, "Remarks in the Capitol Rotunda at the Signing of the Voting Rights Act," August 6, 1965, in *Public Papers of the Presidents of the United States: Lyndon B. Johnson, 1965*, Book II, 840–43, (Government Printing Office, 1966).

51. "Selma to Montgomery March," Martin Luther King, Jr. Research and Education Institute, https://kinginstitute.stanford.edu/selma-montgomery-march.

52. Robin D. G. Kelley, "Watts: Remember What They Built, Not What They Burned," *Los Angeles Times*, August 11, 2015, https://www.latimes.com/opinion/op-ed/la-oe-0811-kelley-watts-civil-society-20150811-story.html.

53. Maria Nolasco, "Ode to Watts: The War on Poverty in South Los Angeles," *Perspectives: A Journal of Inquiry*, vol. 41 (Spring 2024): 61–79.

54. Ibid., 66.

55. "Watts Rebellion (Los Angeles)," Martin Luther King, Jr. Research and Education Institute, https://kinginstitute.stanford.edu/watts-rebellion-los-angeles.

56. Theoharis, "Alabama on Avalon," 49.

57. "Watts Rebellion (Los Angeles)."

58. Robert Richardson, "'Get Whitey,' Scream Blood-Hungry Mobs," *Los Angeles Times*, August 14, 1965.

59. "Special Report: Life Inside a Riot Zone," *Jet*, September 2, 1965.

60. Ibid., 44.

61. Weena Perry, "An Outpost of Strength: The *Los Angeles Times* Performs Law and Order Versus Chaos During the Watts Rebellion of 1965," *afterimage*, July–August 2005, 32–37.

62. Jerry Cohen and William S. Murphy, *Burn, Baby, Burn! The Los Angeles Race Riot, August 1965* (Avon Books, 1966), 25–39; and Nathaniel Montague and Bob Baker, *Burn, Baby! Burn! The Autobiography of Magnificent Montague*, vol. 415 (University of Illinois Press, 2003), 5.

63. Gerald Horne, *Fire This Time: The Watts Uprising and the 1960s* (University Press of Virginia, 1995).

64. Armistead Scott Pride and Jack Lyle, *The Black American and the Press* (Ritchie Press, 1968), xv.

65. Bruce M. Tyler, "Black Radicalism in Southern California, 1950–1982" (PhD diss., University of California, Los Angeles, 1983).

66. "John Buggs Helped Create L.A. Human Relations Commission," *Los Angeles Times*, March 11, 1995, https://www.latimes.com/archives/la-xpm-1995-03-11-mn-41283-story.html.

67. "Dr. King Arrives Here to Study Riot Problems," *Los Angeles Times*, April 18, 1965.

68. Horne, *Fire This Time*.

69. Dick West and Paul Weeks, "Dr. King Hears Watts Protest over Heckling," *Los Angeles Times*, August 19, 1965.

70. Taylor Branch, *At Canaan's Edge: America in the King Years, 1965–68* (Simon and Schuster, 2007).

71. West and Weeks, "Dr. King Hears Watts Protest."

72. Branch, *At Canaan's Edge*.

73. Carson, *Autobiography of Martin Luther King Jr*.

74. Thomas F. Jackson, *From Civil Rights to Human Rights: Martin Luther King Jr. and the Struggle for Economic Justice* (University of Pennsylvania Press, 2007), 241.

75. Carson, *Autobiography of Martin Luther King Jr*.

76. West and Weeks, "Dr. King Hears Watts Protest."

77. Bayard Rustin, "The Watts and the McCone Report," *Commentary*, March 1966, https://www.commentary.org/articles/bayard-rustin-2/the-watts/.

78. Ibid.

79. Ibid.

80. Branch, *At Canaan's Edge*; and Jackson, *From Civil Rights to Human Rights*.

81. Andrew Young, *An Easy Burden: The Civil Rights Movement and the Transformation of America* (Baylor University Press, 2008).

82. "President Johnson and Martin Luther King Jr. on the Watts Riots," Miller Center, December 27, 2016, https://millercenter.org/the-presidency/educational-resources/president-johnson-and-martin-luther-king-jr-on-the-watts-riots.

83. Megan Walker, "50 Years of Static: The Consistent Injustices Facing African Americans in Los Angeles from the Watts Rebellion to the Present," *Toro Historical Review*, August 1, 2016, https://thetorohistoricalreview.org/2016/08/01/50-years-of-static-the-consistent-injustices-facing-african-americans-in-los-angeles-from-the-watts-rebellion-to-the-present-by-megan-walker/.

84. "Out of a Cauldron of Hate–Arson and Death," *Life*, August 27, 1965, 20–34.

85. Pride and Lyle, *The Black American and the Press*, ix, xiii, xiv.

86. *Los Angeles Sentinel*, August 19, 1965.

87. "Violence in the City: An End or a Beginning?," Governor's Commission on the Los Angeles Riots (1965), 29.

88. Rustin, "Watts Manifesto."

89. Martin Luther King Jr., "Beyond the Los Angeles Riots: Next Step, The North," *Saturday Review*, November 13, 1965, 33–55, cited in "Watts Rebellion (Los Angeles)," The Martin Luther King Jr. Research and Education Institute.

90. Kerner Commission, *Report of the National Advisory Commission on Civil Disorders* (US Government Printing Office, 1968), 203.

91. Ibid.

92. Ibid.

93. Hartford, "*Troublemaker,*" 120.

94. McCone Commission report, 154.

95. Pride and Lyle, *The Black American and the Press*, 45.

CHAPTER 5

1. Sally Greene, "The Birth of Black Power," *American Scholar*, April 26, 2021, https://theamericanscholar.org/the-birth-of-black-power/.

2. "'Black Power' Rally Calm," *Los Angeles Sentinel*, December 1, 1966.

3. Ray Rogers, "Defiant Carmichael Declares Goals of Negro Generation," *Los Angeles Times*, November 27, 1966.

4. Lisa Volpe, "Black Power and Acts of Love," *Gordon Parks: Stokely Carmichael and Black Power*, ed. Peter W. Kunhardt Jr. (Gordon Parks Foundation, 2022), 19–20.

5. Doug McAdam, *Political Process and the Development of Black Insurgency, 1930–1970* (University of Chicago Press, 1982), 190.

6. Pride and Lyle, *The Black American and the Press*, 45.

7. *The Tradition Continues: California Black Photographers,* November 10, 1983–January 16, 1984, California Museum of Afro-American History and Culture, 1983; and *Camera and Community: A Celebration by Guy R. Crowder*, 1993, California State University, Northridge.

8. Robert Gottlieb and Irene Wolt, *Thinking Big: The Story of the Los Angeles Times, Its Publishers and Their Influence on Southern California* (G. P. Putnam's Sons, 1977), 344, 379.

9. Sundiata Keita Cha-Jua and Clarence Lang, "The 'Long Movement' as Vampire: Temporal and Spatial Fallacies in Recent Black Freedom Studies," *Journal of African American History*, vol. 92, no. 2 (2007): 265–88.

10. "Watts Secession Urged to Create 'Freedom City,'" *Los Angeles Times*, June 17, 1966.

11. Davis and Wiener, *Set the Night on Fire*, 271.

12. Ari B. Bloomekatz, "Activist Co-founded Watts Summer Festival," *Los Angeles Times*, November 21, 2009.

13. Elaine Woo, "Billy J. Tidwell," *Los Angeles Times*, July 16, 2001, https://www.sfgate.com/news/article/Billy-J-Tidwell-2898712.php.

14. Drew Pearson, "Watts Festival Impresses Poverty Fighter Shriver," *Los Angeles Times*, August 22, 1966; and Los Angeles Public Library Photo Collection, Miss Watts Beauty Contest Winner, 1966, https://cdm16703.contentdm.oclc.org/digital/collection/photos/id/11742/.

15. Betty Pleasant, "Watts Summer Festival Surpasses Expectations," *Los Angeles Sentinel*, August 18, 1966; and Ray Rogers and Dave Larsen, "Bitterness Banished as Watts Stages Gay, Colorful Parade," *Los Angeles Times,* August 15, 1966.

16. Lindsey Baker and T. J. Robinson, "Black Aesthetic," in *Black Power Encyclopedia: From "Black Is Beautiful" to Urban Uprisings*, ed. Akinyele Umoja et al. (ABC-CLIO, 2018), 76–79.

17. Kim McMillon, "Black Arts Movement," in Umoja et al., *Black Power Encyclopedia*, 78–85.

18. Maulana Karenga, "US Organization," in Umoja et al., *Black Power Encyclopedia*, 793–99.

19. "Watts Towers of Simon Rodia State Historic Park," California Department of Parks and Recreation, accessed April 28, 2025, https://www.parks.ca.gov/?page_id=613.

20. Daniel Widener, *Black Arts West: Culture and Struggle in Postwar Los Angeles* (Duke University Press, 2020), 230–33.

21. Regina Jones, interview by Alex Cline, UCLA Center for Oral History Research, Session 2, April 27, 2012, https://oralhistory.library.ucla.edu; and "Little Richard Declares War!," *SOUL* magazine, April 21, 1966.

22. "I'm a Black Communist Woman: Charlene Mitchell on Running for the White House," *People's World*, August 1, 2024, https://www.peoplesworld.org/im-a-black-communist-woman-charlene-mitchell-on-running-for-the-white-house/.

23. Myrna Oliver, "Odessa B. Cox, 79; Helped Found Southwest College," *Los Angeles Times*, November 6, 2001, https://www.latimes.com/archives/la-xpm-2001-nov-06-me-855-story.html.

24. Tyler, "Black Radicalism".

25. Horne, *Fire This Time*, 327; and Montague and Baker, *Burn, Baby! Burn!*, 5.

26. John Floyd, interview by Karin L. Stanford, August 10, 2024.

27. "California: The Deadwyler Verdict," *Time* magazine, June 10, 1966, https://time.com/archive/6875098/california-the-deadwyler-verdict/.

28. Max Felker-Kantor, *Policing Los Angeles: Race, Resistance, and the Rise of the LAPD* (University of North Carolina Press, 2018), 70.

29. Ibid.

30. "Alert Patrol Cruises Area, Eyes Police," *Los Angeles Sentinel*, June 16, 1966, 1; and Betty Pleasant, "Cop Watching Serious Business with Community Alert Patrol," *Los Angeles Sentinel*, June 16, 1966.

31. Joshua Bloom and Waldo E. Martin, *Black Against Empire: The History and Politics of the Black Panther Party* (University of California Press, 2016), 37.

32. Thomas Pynchon, "A Journey into the Minds of Watts," *New York Times Magazine*, June 12, 1966, 34–35, 78–84.

33. "Mrs. Tillmon Appointed NWRO Executive Director," *Los Angeles Sentinel*, January 18, 1973; and Theoharis, *King of the North*, 278.

34. "CORE Slates Demonstration at See's Candy," *Los Angeles Sentinel*, April 14, 1966; and "Core Plans New Citizen Patrol," *Los Angeles Sentinel*, June 22, 1967.

35. Martin Luther King Jr., "Beyond Vietnam—A Time to Break Silence," address, April 4, 1967, American Rhetoric, audio, https://www.americanrhetoric.com/speeches/mlkatimetobreaksilence.htm.

36. Randall Kennedy, "The Prophet as Healer," *American Prospect*, April 3, 2018, https://prospect.org/infrastructure/martin-luther-king-jr.-prophet-healer/.

37. Daniel Schorr interview, *Eyes on the Prize II*, 1988, Washington University Film & Archive, http://repository.wustl.edu/concern/videos/c534ft055.

38. Jack Jones, "Police Hearing Boycotted by Rights Groups," *Los Angeles Times*, June 11, 1966.

39. Horne, *Fire This Time*, 180.

40. "Leaders Picket Manual Arts: Parents Demand Changes," *Los Angeles Sentinel*, September 14, 1967; and "Natural Hair Styles Allowed in City Schools," *Los Angeles Sentinel*, October 5, 1967.

41. "Natural Hair Styles."

42. "Manual Arts Truce Ticks, Ticks: Manual 'Bomb' Ticking," *Los Angeles Sentinel*, October 26, 1967.

43. Augustus Hawkins, "Inside Government: Why Manual Arts Today?" *Los Angeles Sentinel*, November 8, 1967.

44. "High School Dope, Booze Traffic Leads to Inquiry," *Los Angeles Sentinel*, September 21, 1967.

45. "Manual Arts Truce."

46. Larry Pett, "Manual Arts Agitators: Principal of New High School Once Embroiled in Turmoil," *Los Angeles Times*, January 26, 1969; "Natural Hair Styles"; and Theoharis, "WALKOUT!," 116.

47. "East Los Angeles Students Walk Out for Educational Reform (East L.A. Blowouts), 1968," Global Nonviolent Action Database, accessed June 21, 2025, https://nvdatabase.swarthmore.edu/content/east-los-angeles-students-walkout-educational-reform-east-la-blowouts-1968; and Theoharis, "WALKOUT!," 107.

48. "Negro Groups to Study Jefferson High Unrest: Conference of Elected Officials Sets Up Committees on Grievances and Personnel," *Los Angeles Times*, March 16, 1968.

49. Bob Lucas, "Jefferson High Gets Negro Principal," *Los Angeles Sentinel*, March 14, 1968.

50. Theoharis, "WALKOUT!," 119–21.

51. Gustavo Arellano, "How a Jewish Youth Camp Birthed the 1968 East L.A. Chicano Student Walkouts: 'The Young Mexican American Is Tired of Waiting for the Promised Land,'" *Tablet*, March 2, 2018, https://www.tabletmag.com/sections/community/articles/jewish-youth-camp-chicano-walkouts; and Mario T. García, *The Chicano Generation: Testimonios of the Movement*, (University of California Press, 2015).

52. Theoharis, "WALKOUT!," 107, 110, 116–17; and Mario T. García and Sal Castro, *Blowout! Sal Castro and the Chicano Struggle for Educational Justice* (University of North Carolina, Press, 2014).

53. Garcia and Castro, *Blowout!*, 218–19.

54. "1968 East L.A. Chicano Student Walkouts (Blowouts)," Los Angeles Conservancy, July 13, 2023, https://www.laconservancy.org/save-places/issues/1968-east-l-a-chicano-student-walkouts-blowouts/; and "1968 East LA Walkouts," Center for Youth Political Participation, Rutgers University. August 24, 2023, https://cypp.rutgers.edu/1968-east-la-walkouts/.https://www.laconservancy.org/save-places/issues/1968-east-l-a-chicano-student-walkouts-blowouts/.

55. "Rev. Jesse Jackson Visits Breadbasket Ministers," *Los Angeles Sentinel*, April 25, 1968.

56. Theresa Walker, "Martin Luther King Got Tough in Anaheim," *Orange County Register*, April 3, 2011, https://www.ocregister.com/2011/04/03/martin-luther-king-got-tough-in-anaheim/; and John L. Mitchell, "King's Words Resonate at L.A. Church," *Los Angeles Times*, April 4, 2008.

57. "Statement by the President on the Assassination of Dr. Martin Luther King Jr.,"April 4, 1968, American Presidency Project, https://www.presidency.ucsb.edu/documents/statement-the-president-the-assassination-dr-martin-luther-king-jr.

58. "A Special Memorial Edition: Dr. Martin Luther King, Jr.: His Life, His Work, His Death," *Los Angeles Sentinel,* April 11, 1968.

59. George Goodman, "Reagan Dodges Stand on Proposition 14," *Los Angeles Sentinel*, January 6, 1966.

60. Richard Bergholz, "Reagan Triumphs: GOP Scores Heavily in Nation; Finch Beats Anderson; Other Democrats in Tough Battles," *Los Angeles Times*, November 9, 1966.

61. McAdam, *Political Process*, 219–20.

62. Ron Wilkins, interview by Keith Rice et al., June 6, 2019, transcript, session 1, Tom & Ethel Bradley Center, California State University, Northridge, 66.

63. Jerry Rankin, "Heavily Armed Negro Group Walks Into Assembly Chamber," *Los Angeles Times*, May 3, 1967.

64. Bobby Seale, "The Southern California Chapter of the Black Panther Party 1968," LinkedIn Pulse, March 25, 2015, https://www.linkedin.com/pulse/southern-california-chapter-black-panther-party-1968-bobby-seale/.

65. Joe Bingham, "Black Congress Chairman Quits," *Los Angeles Sentinel*, January 30, 1969; and Bloom and Martin, *Black Against Empire*, 169.

66. Wayne Pharr with Karin L. Stanford, *Nine Lives of a Black Panther: A Story of Survival* (Chicago Review Press, 2014), 9–10.

67. Eric Malnic, "Police Accused of Clubbing, Kicking 30 at Panther Office: Panthers," *Los Angeles Times*, December 12, 1969.

68. Gordon Parks, "Whip of Black Power," *Life*, May 19, 1967, 77.

69. Howard Bingham, *Howard Bingham's Black Panthers 1968* (AMMO Books, 2009).

70. Stephen Shames and Ericka Huggins, *Comrade Sisters: Women of the Black Panther Party* (ACC Art Books, 2022), 25.

71. Betty Pleasant, "Cop Watching Serious Business with Community Alert Patrol," *Los Angeles Sentinel*, June 16, 1966.

72. Charles Baireuther, "Cross-Section Rally at City Hall," *Los Angeles Sentinel*, December 18, 1969.

Illustration Credits

Fig. 1: Courtesy of Julian Wasser Estate and Craig Krull Gallery

Figs. 2, 29, and 31, plates 30 and 46: UCLA Library Special Collections; Los Angeles Times Photographic Collections

Figs. 3, 24, and 25, plates 23, 48, 49, and 78: Charles Williams, The Charles Williams Collection / Courtesy of the Tom & Ethel Bradley Center at California State University, Northridge

Fig. 4, plates 38, 47, 51, 58, 67, and 79: Herald-Examiner Collection LAPL / Los Angeles Public Library

Figs. 5, 17, and 36, plates 22, 32, 34, 41, 42, and 73: Harry Adams, The Harry Adams Collection / Courtesy of the Tom & Ethel Bradley Center at California State University, Northridge

Fig. 7: National Museum of African American History & Culture

Figs. 8 and 12, plate 2: *California Eagle* Collections, Southern California Library (Los Angeles, California)

Fig. 9: History of America / Alamy

Fig. 11: USC Archive / Workman and Temple Family Homestead Museum

Fig. 13: Vera Jackson, The Vera Jackson Collection / Courtesy of the Tom & Ethel Bradley Center at California State University, Northridge

Fig. 14: Image Courtesy LAPL

Fig. 15: Courtesy of Johnson Publishing Company / Internet Archive

Fig. 16: © NAACP / Image Courtesy Indiana University

Figs. 18 and 22: Courtesy of *The Los Angeles Times* / Newspapers.com

Fig. 20: Courtesy of the *California Eagle* / Newspapers.com

Fig. 23, plates 37 and 50: The Getty Research Institute, Los Angeles (2005.M.11)

Fig. 26: Independent Star-News / Newspapers.com

Figs. 27 and 28, plate 66: © Howard Bingham

Fig. 30, plate 60: Joe Flowers, The Joe Flowers Collection / Courtesy of the Tom & Ethel Bradley Center at California State University, Northridge

Figs. 32 and 33, plate 84: Guy Crowder, The Guy Crowder Collection / Courtesy of the Tom & Ethel Bradley Center at California State University, Northridge

Fig. 34: Dartmouth College Rauner Special Collections Library

Fig. 35: Courtesy SOUL Publishing, LLC

Plate 1: Security Pacific National Bank Collection / Los Angeles Public Library

Plates 3, 6, 8, and 10: LAPL Digital Collections, Shades of L.A. Photo Collection / Los Angeles Public Library

Plate 4: E. L. Merer / LAPL Digital Collections, Shades of L.A. Photo Collection / Los Angeles Public Library

Fig. 10, plates 5, 9, 12, and 21: UCLA Library Special Collections; Miriam Matthews Photograph Collection

Plate 7: J. Paul Getty Museum, Los Angeles (2001.65.30) © The Watson Family Photo Collection

Plate 11: Bob Douglas, The Bob Douglas Collection / Courtesy of the Tom & Ethel Bradley Center at California State University, Northridge

Plate 13: The Getty Research Institute, Los Angeles (2002.M.42)

Plates 14 and 31: Herald-Examiner Photo Collections / Los Angeles Public Library

Plate 15: Collection Center for Creative Photography © Center for Creative Photography, Arizona Board of Regents

Plates 16 and 17: University of California, Los Angeles Library Department of Special Collections

Plate 18: ZUMA Press / Alamy

Plate 19: Library of Congress, Prints & Photographs Division, Visual Materials from the Rosa Parks Papers, [LC-DIG-ppmsca-47727]

Plate 20: Library of Congress, Prints & Photographs Division, Visual Materials from the Rosa Parks Papers, [LC-DIG-ppmsca-38700]

Plates 24, 25, 40, 44, 45, 74, and 75: Jack Davis, The Jack Davis Collection / Courtesy of the Tom & Ethel Bradley Center at California State University, Northridge

Plates 26 and 43: *Valley Times* Collection / Los Angeles Public Library

Plates 27 and 28: Courtesy of the Archives and Records Services Division, Mississippi Department of Archives and History

Plate 33: CSU Archives / Everett Collection / Bridgeman Images

Plates 35, 61, and 72: J. Paul Getty Museum, Los Angeles (2001.74.3, 2001.21.1, 2000.74.7) Reproduced with permission via Bettmann Archive / Getty Images

Plates 36, 65, and 71: © The Gordon Parks Foundation

Plate 39: © Joe Schwartz Photo Archive / Martin Luther King event

Plate 52: Bob Martin / Los Angeles Public Library

Plate 53: Courtesy of Los Angeles Public Library

Plate 54: Steve Young / Valley Times Collection / Los Angeles Public Library

Plate 55: Cliff Wesselmann / Herald-Examiner Collection LAPL / Los Angeles Public Library

Plate 56: John Phillips / Baldwin Street Gallery

Plate 57: © Bruce Hartford

Plates 59 and 63: *Los Angeles Times* / Getty Images

Plate 62: Photo by Bettman Archive / Getty Images

Plate 64: © Lawrence Schiller

Plate 68: Courtesy Alexander Gray Associates, New York; Stephen Friedman Gallery, London; Galerie Buchholz, Berlin © 2025 Melvin Edwards / Artists Rights Society (ARS), New York / Image courtesy Hammer Museum

Plate 69: Noah Purifoy Foundation

Plate 70: © Harry Drinkwater / Noah Purifoy Foundation

Plate 76: © Ron Wilkins

Plate 77: Wisconsin Historical Society

Plates 80 and 81: Rolland J. Curtis / Rolland J. Curtis Collection / Los Angeles Public Library

Plate 82: © Stephen Shames

Plate 83: © Jeffrey Blankfort

Plate 85: © Tommy Oliver / National Museum of African American History & Culture

Index

Italic page numbers indicate illustrations.